TURKEY
Trip Planner & Guide

TURKEY

Trip Planner & Guide
Paul Strathern

PASSPORT BOOKS

This first edition published 1995 by
Passport Books,
Trade Imprint of NTC Publishing Group,
4255 West Touhy Avenue,
Lincolnwood (Chicago), Illinois 60646-1975
U.S.A.

Conceived, edited, designed and produced by
Duncan Petersen Publishing Ltd, 31 Milson Road, London W14 0YP
from a concept by Emma Stanford

Typeset by Duncan Petersen Publishing Ltd;
film output by Reprocolor International, Milan

Originated by Reprocolor International, Milan

Printed by GraphyCems, Navarra

ISBN: 0-8442-9241-9

Library of Congress Catalog Card Number: 94-73991

Paul Strathern was born in 1940 and took a degree in philosophy at Trinity College, Dublin. He has written five novels and worked for more than 20 years as a travel writer, visiting four continents in the course of his work.

He first visited Turkey in 1962, and has gone back regularly ever since. Over the past 30 years he has survived such unique Turkish rituals as frog racing (for high stakes) with a garrison commander in the mountains of eastern Turkey; a *raki*-drinking marathon in Trabzon with a Kurd and a Mongol; and eating a Hittite pickled egg.

He was instructed in the ways of modern Turkish politics by an embittered former ambassador to Britain in a darkened room in Izmir, and in the truth about the country's earlier history by an Ottoman prince who lives in a small wooden palace with his Peking ducks. He speaks Turkish well enough to get himself into serious trouble, but has despaired of mastering enough to get himself out of it.

Master contents list

This contents list is for when you need to use the guide in the conventional way: to find out about where you are going, or where you happen to be. The index, page, 270, may be just as helpful.

HOWEVER...
There is much more to this guide than the region-by-region approach suggested by the contents list on this page. Turn to page 8; and see also pages 10-11.

Turkey Overall
- master map

Turkey Overall, pages 62–209, is a traveller's network for taking in the whole country, or large parts of it.

Each 'leg' of the network has a number (i.e., Turkey Overall: 1); you will also
find it described as a National Route, plus the number.

The term National Route does *not* simply mean a line on a map. Each route
'leg' features a whole region, and describes many places both on and off the
marked route. Think of the National Routes not only as physical trails, but as
imaginative ways of connecting all the main centres of Turkey and of describing
and making travel sense of the state as whole.

They are designed to be used in these different ways:

1 *Ignore the marked route entirely:* simply use the alphabetically arranged
Gazetteer of Sights & Places of Interest, and the map at the start of each route, as
a guide to what to see and do in the region, not forgetting the hotel and restaurant recommendations.

2 Follow the marked route by public transport (see the transport box), ferry, or
by car. You can do sections of the route, or all of it; you can follow it in any direction. Link the routes to travel the length and breadth of Turkey

Istanbul has a section of its own, pages 38–61.

The routes are broken down into manageable legs. Each leg has a section to itself, beginning with an introduction and a simplified map. The page number for each such section is shown on this master map.

Always use the simplified maps in conjunction with your own detailed maps (suggestions are given on the introductory pages).

On the simplified maps:

RED *marks key sights and centres, not to be missed.*

BLUE *marks important places, certainly worth a visit.*

GREEN *places are for those who aren't in a hurry and want to experience the region in some depth.*

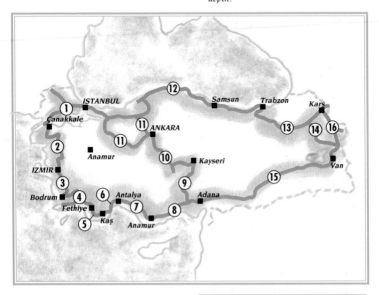

Some practical hints on how to travel red, blue and green are given in the introductory pages and the simplified maps, including key roads and their numbers. Generally, though, there are no absolute rules for going red, blue or green and you are meant to link the places, using a detailed road map, in whatever way suits you best.

The *Turkey Overall* section is ideal for:

■ Planning, and undertaking, tours of the whole country, or parts.

■ Making the journey to or from your eventual destination as interesting and as rewarding as possible.

■ Linking the in-depth explorations of localites provided by the Local Explorations section, pages 210–269

The material in this guide is organized to make a clear distinction between 'mainstream' – more or less regularly visited – Turkey and adventure traveller's Turkey. The first is covered by Turkey Overall: 1 to 12 (plus Local Explorations: 1 to 7); the second by Turkey Overall: 13 to 16, plus Local Explorations: 8.

The Istanbul-Adana-Ankara-Istanbul circuit on this map is the mainstream circuit. Istanbul-Van-Adana is the adventure travel course.

The Local Explorations
- master map

The Local Explorations are strategies for exploring all the interesting localities of Turkey. Also described as Local Tours, they complement the National Routes, pages 8-9. **They are designed to be used in these different ways:**

1 *Ignore the marked route entirely:* simply use the alphabetically arranged Gazetteer of Sights & Places of Interest, and the map at the start of each Local Exploration, as a guide to what to see and do in the area, not forgetting the hotel and restaurant recommendations.

2 Use the marked route to make a tour by public transport (see the transport box), ferry, or by car. You can do sections of the route, or all of it. (In the introduction it tells you how long you might take to cover everything the quickest way, by car.)

If you are driving, you can generally follow the tour in any direction; usually, the route as marked is an attractive and convenient way to link the places of interest; you may well find other ways to drive it. Always use our map in conjunction with a detailed road map (suggestions are given on each introductory page).

The Local Explorations or Tours, pages 210–269, generally follow each other in a north-south/west-east sequence.

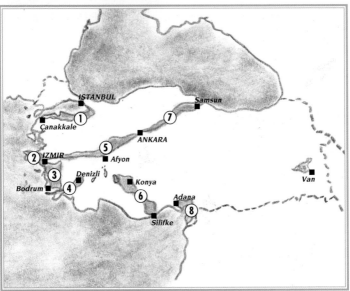

Istanbul has a section of its own, pages 38—61.

The *Local Explorations* are ideal for:

■ Planning single-centre holidays: each Local Exploration encapsulates an area which would make a great holiday. The introductory page to each section is designed to tell you whether the area will suit you: what you can expect; and something of its history, geography, people, customs and food.

■ Entertaining yourself while you are there: each section is packed with ideas for things to see and do. The tour, followed in full, can fill several days, and will always make a memorable journey, but most of the the sights and places of interest make fascinating day or part-day trips in their own right, not to mention the detours.

■ Planning multi-centre holidays: the map on this page shows you at a glance all the interesting parts of Turkey. Combine them at will to experience the different faces of the state; or link them, by means of the national route network.

Conventions used in this guide

A single Turkish *lira* sign – **L** – or several *lira* signs, such as **LLL**, in a hotel or restaurant entry, denotes a price band. Its object is to give an indication of what you can expect to pay. Bear in mind that accommodation offered at any one place may span two or more price bands.

⌂ after a heading in **Sights & Places of Interest** means that there is an accommodation suggestion (or suggestions) for that place in **Recommended Hotels**.

✕ after a heading in **Sights & Places of Interest** means that there is a suggestion (or suggestions) for that place in **Recommended Restaurants.**

Hotels
For a single room (one night), including a private bath or shower where available:

L Less than 300,000TL

LL 300,000-750,000TL

LLL More than 750,000TL

Restaurants
For one person eating a full meal with a half bottle of wine:

L Less than 300,000TL

LL 300,000-750,000TL

LLL More than 750,000TL

(Exceptional inflation means that these figures may need revising upwards in 1996-7)

Hotels and restaurants in this guide are a selection of personal recommendations – not exhaustive lists. They have been chosen to represent interest and quality, or to satisfy specific needs, at every price level.

Opening times of restaurants
Restaurant opening and closing times are intentionally not given in this guide. In Istanbul and the major resorts, restaurant hours tend to conform to general opening and closing hours given on page 27. Outside these centres, and especially in remote country areas, hours become flexible and informal, sometimes varying from day to day at the whim of the owner.

Opening times – museums and tourist attractions
Museums are generally open from 9.30 am until 4.20 pm, Tuesday to Sunday, and closed on Mondays. Palaces keep the same hours, but tend to close on Thursdays. Open-air sites tend to be open from 9 am until sunset, seven days a week.

These rules are subject to local variation and so before setting out on a long journey to see a sight, check first.

Mileages for routes and tours
Are approximate. In the case of the Turkey Overall routes, they represent the shortest distances you could expect to travel, almost always the 'red' option.

In the case of Local Explorations they also represent the shortest possible distance you could expect to cover, excluding detours.

Since the routes and tours are designed to be travelled in whole, in part or indeed not at all, the mileages are given as much for passing interest as for their practical value.

Credit cards
Expensive hotels and restaurants in Istanbul, Ankara and the major resorts of the west and south-west accept the major cards – American Express, Visa, Diners Club and Access. Elsewhere, they have not penetrated. For this reason, hotel and restaurant entries in this guide do not list credit cards accepted. As a rule, expect to pay in cash.

↗ after a place name on a map means that the sight or place of interest is covered in detail in another part of the book. To find out exactly where, look up the place in the **Sights & Places of Interest** gazetteer which follows the map: a cross-reference is given in every case.

Something for everyone

Getting the most from your guide

Here is a *small* selection of ideas for enjoying Turkey opened up by this guide, aimed at a range of needs and tastes. The list is just a start: the guide offers many, many more ideas for what really matters: suiting yourself. You'll find that it takes into account not only your tastes, but how much time you have.

Culture and anarchy – oustanding classical sites, away-from-it-all beaches
Turkey Overall: 5 and 6.

Ancient and modern – great classical cities plus resorts with modern facilities
Turkey Overall: 2 and 3.

Underground cities and great museums
Turkey Overall: 11 and 12.

Oriental city hubbub, island peace
Istanbul city section and Local Explorations: 1.

Unexplored hinterland, Hittite sites
Local Explorations: 7.

Biblical sites
Local Explorations: 8.

Black Sea cities and beaches
Turkey Overall: 14.

Unspoilt Mediterranean coast
Turkey Overall: 8.

Adventure routes
Turkey Overall: 15, 16 and 17.

TURKEY:
an introduction

There's nothing in Turkey that you can't find somewhere else. Greece also has pristine beaches lapped by a translucent turquoise sea and the finest of classical ruins. India, Egypt and Iran also have some of the world's finest mosques. Britain too is lapped by four different seas, and Spain has a string of modern resorts. Italy also has a former capital of the Roman Empire, and Greece likewise contained two of the Seven Wonders of the Ancient World. But only in Turkey do all these wonders come together in one country.

When I first visited Turkey more than 30 years ago I was warned that it was dangerous to stray off the beaten track. I did, and discovered that I'd wandered into an unspoilt hinterland of legendary hospitality. Large parts of the interior were terra incognita to tourists in those days – and remain so to this day. Even in the main tourist regions of the Aegean and Mediterranean coastlines, you're seldom far from some traditional market where herbs, spices, goats and mounds of multi-coloured peppers are sold as they have been for centuries, by people whose appearance is equally unchanged. Or up in the mountains, behind your resort, will be a shepherd playing his flute as the eagles soar above the gorges. But Turkey isn't all picturesque rural backwaters where time appears to have stood still. It also contains one of the greatest cities in the world: Istanbul. Straddling two continents, its superb mosques and palaces look down over the narrows of the Bosphorus, one of the sea's busiest waterways. Here you can see the historic relics of three of the world's great empires. Or, instead of expanding cultural horizons, you can expand your stomach, sampling one of the world's three great cuisines.

Mass tourism came late to Turkey, building up in the 70s, and is very much state of the art. The big holiday hotels in such resorts as Kuşadasi, on the southern Aegean coast, have all the amenities you'll find elsewhere around the Mediterranean. A night out here or in Bodrum can be just as wild, or sophisticated, as anywhere in Greece or Spain. Discos, decibels, down-the-hatch drinking and delirious dawns; or Vermeer-still vistas: the choice is yours. Here Turkey is very much a part of Europe rather than Asia, but with a cuisine more exciting than Italy's, locals more macho than Spanish bullfighters and prices like Greece's in the old days.

When to go, and to which parts

Turkey is, in theory, a year-round destination, with a pleasant winter climate in many regions, as the temperature charts below reveal.

However, the Turks prefer to ignore this fact: many regions, with the exception of the main resort areas, close down outside the tourist season. If you have the choice, go in spring or autumn, avoiding the high summer crowds and heat.

A glance at the temperature charts will reveal that Turkey's temperatures have huge regional variations. In general, the eastern and central regions of the country are very hot in the summer and very cold in the winter. Ankara spent almost three months below zero during a recent winter, yet when I was last there in late October the climate was like that of a (good) summer's day

in north-western Europe. Istanbul, on the other hand, seldom gets too cold, but can become very oppressive in high summer.

Izmir is another matter. Here it becomes very hot in summer, as it does all along the south coast. If you don't like intense heat, avoid as far as possible the southern Aegean coast or the Mediterranean coast during summer. By far the best time to come here is in spring, or autumn, when there are long, warm sunny days, and the evenings aren't too cool. The winters here are pleasantly mild, but places tend to close down.

The north coast along the Black Sea is notoriously wet, according to the Turks. Anyone from Manchester or Amsterdam may wonder what on earth they're talking about. The fact is, it rains a bit up here, but unlike similarly

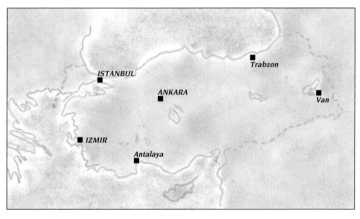

	J	F	M	A	M	J	J	A	S	O	N	D
Istanbul	8	7	11	16	20	25	28	30	24	22	15	10
Ankara	2	-1	5	13	18	22	27	22	24	19	10	4
Izmir	10	11	13	18	23	28	31	32	26	22	17	13
Antalya	13	15	15	19	24	27	33	34	32	24	22	14
Trabzon	10	10	11	14	18	22	26	27	22	18	16	12
Van	5	3	0	7	14	17	24	26	19	13	4	-1

The figures are the average maximum temperature in degrees centigrade for each month.

green spots in the west of Ireland, for instance, the rain does stop. And for days on end the sun shines. The north coast is pleasantly green; it never gets too hot, and seldom too cold. I have swum in the Black Sea in late October, and enjoyed it.

Clothing

Summer in Turkey is usually very hot. Jaunty sporting wear and the latest ghastly shorts are in order for the resorts. If you're there in spring or autumn, bring a pullover in case it gets cool in the evenings. Some may wish to wear cool outfits for dining out. These should be cool in every sense: steamy plunging necklines and temperature-raising see-through blouses are out.

If you're planning to visit any of the ancient sites, where there is often ground to cover, or if you want to walk, pack walking boots. You can get by at most sites with trainers, but they're not practical if you're planning to wander off the beaten track or climb up the rocks to some high citadel. For this you'll also need long trousers, to protect your calves and knees from abrasive undergrowth. If you are walking any distance at all, it is best to wear long trousers, as well as a shady hat with a wide brim. Even on the rare cloudy days you can get badly sunburned in Turkey. This is particularly true if you're going on a boat trip. You may sit in the shade, but you won't be protected from the glare reflected off the sea.

If you are arriving in winter, you should bring a few sweaters and a raincoat for visits to the Aegean or Mediterranean coasts. If you're going anywhere inland during winter, prepare as if for Siberia. Gloves, scarves, boots and a hip flask are essential. The Anatolian hinterland can be very bleak during this season, as even the invading Mongols discovered. (An interlude was declared between the bouts of rape and pillage, and all retired to their felt tents to drink fermented mares' milk in the smoky fug.) The Mongols also had some very interesting hats for this weather: variants are often still on sale in the inland towns – a chance to discover how Genghis Khan kept his ears warm.

Except at very smart spots in the resorts, and places patronized by businessmen in the cities, dress in Turkey is invariably casual. But when visiting a mosque, you should wear clothing appropriate to a place of worship: covered arms, and long trousers or a skirt below the knees. You will be required to take off your shoes, so clean socks are advisable.

Documentation

To enter Turkey you will need a current passport. Citizens of the United Kingdom and Ireland at present require an entry visa, which is acquired on arrival at your port, airport or border post of entry. This costs 100,000TL, but can be paid in the sterling or dollar equivalent if you haven't yet picked up any Turkish money. It enables you to stay in the country for three months.

Visitors from other European countries do not require visas.

Medical and travel insurance

There is no reciprocal agreement between Turkey and the EC for medical care, so EC residents as well as all other nationalities are *strongly advised* to organize private medical insurance for the length of their stay.

This can be obtained at almost all travel agents, and also at airports (where the insurance desk is usually in the departure lounge *beyond* customs.) This insurance invariably covers hospital bills, travel, loss of property, driving accidents and personal injury. But you won't be able to claim from the insurance company unless you have irrefutable documentary evidence to support your claims. Different companies require different documents. However, a local police report on the matter is usually essential.

Money

The currency is the Turkish lira, which is abbreviated as TL. Over the past few years Turkey has suffered from spectacular inflation, which means that you'll get a spectacular amount of TLs for your dollar, pound, mark, guilder and so on. (The rate at time of going to press is around 50,000TL to the pound sterling, 34,000 to the U.S. dollar.)

There are coins with denominations of 5000TL, 2500TL, 1,000TL and 500TL. There are also a few lesser denomination coins around. These are worth more as scrap metal than their

• *Ankara money changer.*

cash advance in TL up to the equivalent of at least £100/$150 (or similar sums in other currencies) at most banks. But be warned: the plastic revolution has hardly penetrated to street level. Very few restaurants, hotels or shops will take credit cards. These are generally acceptable only at classier establishments in the resort and main tourist areas, or at the carpet shops where you have to spend a great deal of money to keep the proprietor interested.

Import and export

At present, those returning to EC countries from Turkey are allowed to bring back the following amounts of duty-free goods: 200 cigarettes, 50 cigars or 250 gms of tobacco; one litre of spirits or two litres of fortified or fizzy wine; two litres of still wine; 60 ml of perfume and 250 ml of toilet water; and other goods up to £32 or $48. Other nationalities are advised to check with their own customs authorities if importing goods from Turkey is a concern.

Those who even think of smuggling drugs should first of all go to see the film *Midnight Express*. Turkish jails are nasty, with nasty inmates (in and out of uniform); sentences are long.

Equally unpleasant consequences (jail, or a *huge* fine if you are *very* lucky) await anyone smuggling out antiquities, bits of ancient monuments, ancient coins or the like. In other words, anything that could end up in a museum. There can be difficulties, too, with ancient carpets: be sure to get a certificate from the salesman which states that your purchase is not an antiquity; it should have the retailer's name and address printed on it.

Local customs: what to expect, how to behave

Turkey is comparatively new to tourism. This means that the country is not yet used to the more outrageous aspects of western European behaviour, except perhaps in the resorts and big cities.

This, above all, is a Muslim country; but for the most part Turks take their religion much as most northern Europeans take theirs. The secular and the sacred co-exist with the minimum of fuss and interference, but what may appear to be casual is in fact deep-

face value (and as such constitute one of the wonders of the Turkish economy). In practice, apart from keeping a couple of 1,000TL coins to pay lavatory attendants, you should find yourself dealing exclusively in notes.

These now start at 5,000TL, and move on through 10,000TL, 20,000TL, 50,000TL, 100,000TL, 250,000TL and 500,000TL. This is just as complicated as it seems: you need to be alert when dealing in such numbers. Not that dishonesty is particularly widespread: indeed, most Turks are astonishingly considerate towards foreigners and their difficulties with the telephone-number currency. You will often be handed back high denomination notes when you have made a simple (but potentially expensive) error. How long this saintly state of affairs will last is anybody's guess.

The wisest way to carry large amounts of money is of course in travellers cheques, which can be cashed at all banks. Eurocheques are now almost as widely accepted.

Credit cards are very useful when hiring a car, or paying for ferry and plane tickets. They also enable you to get a

• *Gold bazaar. The flag honours National Day.*

rooted. It is not wise to criticize the Muslim religion in any way, and your uninformed views are likely to give offence. Listen and learn.

In Turkey you are also not allowed – by law to say anything against Atatürk, the founder of modern Turkey. Public insults in his direction are likely to get you into serious trouble. In private, you may hear certain criticisms, but be wary of adding to them yourself. Most Turks are genuinely proud of Atatürk.

Remote country areas can be very conservative indeed, especially where Muslim fundamentalism has begun to take root. Travellers here should be sure to wear long trousers or a skirt longer than knee length. Women should cover their arms. Those who disregard these conventions are likely to be pestered mercilessly.

It remains extremely unwise for women to travel around on their own in country areas unused to visitors. Even a woman well able to look after herself will find she is soon driven to distraction by the constant male attention. When travelling off the beaten track, it is best to behave and dress with decorum at all times.

Male chauvinism is considered on a par with sanity, though this time-honoured state of mind is beginning to fall from favour with the younger generation, who have started to discover the joys and benefits of treating the opposite sex as human beings. In the cities and resorts, amongst students, profes-

sionals, and urbanized youth, the attitude towards women – as towards most things – will be much the same as anywhere in Europe. That is to say, generally enlightened but with unexpected and often grotesque exceptions. Just be careful.

Contrary to popular calumny, the Turks are, in the main, honest. For visitors this fact is often difficult to reconcile with the practice of bargaining.

Bargaining should be treated light-heartedly, as a kind of game. It is very much a Turkish way of getting to know you – and can be much more revealing and interesting than simply swapping platitudes or talking about the weather. It is like the Olympic games used to be: winning is not the end-all it's more important to have taken part.

If you are going to incur a bill in a hotel or restaurant, and there is doubt about the price, be sure to get the cost fixed right at the outset. Do your bargaining then. You are unlikely to be presented with an outrageous bill if you have demonstrated from the outset that you're financially on the ball. Increasingly, menus in resorts and cities carry prices. These usually mean what they say, yet you can always try bargaining. (The locals will usually be paying less than you, but that's the way it is.)

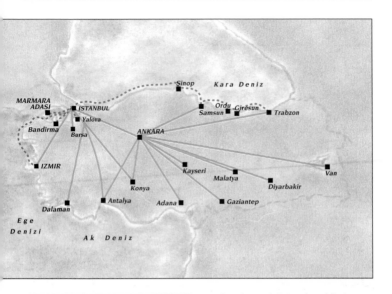

• Above: *internal air routes, and ferries.*

GETTING THERE

By air
This is virtually the only practical means of getting to Turkey at present. There is a wide variety of scheduled and charter flights, most visitors gaining notable bargains by booking package holidays, accommodation and flight included.

The independent traveller should note that there are direct flights from all major European air terminals to many Turkish destinations. These include: Istanbul, Izmir, Ankara, Bodrum and Antalya. All these offer onward services to either Ankara or Istanbul, from either of which you can fly to most major cities in Turkey.

By rail
Severely disrupted because of the civil war in former Yugoslavia. There *is* a train which goes to Turkey via Bulgaria, but the journey takes four days from north-western Europe, often longer due to hold-ups in Bulgaria.

Those attracted by the romance of trans-European rail travel (and why not?) should go for a major rail experience: take a train to Moscow, then change for Odessa. In Odessa, catch a boat across the Black Sea to Istanbul. Set off in spring, and arrive in summer, if you're lucky.

• Opposite: *mosque, Konya;*
above: *bus station.*

GETTING AROUND

Public transport in Turkey is for the most part inexpensive and comprehensive. It's also fairly pleasant and comfortable – especially for those of us who remember 'the good old days'. (I once took a bus journey which lasted for six hours, during which I had an incontinent lamb on my lap; meanwhile the old man who owned the lamb, and who had two on his lap, fell asleep beside me and dribbled into my shirt. It came as a refreshing relief to be set down in the pouring rain at my destination, apparently in the middle of nowhere.)

Car hire, on the other hand, is ridiculously expensive, especially when you compare it with the price of almost anything else in the country.

By air

Flying within Turkey is relatively inexpensive compared with similar flights in Europe. For instance, a one-way ticket from Antalya to Ankara will cost around 1,200,000TL.

By far the most comprehensive network is run by THY – Turkish Airlines. Privatization means that certain smaller companies now run in competition. THY tends to be the most expensive carrier, but is by far the most reliable.

The internal network has two main hubs: Istanbul and Ankara. Flights from Istanbul to most eastern destinations often involve a stopover at Ankara, usually lasting an hour. Indeed, it is almost impossible to find a flight which does not go via either Istanbul or Ankara. This means that if you want to fly from Trabzon to Van (a distance of 400 km), you have to fly via Ankara (1,700 km) and the cost of your ticket increases accordingly.

The planes used on most of these flights are modern and comfortable, and they're usually half empty. But be sure to book at least a couple of days ahead (more, if there's a public holiday or local event). Plastic snacks and watery coffee or tea are de rigeur, as on similar flights throughout the world. Details of flights are available at local THY offices, most travel agents and tourist information offices.

By bus

Turkish long-distance buses are a great institution. They hold the country together: they are cheap, and they connect all the main cities and towns in the land.

Every town has it otogar (from the French auto gare, thus bus station). And each otogar has its formidable array of competing bus companies. As you enter the otogar friendly helpers will attempt to lead you (or if not you, your luggage) to the office of the company which employs them to do just this. Don't be fooled. First make your own tour of the office fronts, where you will see the times and destinations of their particular buses. Choose the time that suits you. Prices are all much the same, and you'll gain little from shopping around. For instance, the four-hour journey from Canakkale to Pergamon costs just 70,000TL.

Some carriers' buses are more comfortable than others', but there's not usually much in it. Two of my favourite firms are Pamakkale and Kamil Koç (the latter means camel coach).

You can get water on most buses, but not much else. On some you will be given freshener towels, which are a great boon. On longer distances the bus will stop at intervals so that you can visit the lavatory, stretch your legs and also have a bite to eat at a restaurant. Most of the buses have comfortable seats with a fair amount of leg room. There is usually air-conditioning, and it usually works. If not, they open the windows, which usually works pretty well. When you buy your ticket, it will have a seat number. Ask for a lower number near the front, where the ride is less bumpy. When you get on the bus, you may find a large unshaven weight-lifter asleep in your seat. Do not attempt to disturb him. The conductor will do this: he is paid to risk his life in this fashion, and is usually very good at it.

These bus trips are no longer an endurance test, as they used to be. However, you'll find that four hours is about as long as you'll want to sit in a bus during one day. The roads often seem to consist entirely of hairpins through breathtaking scenery, while the driver appears to be practising for the Formula One circuit. Best to ignore him, and don't even try to imagine whatever it is he thinks he's doing.

One occasional snag: the bus radio.

American classic taxi, Trabzon.

Turkish music can be delightful, but four hours in a confined space with popular versions of Murat's death throes set to heart-rending quartertones often proves too much for the finely tuned western ear more used to the melodies of Mendelssohn, Meatloaf or Madonna. Ask politely, and the driver will usually turn it down a little. Otherwise, bring earplugs. (Seriously: the wax ones are the best.)

Don't be put off bus travel by my reservations about the music: for the most part it is not intrusive. (I speak here as one who subscribes to Schopenhauer's dictum that a man can be judged civilized in inverse proportion to the amount of noise he can tolerate.) And those *otogars* still, for me, have the romance of old railway station boards listing the route of the Orient Express. Even today, there's a regular bus which runs from Fethiye, on the Aegean coast just opposite Rhodes, all the way to Rize on the Black Sea up by the Georgian border, a distance of over 1,000 km.

By *dolmuş*

This form of travel is another great Turkish institution. Short road hops, which are not covered by the long-distance buses, are undertaken typically by minibus transport (*dolmuş*). It costs only a little more than ordinary bus.

The *dolmuş* has its route marked on the windscreen. There is no timetable: it simply leaves its starting point when it is full up. You can get on or off at any point along the route – by waving to the driver (either from the roadside or from amidst the happy throng inside). You pay a conductor before you set out, or the driver when you get off. (Try to avoid paying with six figure notes.)

Dolmuşes operate between villages, between towns, and often across towns and cities. This mode of transport is not only user-friendly and environment-friendly (only full vehicles use the roads), but also exemplifies the successful working of market forces. Why this system has not been introduced in northern Europe remains a mystery.

Car hire

Expect to pay at least as much as in northern Europe – i.e., more than 1,000,000TL per day for a car from one of the big international firms. Local firms will charge you less, sometimes much less, but are not reliable. And the one thing you do need on Turkish roads is an absolutely reliable car.

Taxis

Turkish taxis are plentiful and inexpensive. In most cities they are yellow, and each taxi has its own number in large numerals on the door. You will find that some taxi drivers are wizards of mental arithmetic, who long to demonstrate their intellectual agility. This is done by forgetting to turn on the meter, and then carrying out calculations in their head involving huge sums of Turkish lira. To relieve cerebral strain in your driver insist that he turns on the meter.

When you get out of the taxi, the driver sometimes asks for a sum which bears no relation to the figure on the meter. He will kindly explain that your journey was of such length that the meter has gone 'over the top' and started again.

Fortunately, such tricks are uncommon. Turkish taxi drivers are usually very pleasant.

By rail

The Turkish rail network misses even the bronze medal in the transport championships. The best trains are the '*ekspresi*' which link Istanbul, Ankara and Izmir, but there are many better ways to travel between these cities. The prices are on a par with buses, if you travel second class. Couchettes (*küşetli*) are available, and travelling overnight can be a relatively painless way to get about.

Off these main lines, rail travel is another matter. The Turkish rail system was originally built by the Germans. In those days it was thought that a Berlin to Baghdad railway would transform the balance of power in the Middle East. It didn't, for various complex geo-political-historical reasons. According to a hoary tale, the German engineers who originally laid the tracks negotiated a deal which specified that they were to be paid by the kilometre. The dictates of the market economy thus encouraged them to take the route of their railway here, there and everywhere. A glance at the rail link between Ankara and Erzurum, for instance, would seem to indicate a large amount of private enterprise by these pioneering engineers.

I once travelled a considerable section of this particular route on a *yolcu* (so-called local train.) I found that I had ample opportunity to strike up a leisurely conversation with one of my fellow passengers, who spoke no English. At this period, my Turkish was still in the embryo stage, so we conversed with the help of my dictionary. The high point of our conversation was reached when he explained to me that we were travelling on '*bir yavaş kayik doğrultusunda Çin.*' I searched through my dictionary, keen not to interrupt the flow of our conversation, and discovered that I now knew the Turkish phrase for a 'slow boat to China.'

Turkish railways certainly meander (this word in fact orginates from the name of a river in Turkey). Despite this, the rail network still manages to miss out considerable tracts of the country – such as the entire north coast, the entire south coast, and the entire west coast with the exception of Izmir.

Turkish railways should be regarded as an experience, rather than a form of travel.

By ferry

Turkish ferries are very good indeed, but alas their network is pitifully inadequate. Neither the Mediterranean (south) coast nor the Aegean (west) coast has a local service.

Turkey's internal ferry service is run by Türkiye Denizkilik Işletmesi, which is widely referred to as Turkish Maritime Lines (TML). This company runs a number of short-hop services in the Sea of Marmara, including services from Istanbul to the Princes' Islands, to Yalova and Bandirma on the south Maramara coast, and to the Marmara Islands. There is also a daily service connecting Istanbul and Izmir.

During the summer (usually March to mid-October) there is an excellent regular service between Istanbul and Trabzon, which calls at the Black Sea ports of Sinop, Samsun, Ordu, and Giresun. This makes for a great mini-cruise, and you can often meet up with some interesting fellow passengers. The long-distance ferries have a range of air-conditioned cabins, but the food is ordinary and relatively expensive. Be sure to bring your own wine or *raki*.

Details of times and prices for all these ferry routes are available at tourist information offices. Do not rely on printed brochures, as these are published much too far in advance to keep up with the whims of Turkish shipping.

ESSENTIAL PRACTICAL INFORMATION

Accommodation

Accommodation in Turkey is inexpensive. Even the classiest hotels in Istanbul charge considerably less than you'd pay for similar accommodation in London or Hamburg. But be warned: the lower end of the scale can be very low indeed. You pay practically nothing, but accommodation is *extremely* basic, not always very clean, and you may find yourself coming away with a small wildlife preserve of intimate guests.(My hotel recommendations in this guide don't include *any* hotels of this kind: entomologists and creepy crawly lovers will have to explore for themselves.)

Prices should be displayed by law somewhere in the hotel – but often this is in some obscure part of the building not frequented by guests. Always establish the price before you take a room.

Banks and currency exchange

Turkish banks are open from Monday to Friday, 8.30 am–12 noon, and 1.30 pm –5 pm.

Irritatingly, the foreign exchange departments often don't open until at least 20 minutes after the official opening time (because they are 'waiting for the list of official rates'), and usually pack up shop some 20 minutes before closing time (for no reason at all in c, as the jazz number goes.) The good news is that in many of the resort centres certain banks stay open in the evenings and at weekends to exhange foreign currency. Banks mostly charge no commission (komisyon). The currency exchange booths which are open at competitive hours in most resort centres do charge commission. Be careful, some charge a lot.

You can also change money at most Post and Telephone Offices (yellow sign marked PTT). Hours at these offices vary throughout the country, but you can usually rely on 9 am–5 pm, Monday to Friday.

All these places will have display boards giving the current rates of exchange for all major currencies.

Breakdowns

There is no such thing as a national motoring organization. In case of breakdown, contact the people you hired your car from, or follow the procedure they require. If you have brought your own car, be sure to take out AA or RAC membership with the appropriate cover. Both these organizations have lists of reliable garages.

You can pick up spares for most European cars in the big cities. The small local repair shops are on the whole highly efficient and highly ingenious. Be sure to fix the price for any repairs beforehand, and stay in close touch whilst these repairs are being carried out. Then you will find that such places are also amazingly inexpensive.

Diarrhoea

A fact of life if travelling off the beaten track in Turkey, and common enough in the main resort areas. The ultra-careful traveller can sometimes avoid 'traveller's stomach' by never drinking tap water (unless boiled or purified with tablets); never having ice cubes in drinks; never eating fresh fruit (especially unpeeled) and only consuming freshly cooked food and vegetables (previously cooked and re-heated food is as likely to cause gastro-enteritis as uncooked food).

Your symptoms will range from mild nausea and loss of appetite through diarrhoea and vomiting to full-blown food poisoning with chills, headache, weakness and malaise.

Self-help: children will need immediate fluid replacement. Use glucose-salt solution if possible, but any fluid will help. For adults, the discomfort and inconvenience can be relieved by taking anti-diarrhoeal drugs, but remember also to take plenty of fluids.

Camomile tea (in Turkish *papatya çay*) may be helpful against a queasy stomach. You can find it in some teahouses and herb markets often sell dried camomile.

Above all, give your inflamed gut a rest by stopping solid food for at least 24 hours. Eating will only aggravate the problem and delay recovery. As soon as you feel able, start eating again with dry bread or toast. Avoid fatty food and milk, which can worsen the symptoms.

Electricity

The Turkish current is 220 volts, 50 AC, the same as in Europe. Plugs are two-prong, but to make life difficult, they come in two sizes, which don't fit each other. Most are the small size, like those found over most of continental Europe. The larger size is the same as

Essential practical information

• *Lottery tickets for sale, Ankara.*

that used in Germany and Austria.

Embassies and consulates

All the main embassies are in the capital, Ankara; there are consulates in Istanbul. They tend to open at eccentric hours, and are always closed on the slightest pretext of a holiday, either at home or in Turkey. Be sure to ring and enquire before making the effort to reach a closed door. There will usually be at least an answerphone service giving minimal details in a bored voice.

Australia Embassy: 83, Nene Hatun Caddesi, Gazi Osman Paşa, Ankara; tel. 312 136 1240.
Canada Embassy: 75, Nene Hatun Caddesi, Gazi Osman Paşa, Ankara; tel. 312 136 1275/9.
France Embassy: 70, Paris Caddesi, Kavaklidere, Ankara; tel. 312 126 1480.
  Consulate: 8, Istiklal Caddesi, Taksim, Istanbul; tel. 216 143 1852.
Germany Embassy: 114, Atatürk Bulvari, Kavaklidere, Ankara; tel. 312 126 5465.
  Consulate: Inönü Caddesi, 56, Selim Hatun Camii Sokak, Ayazpaşa Taksim, Istanbul; tel. 216 151 5404.
Netherlands Embassy: 16, Köroğlu Sokak, Gazi Osman Paşa, Ankara; tel. 312 136 1074.
  Consulate: 393 Istiklal Caddesi, Tünel Beyoğlu, Istanbul; tel. 216 149 5310.
U.K. Embassy: 46/A, Şehit Ersan Caddesi, Çankaya, Ankara; tel. 312 127 4310.
  Consulate: 26, Meşrutiyet Caddesi, Tepebaşi, Beyoğlü, Istanbul; tel. 216 149 8874.
U.S. Embassy: 110 Atatürk Bulvari, Kavaklidere, Ankara; tel. 312 126 5470.
  Consulate: 106, Meşrutiyet Caddesi, Tepebaşi, Beyoğlü, Istanbul; tel. 216 151 3602.

Emergencies

Police: telephone 155; fire: telephone 110; ambulance: telephone 112.

If you have an accident, ring the police at once. In most cases, especially if you are not to blame and everyone else is being genuinely unreasonable, the police may well be very helpful. Surprisingly, the police will often take your side against local opposition, if your case is good.

Most visitors to Turkey will have an air ticket linked with some travel operator or organization. Its representative will be named on the folder accompanying your ticket. If you do find yourself in trouble, this is by far the best person to contact.

Be sure to report any accident or loss to the police as soon as possible, and obtain an official piece of paper recording that you have done this. Otherwise you won't be able to claim on insurance.

Late night activities

In the big cities and the resorts there are usually a number of late-night bars. These stay open until around 4 am. Dis-

Some international dialling codes from Turkey:	
Australia	61
Austria	43
Canada	1
Irish Republic	353
France	33
Germany	40
Netherlands	31
U.K.	44
U.S.	1

• Sunday card game, Istanbul.

cos usually close 3–4 am. Most big cities have a thriving red light district. The north-east Black Sea coast is at present suffering from an invasion of 'Natashas' from Russia. Homosexuality is widely practised but not talked about, and there are few gay bars. Aids is not yet widespread in Turkey, but VD is. Condoms (Turkish: *preservatif*) are available in chemists.

Lost property
Contact your tour representative or the police (see Emergencies, above).

Measurements
Turkey uses the metric system, in line with EC countries:
One litre = 1.7 pints (1 Imperial gallon = 4.54 litres); 1 U.S. gallon = 3.73 litres.
One kilogramme (1,000 grams) = 2.2 lbs.
One kilometre (1,000 metres) = 0.62 miles. To convert kilometres to miles, multiply by five and divide by eight, and vice-versa.

Medical matters
Most large towns and resort areas have a chemist (Turkish: *eczane*) that is open at night. There will also be a dentist on call. If in doubt, ring the local hospital (Turkish: *hastane*).

Many consulates keep a list of doctors and dentists who have proved reliable when treating their nationals.

In most towns there is a Red Crescent Clinic (*Kizilay*) – the Islamic equivalent of the Red Cross. Costs are low, and controlled by the government. The word for hospital is *devlet hastansi*. Turkey uses the international 'H' road sign to help locate hospitals.

All towns and large villages have a doctor within reach. The sign for doctor is *tibbi doctor*. All large resort hotels have a doctor on call, who will usually come quickly: contact reception. In case of an emergency, ring 112.

Opening hours
Shops are usually open from 9 am til 7 pm, Monday to Saturday. These are *minimum* hours. In resorts and tourist areas shops will often stay open until 11 pm, and also open on Sundays. The same is true of bazaars.

For bank opening hours, see Banks and currency exchange, page 25. For Post Offices, see Post and telephone, below.

Museums are usually open from 9.30 am until 4.30 pm, Tuesday to Sunday. They are usually closed on Mondays. Palaces keep the same hours, but tend to be closed on Thursday. Open-air sites tend to be open from 9 am until sunset, seven days a week.

Most offices are operational from 9 am until 6 pm, Monday to Friday. Government offices theoretically open half an hour earlier and close half an hour earlier. The lunch hour is rigorously observed in all Turkish offices, and appears in many places to amount to a complete cessation of activity from around noon till mid afternoon. If you want action, or (heaven forbid) decisive and speedy action, don't even think about ringing during the afternoon.

Post and telephone

Post Offices have a large yellow sign with PTT outside. In the big cities they are open from 8 am until 9 pm, Monday to Saturday. On Sunday they are open from 9 am to 7 pm. Smaller Post Offices are theoretically open from 8.30 am until 5 pm, Monday to Saturday, but these hours vary considerably. (Sometimes they are open even longer – but sometimes they are not.) In Post Offices you can post letters, buy stamps, make metered phone calls (national and international) and *usually* change money.

Postal charges are minimal, but constantly rise to keep pace with inflation. At present it costs 500TL to send a letter or postcard to Europe, and 700TL to send one to North America. A postcard will sometimes take five days to reach a western European destination, but don't count on this. It is not unknown for holiday cards to arrive with the Christmas mail. All public telephones, except metered ones in post offices and hotels, use jetons or phone cards. Jetons cost 500TL and can be bought in Post Offices, as can telephone cards.

To make a local call, put a jeton in the phone and then dial. The light will begin to flash and a warning bleep will sound when you need to feed in more jetons. Phone cards come in 30, 60, 120 and 180 units (the latter two being the only practical ones for international calls). To make a local call, dial the local number *only*. For a non-local call dial 9, wait for the buzz sound, then dial the complete number.

To make an international call, dial 99, then your country code, followed by the city or district code *minus* the opening nought, then the number. International calls from Turkey to northern Europe are not cheap. At present they cost about 20,000TL per minute. Rates don't seem to change at different times of day.

Much the best way to ring is by metered phone in a Post Office, where you can actually see the meter. Hotels tend to charge way over the odds for metered calls. If you need assistance with telephoning, or want directory enquiries, once again it is best to visit a Post Office, where there is a fair chance of finding someone who can get by in English or German.

Most Turkish telephone operators (and inevitably all the ones you'll have to deal with) do not speak English.

Two years on, the Turkish telephone numbering system is still being updated. This means that although the phone numbers in this guide are the most up to date, you may nevertheless have difficulty in obtaining some of them, both in cities and small villages.

Public holidays

From the evening before public holidays all public transport is booked solid. *Avoid travelling at all costs on these days.*

On public holidays all banks, Post Offices and many shops are closed. Museums are also liable to be closed, but most of the larger historic sites stay open. There are usually a few smaller shops open, too; otherwise, except in tourist areas, everything comes to a standstill.

- January 1 (New Year's Day).
- The beginning of the 40-day feast of Ramadan and Şeker Bayramı, the end of Ramadan: these two dates are calculated according to the Muslim calendar, and are thus not fixed. At present Ramadan starts in mid-February and finishes towards the end of March. However, Ramadan arrives about twelve days earlier each year.
- April 23 (Independence Day).

• May 19 (Atatürk's birthday).

• Kurban Bayrami, a religious holiday which takes place 68 days after the end of Ramadan.

• August 30, celebration of Victory over the Greeks at battle of Dumlupinar in 1922.

• October 29 (Republic Day).

• November 10, anniversary of Atatürk's death in 1938. The entire country observes a minute's silence at 9.05 am, the moment of his death.

Rush hours

The concept of rushing is alien to the Turkish character. However, in the big cities an all-too-recognizable clogging up of all traffic and an increase of philosophical debate between drivers of vehicles takes place each morning between 7.30 am and 9.30 am. The afternoon rush hour tends to last from just after 5 pm until well after 6 pm. Friday evening rush hours – especially in summer and/or before public holidays – may be quite dramatic.

Smoking

Smoking is still avidly practised in Turkey. Men and women smoke, and there are very few non-smoking areas. Buses and *dolmuşes* (see pages 22 and 23) are non-smoking zones, but this doesn't stop the driver, and thence his passengers. Indication of non-smoking signs by you is taken as a harmless foreign eccentricity, and ignored.

Time

Despite extending more than a thousand kilometres from its eastern border to its western border, the entire country operates on one time zone. This means that in winter the light starts to fade in the east just after three o'clock in the afternoon. Turkey is two hours ahead of Britain and one hour ahead of continental time, except for a brief period during October when it keeps the same time as the rest of Europe and is one hour ahead of Britain. For some time there has been pressure to eliminate this anomaly, but so far Turkey and Britain have stoutly managed to uphold it.

Tipping

Most restaurants simply add 10 to 15 per cent to your bill. Unfortunately, this has nothing to do with the service you have received, and the money does not go to the waiter. If your waiter has been pleasant, and you wish to reward him, you will have tip him personally.

Taxis now expect a tip. Usually it's best just to round up your bill to the nearest 1,000TL.

Some will tell you that in a *hamam* (Turkish Bath) you need to tip (up to 30 per cent). This is not so. You will have to pay for extras, such as massage or tea. However, in some tourist spots the attendants are now beginning to expect a tip: give 10 per cent.

Pre-history

Anatolia, the old name for the area of the Mediterranean basin now occupied by Turkey, has been inhabited since around 7000 BC. The first Stone Age settlements eventually grew into comparatively civilized Neolithic communities, such as the city of Çatal Höyük, 60 km SE of Konya.

Development was tediously slow, and for the next 5,000 years or so not much happened (from our perspective, at least). Then, around 2300 BC, in the midst of the Bronze Age, a people called the Hatti began building cities in central Anatolia. Their capital was Kültepe (modern Kanesh), some 20 km NE of Kayseri.

The Hatti appear to have evolved their own primitive culture and established extensive trading links, exchanging copper for cloth and tin from neighbouring peoples. Around 2000 BC the Hatti were overrun by the Hittites, an Indo-European people who probably arrived in Anatolia from the lands on the far side of the Black Sea and the Caucasus.

The Hittite Era

The Hittites established the first major empire in Anatolia, but they appear to have absorbed much of their culture, technical abilities and religion from the indigenous Hatti.

The Hittites established their great capital at Hattuşaş (modern Boğuzkale), just over 200 km E of Ankara. In time, the Hittite empire came to rival even that of Ancient Egypt, and in 1328 BC the two empires clashed in a great battle, the first of its kind in world history. This battle took place before the rules for such contests had been established, with the result that both sides came away claiming that they had won.

The Hittite Empire began falling apart with the arrival in the 13thC BC of the mysterious Sea People, who were almost certainly Iron Age settlers from the Greek islands. By now several local semi-independent kingdoms had been established along the west coast. One of these was Troy, which posed a serious threat to the Greeks in the Aegean and their trade with their colonies in the Black Sea. As a result of these prosaic factors (rather than the beauty of Helen, whose face according to the legend launched a thousand ships) the Greeks fought a war against the Trojans. The fall of Troy probably took place in 1275 BC, after which the Greeks began to colonise the west coast.

The Greeks

Ionia, as this region became known, produced several of the greatest Greek cities, such as Miletus and Ephesus. Some of them had colonies as far afield as the Black Sea and Egypt. It also played a crucial role in the development of Ancient Greek culture. Hippodamus, the great architect of Miletus, developed the grid plan, and this same city also produced Thales, who is now generally considered to have been the first philosopher.

In 547 BC the Persians invaded from the east and overran Anatolia. Just over 200 years later, in 334 BC, the Greeks invaded from the west under Alexander the Great, and the entire region fell under his control. After Alexander died his empire in Anatolia fragmented as his generals struggled for power. This was the era which saw the greatness of Pergamon. But by now Roman power was beginning its inexorable spread eastwards.

The Roman Era and the spread of Christianity

In 47 BC Julius Caesar led his armies into the Pontus (the kingdom bordering the Black Sea), and fought the Battle of Zela – after which he boasted: "Veni, vidi, vici." ('I came, I saw, I conquered.') By the end of the first century AD the Romans had conquered all of Anatolia as far as Armenia. This they named Asia Minor.

Already Christianity had begun to spread westwards along the Mediterranean coast, and north along the Aegean coast. Indeed, it seems likely that both St John and St Luke lived for a while in Ephesus, and that the Virgin Mary may have died nearby. St Paul played a major role in the spread of Christianity, journeying through Anatolia between 47-57 AD. As we know from the Bible, wherever he went there was always trouble – but it was largely through his efforts that Christianity proved to be no passing fad.

During the following centuries, the Roman Empire started falling apart in glorious fashion, and Christianity began to offer solace to its disillusioned citizenry and slaves. In the 4thC the Emperor Constantine became a Christian himself, and Christianity became the official religion of the Empire.

In order to preserve his crumbling Empire, Constantine shifted its capital from Rome to Byzantium (modern Istanbul.) This city soon became known as Constantinople, named after him.

The Byzantine Empire

The Roman Empire now split into two, with Constantinople as capital of the Eastern Empire, or Byzantine Empire as it later became known. For a while this new empire flourished. In 537 the Emperor Justinian built Aya Sofya, which for almost a thousand years was to remain the largest church in Christendom (enclosing a greater space even than the great Gothic cathedrals of medieval western Europe.)

Yet within two centuries, the Byzantine Empire found itself under threat on all sides. The Lombards and the Goths conquered its far-flung territory to the west; the Persians and the Arabs threatened in the east.

The Arabs had found a new religion, given to them by the prophet Muhammad. Under the banner of Islam, Arab raiders now spread throughout the Middle East. In 663 Arab raiders even managed to reach the shores of the Bosphorus, before they were finally driven back.

The Byzantine Empire had now lost all connection with Rome and had become essentially Greek in character. From this split derives the difference between the Roman Catholic Church and the Orthodox Church (which to this day remains the prominent religion in Greece and Russia). The Arab raiders of the 7thC disappeared from Asia Minor almost as quickly as they had appeared. But as they did so they passed on their religion to the Selçuks, a Turkoman tribe from central Asia who were moving in from the east and had conquered Baghdad in 1055. (The original Turkoman tribes were nomads who came from Mongolia, where they happily lived a homeless and nameless existence until the Chinese called them Tu-kueh.)

In 1071 the Selçuk army confronted and defeated the Byzantine army at Manzikert (Malazgirt) in eastern Turkey. From this power base the Selçuks continued to expand into Anatolia. A century later they established the Sultanate of Rum with its capital at Konya.

The Byzantine Empire now scored a devastating own goal. The alleged purpose of the Crusades was to take the Holy Land (modern Israel) for Christendom. The Roman and Byzantine churches should have united in this aim. The First Crusade had indeed helped the Byzantines to push back the advancing Selçuks, but by the time of the Fourth Crusade, things had changed. By now any Christian brotherly love between the Roman and the Byzantine churches had degenerated into the usual emotions with which Christian sects regard each other. In 1204 the soldiers of the Fourth Crusade, allegedly on their way to the Holy Land, arrived in Constantinople and sacked the city. Amidst scenes of great hilarity and rejoicing a prostitute was temporarily set on the emperor's throne in Aya Sofya.

During this period the Selçuk Sultanate of Rum controlled most of central Anatolia. Within a few years it found itself under serious threat from the east. The Mongol hordes of Genghis Khan had begun pouring out of eastern Asia, wreaking havoc and destruction wherever they passed. When they reached Anatolia, they were confronted by the Selcuks. In 1243 the Mongols defeated the Selçuks at the Battle of Köse Dağ.

This left a power vacuum in Asia Minor. The Mongols were a largely negative force of no lasting influence; the mortally wounded Selçuk Empire now gradually disintegrated, and in the west the Byzantines were more interested in Byzantine intrigue and preventing prostitutes from keeping the emperor's throne warm than maintaining an Asian empire.

Despite this lack of a single controlling power, Asia Minor now witnessed the two crucial developments which were to alter the entire character of this region until the present day.

For the next two centuries, the Turkomen people continued to migrate into the region, and Islam continued to spread.

One warrior band of Turks which moved into the region had a leader called Osman. From the end of the 13thC the dynasty which ruled this tribe came to be called the Osmanlis, after Osman. (In the west the name Osmanli was corrupted to Ottoman.) Osman was succeeded by his son Orhan, who expanded his territory to the southern shores of the Sea of Marmara, where Bursa became the first capital of the fledgling Ottoman Empire. At the start of the 15thC the Ottomans moved their capital to Edirne, in order to rule their growing empire whose territories had now expanded into the Balkans.

The Byzantine Empire was virtually surrounded and cut off from contact with western Europe. Eventually a huge Crusader army was despatched from Hungary to stem the Ottoman threat. This was confronted by the ruthless fratricide Sultan Beyazit I, known as 'lightning' for the speed of his military manoeuvres. The Crusader army was routed at Nicopolis (in modern-day Bulgaria) in 1396.

It seemed that Constantinople was doomed. But Beyazit I had reckoned without the Mongols, who now unexpectedly returned, this time led by the fearsome Tamerlane of Samarkand. The Ottoman Empire was badly overexposed on the eastern front, but Beyazit marched his army east to confront the invader. The two armies met at the Battle of Ankara (1402), and the Turks proved no match for the Mongols. So great was their defeat that the Mongols even succeeded in capturing Beyazit himself. According to their quaint custom, he was then stuffed into a cage and hauled along behind the Mongol army as it continued pillaging its way through Anatolia. It took him a year to die.

After this, the fun seemed to go out of it for Tamerlane and his rampaging hordes. Not long afterwards they decided to return home – where according to one story their sex-starved wives set upon them in much the same fashion as they had set upon the wives of those they had conquered.

This left Asia Minor clear for the Ottomans. Sultan Mehmet II ascended to the throne in 1451, and immediately began making plans for the conquest of Constantinople. This he finally achieved in 1453 – the most significant event in the eastern Mediterranean since the end of the classical era. Henceforth Mehmet was known as Mehmet the Conqueror.

The fall of Constantinople marked the end of the Byzantine Empire. This city now became the new capital of the Ottoman Empire, which soon entered its greatest phase. Under Suleiman the Magnificent, who reigned for almost the entire first half of 16thC, the Ottoman Empire expanded to cover an area comparable to the great world empires which had preceded it: that of Alexander the Great, and the Roman Empire. At its height, Ottoman rule extended though three continents. In Africa it ran along the north coast from Morocco (and into Spain) to Egypt, as well as a thousand miles up the Nile. In Asia it extended east to the shores of the Caspian and the Persian Gulf, and as far south as Yemen. In eastern Europe, Turkish troops reached the gates of Vienna. And the Turkish fleet under the notorious Barbarossa ruled virtually the entire Mediterranean.

Yet no sooner had Suleiman died than the empire began its long decline, starting with the reign of Selim the Sot, the ill-starred son of Suleiman's great love, the concubine Roxelana. Eventually, against all precedent, Roxelana had persuaded Suleiman to marry her. Such was her scheming power over Suleiman that she persuaded him to execute his grand vizier (a post similar in executive power to prime minister), his heir (one of his sons by a previous marriage), and even one of her own sons. This left the hapless Selim.

From now on events generally went from bad to worse. Intrigue, interference from the harem, and ineptitude, all played their part. With few exceptions the sultans were mediocrities. Amongst those who were not mediocrities, there were some spectacular incompetents – such as Ibrahim the Mad and Mustapha I. Despite all this, the empire managed to hold together. In 1683, the Turks even managed once again to lay seige to Vienna – after which the first croissant (crescent) was baked as a celebration of the Viennese triumph over the forces of the crescent (Muslim) flag.

On the whole, the Ottoman Empire was exemplary. Its extremely easy-going 'rule' often consisted of little more than collecting a regular tribute to the sultan. The lifestyle of the locals was not interfered with, and if they converted to Islam they could even rise within the administration. Opposition was admittedly often dealt with in drastic fashion: mass slaughter of the population was the usual response. But on the whole the people of the Ottoman Empire were only too glad to be ruled by the Turks for four centuries or so. This was a period of stability, when they were not either involved in a war with their neighbours, or being ruled by some gruesome tyrant of their own. One only has to look at the history of the Middle East before and since the Ottoman Empire to realize the beneficial effects of such somnolent rule.

By the 18thC the decline of the Ottoman Empire was beginning to match that of the Roman Empire, both in terms of endurance and historical spectacle. Egypt was being 'looked after' by the British, who had also 'leased' Cyprus; the Greeks had been reluctantly granted a small part of their country in which to be independent; and the west coast of the Balkans almost from Albania to the Peleponnese was run virtually as a private kingdom by the Sultan's appointee, the notorious Ali Pasha.

The sight of this collapsing empire soon aroused the interest of the European powers, who were all greedy to extend their own vast empires. The Russians, the French, and the British each began jockeying for position. The result was the Crimean War. Then the Germans and the Austro-Hungarians joined in. The rivalries this engendered and the treaties all these countries consequently signed with one another were to pave the way for the First World War.

Meanwhile, some decided that it was time the Ottoman Empire 'caught up' with the rest of the world. Revolution had been unthinkable in the old empire, let alone an Industrial Revolution. Turkey and its empire were a preserve in which time had stood still. Reform was long overdue.

During the course of the year 1876, after no less than two mentally deficient sultans had been deposed, the remarkable Sultan Abdul Hamid II was appointed to the throne. By the end of the year a constitution was proclaimed. There followed a slight rush of blood to the head, involving a brief but disastrous war with Russia. After this Abdul Hamid decided to dismiss parliament and revoke the constitution, which had been in place for all of two years. He then retired to the Yildiz Palace in Istanbul and ruled in isolation for the next 40 years.

Abdul Hamid II was opposed by the Young Turk movement, which wanted European-style reform. He tried exiling their leaders, but by 1908 they had gained sufficient support to force the readoption of the constitution. This brought widespread rejoicing, but also a revolt by junior officers who were against this lurch towards western influences. The revolt overthrew the government, and was supported by Abdul Hamid II. Abdul Hamid's much vaunted secret police had advised him extremely badly. The officers were in turn ousted by the Young Turks, who forced Abdul Hamid II to resign in favour of his younger brother, who took over as a puppet ruler. From now on the Ottoman Empire was ruled by a triumvirate of Young Turks. Cultural and political freedom flourished briefly, but within four years an even more severe and inept dictatorship was in control.

By now the Balkan states were working themselves up for the Balkan War, which broke out in 1911. Initially, everyone united against the Turks, but as soon as they had achieved independence they immediately went to war against each other *and* the Turks. (One of the essential ingredients of a Balkan War is that there should be more than two sides.)

Various Balkan armies advanced to within a few kilometres of Istanbul, and were then driven back. Various political assassinations took place in Istanbul (predictably, the minister of War didn't last). Then the Turks took advantage of the free-for-all amongst the Balkan countries and grabbed back some of Thrace.

The First World War

These events were overtaken by the outbreak of the First World War in 1914. The Young Turks knew perfectly well that Turkey's only hope was to remain neutral and stay out of the fighting. But as a result of the usual intrigue (it was discovered that someone had signed a treaty with the Germans), and some skilful diplomatic moves by the Germans (who 'loaned' the Turks two warships and then sent them across the Black Sea to shell the Russian port of Odessa), Turkey soon found itself in the war – and on the wrong side, at that.

The First World War was a disaster for Turkey. The defence of Gallipoli in 1915 against the invading French,

British and Commonwealth forces was the only redeeming military action. (For further details see the entry for Gallipoli, page 66.) A low point was reached with the Armenian Massacre of the same year, the second genocide of the 20thC (after the massacre of natives by the Belgians in the Congo). Unforgivably, attempts are still made to deny or justify this sickening event in which over a million Armenians lost their lives. (For further details see the entry for Van, page 208.)

By the end of the war the Ottoman Empire had collapsed and Turkish territory had shrunk to virtually its present borders. The country was in a deeply disillusioned state. Seizing their opportunity, the Greeks invaded, covertly encouraged by the victorious European powers. The Greeks took Smyrna (modern Izmir) and began moving into the Anatolian hinterland.

The shock of this invasion by their former colony roused the Turks from their torpor. The heroic general who had led the Turkish forces at Gallipoli, Mustafa Kemal, began organizing armed resistance. The Turkish War of Independence lasted from 1920 until 1922. It ended with complete Turkish victory.

In 1922, as the Turkish army drove the Greek Army and thousands of Greek refugees into Smyrna, the city caught fire. In the resulting confusion and panic a full-scale massacre took place. (For further details see Izmir, page 221.)

After this conflict and the so-called Smyrna Massacre, it was agreed between the Turkish and Greek governments that there should be an exchange of minority populations between the two countries. As a result, half a million Muslim Turks living in Greece were deported to Turkey, and well over a million Orthodox Greeks living in Turkey were deported to Greece. As can be imagined, this uprooting of populations, many of whom had been settled for centuries, caused widespread heartbreak and economic hardship.

After the victory in the War of Independence, Mustafa Kemal was the hero of the hour. Whilst fighting the War of Independence he had defied the sultan (and had even been condemned to death in his absence.) But by now he had the support of almost the entire country. In 1922 the sultan was deposed and the sultanate was abolished. On 29th October 1923 Turkey was declared a republic and Mustafa Kemal became its first president. In order to make a complete break with the old Ottoman Empire, the capital was moved from Istanbul to Ankara, and Mustafa Kemal set about a programme of reform. His aim was to modernise the country along European lines.

In 1925, in a series of moves against the power of the conservative religious heirarchy, Mustafa Kemal closed down the Islamic religious brotherhoods, and banned the wearing of the fez and the veil. From now on women would be equal citizens with men – a truly revolutionary measure. In an attempt to overcome illiteracy, the Latin alphabet was introduced instead of Arabic script for the Turkish language.

Atatürk

These reforms met with considerable opposition, and there were a number of attempts on Mustafa Kemal's life. After surviving these, he put down the opposition ruthlessly. Mustafa Kemal became a dictator, partly out of necessity, but his heart was in the right place. He assumed the name Atatürk, which means father of the Turks.

Meanwhile in Europe other dictators had arrived on the scene. Ironically, Atatürk was to benefit greatly from the injustices of his fascist European peers. The years after 1933 saw a large influx of Jewish intellectuals and scholars from Germany. Many of these were given posts in Atatürk's reformist administration. But Atatürk had lived a hard life, and in 1938 after just 15 years of rule he died at the age of 57.

Fortunately, Atatürk's foresight did ensure that the administration continued on the course he had mapped. In spite of heavy pressure from both the western allies and the Germans, Turkey maintained a neutral stance during the Second World War, thus avoiding the European cataclysm.

Such unaligned neutrality became impossible, however, after the end of the war. In 1945 Stalin threatened to occupy parts of eastern Turkey and demanded military bases along the seaway linking the Black Sea and the Mediterranean. Turkey turned to the United States for help. President Truman promised military support together with economic aid.

In 1950, Turkey became for the first time a multi-party democracy. The result of the first election was power for Adnan Menderes and his Democratic party. Menderes began by being largely populist, but as the years went by his government became increasingly corrupt and repressive, even suspending a number of Atatürk's reforms. In 1960 this was used as an excuse by the military for a coup, which later resulted in Menderes' execution, and mass arrests.

A new constitution was written, and the country attempted to make a fresh start. A period of ineffectual government followed, with various attempted coups. By the mid-Sixties the economic situation was so bad that large-scale emigration began – mainly to the booming factories of Germany. This absentee labour force remains an important factor in the Turkish economy. At present there are more than a million Turkish *gastarbeiter* in Germany who between them contribute the equivalent of more than 5 billion pounds sterling or 7.5 billion U.S. dollars each year to the Turkish economy. The constant return of emigrants who have worked in Germany has also made a profound impact Turkish society, continuing the Europeanisation started by Atatürk.

In 1974 the Greek military junta attempted to take over the independent island of Cyprus. For many years the Turkish and Greek communities on the island had lived a fraught co-existence, and this was the last straw for the Turks, who staged a military invasion and occupied the northern half of the island. The Cyprus problem has continued to plague the traditionally uneasy relations between Greece and Turkey. 1983 saw the election of Turgut Özal and his Motherland Party. Under Özal's leadership, a period of economic growth continued throughout the eighties (with just a few hiccups). This culminated in Turkey applying for membership of the European Community, and a determined attempt to patch up relations with their Greek neighbours.

At the outbreak of the conflict in the Persian Gulf, Turkey joined in the United Nations sanctions against the regime of Saddam Hussein, suffering considerable economic set-back. The situation worsened after the war when many thousands of Kurdish refugees crossed the border from Iraq into Turkey. Relations between the national government and the Kurds worsened, and there has been continuing agitation by the Kurds for independence ever since.

Despite this, Turkey has continued to experience a major tourist boom, especially along the Aegean and Mediterranean coasts. The economy, too, has managed to weather the storms and now looks set for further expansion. At the same time a new generation of younger Turkish politicians, many of them educated in the United States, has begun to make its presence felt on the political scene. The culmination of this trend was the election of Tamsu Çilar as Turkey's first woman prime minister in 1993.

SOME KEY CULTURAL THEMES

The Turkish language

Turkish is one of the Turkic group of languages which are spoken throughout the central Asian region by the Turkoman peoples. Through the centuries it has absorbed many words from Persian, Arabic and latterly European languages.

There's no point in pretending that Turkish is easy. So what do you do when you're confronted with a language that looks like a computer malfunction?

The first essential is to learn how to pronounce it. This apparent impossibility becomes much less challenging once you realize that Turkish is actually the easiest of all languages to pronounce. Unlike most other languages, it works in an absolutely rational fashion.

Each letter is pronounced in just one way. (Compare this with, say, the English pronounciation of 'h' in 'the', 'enough', 'ham' and so forth.)

A few hints with the vowels:

a is pronounced as in star
e as in let
i as in hit
o as in rot
u as in true

The difficulties with all those accents disappear once you realize what they are for:

s is pronounced as in sum.
ş as in shoot.
c is pronounced as a j, as in joke.

35

ç as a ch, as in chump.
ö as ur, as in burp.
ü as ue, as in glue.
g is pronounced as in go.
ğ is mostly silent, or as a y between two vowels.

A few further hints:

h is always pronounced, as in happy.
j is pronounced the same as the s in measure.
v is softened, so it's almost like a w.

Otherwise, most letters are the same as in English.

With this knowledge, you are further ahead than you may realize. Turkish has borrowed many words from European languages, and if you can pronounce Turkish properly, you can often identify the borrowed words, many of which can be useful to the visitor. They usually arrive in Turkish in phonetic form. A few examples:

Koç = coach
Otogar = auto gare = bus station
Kuaför = coiffure = ladies' hairdresser

And from French:
Şarküteri = *charcuterie*
Höparlor = loudspeaker

Here are a few for you to work out on your own:

Sosyal Demokrat
Büfe
Recepsiyon
Hidrolik
Sinema
Beysbol
Nükleer

and two of my own favourites: *Kanguru* and *Psikiyatrist*

As for progressing any further in the language, all I can suggest is an intimate relationship with a patient Turk (or as a last resort, a phrase book).

Religion

The religion in Turkey is Islam. The Turks are for the most part deeply religious, and like any such nation are bound to have their fanatics. However, Muslim Fundamentalists at present make up a small (though vociferous) percentage of the population. The greatest concentration of Fundamentalists tends to be in the south-eastern cities, but amongst any larger gathering of students you will recognize a few of their bearded male and shrouded female adherents.

For the most part, religion is taken in a devout but surprisingly easy-going fashion by the Turks. There is a similarity here to the Church of England, and like many Englishmen Turks are not keen to discuss religion, especially with foreigners. A Muslim looks upon Islam as the ultimate revealed religion, and thus its tenets are *beyond discussion*.

Contrary to popular misconception, Islam is not *in itself* against Judaism or Christianity. Indeed, its believers hold that Islam has grown out of these religions and superceded them. Most Jewish and early Christian saints are also considered holy by Muslims, as are the Jewish and Christian holy places. It is mainly racial conflict and history (from the Crusades to the present situation in the Middle East) which have led to conflict between the religions.

Islam was founded by the prophet Muhammad, who was born in Mecca (now in Saudi Arabia) around 570 AD. In 610 Muhammad heard the voice of God while he was meditating. He became the Messenger of God, and communicated God's Holy Word in the Koran, which is the Muslim equivalent of the Bible.

The most sacred part of the Koran (and similar in force to the Judao-Christian Ten Commandments) is the Five Pillars. These are the kernel of Islamic belief and practice, and are as follows:

Speak, understand and believe: 'There is no god but God, and Muhammad is his prophet.'

Perform ritual washing and say prayers at the five appointed times each day.

Give alms to the poor.

Keep the holy month of Ramadan sacred by fasting. (The Turkish word for Ramadan is Ramazan.)

Make a pilgrimage at least once in your lifetime to Mecca, if you can. (This pilgrimage is known as the Hajj.)

Besides being a prophet, Muhammad was also a great military leader. By the time he died on June 8 632 at Mecca, he had virtually united all the nomadic peoples of the Saudi Arabian peninsula. This led to the Arab conquests which spread over the Middle East, bringing the Islamic faith in their wake. The Selçuk Turks, a Turkoman tribe from Mongolia, were the first Turks to convert to Islam. (For further details see page 31.)

This conjunction of warrior and religious leader may possibly have played a role in the Islamic attitude towards holy war, known as *Jihad*. (The Christians have been under the impression that they have fought many holy wars, despite the fact that their religion specifically forbids such practice.)

Likewise, Islam's repressive and primitive attitude towards women may just possibly be an echo of 7thC desert nomadic practice.

Turkish baths (*hamam*)

No trip to Turkey is complete without a visit to the *hamam*. This is both a refreshing and deeply relaxing experience, as well as a cleansing one. (For Turks, this is so in both the physical and the spiritual sense.)

Most towns will have at least one public *hamam*. These are strictly segregated (though in some of the smaller *hamams* this will be done on a rota basis, rather than having different areas for men and women).

When you enter the *hamam* you first go to the changing area, where you are allotted a locker for your clothes and valuables. You are given a *peştamel,* a Turkish version of the sarong, which you wrap around your soon-to-be-reduced waist. This article should be worn at all times. Turkish baths are sociable but modest establishments. Often you are also given a pair of *takunya* (clogs).

Proceed to the *hamaret*, which is where it all happens. This is the main bathing room, usually constructed of marble. The atmosphere in here is quite warm and steamy – something of a disappointment for those who were expecting some kind of ritual trial by heat. But have no fear, the trials to come will prove no disappointment.

The central area of the *hamaret* is occupied by the *göbek taşi* which means navel stone. This is a raised

stone platform (usually marble-clad), beneath which is the heating fire. This stone will be hot, or sometimes *very* hot. Lay yourself down on it, if you can. If at first you don't succeed, then you'd better try again: this bit, after all, is the main purpose of your visit.

Within a few minutes you will be aware of the sweat streaming from every pore in your body. A deeply satisfying sensation. As a respite, you can pour water over yourself from a scoop. This cools you down so that you can start the process all over again.

If you feel daring, you can also have a massage. This will feel as if every bone in your body is being disjointed, but does you an *immense* amount of good (so I'm assured by enthusiastic, masochistic friends).

The same sadist who applied your exquisitely excruciating massage can also give you a rub-down with a *kese*, a sharply whiskered glove. This scrapes the engrained grime and layers of (allegedly) dead skin from the smarting surface of your body. Meanwhile your raw flesh continues to emit streams of sweat. Like all painful exercises in life, these assaults on your anatomy will cost you extra money.

It's worth spending around an hour in this steamy inferno. Afterwards, you will feel an amazing sense of well-being. Enveloped in your aura of purity you can now return to the changing room. Here you can be served tea or mineral water, which allegedly replaces the liquid you have lost, but in fact simply dribbles from your pores.

Turkish literature

Sadly, few modern Turkish writers are available in translation. An exception is Yaşar Kemal, whose best-known work is *Mehmet My Hawk*. You may find this somewhat rural for your taste. More interesting is *The Sea-Crossed Fishermen*, by the same author, which is set on the coast by Istanbul.

By far the most readable modern Turkish writer is Sait Faik, who wrote stories of Istanbul low life. Faik was a psychologically interesting loner, whose drinking bouts and homosexual inclinations led him to know and to empathise with the sufferings of Istanbul's underclass. He died in 1954, and his finest translated work is the collection called *A Dot on the Map*.

Istanbul:
introduction

Istanbul can claim with justice to be the world's greatest historical city. In its time, the city standing on this spot has been capital of three of the world's great empires: the Roman Empire, which gave way to the Byzantine Empire, and the Ottoman Empire.

The city itself spans two continents, Europe and Asia, with the dividing channel of the Bosphorus running through the middle. The ancient heart of Istanbul lies in Europe – but the moment you set foot in it you are aware that this is like no other European city. You have arrived in the Orient.

By far the best way to arrive in Istanbul is by sea. As you approach across the Sea of Marmara, the minarets and domes of the great mosques rise from the horizon in spectacular fashion. As you sail closer, the growing city embraces the skyline, surrounding you, until finally you dock in its very heart – the waters all around you alive with ferries, fishing boats, liners, freighters, the quayside below teeming with porters, vendors, carters, stall-owners, the nearby bridges thronged with hooting cars, buses, lorries, taxis.

Istanbul is a city such as cities used to be. No other city in Europe still has a street life like this. The pavements are alive with shoeshine boys, perfume sellers, vendors hawking trays of fresh mussels, rings of sesame bread, stalls selling fruit, frying fish, nuts, roasting corn cobs – as well as the more traditional market hucksters selling traditional modern fake watches, intricately useless toys and gadgets, noise-making electronicware and simple computers for up-to-date simpletons.

There are crowded mazes of alleyways, modern boulevards, labyrinthine covered bazaars, historic palaces, green gardens with fountains, and of course mosques of all sizes. A man who is tired of Istanbul is not tired of life – he is only human. The entire city is one huge culture

• *The Blue Mosque.*

shock. Even when you live here, every morning is a bright new high-decibel event of exhausting proportions – starting at first light with the dawn calls to prayer ringing out from the minarets all over the city.

Go easy, taking it in gradually, in absorbable portions – and the city of Istanbul will provide one of the great experiences of your life. Try to take it all in at once and you'll be overwhelmed. Even New Yorkers can suffer city-saturation here.

Yet if you stand on the terraces of the sultans at Topkapi Palace looking down over the Bosphorus, or pause on Galata Bridge to gaze across the Golden Horn towards the grand mosques at sunset, or drive over one of the great suspension bridges and look down on the shores of two continents, you'll see unforgettable cityscapes such as are matched nowhere else on the globe. All rivetting dreams have a sub-strata of nightmare.

Istanbul is Turkey's main city and port, though it ceased to be the capital more than 70 years ago. It remains the nations's main commercial centre, and its population is estimated to be rapidly approaching ten million. Compared with some of the world's great urban centres, this may not appear such a high figure – but it certainly does at ground level, where it seems you run into just about everybody.

This is also Turkey's cultural centre, and as any local will tell you, it is also home to the nation's greatest football teams. The sport comes a close second to Islam as Turkey's religion. When an important match is being played, the nation comes to a standstill, all male eyes glued to the café TV screens.

USING THIS SECTION

Don't, during the first days of your first visit to this teeming oriental city, try to discover it on foot, especially if it's summer. Walking may well be the best way to explore Florence, Paris or Rome; here, you'll end up overheated, disoriented and quite possibly depressed and disturbed by the culture shock.

The main sights of Istanbul are listed and described in alphabetical order on pages 42-57 as conventional, gazeteer-style entries. The most comfortable way to tackle the city is to turn straight to these pages and take in the classic tourist sights in leisurely fashion, getting to and from them with least commotion, by taxi or *dolmuş* (see pages 23 and 24).

If after a day or two you feel like exploring in greater depth, consult my two walks, starting on pages 54 and 56 (which are best taken very early in the morning or late in the afternoon to minimize aggravation and heat).

Following these two city walks, starting on page 58, are interesting sights outside Istanbul, but within easy reach. Hotel recommendations begin on page 45 and restaurants on page 60.

ARRIVING

If you fly to Istanbul you will land at Atatürk Airport, to the west of the city. This has a domestic and an international terminal separated by 5 km. Both are connected to the city centre by a regular bus service, which costs 15,000TL. The journey should take 20 minutes, but the route is prone to hold-ups and often takes longer. Much better to take a taxi direct to your hotel, which will cost around 130,000TL. (These prices were correct at time of going to press, but subect to dramatic rises because of the extreme weakness of the TL.)

If you travel to Istanbul by boat, you will arrive in the heart of the city. From here it's best to take a taxi to a hotel. This should cost you just 40,000TL maximum.

Buses arrive at either of the two main *otogars* or bus stations. Buses from Europe arrive at the Topkapi *Otogar*, which is 5 km from the city centre. There are buses from here into town. But to avoid adding to the complexities of your first encounter with Istanbul, you're far better off taking a taxi to your hotel. This should cost less than 50,000TL. If you're travelling to Istanbul from Asia, your bus will arrive at the misleadingly named Harem *Otogar*. From here there is a regular cheap *dolmuş* service (see below) to Kadiköy, where you can catch a ferry across the Bosphorus to the city centre.

Istanbul's European railway station (Sireki) boasts a service from London, and its Asiatic railway station (Haydarpaşa) boasts a service from Moscow. These are at present idle boasts, owing to the civil wars in former Yugoslavia and in Georgia. If you make it to Istanbul by train, you will be far too experienced a traveller to need further advice about onward transfer.

PUBLIC TRANSPORT

Getting around Istanbul can be comparatively painless. Taxis are cheap and plentiful (they're yellow, and driven by absent-minded types who must always be reminded to switch on the meter). Even cheaper is the comprehensive *dolmuş* service. In Istanbul the *dolmuş* vehicles are mini buses and large old American cars. They are essentially shared taxis with fixed routes which ply up and down the main streets; destinations are marked in the window. You wave down the driver, pay for how far you want to go along the route, and get out when you reach your destination. As everyone else does this too, it makes for quite a lively and amicable journey.

Journeys across the Bosphorus can be made by one of the many antiquated ferries. From Asia to Europe it's free, but the intercontinental trip from Europe to Asia will cost around the same as a glass of tea. Smaller boats also ply some of the routes – for those who want that authentic nautical encounter with a supertanker in mid channel.

Istanbul's bus system is cheap and comprehensive, but highly complicated unless you really know your way around. There is also an excellent metro system, which runs everywhere except where *you* want it to go (it's intended for commuters, not tourists). The Istanbul train system suffers from a similar defect.

ACCOMMODATION GUIDELINES

The best area in which to look for a hotel is the Sultanahmet district, the old

• *The Blue Mosque.*

quarter in the heart of ancient Istanbul. Many of the hotels and *pansiyons* have superb views of the grand mosques and of the Sea of Marmara. There are also some good places to stay further east around Topkapi.

The heart of the modern city is around Taksim, where standards go up, along with prices. Out of the heat, and only an hour or two away by ferry, are the Princes' Islands (page 59), which also have some reasonable accommodation.

NEIGHBOURHOODS TO AVOID

Walking the streets of Istanbul with the flood-lit minarets rising against the stars is one of the romantic treats of the city. Women (and to a lesser extent men) should avoid doing so on their own, unless they stick to populated, well-lit districts.

The small streets south of the Galata Tower of Yuhsek Kaldirim Caddesi fulfil both these criteria – but they are also the red light district, and attract the usual astute investors who prefer to abandon their emotional life in favour of market forces. If you don't wish to be mistaken for a commercial operator (male or female) in this field, wander elsewhere.

SIGHTS & PLACES OF INTEREST

BLUE MOSQUE, THE
(SULTAN AHMET CAMII)

By Hippodrome. Visitors must remove shoes.
The renowned Blue Mosque is in fact grey. It derives its name from the colour of the 17thC Iznik tiles inside, of which there are more than 20,000. Those on the balcony are meant to mirror the colour of heaven.

The Blue Mosque was started in the early 17thC by the 19-year-old sultan Ahmet I, who wanted Muslim Istanbul to have a building to rival the Christian-built Aya Sofya. To this day they stand opposite each other, and none but an aesthetic numbskull would mistake which is the greater building. The soaring minarets and graceful domes of the Blue Mosque only serve to emphasize the crude exterior barrenness of its so-called rival.

Yet curiously, where Aya Sofya succeeded, the Blue Mosque failed. Aya Sofya's unsupported dome, which was far larger and erected more than a thousand years previously, was not to be emulated by the sultan's architects, who were unable to solve the problem of supporting the mosque's far smaller central dome. It is in fact supported by four fat, clumsy pillars – aptly named the **Elephant Foot Pillars** – whose 16-m girth disfigures the lofty inner space of the mosque.

At the entrance to the mosque there is a **ramp**, built to enable Sultan Ahmet to ride his horse into the mosque, so that he wouldn't have to dismount before entering the Royal Box.

But on one point the will of Sultan Ahmet did not prevail. When it was seen that the Blue Mosque had no fewer than six minarets, there was consternation: it equalled the number of minarets on the great Elharam Mosque at Mecca. So eventually, rather than tear down one of the minarets and ruin the proportions of his new mosque, Ahmet paid for a seventh minaret to be built

• *Opposite: Saint Sophia.*

BACKGROUND

Istanbul's history started quite recently, compared with that of many cities in the eastern Mediterranean. Archaeologists have recently uncovered evidence of Mycenaen remains dating from the 13thC BC, but the city's generally accepted origins date from much later. According to the tradition recorded by the Roman historian Strabo, the city was founded in the middle of 7thC BC by colonists from Megara in Greece. Their leader was called Byzas, and it was from him that the city received its first name: Byzantium.

This original settlement was at the tip of land now known as Seraglio (Sarayburnu) Point, which stands at the end of the peninsula between the Golden Horn, the Bosphorus and the Sea of Marmara. According to legend, Byzas was instructed to found a city by the Delphic Oracle at the site 'across from the city of the blind people'. This is usually taken to refer to the city of Chalcedon across the Bosphorus, whose inhabitants must have been blind to miss the strategic advantages of founding their city on the opposite peninsula.

The site of Byzantium was eminently defensible, being protected by the sea on three sides. However, this didn't prevent it from being beseiged by the invading Persians in the early 6thC BC, and again 200 years later by the army of Philip of Macedon (father of Alexander the Great). The city was also sacked by the Roman Emperor Septimus Severus in the 2ndC AD, though he later rebuilt the city's defensive walls and constructed the Hippodrome, the ancient Roman stadium whose outline can still be seen beside the Sultanahmet Mosque.

Throughout the classical era, Byzantium was strategically important, guarding the entrance to the Bosphorus and the route to the colonies of the Black Sea. But it never played a leading role, and remained subservient to other more powerful cities. All this was to change in the early 4thC AD. By now the Roman Empire was racked by civil wars, and was generally falling apart. The Emperor Constantine therefore decided to move his capital to

Byzantium: no idle choice, since the power centre of the Roman Empire had shifted to the east, and the superstitious Constantine noted that, like Rome, Byzantium was a city built on seven hills. Indeed he considered calling his new capital New Rome, but in the end decided to dispense with such modesty and called it Constantinople.

The Roman Empire split in two, with Constantinople as the capital of its eastern half. Then Rome fell to the barbarians and Constantinople became capital of all that remained of the ancient empire. Through the dark ages, this eastern empire remained an outpost of Roman civilization, but in character was soon much more Greek than Roman, and became known as the Byzantine Empire.

This too eventually entered its own long period of decline, characterized by political factionalism and plotting of extreme deviousness, as a result of which the word Byzantine has entered the English language as a byword for arcane complexity, especially with regard to intrigue.

Finally, in 1453, the Ottoman sultan Mehmet II overran Constantinople, bringing the Byzantine Empire to an end. The city now became the capital of the Ottoman Empire, which at its height was to extend from the gates of Vienna to the tip of Arabia. The city was still referred to by the conquering Turks as Konstantiniyye, but through the centuries it gradually came to be known as Istanbul. Surprisingly, it wasn't officially given this name until 1930, by which time the Ottoman Empire had ceased to exist.

In 1923, when Mustafa Kemal (later to be known as Atatürk) became president of the new Turkish Republic, he moved the nation's capital to Ankara, a symbolic break with the country's Ottoman past.

Since the Second World War, Istanbul has rapidly expanded. Nowadays, its modern sector boasts apartment blocks, high-rise office buildings, prestige edifices and spectacular suspension bridges, which make it very much a 20thC metropolis – but the old Ottoman city of the grand mosques and palaces still remains very much a feature.

at the Elharam Mosque.

The interior is refreshingly uncluttered: an empty floor merely strewn with huge carpets. The present stained glass windows are distinctly garish, but they manage to illuminate the interior to good effect. The originals were made of the best Venetian glass and are said to have rendered the lofty interior rather dim. Yet despite the air of emptiness, the lack of ethereal gloom and the Elephant's Foot Pillars, the interior of this mosque retains a distinct air of spirituality far more compelling and immediate than one encounters in the trophy-laden interiors of

many a western European cathedral.

DOLMABAHÇE PALACE

On the Bosphorus shore at Beşiktaş. This was the modern palace of the sultans, built in the mid 19thC by Sultan Abdül Mecid. It stands on a historic site: the harbour from which Mehmet II launched his final attack on Constantinople in 1453. By the 19thC this harbour had silted up and been turned into a royal park, complete with oriental pavilions: *dolmabahçe* means filled garden.

It is customary to ridicule the Dolmabahçe Palace as a copy of European bad taste. The place is certainly a gross disappointment compared with the Topkapi Palace which it displaced, but it is easily outclassed in matters of bad taste by many British, French and German royal residences of the period.

Unfortunately, you are obliged to go on a conducted tour. This lasts for just under an hour, and the guides share the crippled aesthetic sense of the late Ottomans. Choose a Japanese-speaking tour, and gaze at leisure over the heads of your companions without meaningful interruption.

Best of all is the **Throne Room**, whose ceiling is almost 40 m high. This is dominated by the largest (four-and-a-half tons), most tasteless chandelier ever made – presented appropriately enough by Queen Victoria, who evidently had her own ideas on heavyweight oriental décor.

The royal proceedings in the Throne Room would be watched from behind a grille by inferior beings such as members of the harem and the international press, who needless to say were *strictly* segregated from each other.

Other points of interest include **Sultan Adbül Aziz's gargantuan bed**, the living quarters of the majority of its occupants (the **Harem**), the **sultan's bath** (a veritable reservoir), the occasional **views out over the Bosphorus**, and the **room where Atatürk died** on the morning of November 10 1938 (the palace clocks are kept at 9.05, the time of his death).

The Dolmabahçe Palace was intended to demonstrate to the world that contrary to rumour the Ottoman Empire was far from bankrupt. Its enormous cost almost succeeded in turning the rumour into fact.

THE BOSPHORUS (BOĞAZIÇI)

The narrow strip of water which divides Europe from Asia, linking the Black Sea to the Sea of Marmara, is about 30 km long and 3 km wide, with a very swift southerly current. This last is caused by the great rivers which flow into the Black Sea: the Danube, the Dnieper, the Dniestr and the Don.

Since ancient times the Bosphorus has had great strategic importance as the only waterway connecting the Mediterranean with the Black Sea.

Bosphorus literally means 'ox ford', and has the usual bovine associations you'd expect of the name. The goddess Io is said to have swum across its waters after turning herself into a cow.

It is now one of the busiest shipping lanes in the world.

THE GOLDEN HORN (HALİÇ)

This is the strech of water which runs west off the Bosphorus just before it enters the Sea of Marmara. It bisects the heart of European Istanbul and is always a picturesque clutter of shipping. The teeming Galata Bridge crosses it and it is overlooked from the south by many of the grand mosques.

It got its name because its waters twist like a horn and turn golden in the dawn. Before being flooded by water from the Bosphorus this was a 7 km-long river valley.

RECOMMENDED HOTELS

Hotels in Istanbul tend, unsurprisingly, to be more expensive than anywhere else in the country. But it's worth paying a little bit extra as there are some exceptional places to stay; likewise, the fleapits of Istanbul are *real* fleapits, recommended only to entomologists.

Kalyon Hotel, LL-LLL; *Kennedy Caddesi; tel.* 216 517 440.

One of the best locations in the city – looking out towards the Asian shore where the Bosphorus flows into the Sea of Marmara. A must for nautical buffs, the Kalyon (whose name means galleon) also has a gourmet restaurant. In the summer their outside terrace overlooking the sea is a great spot for musing.

Pera Palas Hotel, LLL; *98 Meşrutiyet Caddesi in Tepebaşi, north of Golden Horn; tel.* 216 151 4560.

This is the famous 'Orient Express' hotel – built in 1892 to accommodate the train's celebrity passengers and travelling royalty. Agatha Christie stayed in room 411, the suite where Atatürk stayed is now a museum. Royalty, prime ministers and the Greta Garbos of this world made do as best they could in what was left.

Still maintains an air of gracious elegance, despite becoming a favourite with foreign correspondents. Internationally famous bar, excellent outdoor dining, great *hamam* (Turkish bath).

Hotel Grand Lord, LL; *22 Azimkar Sokak; tel.* 216 517 7630.

Large, well-equipped hotel in Aksaray, just a couple of hundred metres from the seafront; also handy for the airport road. Very helpful desk staff who speak English and German.

Hotel Antique, LLL; *Küçük Ayasofya Caddesi, 17 Oğul Sokak; tel.* 216 516 0997.

Between the Hippodrome and the Sea Wall. Friendly spot with clean, well-equipped but midget-sized rooms. The big bonus here is the views out over the Sea of Marmara. A tiny terrace upstairs, where breakfast is served, has breathtaking views of the sea and Blue Mosque. Stunning sunsets. If you're planning to run away for a secret tryst in Istanbul, this is the place to which you should run.

Rose Pansiyon, L-LL; *Aksakal Sokak, Küçük Ayasophya Caddesi; tel.* 216 518 9705.

Friendly, well-run budget accommodation close to the seafront and within easy walking distance of the sights in the heart of the old city. The bar, which runs to late hours, is a useful spot for meeting fellow travellers.

Hotel Dünya L; *79 Meşrutiyet Caddesi; tel.* 216 144 0940.

For those who want low-budget accommodation, this is about as low as you'll want to go. The rooms are clean but have a distinctly worn-out look, as do the staff. Ask for a room at the top, where there are great views out over the sea.

If the above is full, another similar spot with similar prices is nearby:

Hotel Erişen, L; *Galipdede Caddesi, 10 Şahkulu Sokak; tel.* 216 149 9169.

This one has few redeeming features bar the price and the fascinating seediness of the surrounding street life. You will receive an inappropriately jokey welcome to the gloom, and will doubtless respond similarly when informed of their joke prices.

If you fancy staying on an island in the Sea of Marmara within easy reach of the city, try:

Hotel Splendid, LLL; *23 Nisan Caddesi, Büyükada; tel.* 212 382 6950.

Superb Belle Epoque hotel with all you'd expect of a bygone era: large public rooms, discreet service, slightly faded elegance. One bogus touch: the plumbing works much better than it did in the good old days.

GRAND BAZAAR, THE (KAPALI ÇARŞI)

North of Yeniçeriler Caddesi. The Grand Bazaar of Istanbul is the largest shopping mall in the world, but any resemblance between it and the covered shopping precinct in your local town is purely fortuitous.

The Bazaar was started by Mehmet II not long after he conquered Constantinople. According to a long-standing tradition, it was used as his stables – and some maintain that its stalls still contain a large amount of its original product. The bazaar quickly grew, and grew, becoming more and more popular with locals and visitors alike. Nowadays it remains as popular as ever – with the locals convinced that they are fleecing the visitors, and the visitors convinced they are getting great bargains from the locals. Frequently both are correct.

The Grand Bazaar has suffered from all kinds of calamities during its long history – closed in time of pestilence, flattened during an earthquake, and frequently catching fire. The last fire was just a few years ago when a gas cylinder blew up – since when all gas cylinders have been banned from the bazaar.

When you first enter the Grand Bazaar, it seems like an incomprehensible maze. In fact, it's laid out in a surprisingly logical grid pattern. However, even when you are aware of this, it makes precious little difference – the place remains an incomprehensible maze. Your best bet is simply to remember the name of the gate you came in – for example Örücü Kapisi (The Gate of Knitters) – and when you want to get out, simply start asking for directions to it. This will take time, but at least you'll end up back where you started.

Each area of the bazaar specializes in different wares. So that, for instance, the silver shops will tend to be in one street, the carpet dealers in another. Inevitably, the most interesting part is plumb in the middle. This is the **Iç Bedesten** (Old Bazaar). It contains the finest silverware and antique shops.

Just west of here on **Takkeciler Caddesi** you'll find the best range of **carpet shops**. East off this street, to the south of Iç Bedesten on Keseciler Caddesi, you'll find a range of shops selling **bags and leatherware** (which are inexpensive in Turkey).

Head west from central Iç Bedesten along Zennneciler Sokağı and in 50 m or so you come to Şark Kahvesi, a pleasant café where you can have a bulb of sweet tea and recover your wits.

Continue south-west from here along Fesçiler Caddesi for almost 100 m and you come to **Sahaflar Çarşisi** (the Ancient Book Bazaar) which is well worth a browse. A word of warning: the shopkeepers here have a long-standing tradition of rudeness which is stoutly maintained, even if you make expensive purchases.

Remember, when you see something that you wish to buy you are *expected* to bargain. Nobody is offended – unless of course you go about this in an offensive fashion. Bargaining is meant to be fun for all concerned. Look upon it as a game, and you may find that you actually enjoy wasting your time in this futile manner. Then you will have begun to understand what it's all about.

HIPPODROME, THE

Beside the Blue Mosque. Known in Turkish as At Meydani, The Square of the Horses – this was the original Roman circus of Byzantium. The 500 m-long arena was used for *Ben Hur*-style chariot races before audiences of up to 100,000. Now all that remains is a park, which follows the outline of the original track, with a number of ancient monuments running down its centre.

On the western side, just north of the rather boring Museum of Turkish and Islamic Art, there is a large, pleasant café terrace.

The original Hippodrome was built in the early 3rdC AD by the Roman Emperor Septimus Severus. (He had previously just sacked the city, but wanted to make it up with the locals.) Later, when Constantine made Byzantium his New Rome, he added to the grandeur of the Hippodrome by shipping in public statues and monuments pilfered from the former capital. One of these was the **Egyptian Obelisk** (Dikili Taş), which can still be seen. Even in Constantine's time this was a very ancient monument indeed, having first been erected in ancient Egypt in the 15thC BC.

Also still standing here is the distinctly odd-looking **Serpentine Column** (Yilanli Sütan). All that remains to be seen nowadays is the ungainly black

stump of a bronze which once depicted three entwined serpents. But this remnant lump of bronze has a fascinating history.

In the 5thC BC the Persians invaded Greece and were defeated at the Battle of Plataea. In thanks, the Greeks melted down some Persian shields, cast them into a bronze statue of three entwined serpents, and dedicated the statue to the God Apollo, placing it at his shrine in Delphi. It was brought to Byzantium by Constantine, and placed in the Hippodrome.

When Mehmet II conquered Constantinople (as it had then become) in 1453, he went to great lengths to prevent his troops from plundering the city too severely. His own one recorded act of vandalism was purely symbolic. He cut off a head from the Serpent Statue as a blow against infidel idolatry. The other two heads are said to have been torn off by vandals in the 18thC, and may yet be discovered (erroneously labelled by a great expert) in some European collection.

• *Making red pepper sauce, Istanbul.*

Almost as interesting is the fate of a statue which is no longer here. This was of four life-sized bronze horses, and was also brought by Constantine from Rome, though precisely from where, and what exactly these horses commemorated, remains in dispute. When the Crusaders sacked Byzantium in 1204 they carried off this statue in triumph back to Venice. Here it remained for 600 years until Napoleon conquered Venice. He then shipped it to France, where it adorned the Arc de Triomphe in Paris. When Napoleon was defeated, it was duly returned to Venice, where today it stands at the entrance of St Marks's Cathedral. (For this historical cycle to be completed, the Turks would only have to conquer Venice, and the Romans then conquer Istanbul.)

The ancient chariot races at the Hippodrome were conducted very much in the manner of modern football matches. It didn't really matter who won on

MIMAR SINAN (1489-1588)

The greatest architect of the Ottoman Empire.

Curiously, this essentially Islamic artist was born of Greek Orthodox parents, and was almost certainly Greek or Armenian. However, at an early age he was press-ganged into the Ottoman army, where he served in the crack Janissary corps and was converted to Islam. Eventually he became a military engineer, and it was here that his talents were first noticed.

Fortunately, Sinan's career coincided with the high point of the Ottoman Empire. He was to serve under three sultans, Suleiman the Magnificent, Selim II and Murat III. But his greatest work was done for Suleiman. After leaving the army he played a leading part in the huge building programme which took place in the mid-16thC Ottoman Empire. By the end of his career Sinan had built nearly 80 mosques, more than 30 palaces and a similar amount of public baths, in excess of 50 schools, as well as innumerable fountains, tombs, granaries, and several aqueducts, waterworks and numerous bridges.

Sinan's finest early work was the **Şehzade Mosque** in Istanbul. As with all his great mosques, this harks back to his Greek Orthodox origins. It is based on the original Byzantine style, especially that embodied in Aya Sofya. But Sinan was able to transform this rather leaden, simplistic style into something of great elegance and aesthetic beauty – as well as making use of the Byzantine mastery with domes.

The Suleymaniye Mosque (see page 50) in Istanbul is generally regarded as his masterpiece and the finest architecture of its kind. Though Sinan himself considered his **Selimiye Mosque** in Edirne, completed 1575, to be his greatest work after the Suleymaniye Mosque. For further details see page 65.

the field. The main battles took place between the hooligans on the terraces. There were two sides, the Blues and the Greens, which took their colours from the teams of charioteers. Just like modern hooliganism, there were the usual undertones of racism, religious factionalism and politics.

As in Britain today, the Blues were the conservative hooligans who were all in favour of the established church, and the Greens consisted of all kinds of odds and sods who wanted to reform just about everything. All went well, and everyone enjoyed their weekly bouts of mindless violence, until one day the two factions became so disgusted with the authorities' feebleness in face of this anarchy that they joined forces and staged a full-scale revolt.

Besides raising a riot, this also razed much of the city to the ground – including its main church. Fortunately, this now left room for the building of Aya Sofya, and everyone went home happy. The authorities began building, and the hooligans retired to their separate ends of the Hippodrome for the new chariot-racing season.

KÜÇÜK AYASOFYA CAMII

Just west of Küçük Ayasofya Caddesi where it enters the old walls off Kennedy Caddesi.

The name of this mosque literally means Little Santa Sofya – and that's precisely what it is. The building was originally a church, and is said to have been built as a trial run for Aya Sofya by the Roman Emperor Justinian in the early 6thC. Its reduced size, and its delightful setting in a leafy courtyard, make it much more attractive than its overblown successor.

Around the courtyard are the original monks' cells, each one with its own fireplace and chimney. Outside this courtyard is one of the more run-down sections of Istanbul, where you can see some magnificent old ramshackle wooden houses.

The church was turned into a mosque after the fall of Contantinople, and restored at the start of the 16thC by the Chief White Eunuch at the Sultan's court, whose tomb can be seen on the left, just inside the gate to the courtyard.

This is one of the hidden gems of Istanbul but try to get here either very early, or very late, as one coachload of visitors can entirely ruin the atmosphere of the place.

OLD CITY WALLS, THE

From the Golden Horn at Ayvansaray south to the Sea of Marmara at Yedikule.

The ancient city of Byzantium had sea on three sides, but it always needed a wall to defend the landward side. One of the earliest walls was probably built by the Roman Emperor Septimus Severus somewhere near the Hippodrome.

Two centuries later Theodosius II completed the great walls which run from the upper reaches of the Golden Horn down to the Sea of Marmara. Much of this vast wall remains standing to this day – as you will notice if you drive into the city from the west. The city's defences were further strengthened by sea walls which ran along the Marmara shore – and large sections of these too still remain. For centuries the Golden Horn was protected by a chain across its mouth to keep out ships, until this shore too was fortified by a wall.

Ironically, the first threat to the sea walls of Istanbul came not from an enemy, but from the weather. In 763 AD the winter was so severe that the Bosphorus froze over. When spring arrived, the sea became choked with ice floes from the Black Sea. Finally the floes unclogged, but the rushing current carried two icebergs into the Golden Horn. They were so large – taller than the defensive walls – that they crushed the walls. This unlikely story is even supported by historical evidence.

Five hundred years later the Crusaders sailed their ships up to the sea walls and scaled them with ladders, and two hundred years later Mehmet II also breached the walls along the Golden Horn before his defeat of Constantinople.

The great land walls initially proved little better. They were barely completed when they were flattened by an earthquake in 473. This was bad timing indeed, as Atilla the Hun was at that moment on his way. In an unusual show of solidarity, the city's two rival hooligan factions, the Blues and the Greens, (see Hippodrome, page 47) combined forces to produce 16,000 volunteers, who set to work and rebuilt the entire land wall in less than two months. This miscreants' masterwork was not to be breached until the fall of Constantinople in 1453.

It is still possible to walk along these walls for their entire 6-km length, and there are several interesting sights.

In all, this walk will take you an entire day. It should not be done alone, nor outside daylight hours. Parts of the walls are unexpectedly remote from immediate urban contact, and a number of gypsy encampments have sprung up along the way. You should come to no harm with the gypsies – indeed, I have been welcomed. However, be sure to proceed politely and carefully along these stretches.

Some sights to watch out for on the way:

Tekfur Saray

Just south of Eğrikapi Gate. The last remaining Byzantine palace in Istanbul, now just a ruin. This neighbourhood was the site of the first imperial residences around the end of 5thC. Tekfur Saray is now a ruin, but was once the palace of Constantine Porphyrogenetus.

Ayvan Sarayi

Right by the Golden Horn. One of the two remaining towers of this palace was the prison of Michael Anemas, who plotted to overthrow the Byzantine Emperor Alexius I Comnenus. After Anemas was caught he had his beard plucked out hair by hair, and was then crowned with a wreath of sheep's guts and led in mockery through the streets. Fortunately, the emperor's daughter took pity on him and intervened just before his eyes were due to be plucked out, much to the disappointment of the eagerly awaiting crowd.

From this palace the last Byzantine emperor, Constantine XI, rode to his defeat at the hands of Mehmet II in 1453.

Yedikule

By the Sea of Marmara. This is the **Castle of the Seven Towers**, which was completed by Mehmet II four years after his defeat of Constantinople.

For many years the Ottoman Empire adopted a realistic approach to diplomacy. When any European country sent an ambassador to Istanbul, he was immediately locked up in the Yedikule as a spy. The ambassadors were kept

ISTANBUL AND THE OLYMPICS?
Recently, the city put in an unsuccessful bid to host the Olympic games, and intends to try again in the future. This has done great things for civic pride, but no one has yet come up with a convincing proposition as to where exactly the games would take place, let alone where the competitors and host of visitors would be accommodated.

in the **Tower of Inscriptions**, where-Russian, French and German ambassadors have duly inscribed their names on the walls. Less fortunate prisoners, without diplomatic immunity, were despatched to the second of the two prison towers – which contained a well-equipped torture chamber, an execution platform and a 'Well of Blood'.

SAINT SOPHIA (AYA SOFYA)

Sultanahmet Square. This famous pink edifice is something of a monstrosity on the outside; the ambition of its founder overwhelmed his architects. It was built by the Emperor Justinian in the 6thC, and in its time was the greatest cathedral in Christendom. Its cost all but bankrupted the empire, but Justinian was well pleased with his 'Eye of the Universe'. For more than a thousand years it remained the largest enclosed space on Earth. The name, Hagia Sofia in Greek and Aya Sofya in Turkish, means Divine Wisdom.

Indeed, it is the inside of this church which is its glory. The dome is more than 30 m wide and some 60 m high, yet it receives no direct support from the outer walls. Instead, it is supported by an ingenious system of piers, arches and half-domes. Not surprisingly, it has collapsed a number of times. The lofty interior space is nowadays rather gloomy, but this only contributes to its feeling of serenity and great age. High above are the spacious **galleries**, and gazing down from the walls are **mosaics of the saints**. On the east wall there is a large **mosaic depicting Christ** accompanied by one of the Byzantine emperors and his wife 'the most worshipful' Zoë.

Zoë was to become empress in her own right, and during her reign had a succession of husbands: each time she re-married, the mosaic face of her consort would be replaced by that of his successor.

The building has been sacked several times during its long history. Most memorable was the desecration carried out by the Crusaders in 1204, when a prostitute was placed on the patriarch's throne and made 'to sing profane songs and perform lewd dances for the amusement of the revellers'. But when Mehmet II conquered Constantinople in 1453 he personally intervened to halt the looting of Aya Sofya, and even prayed here. The church's Christian relics were then removed and Aya Sofya became a mosque – which it remained until the 1930s, when it was turned into a museum.

SULEYMANIYE MOSQUE, THE (SULEYMANIYE CAMII)

*Just north of Istanbul University.*This is the largest, and also the finest, of all the great mosques in Istanbul. It was completed in 1557 for Suleiman the Magnificent by his master architect Mimar Sinan. Its superb domes and minarets dominate the skyline above the Golden Horn: they are best seen at sunset from the northern quayside across Galata Bridge: one of the world's most romantic city skylines.

The simple **tomb of Mimar Sinan** is in the garden on the corner of Mimar Sinan Caddesi. It was designed by Sinan for himself, and reflects the modest lifestyle of this hard-working, pious genius. (Further details about his life and work are on page 48.)

In the mosque's main cemetery you can see the **tomb** of Sinan's great benefactor **Suleiman the Magnificent**, who is buried alongside his redoubtable wife Roxelana.

The lofty, spacious interior of the mosque is somewhat ruined by 'restoration' work that was carried out in the 19thC by the notorious Fossati brothers from Switzerland. One can only assume that the sultan who employed these two baroque boors was indulging in some kind of unconscious atavistic revenge.

• *Opposite: audience chamber,*
Topkapi Palace.

TOPKAPI PALACE

Just off Sultanahmet Square. This – one of the three 'obligatory' sights of Istanbul (along with the Blue Mosque and Aya Sofya) – was the original sultan's palace, the ruling nerve-centre of the Ottoman Empire. It was the residence of the sultan, his harem and his ministers, and also housed the sultan's treasure house. (The original and strictly correct meaning of the term harem is, incidentally, private living quarters, rather than their female occupants.)

The Topkapi was started just three years after the Ottoman conquest of Constantinople and completed six years later in 1465 – though it was to see many additions during the following centuries. It appears to be laid out in a haphazard succession of courtyards, somewhat resembling the Alhambra in Granada. In fact, its layout was planned with immense care, and the result resembles a number of enclosed gardens, one giving on to the other, with adjoining areas of residence, a throne room, a library, the harem, beautiful terraces overlooking the city, and so forth. Its atmosphere is like a blend between an extensive Oxford college and an oriental garden, and has none of the overbearing grandeur of a European palace. Everything is human-sized, rather than monumental, which makes it much easier to imagine what it was like to live here. (Until you hear what some of the sultans actually got up to.)

The approach to Topkapi is through the fortified **Imperial Gate**, and at once you enter a peaceful world far from the hurly-burly of urban Istanbul; though alas during the season you now merely forsake the rich clamour of the streets for the more rarefied Babel of dozens of guides pontificating to their international flocks.

You will be surprised to find that the **First Courtyard** of this most Muslim of palaces contains a church: **Aya Irini** (the Church of Divine Peace). The original church here predates even the founding of Constantinople, and was the meeting place of the Second Ecumenical Council in 381 (the one which ratified the Nicaean Creed). In this courtyard there are also the **palace bakeries** and the **Imperial Mint**.

From here you pass through the **Gate of Salutations** into the large **Second Courtyard**, whose pathways fan out before you through leafy shade. On the right are the **palace kitchens**, where 2,500 servants would busy themselves preparing the sultan's dinner (few sultans were renowned for their sylph-like figures). You can view some of the cooking utensils used by the sultan's cooks, as well as a superb collection of porcelain which includes some Chinese masterpieces.

On the left of the **Second Courtyard** is the place which most of the visitors have come to see. Unfortunately, the **harem** (additional fee) is something of a let-down – and not just owing to the absence of its female occupants. Nowadays you have to go on a guided tour, which isn't even conducted by a genuine eunuch. Despite the disappointment, as you wander through you can't help imagining what the place was like in the bad old days, before it was considered beyond the pale of political correctness. This was where the sultan kept his wives, odalisques, concubines and cuties – all jealously guarded by fearsome scimitar-bearing eunuchs, who would in a trice reduce any intruders to a similar sexual status to themselves.

The harem was once the home of the fabulous Roxelana, wife of Suleiman the Magnificent, who used her wiles to persuade her husband to murder both his Grand Vizier and his heir, so that her son could succeed to the throne.

Sultan Ahmet III's dining room (within the harem) is said to contain a series of inspired erotic murals, but sadly this ocular feast is not open to the public. Nor, unfortunately, is the notorious **Cage**. Indeed, it is only your imagination (inspired by the tales of what went on in the harem) which really make it worth a visit. Prior to Ahmet I's accession, all brothers of the sultan would be murdered as soon as he succeeded to the throne, in order to eliminate any royal pretenders. Instead, Ahmet I had all his brothers locked up in a wing of the harem, together with their concubines and a retinue of deaf mutes. This became known as the Cage, possibly because of the monkey-like activities of its inhabitants. The royal princes would remain locked up here for years, often with highly detrimental effects on their mental health. Occasionally, when the sultan died without leaving a suitable heir, one of the inmates of the

• *Revan Köskü, Topkapi Palace.*

Cage would emerge to take on the throne. It is no accident that the Ottoman Empire had more than its fair share of paranoid and potty rulers.

No visit to Topkapi woul be complete without seeing the harem, even if it fails to live up to expectations. What would? Just inside the **Third Courtyard** you come to the **Throne Room**. Behind this is the delightful small building which housed the **Library of Ahmet III**, who used to while away his hours here reading, before retiring to dinner in his erotic dining room in the harem. The far right-hand corner of the Third Courtyard contains Topkapi's second most popular spot with visitors: the **Treasury**. This contains the celebrated **Spoonmaker's Diamond**, as well as a collection of gaudy jewel-encrusted objects which to my eye seldom rise above the level of childish baubles. The high point of tawdriness is achieved by a uselessly over-ornamented flintlock rifle which is probably worth as much as the entire takings of a Madonna concert, and is culturally of a similar value. But don't despair: the Treasury contains the finest sight in all of Istanbul.

This is the **Mehmet II Pavilion**, a delightful open pillared terrace which looks out over the entrance to the Golden Horn and across the Bosphorus to the Asian shore. It is one of the most romantic spots on earth: fit indeed for a sultan.

Beyond the Third Courtyard there is a **Fourth Courtyard**, beneath which is a pleasant café-restaurant which also has a spectacular view out over the Bosphorus. The food in the café section is good, if pricey. Avoid the pies and go for the puddings.

On the far (north-western) side of the Fourth Courtyard is another delightful **terrace**, looking out over the Golden Horn and the skyline of the grand mosques. This has an enticing pool which was a great favourite with Sultan Ibrahim the Mad, who ascended to the throne after spending more than 20 years in the Cage. Ibrahim's favourite pastime was disporting with members of his harem in the pool, but unfortunately he became jealous and had all his 280 concubines sewn into sacks and cast into the Bosphorus. One managed to claw her way out of her sack, was picked up by a passing French ship, and eventually sold her memoirs for a fortune in Paris. History is not without its occasional happy endings.

The final spot not to be missed is a charmingly tiled **public lavatory**. This is in a little corner courtyard by a staircase next to the quarters of the White Eunuchs, on the left of the Third Courtyard. You may find the division between the sexes here a trifle lackadaisical, but then what else would you expect in a White Eunuchs' lavatory. Warning: in season, Topkapi is crowded at all times.

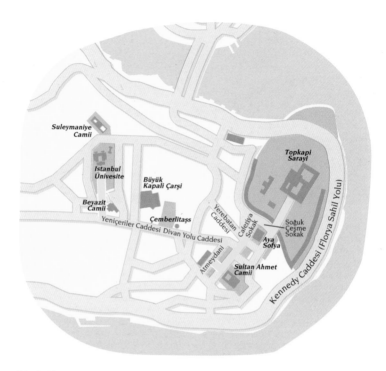

Istanbul is not an ideal city for walking. In the summer season it is usually too hot, and the streets tend to be very crowded. Few can go for long under such conditions without reaching saturation point.

The second of the two walks I've devised – **The Sea Walk** – is designed to get around these difficulties: much of the route is relatively free from crowds, and such cool air as there is will tend to come off the sea.

The first walk – **The Land Walk** – is best undertaken in the cool of the early morning.

Both routes are through the old city, which is by far the best area for walking.

Land Walk

This takes you past most of the city's major tourist sights. The distance is less than a couple of kilometres, but much of this is through busy streets.

Start In the First Courtyard outside the gate into **Topkapi Palace** (for further details of the Topkapi Palace, see page 52). From here, walk south-west, back through the leafy courtyard, and out of the gate in the walls. You now cross the wide Soğukçeşme Sokak.

Once across, walk a short distance to your right (north-west), and soon turn left down Caferiya Sokak. This leads alongside **Aya Sofya** (see page 42), whose main entrance you will see on your left.

Continue south-west along Caferiye Sokak, and cross Yerebatan Caddesi. On your left you will see some gardens with a fountain playing, and ahead you will see the Sultan Ahmet Camii, popularly known as the **Blue Mosque** (see page 44).

The square across the road to the north-west of The Blue Mosque is Atmeydani, the ancient **Roman Hippodrome** (see page 47). On the far side of the Hippodrome is the disappointing

• *Old quarter, Istanbul.*

Museum of Turkish and Islamic Arts and just north-east of here is a pleasant café terrace where you can have a refreshing drink and rest your feet, for you have now completed nearly half the route.

From the café terrace head north across the park for Istanbul's main street, called Divan Yolu Caddesi. Here turn left, westwards.

In 200 m on your right you will see the celebrated **Burnt Column** (Çemberlitaşş). This is one of the city's oldest monuments, and was put up by the Emperor Constantine in 330 AD to commemorate Istanbul becoming capital of the Roman Empire. It almost collapsed during an earthquake in 416, and has long since been stripped of its original marble coating. According to a centurìes-old legend, when this column fell it would mark the end of Ottoman rule in Europe. The Ottoman Empire has long since vanished, yet the column still stands. Some maintain this dis-

proves the legend – but in fact Turkish territory still extends 200 km into Europe.

From here, continue down Divan Yolu for a hundred metres or so, and then take one of the turnings to the right, which will lead you in a few yards into the **Grand Bazaar** (see page 46).

Continue down the main street, which here becomes Yeniçeriler Caddesi, and on your right in 50 m or so you will see the **Beyazit Camii**, one of the city's main mosques. Further across the square to your right is the marble entrance to **Istanbul University**.

From here you can take a taxi back to base. If you have energy to spare, you may wish to continue north through the university, reaching, in about 400 m, the Suleymaniye Camii (see page 50).

you may wish to continue north through the university, reaching, in about 400 m, the Suleymaniye Camii (see page 50).

Sea Walk

This route takes you along Istanbul's sea wall and across the Golden Horn. It is about 2.5 km in length, and takes you past a number of major sights, but its main point is the views.

If possible, start this walk just as the heat of the sun is beginning to die down in the afternoon, so that you end up across Galata Bridge as the sun is setting beyond the skyline of the old city.

Start Outside the Blue Mosque (Sultan Ahmet Camii, see page 44). Head for Atmeydani, the square which lies directly north-west of the Blue Mosque. This square was Byzantium's Hippodrome (see page 47).

Leave the Hippodrome by its southernmost exit and continue down the hill. At the major fork in 50 m or so, keep right down Kaleci Caddesi. This leads you into a rather run-down little area

which has some fine ramshackle old wooden houses. If you get lost, follow the yellow signs for Küçük Ayasofya Camii (see page 49).

As you leave Küçük Ayasofya turn right and continue to the main road, Aksakal Caddesi. Here turn right, which leads you down under the railway bridge to the sea front. Cross busy Kennedy Caddesi to the promenade along the sea front. Here turn left, eastwards.

You are beside the Sea of Marmara, and it is usually filled with ships: some waiting to enter the port of Istanbul, some laid up. Ahead you will see ships entering and leaving the Bosphorus. Many of these will be Russian and Ukrainian ships plying from the Black Sea ports.

There are a few cafés along this stretch of the promenade. Their parasols provide welcome shade, but their prices are a little over the odds owing to the location.

Continue east along the sea front. To your left you will see the domes and minarets of the Blue Mosque. You will also see continuous stretches of the water is the entrance to the Bosphorus. Look north up the Bosphorus and to your right you will see the little island on which stands the white **Maiden's Tower** (Kiz Kulesi, sometimes erroneously known as Leander's Tower). This romantic little structure has a suitably romantic little legend attached. Once upon a time it was foretold that the sultan's daughter would die of a snake bite on her 18th birthday. In order to forestall this, the sultan had her placed on this tiny island, where there were no snakes. But on her birthday an old lady arrived with a basket of fruit – and guess what was hiding amongst the figs.

Further down the Bosphorus you can see the great **Bosphorus Suspension Bridge** – the first bridge in the world to link two continents.

You now pass a tall white lighthouse. Beyond the ancient stretch of wall to your left is the **Topkapi Palace** (see page 52).

Continue along the seaside promenade beside Kennedy Caddesi which leads you round Seraglio Point (Sarayburnu), where there is a **statue of Atatürk**. This was the spot where Byzas stepped ashore to found Byzantium more than 2,500 years ago.

As the road curves further to your left you will see the Golden Horn and Galata Bridge. Across on the opposite quayside is the city's main liner berth. Ahead of you, at Sireki, is the bustle of the city's main ferry berth, with a constant flurry of ferries departing for the Asian shore and points further up the Bosphorus. Continue down the main street to the quayside.

Here you will find constant activity, with vendors selling all kinds of fish, sweetcorn and kebabs. You will also see fishermen selling fresh fish from their boats. Continue down the Golden Horn, and turn right over Galata Bridge. This takes you across the Golden Horn, with fine views back over the old city skyline.

On the other side of Galata Bridge, turn immediately right, down to Rihtim Caddesi, the street which runs along the quayside. By the water there is a lively fish market and across the road are a number of cafés and fish restaurants. One of my favourite pastimes in Istanbul is to sit here with a large glass of beer and a plate of prawns watching

• B*osphorus catch.*

the spectacular crimson glow of the sunset fading behind the sillhouettes of the mosques on the far shore.

If you arrive here earlier in the day, and still have energy to spare, continue north along the main street leading from Galata Bridge. This leads to Yüksek Kaldirim Caddesi, where you will see the **Galata Tower** (Galata Kulesi) on your left in 200 m or so. Take the lift to the top of this tower for one of the best views of the city (the tower closes at six). Galata Kulesi was built in 1348 by the Genoese as a watchtower – replacing one which had been built on this spot a thousand years before.

Those who wish for less elevated views of city life will doubtless turn off Yuksek Kaldirim Caddesi before they get to the Tower. These streets lead into Istanbul's once world-famous **red light district**, Iki Buçuk. Iki Buçuk is Turkish for two-and-a-half: the necessary amount of lira each sailor grasped in his tattoo-embossed fist as he strode ashore. How times have changed.

BELGRADE FOREST, THE

Some 20 km N of the city, inland from the European shore of the Bosphorus. Reached by dolmuş from the northern Bosphorus suburb of Çayırbaşı. This is the nearest region of genuine greenery to Istanbul. The forest used to be a hunting ground for the Ottoman sultans, and its reservoirs have long been the source of Istanbul's water. Nowadays its lakes and woodlands are a popular picnic spot with rurally deprived barbecue enthusiasts and pyromaniacs. There are a number of fine lakeside and woodland walks which pass through more remote regions of the forest.

And the curious name? In 1521 Suleiman the Magnificent conquered Belgrade, and imported a group of expert Serbian well-diggers to create reservoirs. Homesick for their Serbian sumps, these immigrants called their new home Belgrade. A prosaic but unlikely tale, which I am assured is true.

BLACK SEA RESORTS

Like the Princes Islands (page 59), these are Istanbul's 'lungs'. The bonus here is that the swimming beaches are good and the water of the Black Sea is upstream from Istanbul and thus much cleaner than the Sea of Marmara's.

The nearest resort is **Kilyos**, on the European shore, which is just over 30 km north of the city. The most pleasant way to get here is to take a ferry up to the Bosphorus suburb of Sariyer,

• *Ferry, Bosphorus.*

from where you can catch a *dolmuş* for the 25-minute ride to the coast.

Kilyos has a bay, cliffs and a sandy beach overlooked by a Genoese castle – which unfortunately cannot be visited, as it is still used by the Turkish army as a bastion of defence against a Russian invasion. Afficionados of internationalese will hardly be able to refrain from eating at the Şanzelize, whose name is intended to remind the French of the Elysian fields of home, but whose *cuisine* is in no way similarly mangled.

The best resort on the Asian shore is **Şile.** This is a *déjà vu* of what a seaside holiday spot used to look like. It has a long sandy bay, cliffs, a fishing harbour filled with ferocious-featured sailors in gum boots, a little island with a ruined castle and even a lighthouse freshly painted with black-and-white stripes to stop the seagulls from flying into it. What more could you ask for? Perhaps a retired classics bore to inform you that in ancient Greek times this place was known as Kalpe, and that Xenophon called in here with his Ten Thousand mercenaries on his way from Persia.

On hot summer weekends these resorts tend to be visited by at least half a dozen Xenophons, all with their armies of mercenaries, baggage, field kitchens and auxiliary troop entertainers in tow.

PRINCES' ISLANDS (ADALAR)

In Sea of Marmara, off N Asian shore.
These islands make a pleasant seaside retreat from the heat and clamour of Istanbul. You reach them by ferries which leave from Sireki and Kabataş. From Sireki the ferry takes two hours, from Kabatas the express ferry takes less than an hour, and the hydrofoil from here takes just over half an hour. Most services are linked to either Heybeliada or Buyukada, which in turn are linked to the other islands by smaller ferries. There are nine islands in the archipelago. Featured below are the four main ones, followed by one of the smaller ones.

Büyükada

This is the largest of the islands (its name means large island). It has long been a place of exile, especially for Turkish royalty. The last famous exile was Trotsky, who lived here for four years until 1933. He stayed at the Savoy Hotel (which burned down several years ago), where he spent his time writing his *History of the Russian Revolution*. During his stay he conducted all kinds of cloak-and-dagger negotiations, and is even rumoured to have corresponded with Winston Churchill. His stay ended unhappily after his daughter committed suicide.

The main form of transport on Büyükada is by horse-drawn carriage. Cars are forbidden, except to the police and the refuse collectors. You can also hire bikes to tour the island. There are two 'mountains', a wood, several settlements, and a number of hilarious Victorian villas. But alas, no swimming beaches worth recommending.

Each hill has a former Greek Orthodox monastery on top. **The Monastery of St George** on Yüce Tepe, the southernmost peak, was used as a madhouse 500 years ago. Here you can still see the rings in the stone floor where the inmates were chained, but the other contemporary therapeutic implements have since been lost.

Heybeliada

Lies to the west of Büyükada, and is the second largest island. This one does have some pleasant beaches (unlike Büyükada, above), and for this reason is packed during summer weekends. At other times it appears to be populated

• *Pomegranates.*

mainly by cats, who are touchingly tolerant of the human residents. (Unlike many Mediterranean people, the Turks treat their cats well and take them very seriously. This attitude is not always reciprocated.)

You can make a grand tour of the island by horse-drawn carriage, but far better is to go for a walk in the woods, and then head for the northern shore, where there are a few remote beaches.

Burgazada

The next island to the west, after Heybeliada. For centuries Burgazada was home to Greeks and Jews, who still return here during the summer in considerable numbers. Indeed, a knowledgeable Turkish friend of mine claims that until recently the rare Ladino was spoken here. This is the language brought to the Levant by the Sephardic Jews who were expelled from Spain in 1492. It is a mixture of the ancient Castilian Spanish spoken in Cervantes' time, and elements of Hebrew. Sadly, it is now almost extinct.

Just above the harbour is the Greek Orthodox **Church of St John the Baptist**, with its characteristic dome. (The island also has a Catholic church and a synagogue, as well as the inevitable mosque. All of these are said to have regular worshippers.)

By far the most interesting sight on

59

the island is the **museum** which was once the home of the Turkish writer Sait Faik, who is sometimes unfairly likened to Mark Twain. A fitfully inspired author, Faik recorded an Istanbul low-life that has now all but disappeared. The museum contains everything, right down the maestro's pyjamas.

Kinaliada

The name means Henna Island, from the colour of its cliffs. Compared with the others, it is fairly barren – though it does have fields of lavender. Again, this is a pleasant place for walking, with unbroken views west to the Bosphorus entrance and Istanbul, and east to the other islands.

Köpek Adasi

The smallest and saddest of the islands. Its name means Dog Island. For many years, all the stray dogs in Istanbul would be rounded up at regular intervals and taken on a one-way trip to the seaside here. In the end the sound of their pitiful barking melted even the icy heart of Istanbul's municipal führer, and this doggedly cruel practice was discontinued.

RECOMMENDED RESTAURANTS

For once Ernest Hemmingway was right when he claimed that Turkish cooking had produced one of the world's three great *cuisines* (along with French and Chinese). And the best place by far to sample this *cuisine* is Istanbul. Even better news is the fact that generally you don't have to pay over the odds.

Unusually, the classiest *cuisine* in the city is to be found in the restaurants of the top-class hotels. But be warned: some of these *are* expensive.

Below this level, standards remain exceptionally high, and prices reasonable. You'll be amazed at the sheer variety of dishes on offer in even quite modest restaurants. There are no language difficulties here – just point to what you want.

Turkish wine is in general reliable, but little more. It is comparatively expensive, and will often cost as much as your entire food bill. Otherwise try beer, which is much cheaper.

Those who wish to save on dining out will be pleased to discover that genuinely inexpensive eating places abound; and further still down the scale, fast-food joints are both cheap and nourishing.

A serious warning: you will see all kinds of frying fish on sale from stalls on the streets. This is usually fresh, but use your discretion, especially on a hot day. You will also see boys selling trays of mussels and lemon. These can be delicious, but are not always as fresh as they should be. Bad luck here is *disastrous*.

Revan, LLL; Sheraton Hotel, Taksim Parki; tel. 216 231 2121.

This place is fit only for superlatives – which include the view and the service, as well as the food and the bill. Authentic music adds to the Ottoman-style atmosphere.

For those who want to try something a little less expensive, but equally exotic, each evening in summer the Sheraton runs a boat which cruises the Bosphorus while you dine on a first-class buffet. Ring the Sheraton for details. The boat leaves from just below Dolmabahçe Palace; four hours later you return feeling bouyant, but lower in the waterline.

Köşem Cemal Restaurant, LL; Kumkapi Meydani; tel. 216 520 1229.

The Kumkapi district is famous for its fresh fish, and this restaurant is in the square at the heart of it. They serve an excellent *kiliç şiş* (swordfish kebab), and the fish of the day is justly renowned. There are also some pleasant Marmara wines on offer.

Haci Baba Restaurant, LL; 49 Istiklâl Caddesi; tel. 216 144 1886.

On the main drag running south from Taksim Square towards Galata Tower. Excellent *cuisine* at an affordable price. Try dining in the relaxed open-air section at the back. Good wines, and an exotic range of *mezze* – small dishes similar to *hors d'oeuvres*. Friendly service.

• *Starter, up-market restaurant.*

There are a number of comparatively inexpensive fish restaurants along the Bosphorus just over Galata Bridge on the Karaköy shore at Rihtim Caddesi. These serve good fresh fish, but be sure to ask the price first. Irritating touts patrol outside, persistently attempting to solicit your custom.

The best of the bunch is probably **Yildizlar**. If you just fancy a beer and a plate of prawns while you watch the sunset, try one of the cafés closer to the bridge.

The best inexpensive restaurant in the Sultanahmet district by the main mosques is:

Vitamin Restaurant, L; 16 *Divan Yolu Caddesi; tel.* 216 526 5086.

As you enter you will see the trays of exotic dishes laid out on your left. Indicate which ones you want, and you will be served by the singing chef. I once heard him claim he could yodel in Dutch. At night, beyond the open doorway and operatics, you can see the floodlit minarets of the Blue Mosque. Non-opera buffs can dine upstairs.

World Famous Pudding Shop, L; 24 *Divan Yolu Caddesi; no booking.*

This spot achieved world fame during the days of the hippy trail to India. It was where flower power turned into flour power as the freaks fattened up for the long overland journey. The place has smartened up (a little), but still retains something of the old atmosphere (minus exotic odours). The menu has expanded and now includes a range of all kinds of dishes, as well as a few ex-world famous puddings. Not to be missed – for sociologists and socializers alike.

If you want to have a friendly drink and see a few of the local in-crowd, one of the best places to go is:

Bukalemun, LL; 22 *Dereboyu Caddesi; tel.* 216 159 1972.

This is out at Ortaköy, which is just north of Dolmabahçe Palace before the Bosphorus Suspension Bridge. It is owned by the famous Turkish artist Bedri Baykam, who believes in parking his works on the trendily scruffy walls. There's frequent live music (Turko-mod), and a regular live clientèle doing their best to look coolly dead.

Between Istanbul and Çanakkale
European Turkey:
Gallipoli and Edirne

240 km; map GeoCenter Euro-Country, Western Turkey, 1:800 000

This section covers the region west of the Bosphorus and north of the Sea of Marmara: European Turkey. It once formed part of ancient Thrace, now known as Trakya by the Turks. The two main places of interest are the Gallipoli (Gelibolu) Peninsula and the ancient capital city of Edirne. There are also three distinct and interesting coastal stretches: the western Black Sea coast, the northern shore of the Sea of Marmara, and the western Aegean coastline. Each of these has its charms, with parts relatively unspoilt – though they hardly match the spectacular beauty to be found along other stretches of Turkey's long coastline. For this reason they attract little foreign tourism.

If you're planning to travel through this region you'll probably start from Istanbul. Route E80 west from Istanbul follows the north coast of the Sea of Marmara. This can be dreary in parts, as Istanbul seems to sprawl on for ever. Seventy kilometres beyond Istanbul you can either continue west along the E84 for the Gallipoli Peninsula (Gelibolu Yarimadasi), or take a detour by keeping north-west on the E80 for Edirne, the ancient Ottoman capital. It's well worth travelling these extra miles to Edirne if you have time: this city may be off the main tourist trail, but it has the finest mosques in Turkey outside Istanbul.

From Edirne you head south along the E87 for Gallipoli (Gelibolu). The town lies at the beginning of the peninsula, on the shore of the Dardanelles (Çanakkale Boğazi). This strategic neck of land was the site of the disastrous Gallipoli campaign in 1915, where the ANZACs fought so bravely to no avail and Atatürk first became a hero leading the Turkish forces. There are many moving monuments to the fallen along the unspoilt shores of the peninsula.

From here it's just a short ferry ride across the straits to Çanakkale. If you have time on your hands here you can catch a ferry to Gökçeada, the largest of the Turkish Aegean islands. This is mountainous, mostly unspoilt and has several fine beaches.

The short route along the northern shores of the Sea of Marmara is just 240 km. It's possible to cover this and view a few of the Gallipoli sights all in one day. But if you want to see Edirne, take a little more time seeing the Gallipoli sights, and perhaps visit Gökçeada, you should allow five days.

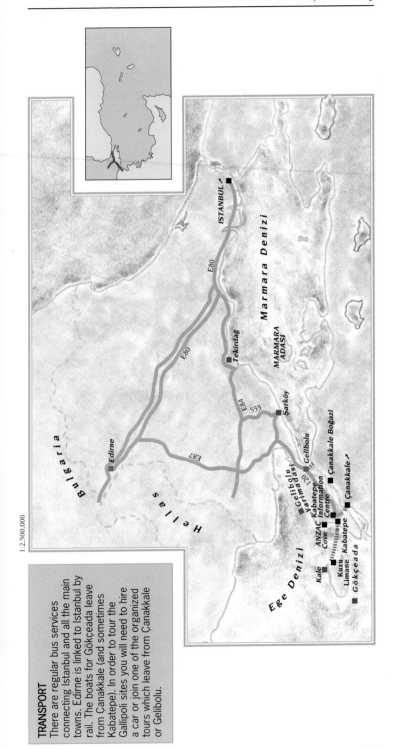

TRANSPORT

There are regular bus services connecting Istanbul and all the main towns. Edirne is linked to Istanbul by rail. The boats for Gökçeada leave from Çanakkale (and sometimes Kabatepe). In order to tour the Gallipoli sites you will need to hire a car or join one of the organized tours which leave from Çanakkale or Gelibolu.

63

SIGHTS & PLACES OF INTEREST

ÇANAKKALE

A useful base from which to visit Gallipoli (page 65), and Troy (see Turkey Overall: 2. It is covered in detail in Local Explorations: 1.

EDIRNE ⭢ ✕

Close to Greek border, some 250 km W of Istanbul on Rt E80. The traditional capital of the ancient province of Thrace, which once extended over northern Greece, European Turkey and Bulgaria. After Istanbul, Edirne is the main city in European Turkey. As you approach across the plains you will see its famous skyline – the looming domes and thin minarets of mosques rising above the city. Despite this oriental appearance, Edirne has a slightly eastern European feel: on your radio you can pick up music which sounds like that of the distant steppes.

Archaeologists maintain that there has been a settlement here for some 6,000 years. The 'modern' city was founded by the Roman emperor Hadrian in the 2ndC AD. It was named Hadrianopolis after him, and its present name is a Turkish reduction of this mouthful. In 1361 the Ottoman Sultan Mehmet I took Edirne, and soon made it his capital. Ninety years later Mehmet II set off down the road to attack Constantinople (Istanbul), the capital of the Byzantine Empire. After a 50-day siege Constantinople fell – and the new Ottoman capital became Istanbul, though the new name did not immediately become universal.

In the following century, Suleiman the Magnificent would spend his summers in Edirne, bringing with him his hunters and his harem. He would stay for several months, only returning to Istanbul 'when the croaking of the frogs became unendurable'. During this period Edirne was one of the greatest cities in the world, the peer of Baghdad, Brugge and Naples. It boasted nearly 300 mosques and more than 100 public fountains (homes for all the frogs).

RECOMMENDED HOTELS

EDIRNE

Finding reasonably priced accommodation can be difficult in Edirne. The city is not yet fully geared to tourism. But it's worth paying a little extra to stay at one of the most atmospheric hotels you'll find in Turkey:

Hotel Rüstempaşa Kervansaray, LLL; *Iki Kapili Han Caddesi 57; tel. 284 212 2195.*

This hotel is housed in a 16thC caravanserai (traditional inn) which was built in the reign of Suleiman the Magnificent by his great architect Sinan for Rüstem Paşa, the grand vizier. Camel caravans heading down the Via Egnatia (the old Roman road which connected Byzantium to Rome) would put in here for the night.

One word of warning: *demand* a room as far away as possible from the night club, unless you keep Draculan hours.

For a less expensive night try:

Otel Saray, L; *Eski Istanbul Caddesi 28; tel. 284 212 1457.*

A spartan spot, but this is much more your authentic Edirne, which remains impervious to the blandishments of tourism.

GELIBOLU

There are a number of adequate inexpensive hotels by the harbour. Try:

Hotel Yilmaz, L; *Liman Caddesi 6; tel. 286 566 1256.*

Simple accommodation in a clean and friendly spot. Be sure to book ahead in August.

GÖKÇEADA

There are inexpensive hotels and *pansiyons* at both Kuzu Limani (where the boat puts in) and Kale (on the other side of the island).

ŞARKÖY

Sohbet, L-LL; *by the harbour; tel. 282 518 1400.*

Turn left at the front. Away from the decibel-rich epicentre of town.

There are many fine things to see in Edirne. For a start, it has the greatest mosques outside Istanbul. The best known of these is **Selimiye Camii**, which dates from 1575 – the masterpiece of the great Levantine architect Sinan, which he completed when he was 85 years old for Selim the Grim. This mosque is said to have 999 windows, because Selim didn't want to tempt fate. Its four graceful minarets are over 70 m high, making them second only to those at Mecca.

Edirne's other great mosque is across the Beyazit Bridge over the Tunca River in the outskirts of town. Here you come to **Ikinci Beyazit Külliyesi** (the Beyazit mosque complex). This was built as a huge welfare institution for the poor, the sick and the mentally ill – the largest of its kind in the Ottoman Empire. Some of its buildings now house a section of the local university. This is an atmospheric spot, with silent courtyards, cells and halls, the mosque itself with hidden gardens. It was completed for Sultan Beyazit II in 1488 by his chief architect, Hayrettin.

Be sure also to see the **ruins of the Sultan's Palace** (once almost as large as the Topkapi in Istanbul), the **ancient bridges across the Tunca River** (built for mule carts, but still in use for irritable car-drivers), and the **Museum of Turkish and Islamic Arts**. Here, besides the usual exhibits, you will come across some portraits of celebrated Turkish wrestling champions.

If you visit Edirne in June, be sure to attend the amazing **Kirkpinar Championships**, which attract contestants from all over Turkey. The contestants are smeared from head to foot with olive oil, wear curious leather pants, and wrestle with no apparent rules until the loser collapses or is pinned to the ground by his fearsome, heavy-breathing opponent. This sport is known as *yağli güres,* a name which tellingly evokes what the two contestants do to each other. This is a uniquely Turkish event, and attracts a large and fanatic cross-section of the population, including a voiciferous contingent of gypsies. Photography is not encouraged, unless you happen to be James Fox, the Paris-based photographer, whose expressive studies of this sport have brought it to the attention of the wider audience it deserves.

GALLIPOLI PENINSULA (GELIBOLU YARIMADASI)

Over three quarters of a century after the carnage (see The Gallipoli Campaign, page 66) this region is now a landscape of bucolic calm and beauty, with pine forests, picturesque beaches and coves, and undulating farmlands – but reminders of the grim past remain. There are several large cemeteries and a number of memorials.

If you wish to make a tour of this area, the best place to start is at the **Kabatepe Information Centre**, which has a number of old photographs and relics. This is 4 km south of the village of Kemalyeri, which is inland three quarters of the way down the peninsula on the Aegean (western) side. Just northeast of here is **ANZAC Cove,** with three cemeteries nearby. Around the cove and the cemeteries you can still distinguish some of the trenches. You will also find an extraordinary monument on the hillside above the beach. This contains the words of the open letter which President Atatürk (formerly a commander of the Turkish troops in the campaign) wrote to the Australian people just 16 years after the end of the war:

Those heroes who shed their blood and lost their lives – you are now lying in the soil of a friendly country. Therefore rest in peace. There is no difference between the Johnnies and the Mehmets; to us they lie side by side, here in this country of ours... After having lost their lives on this land they have beome our sons as well.

At the southernmost tip of the peninsula (Cape Helles) there is the **British Naval Memorial** and a large cemetery filled with crosses. North-east of the nearby village of Seddülbahir is the **French Cemetery**, and a couple of kilometres east you come to the large **Turkish Monument** with its imposing pillars.

By far the best way to visit the Gallipoli sights is on one of the organized tours, which leave from Gelibolu and Çanakkale. The best of these is Troy-Anzac Tours, Yali Caddesi, Çanakkale; tel. 196 15849.

Their guides are exceptionally well informed and can make your visit an informative and moving experience.

THE GALLIPOLI CAMPAIGN

This grotesque catastrophe of the First World War took place in 1915. It probably cost the lives of half a million men, and it is almost impossible to exaggerate the farcical blend of classic military incompetence and sheer heroism which characterized this event.

The British Admiralty, under its First Lord, Winston Churchill, came up with a plan to eliminate Turkey from the war and enable the Allies to link up with the Russians. The entire British cabinet agreed upon this plan, with the exception of Lord Fisher, who was the only man present who knew what he was talking about. Fisher resigned in disgust, and Churchill despatched the fleet to sail up the narrow straits of the Dardanelles and bombard Istanbul into submission.

During the first months of 1915 the British and French navies made various attempts to breach the Dardanelles. One of the initial sorties managed to get almost six miles up the straits before being repulsed by the Turkish guns and mines.

Subsequent sorties were less succesful, and it soon became clear that this plan of attack was futile.

So Churchill cooked up another, even more disastrous scheme. Meanwhile, all element of surprise had vanished, and the Turks rapidly set about defending the area. Churchill's new scheme involved British, Commonwealth and French troops making simultanous landings on the Gallipoli peninsula and nearby, joining forces, and knocking out the Turkish guns which guarded the Dardanelles. On April 25, 1915, in a combined operation, British troops landed on the tip of the Gallipoli peninsula at Cape Helles, the French landed on the other shore at the mouth of the Dardanelles below Çanakkale, and the ANZACs (Australia and New Zealand Corps) landed further up the Gallipoli Peninsula on the Aegean shore.

In each case the Turks were waiting, and in each case the Allied commanders excelled themselves in displays of bungling incompetence. Half the French force was slaughtered on the first day, the ANZACs were put ashore at the wrong place, and the British were forced to storm cliffs under fire and then received no further orders when they reached the top, where they became even more of a sitting target. The ANZACs showed exceptional heroism under suicidal circumstances, and the bravery of the other Allied forces was of a similar calibre. Meanwhile, back at headquarters, their commanders demonstrated that military incompetence of an exceptional order was not the exclusive preserve of the commanders running the war in the trenches in France.

What is sometimes overlooked is the fact that the Turkish troops fared little better. Many of them were raw teenage recruits and peasant boys from Anatolia. Few had any more than the most rudimentary training, and their equipment was far inferior to that of the Allies. But one of their commanders, Lt-Col Mustafa Kemal, was to prove a perceptive tactician and a great leader of men. His personal heroism under fire was reckless to the point of lunacy (he would direct his men in full view of the enemy guns), and he managed to inspire his troops with the most uncompromising appeals to patriotism: 'We have not come here to fight, we have come here to die.' Not surprisingly, such brilliant military tactics led to much the same result as the incompetence of the Allied commanders. The brave Turkish recruits died in equally huge numbers. But the Allies failed to break through, remaining cooped up in narrow beachheads.

Despite the obvious, the Allies persisted, and went on persisting. In all, this outrageous and utterly futile carnage was to continue for nine months. Still nothing had been achieved, when it was decided to evacuate the last brave survivors from the beachheads in January 1916. By now a quarter of a million men had died on the Allied side, and the Turkish army had lost a similar figure.

As a result of the Gallipoli Campaign, Lt-Col Mustafa Kemal achieved heroic status throughout Turkey. He was promoted to general, and later became a rallying figure for the entire nation in its eventual defeat. He took

GELIBOLU (GALLIPOLI TOWN) 🚢 ✕

On the NW shore of the Dardanelles. A pleasant small seaside town on the Dardanelles, which makes an ideal base for exploring the Gallipoli Peninsula. It has a picturesque harbour with cafés, and there's a ferry across the water to the Asian shore.

South of here the straits narrow down to just over 1 km, and the current becomes swifter accordingly. (This is the only outlet of the Black Sea, which receives the waters of no fewer than three of Europe's great rivers: the Danube, the Dnieper and the Don.) According to an ancient Greek legend, the youthful Leander would swim this

• *Top left:* Atatürk *statue,* Gallipoli; *above:* ANZAC *Cove.*

on the name Atatürk (which means father of the Turks), and as such became president and founder of modern Turkey. Meanwhile, many saw this as the end of Churchill's political career – until (astonishingly, given his record) he was recalled 25 years later and proved himself the greatest war leader Britain has ever known.

The date of the Gallipoli landings, March 25, is still proudly commemorated as ANZAC Day in Australia and New Zealand – a reminder of the day on which the Aussies and the Kiwis learned their lesson about trusting the mother land, a lesson which they have never forgotten.

channel each night for a tryst with the priestess Hero, who lived in a tower on the European side. Hero would light a lantern to guide her lover across the water, but one night in a storm the light blew out and Leander was drowned. When Hero heard what had happened, she threw herself from her tower into the waters and she too drowned.

Since that time swimming the Hellespont (otherwise known as the Dardanelles or Çanakkale Boğazi) has been regarded as a classic challenge. Byron swam it in 1810. He was a strong swimmer, but only just managed to defeat the current. Afterwards he unchivalrously expressed reservations about his legendary predecessor's nightly feats: 'I doubt whether Leander's conjugal powers must not have been exhausted in his passage to Paradise.' More recently, this strait was swum by the celebrated swimmer Charles Sprawson, author of *Haunts of the Black Masseur*, the finest book on swimming ever written.

Even if you are a strong swimmer you should not attempt this crossing, as I did several years ago, in an amateur fashion. Never have I grasped the shore of Asia to my bosom with greater thanks. My one-hour walk upstream in soggy bathing togs, to the spot where I had disembarked so blithely, was the occasion for profound reflection upon the absurdity of the human condition from which I had so nearly departed.

GÖKÇEADA ⇹

Off coast of Gelibolu Peninsula. Turkey has just two Aegean islands, and this is the largest (just over 20 km long and 10 km wide). It is a beautiful but distinctly sad spot. The island is mentioned in Homer by its Greek name (Imbros), and managed to remain Greek in all but name until recent decades when Greece and

Turkey almost came to war over the Cyprus question.

On account of the island's strategic position at the entrance to the Dardanelles, a large Turkish garrison was moved in. Greek schools and churches were closed, and the local Greek population were 'encouraged to leave'. Of the original 6,000 Greeks, less than one in 20 now remains. An open prison was established here – from which the real-life hero of *Midnight Express* managed to escape (an unlikely episode which bears no relation whatsoever to the even more unlikely episode portrayed in the film).

Ferries to Gökçeada run from either Çanakkale or Kabatepe on the western Gelibolu Peninsula (usually the former in summer, the latter in winter, but there is an element of whimsy in these arrangements). Because the island is a military zone, you will need a pass to visit it. You must apply for this at the Passport Office in Çanakkale. Allow at least two hours for an intriguing bureacratic process, which includes some testing questions concerning your pedigree, documents stamped with venom or

---

RECOMMENDED RESTAURANTS

EDIRNE

Edirne is no star of the culinary scene. The local speciality is a fried liver dish which I have so far succeeded in avoiding. (Daring diners tell me it's quite pleasant.) However, the city makes up for this unfortunate blemish by being strong on puddings and cakes, which are best sampled at:

Cafe M Restaurant, L-LL; *Saraçlar Caddesi, Vakif Iş Hani; tel. 284 212 3448.*

This is upstairs, and is *the* place to see and be seen in at Edirne. Ignore the gilded youth and tuck in to your cholesterol-rich goodies, or join in the deep philosophical discussions (football, disco, latest Madonna and so on). This establishment should not be mistaken for the next-door Muharipler Café (which means The Old Soldiers' Café) where the 200 per cent conservative male clientele are not in the least interested in the logical conundrums of Madonna.

For those who wish to dine on more substantial fare whilst discussing Kant's categorical imperatives, there is only one choice:

Aile, LL; *Saraçlar Caddesi, Belediye Iş Caddesi; no booking.*

Up the stairs in the building by the PTT, with its entrance door in the side street. Having found this spot, you'll be surprised at how big it is – complete with sprouting greenery and a football team of swift-swerving waiters. They have a wide-ranging menu with several good (as distinct from liverish) regional specialities.

GELIBOLU

By far the best place to eat in town is one of the restaurants by the water. My favourite here is:

Restaurant Imren, L; *by the sea; no booking.*

Just the place for a plate of fish and a bottle of cold wine as you watch the nautical world go by.

flourishes depending upon the mood of your interrogator, a visit to the suitably Kafkaesque Emniyet Mürdürlüğlü, and sometimes even the surrender of your passport. But no real harm is meant, and this entire show won't cost you a penny. The boat arrives at **Kuzu Limani**. The best place to stay is on the other side of the island at **Kale**, which has a ruined 15thC castle overlooking the beach and some restaurants and *pansiyons* along the front. Gökçeada literally means sky island, and inland the mountains rise higher than 600 m. It's a great place for walking and there are some fine remote beaches.

ISTANBUL

See pages 38-61.

ŞARKÖY 🛥

On the north-western coast of the Sea of Marmara. Like all self-respecting seaside spots it has prom, beaches, a picturesque fishing harbour, plenty of inexpensive guest houses and thousands of visitors every summer. Almost all of these are Turkish, who will be respectfully tolerant of your quaint habits. Some 30 km across the water you can see

• D*ardanelles' narrowest point, from Çanakkale.*

Marmara Island – where an equal number of Turks on holiday will be staring back at you across the water.

TEKIRDAĞ

On the central north coast of the Sea of Marmara. A grim blot. It has an irregular ferry link with the Marmara Islands, and even a tourist office to deal with the odd unfortunate who thought it looked interesting on the map. Should you fall into the latter category, you will be pleased to hear that this town was the last resort of the famous Hungarian patriot Rakoczy, who died here in 1735 having decided not to become King of Poland after all. His house is now a **museum**. In it you can see momentos of this leader who raised a peasant army to take on the might of the Habsburgs. (The *Rakoczy March* in Berlioz's *Damnation of Faust* is the song his army used to sing on its way to battle. Anyone who can come up with an even more obscure fact about this spot deserves to be banished for a week's holiday here.)

69

<u>Western Turkey</u>

Between Çanakkale and Izmir
Northern Aegean Coast

340 km; map GeoCenter Euro-Country, Western Turkey, 1: 800 000

Turkey's northern Aegean coastline offers some of the finest scenery and sights in the country. You can visit Bozcaada, Turkey's most lively Aegean island, or the smaller islands off the resort of Ayvalik. You can see three of the best-known archaeological sights in the entire Mediterranean: Troy (Truva), Pergamon (Bergama) and Assos. They are sometimes overrun with visitors, so I have included in this section a number of lesser-known ancient sites. These are not so spectacular in themselves, but have their own quirky history and you can often experience much more of a sense of place when you are standing alone in the sun overlooking the sea beside such deserted, millennia-old ruins.

If you're planning to tour the region, an obvious starting point is Çanakkale on the Dardanelles. From here Rt E87 runs south towards Troy, a site whose exciting history can lead you to expect more than you'll actually see here.

Continue down the E87 and you'll come to the turn-off for ancient Assos, where the philosopher Aristotle once lived. Even further down the E87 you pass the resorts of Kücükkuyu and Ayvalik, and finally you reach Bergama, the site of Ancient Pergamon, which for me has the finest classical ruins in Turkey.

South of Bergama you pass Myrina, and then arrive at Izmir, the third city in the land after Istanbul and Ankara, a busy port and commercial centre. You can cover the route easily in three days, though you should allow a few days more if you want to see all the sights.

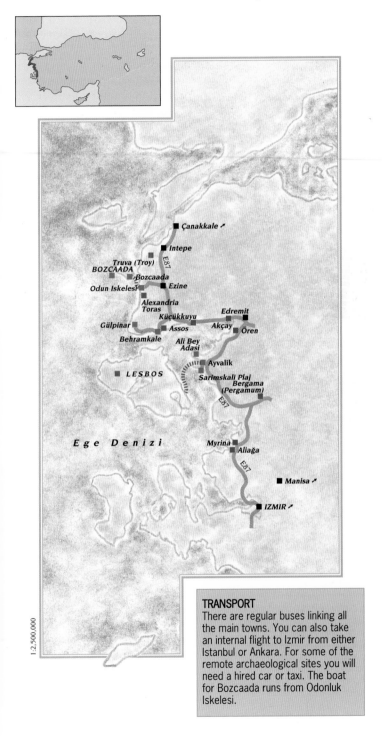

1:2,500,000

TRANSPORT
There are regular buses linking all
the main towns. You can also take
an internal flight to Izmir from either
Istanbul or Ankara. For some of the
remote archaeological sites you will
need a hired car or taxi. The boat
for Bozcaada runs from Odonluk
Iskelesi.

SIGHTS & PLACES OF INTEREST

AKÇAY
And Ören, see Edremit, page 81.

ALEXANDRIA TROAS
Just S of Odonluk Iskelesi, 20 km or so off Rt E87 at Ezine. This extensive but rather overgrown wilderness of rubble was once an important city with walls more than 10 km long and covering some 400 hectares.

The city was founded in the 4thC BC by one of Alexander the Great's generals, Antigonus I Monopthalmos. (The name suggests that he had only one eye, but I can find no other evidence for this.) He named the city Antigonia after himself, and filled it with citizens shipped in from nearby villages in the region, which used to be known as the Troad.

Later the city was conquered by another of Alexander the Great's generals, who renamed it after his ex-boss.

The city then thrived to such an extent that the Emperor Constantine initially decided it should be the capital of his empire, but then changed his mind and chose Byzantium (now Istanbul) instead. In fact, as some scholars have pointed out, this could possibly have been a better site.

St Paul visited the city on two occasions. According to the Bible, on his first visit he had a vision which prompted him to leave at once for Macedonia. On his second visit no such vision occurred and he stayed on to preach to the assembled citizens. This he did with such zeal and at such length that he went on long after midnight. One of his listeners became so engrossed by this marathon sermon that he fell asleep and toppled out of a third floor window. St Paul leapt to his rescue, wrapping him in his cloak. He bent over the unfortunate young man and then reassured the crowd: 'His life is yet in him' (Acts 20, 10). Later, when St Paul had left the city, he wrote back asking for his

---

RECOMMENDED HOTELS

AYVALIK
Kiyi Motel, L; Gümrü Meydani 18; tel. 266 311 6677.

Just off the seafront square with excellent views over the harbour. Highly recommended for those who relish the sight of a port in full working order (with much pottering throughout the day, but little actually happening). Monastic accommodation.

If you want a balcony overlooking a sandy beach with views out to sea (and not a rusty fishing boat in sight) you will probably prefer to stay down at Sarimsakli Plaj:

Otel Ankara, LL-LLL; tel. 266 311 1195.

Smart beach-front hotel with many comforts, restaurant and more than 100 rooms. Can be heavily booked with tours at the height of the season (when you'll be expected to have meals here as well). Friendly atmosphere, ideal for families – but be sure to ask for a balcony room looking out over the sea (not all of them do).

If you want to stay on Ali Bey Island,

try:

Günay Motel, LL; Ali Bey Island; tel. 266 327 1048.

In the village where the boats arrive from Ayvalik.

BEHRAMKALE
The smart little resort close to Assos. If you want to join in the swing of this swinging spot, try:

Hotel Behram, LL; by the port; tel. Behramkale 2758.

Attracts a lively crowd of Turkish and international holidaymakers. Many rooms have views out over the sea, but some don't, so be sure to ask. Booking essential in high summer.

Behramkale is a boom resort, with all kinds of mixed building metaphors ooozing from the ground. Some of these may well prove worth staying in. When you have a good view, you're not usually too concerned about the awfulness of what might appear in the mirror.

If you want to stay in the upper village, close to the site and away from the sea, the best place to stay is:

cloak (Timothy II, 413).

After Constantine meanly (and ill-advisedly) decided to position his capital at Constantinople, the fortunes of Alexandria Troas began to decline. But after the Ottomans overran Constantinople and renamed it Istanbul, they began referring to Alexandria Troas as Eski Istanbul (Old Istanbul) – an indication of its former importance.

By now large sections of the city were deserted, and the Ottomans began shipping the finest pieces of the ruins to build their new capital at Istanbul. In this way marble from Alexandria Troas came to be used for building the famous Blue Mosque (Sultan Ahmet Camii).

Even two centuries ago the ruins here remained fairly impressive, with high walls and towers, and a number of temples – but by this time, according to a passing English traveller, it had become a haunt of pirates and bandits. Today these have all vanished to more popular sites.

ALI BEY ADASI

See Ayvalik, *page 74.*

ASSOS

At *Behramkale, 36 km W of Küçükkuyu off Rt E87 down a difficult road.* As you approach Behramkale you will see to your left a fine 14thC Ottoman bridge, with its characteristic hump-back. The modern village occupies the northern section of the old city, and to reach the upper part of the site you have to walk up through the village's narrow streets. During summer this can be a pain – running the gauntlet of pestering crochet and lace sellers. (These young people have been taught to regard you as their legitimate prey: they depend upon you for their livelihood. This is the sharp end of the tourist dilemma.)

Ancient Assos was probably founded around 800 BC by colonists from the island of Lesbos, just across the water. The city had its golden era in the 4thC BC when it was ruled by the eunuch tyrant Hermias. Contrary to his

---

Gök Köşe Pansiyon, L; *upper village; no booking.*

A friendly spot which charges reasonable rates.

BERGAMA

For Pergamon:

Hotel Efsane, LL-LLL; *Izmir Caddesi 86; tel. 232 631 2963.*

On the road which links Bergama to Rt 230 (Balikesir-Edremit). The moderate bonus here is a moderate-sized pool to cool off in after your long day in the early centuries BC.

BOZCAADA

The island attracts many holidaymakers in season, and you may experience great difficulty in finding a room unless you book ahead. On the other hand, in winter the place closes up almost completely – though you can usually find a room somewhere. The best hotel on the island is:

Zafer Motel, LL; *Bozcaada Town; tel. 286 695 1078.*

On the headland by the ferry berth, with well-equipped rooms at very reasonable rates.

Those who prefer more typical, 'unspoilt' island accommodation at island rates should try:

Gümüş L; *Bozcaada Town; tel. 286 695 1252.*

This building used to be a school, and retains a slightly austere ambience. But it's clean, and as conducive to sleep as it probably was in its previous incarnation.

TROY (TRUVA)

There is a rather ordinary *pansiyon* in the village by the site:

Yarol Pansiyon, L; *Tevfikiye.*

Achilles would have found this accommodation luxurious, though probably far too clean.

Much better can be found at Intepe, 12 km or so up Rt E87 on the way to Çanakkale:

Tusan Güzelyali LL; *Intepe; tel. 286 223 8210.*

Large modern hotel by the beach. Attracts groups, so be sure to book in advance, and bring earplugs on disco night. Adequate restaurant, friendly atmosphere.

somewhat forbidding characterization and job-description, Hermias seems to have been quite pleasant. In his youth he studied philosophy under Plato at the Academy in Athens. After momentarily setting aside his philosophic education in order to seize power in vicious fashion, Hermias established himself as ruler of Assos – and decided it would be a good idea to run the place on philosophic lines. Here was the opportunity to put into practice the teachings of his master, Plato.

Hermias summoned Plato's star pupil Aristotle, and gave him the job of philosopher-in-residence, with a brief for setting up Plato's ideal republic. At the same time, a number of poets, geometers and wandering wise men were invited to the court which soon became a great centre of the arts, philosophical disputation and other forms of intellectual bickering. Aristotle was by now middle-aged and a confirmed bachelor. But soon he was so enjoying himself that he decided to get married to a woman half his age called Pythia. Some classical historians claim that Pythia was a concubine of Hermias, whom the tyrant offered to the philosopher in a moment of generosity. However, owing to Hermias' sexual status, this seems an unlikely story. She was probably either Hermias' half-sister or his niece. On the other hand, the tyrant probably did offer her to Aristotle, and this may have been the sort of offer you couldn't refuse when it was made by the local tyrant (even if he was a philosophy-loving fellow at heart). Either way, Aristotle was delighted: and he and Pythia lived together happily ever after (really).

Hermias came to a bad end: captured by the Persians and crucified. Aristotle and Pythia escaped the Persians by skipping across to the island of Lesbos, where Aristotle abandoned the idea of setting up an ideal republic and instead took up classifying the local flora and fauna.

During the Roman era Assos was visited by St Paul, who met St Luke here. (It has even been suggested that Luke may have painted his celebrated icon of the Virgin Mary at Assos – the only representation of this oft-depicted figure by someone who had actually seen her.)

After the Roman era Assos fell into decline, overshadowed by the nearby city of Alexandria Troas (see page 72). The city was taken by the Ottomans in the 14thC, 'discovered' by American archaeologists in the 19thC, and was finally overrun by tourists just a few decades ago.

This is a very impressive site – both for its fine ruins and its stunning **views** out over the Gulf of Edremit towards Lesbos. Parts of the site are also heavily littered with **ancient pottery shards**, which you are not allowed to remove. The ruins are crowned by a **mosque**, which was completed in 1389. This was built out of blocks from the Roman and Byzantine ruins which littered the site, and above its door you can see a lintel incongruously carved with Greek crosses and a Christian inscription.

Just beyond is the superb **Temple of Athena** (which you may not wish to know was recently erected by American archaeologists, but using original material). This was first built in the 6thC BC and has several columns still standing. Beyond here is the ancient **agora** or market place, the remains of a **theatre**, a **gymnasium**, the ancient Greek **walls**, and a **necropolis** with some ancient Greek and Roman tombs.

Below the site, by the sea, is the **lower village of Behramkale**, a beautiful small resort, set beneath cliffs, with its own harbour. It has several hotels and *pansiyons*, and is a great favourite with the Turkish smart set and attendant intellectuals (who seem to be rather more well-heeled than their counterparts in Europe). Swimming opportunities here are poor, but pleasant beaches start a few kilometres along the coast to the east.

A word of warning: driving down to Behramkale port from Assos after watching the sunset should be undertaken with extreme care, as this road can be hazardous after dark.

AYVALIK ⌂ ✕

43 km S of Edremit, and 2 km W off Rt E87. Not to be mistaken for the little town of Ayvacik, which is inland on the other side of the Gulf of Edremit and has an interesting country market.

There's nowhere quite like Ayvalik on the Aegean coast. The town straggles along the shore of the Gulf of Edremit at the point where it is littered with more than a dozen islands and islets. The largest of these is **Ali Bey Adasi**

(Island) (or Cunda). This can be reached by a causeway, but by far the quickest and best way to get there is by boat from the quayside at Ayvalik. Ali Bey Island has a harbour, lined with restaurants. The backstreets are a revelation. These are in part deserted and lined with delapidated houses (including a derelict church). This was where the local Greeks lived until the exchange of populations in 1922. Both Ayvalik and Ali Bey Island had large Greek communities, but even now that they are long

• *Ayvalik.*

gone you can sometimes still hear Greek spoken on the streets. This is because many of the Turks who were shipped in from Greece in the 1922 exchange were Greek-speaking Muslims from Crete. There are a number of hotels and *pansiyons* by the harbour. The best beaches on the island are along the northern shores, and some of these can be relatively peaceful, even at the height of the season.

• *Cobbler, Bergama.*

Ayvalik itself tends to be rather more crowded. It is a popular resort with holidaymakers from Izmir, and has recently suffered from a rash of villamania. Actually, it has always been a popular holiday spot, even in the pre-1922 days when Izmir was a largely Greek city called Smyrna. The potty old bourgeois villas lining the front to the south of the town centre are the former summer homes of Smyrna Greeks.

A few kilometres further south you come to the unappetisingly named but attractive **Sarmiskali Plaj** (Garlic Beach). This is the best beach in the Ayvalik area and has now attracted a number of smart hotels filled by the European package trade.

The port at Ayvalik is given over to more than just holiday traffic. It has fishing boats, as well as visits from rusty old freighters, which come to collect the olive oil. The region around Ayvalik is said to produce more than three quarters of Turkey's olive oil. Though one old local I spoke to said that nowadays it produces less than half this, whilst another at the table insisted that it produced *all* the olive oil in Turkey, because no other olive oil in Turkey was worth having.

From the harbour there are also regular ferries across the water to the Greek island of **Lesbos**. The journey takes just two hours, so it is possible to make it a day trip. The boat leaves at 9 am, back at 7 pm; daily except on Sundays in summer, infrequent and unpredictable in winter. Various niggling extra charges are included because neither country wishes to encourage this contact.

Sunset watchers and other assorted romantics, heliophiles and viewmongers should head out to **Şeytan Sofrasi** (the Devil's Table), south of town. It overlooks the bay – with its islands, the distant profile of Lesbos, and in early evening the spectacular infernal glow of Şeytan's hellfires being stoked beyond the western horizon.

BEHRAMKALE 🛏

See Assos, page 73.

BERGAMA AND ANCIENT PERGAMON 🛏 ✕

46 km S of Ayvalik: take Rt 240 E off Rt E87, then turn N following sign. Two millennia ago this was the greatest city in Asia Minor, and an aura of greatness still clings to its superb ruins. Troy attracts visitors because of its legendary Homeric associations, and can prove something of a disappointment when you actually see it. But you won't be disappointed with Pergamon – the ruins here rival even those of Athens.

This site can be seen in a day, but if you're at all interested in ancient ruins you should allow longer.

History

The city was probably founded by Aeolian Greeks in the 8thC BC. It is mentioned by the ancient Greek writer Xenophon, who arrived here in desperate circumstances in 399 BC. He had just tramped all the way across Asia Minor from Mesapotamia with the remnants of his army.

Loot, in the form of almost 10,000 gold talents, laid the foundations for Pergamon's rise to greatness. After the death of Alexander the Great in the mid 4thC BC, his general, Lysimachus, deposited his vast fortune of ill-gotten gains in the safe-keeping of the officer in charge of the city, a eunuch called Philetarus.

Not long after this, Lysimachus was killed while away in the Middle East in the course of a battle with the Syrians. When Philetarus heard the news he decided to hang on to the loot. He used it to bolster his position and make a few improvements in the city. After he died, his nephew Eumenes took over and continued the good work. Eumenes managed to hold back the Gauls who were at that time marauding through Asia Minor, and established Pergamon as the capital of his own private kingdom. When he died, the grateful citizens made him a god and declared him to be immortal (a bit late, it would seem). And so the great Pergamon dynasty began, and the city continued to flourish.

Then in 190 BC Eumenes II defeated Antiochus the Great at the Battle of Magnesia, and Pergamon succeeded to Antiochus's empire. The city suddenly found itself ruler of a territory almost as great as half of modern Turkey – stretching as far as modern Konya in the east, and including various far-flung possessions to the west, such as the island of Aegina off Athens. The city now became a great centre of culture and the arts; and its buildings soon became the envy of the entire Hellenistic world.

A library was founded here which was to became a rival to the great library in Alexandria. Indeed, Alexandria eventually became so jealous of Pergamon's library that the Egyptians refused to export any more papyrus to the city, so that its library would have

A LOAD OF OLD STONES?

The German pillaging of Pergamon is matched only by Lord Elgin's similar exploits at the Acropolis in Athens, which date from the same period. These patronizing westerners were under the impression that they were protecting their cultural heritage from the neglect or rapaciousness of the ignorant locals. And they were proved right – as is made plain by the fate of those sites which weren't so 'protected'. These were often ravaged wholesale for building materials during the 19thC and early 20thC.

Despite this, there now seems little justification for these archaeological treasures not to be returned to where they belong.

no material for any further books. Eumenes asked his master craftsmen to come up with a substitute, and they invented a new early form of paper made from treated animal hides. This came to be called *pergamene*, the origin of our word parchment. Pergamon's new technological wonder soon proved to be even better than the Egyptian papyrus because both sides could be written on, and sheets of it could be bound into codices (the earliest form of book) – unlike papyrus, which could only be rolled up into scrolls.

When the philosopher Aristotle died, there was great competition between Pergamon and Alexandria over which should get his private library of scrolls (at the time the finest collection of knowledge outside these two great libraries). Pergamon eventually won when Eumenes offered to pay their weight in gold.

It was during this period of prosperity that the great Altar to Zeus was constructed, the huge 80-row theatre was carved into the hillside, and the terraces were laid out below the city's acropolis. When the classical geographer and historian Strabo visited Pergamon, he compared these terraces to a pine cone – a likeness which appears to have occurred to him alone.

The last king of the great Pergamon dynasty was Attalus III, who ruled from 138 to 133 BC. By all accounts, Attalus

• *The theatre, Pergamum.*

was a typical end-of-the-line character. Scholarly by nature, he became a recluse, studying medicine and plant life. He specialized in inventing new types of poison, which he would try out on convicted criminals. He died after reigning for just five years, and in his will left his entire empire to the Romans. The citizens of Pergamon were naturally indignant, but the Romans moved in quickly before the citizens could contest their ex-ruler's will. The Romans would almost certainly have taken Pergamon anyway, and Attalus' will ensured that this came about with the minimum of bloodshed.

During the Roman period the city was taken briefly by Mithradates Eupator, the neurotic king of the Pontus (for his case-history see Sinop in Turkey Overall: 12), but the Romans soon regained control.

Galen, the great physician of the classical era, was born at Pergamon in 129 AD. He wrote a number of medical treatises, which were to remain accepted as standard practice in the treatment of certain ailments and illnesses until well into the 16thC. Galen was more than just a briliant theorist: he eventually went to Rome where he treated a couple of emperors. They didn't survive, but miraculously he did. Pergamon gradually began to decline towards the end of the 1stC AD,

because of growing commercial competition throughout the Aegean.

The city is mentioned in the last book of the Bible, the Book of Revelations. Here St John the Divine describes it as 'the place where Satan has his altar'. (This almost certainly refers to the great Altar of Zeus.) After the collapse of the Roman Empire, Pergamon became the seat of a Byzantine bishop; then the city was sacked by Arab raiders in 717. After that it was sporadically occupied by the Crusaders and the Selçuks, and finally became part of the Ottoman Empire when it was taken by Orhan in 1336.

The ancient city was 'forgotten' for centuries, and only rediscovered by accident. In 1871 the German engineer Karl Humann was laying out the Istanbul-Izmir railway and needed some building materials. His labourers went off and came back with some blocks of marble. Humann was astonished at the ancient carvings on the blocks, and asked where they had come from. The sight which he saw was to change him overnight from an engineer into an archaeologist.

A number of experts soon arrived on the scene, and proceeded to transport

• *Opposite: Trajan's Temple, Pergamon.*

all the best bits to Berlin. German archaeologists have been painstakingly working here ever since. Meanwhile, the Turkish government has been demanding that its property be returned, but with no success.

The ancient city of Pergamon was protected by a superb acropolis which dominated the fertile plain below. This was watered by two rivers, as it is today, so Pergamon's harvest remained rich, even when the rest of the Aegean was suffering from drought.

Viewing the site

The modern town of Bergama covers part of the ancient city. Bergama's **old quarter** is an interesting maze of streets, but its modern section is largely devoted to helping overheated tourists divest themselves of their excess financial baggage. Carpets, leather goods, metalware and so on are available: you name it, they'll name their optimistic prices.

But do visit the **Archaeological Museum** which has a number of finds that never made it on to the Berlin express. It also has a pleasant café in the courtyard, with tables incorporating bits of ancient pillars.

Another sight worth seeing in town is **Kizil Avlu** (the **Red Basilica**). This red-brick building began life as a temple of the Egyptian god Osiris, but later became a Roman temple, then a Christian church, and it now contains a mosque. It straddles the river, which still runs through the original pipes beneath the building.

The classical site is awe-inspiring, with much to see. Best of all is of course the **acropolis**. Look at the locally available, meticulously detailed reconstruction drawing done by Dr Wolfgang Radt, and you can see that this must have been almost the equal of the Acropolis at Athens.

On the other hand, the remains of the **library** are rather sad – it is now just a few stones. (In the end it lost out to Alexandria. In 41 BC the Alexandria library was destroyed by fire – arguably the greatest cultural loss in the history of western civilization. But Mark Antony then stole the 200,000 volumes from the Pergamon library in an attempt to make up for this loss. It was also an attempt to impress his paramour Cleopatra, who didn't read a single one of them.)

Nearby is the awe-inspiring **theatre**, which could seat 10,000 spectators. There are also two other theatres further down the hillside. According to an expert who once led me around here, the valley below would sometimes be dammed so that the spectators could watch mock sea battles between triremes manned by galley slaves and gladiators – though he had previously rather undermined my confidence in his expertize by claiming that Cleopatra was really a man.

The magnificent **Altar of Zeus**, the largest of its kind anywhere, must have been some sight in its day. (And still makes quite a sight – both here, and in Berlin, which has the best bits.)

Also not to be missed are the **Temples of Athena and Dionysus**.

Just over a kilometre away across the valley is the **Asclepion**, which was founded in the 4thC BC and dedicated to Asclepios, the son of Apollo, the god of healing. This was the great medical centre where Galen studied.

BOZCAADA 🛥

NW of *Odonluk Iskelesi*. The smaller of Turkey's two Aegean islands. (the other is Gökçeada.) Since it is a military area you will need a pass, which is obtainable in Çanakkale (see under Gökçeada in Turkey Overall: 1). The ferry to this island leaves from Odonluk Iskelesi, west off Rt E87 from Ezine.

Bozcaada is small (about 12 km by 5 km) and relatively flat. It is much more popular than Gökçeada: even Greeks who used to live here come back to see their old home and visit their few remaining relatives. Since the Second World War the Greek population has dwindled from 50 per cent to a few dozen aged survivors.

The island's history goes back a long way. It was mentioned in myths of the Homeric era, under its Greek name, Tenedos. This is where the Greeks hid, along with their fleet, when they left the wooden horse at Troy and deceived its inhabitants into thinking that they had abandoned their siege. Nowadays, as then, the island is renowned for its wines. (To my taste, the light white is much better than the red.)

The boat puts in at the island's only town, which is also known as **Bozcaada**. This is dominated by a surprisingly large and well-preserved **castle**, which has been added to by almost all the conquerors of the island. Major work was done by the Byzantines, the Venetians and the Genoese, before it was massively refortified by Sultan Mehmet II.

The town below it is a delight, with cobbled streets and overhanging balconies that inevitably remind one of the old pre-tourist days in the Aegean.

Inland there are low hills and vineyards. The coastline has a number of pleasant beaches. The best are along the south coast, but these are also the most popular. Near one of these is **Ayazma**, the sacred spring which gave the island its present name.

ÇANAKKALE
A useful base for tackling the major sights in this section; covered in detail in Local Explorations: 1.

EDREMIT
39 km E of Küçükkuyu on Rt E87. This dreary spot was sacked by Achilles, who had the right idea. The resorts down the road on the coast – **Akçay** and **Ören** – are pleasant enough, but tend to be overrun by Turkish holidaymakers during the season.

GÜLPINAR
20 km W of Assos down very third class roads. There are a number of minor classical sites around here. To find them you will need a detailed map, and must be prepared to ask the way. There is a sign in the village to the nearby 2ndC BC **Temple of Apollo Smintheus** (Apollo as the god of mice).

According to legend, a clan of Cretans, led by their hero Teucer, fled their native island during a famine. Before they left, the local soothsayer promised that all would be well if they settled in the land where they were attacked by the 'sons of the earth'. Teucer and his band put into Gülpinar exhausted, and fell asleep on the beach. They were awakened by the sound of their kit and weapons being gnawed by mice. At once they realized that they had arrived at the right place, and set up a Temple to Apollo Smintheus. Archaeologists are still at work here, and they have yet to come up with a better story.

The sites in this neighbourhood are not spectacular, but you'll usually find

that you are alone when you finally arrive at one of these remote locations – giving you a pleasant, proprietorial feeling of achievement. (It must have been like this for those who originally discovered the great ruins.) On your detailed map look out for **Satnibes, Hamaxitos** and **Polymedium** (not a new form of weatherproof paint, but a site down the road near Bademli).

This small peninsula has a number of remote beaches and an unspoilt little fishing village at **Babakale**. This even has its own ruined 400-year-old castle, which used to be a haunt of pirates.

For those who insist upon going to extremes, the cape here is the westernmost landpoint of mainland Asia, a mere 9,600 km from its easternmost point at Cape Dezhneva in eastern Siberia: presenting one of the world's last great unconquered challenges.

INTEPE 🏨
See Recommended Hotels, under Troy.

IZMIR
See Local Explorations: 2.

KÜÇÜKKUYU
42 km W of Edremit off Rt E87. A resort on the northern shore of the Gulf of Edremit. It has a picturesque little harbour and there are some pleasant swimming beaches nearby. Ideal for a spot of lazing, or as a base for visiting Assos and exploring the scattered minor sites beyond (see Gülpinar, this page). When asking the way to this town it is better to write its name down on a piece of paper, or misguided attempts to pronounce it could easily lead you into adventurous situations which you had not anticipated.

LESBOS
See Ayvalik, page 66.

MANISA
See Local Explorations: 5

MYRINA
6 km N of Aliaɟa, 2 km W off Rt E87. If you see a small ancient Greek terracotta figure in a museum, there's a fair chance that it came from Myrina. Just a century ago archaeologists dicovered a vast necropolis here with more than 5,000 tombs dating from the first two centuries BC. Amazingly, these had

remained unpillaged (until the archaeologists came along).

In the early classical era it was customary for the dead to be buried with a small terracotta figure. These could represent anything from an animal to a deity, or even a busty female figure. Some were recognizable as children's toys – dolls, for instance, complete with movable arms. These figurines sometimes represented treasured possessions (toys, busty females) or were indicative of the deceased's character (Dionysios was a favourite for the boozers, Priapus for those who favoured earlier bedtime).

Myrina was probably founded around 2000 BC, and is said by Strabo to have been named after a 'much-bounding' Amazon named Myrina. What precisely this bounding was all about has continued to excercise the minds of scholars. The city flourished until it was destroyed by an earthquake in the 1stC BC and rebuilt by the Emperor Tiberius and renamed Sebastopolis, which means city of the emperor.

The ruins here spread over the hillsides, but are largely covered in a tangle of undergrowth which sometimes makes them difficult to distinguish. However, it can be a relief to explore these minor sites where you find yourself alone with your musings on the vicissitudes of history (as distinct from taking part in large-scale historical migrations amongst hordes at Troy and Pergamon).

ODONLUK ISKELESI

On the coast, W off Rt E87 at Ezine. This is where the ferry leaves for the island of Bozcaada (see page 80). You can have a swim at the pleasant sandy beach while you wait for the ferry, and there are a number of café-restaurants by the sea. It's also only a couple of kilometres from the ruins of Alexandria Troas (see page 72).

SARMISKALI PLAJ

See Ayvalik, page 74.

TROY (TRUVA) ⚓

32 km SW of Çanakkale, W off Rt E87. The most legendary city of them all. In Homer's *Iliad* we learn that Paris, the son of King Priam of Troy, sailed to the Peleponnese and ran off with Helen, the beautiful wife of King Menelaus of Sparta. Enraged, Menelaus joined up with King Agamemnon, Achilles, Odysseus and a combined Greek force. Together they set sail in a vast fleet for Troy, in order to fetch Helen back (hence Helen's beauty being described as 'the face that launched a thousand ships'). The Greeks were to besiege Troy for ten long years, during which several notable battles took place on the plains below the city walls. Homer records how Hector killed Petroclus, how the invincible Achilles avenged this by slaying Hector, and how Paris avenged this by shooting an arrow into Achilles' one weak spot, his 'Achilles heel'.

Then one day the Greeks decided that they'd had enough, and sailed away. Behind them they left a gift for the citizens of Troy in the form of a large wooden horse. The Trojans, celebrating at the end of the long siege, spilled out of the city. They gazed in wonder at the wooden horse, then joyfully dragged it up the ramp through the city gate. The horse was so large that part of the gate had to be knocked down so that they could get it in.

It was all a Greek subterfuge. That night, when the drunken Trojans lay asleep, some soldiers concealed in the wooden horse slipped out and opened the city gates to let in the Greeks, who had sailed back under cover of darkness. Troy fell, and the Greeks triumphantly carried off Helen back to Greece.

It is from this story that we get the saying 'Beware Greeks bearing gifts' – but not the saying 'Never look a gift horse in the mouth' (had the Trojans disobeyed this advice, they might have noticed a few wary eyes peering up at them from within).

This was the most crucial early encounter between the mainland Greeks and the inhabitants of Asia, and it resulted in a European victory. When the Persian king Xerxes marched on the Greeks in the 5thC BC he specifically mentioned that one of his aims was to avenge the defeat of Troy.

Two centuries later Alexander the Great honoured the Greek victory at Troy on his way to conquer Asia. And in 1453, after Mehmet II had conquered the Byzantine Empire, he visited Troy and declared that the Greek victory had been avenged.

The Greek victory at Troy thus

• *Carpet shop, Bergama.*

played a crucial role in the subsequent history of the region. Yet did this much-vaunted event actually take place? Homer wrote the *Iliad*, which describes the events at Troy, some five hundred years after the event. Indeed, scholars have long suspected that this conflict had nothing to do with the abduction of Helen. In their view it was probably just a commercial dispute over who controlled the rich trade pouring through the Dardanelles from the Greek colonies in the Black Sea.

Homer's story came to be regarded as no more than a poetic fiction. In 1705 the German scholar Friedrich Wolff went so far as to 'prove' that there had been no Trojan war at all, and that Troy had never even existed. (He also went one step further and 'proved' that Homer didn't exist either, but was unable to prove that the *Iliad* didn't exist: too many people had read it.)

Then in 1871, much to the disbelief and irritation of the academics, the German Heinrich Schliemann claimed that he had discovered the site of Troy. Schliemann was an extraordinary man. He had been born in 1822 in Mecklenburg. A poor, not particularly bright boy, he had set about educating himself by reading the Greek myths, which fascinated him. After leaving home he became a millionaire in the California

gold rush. At the age of 42 he retired and set off to find Troy, using the visual references in Homer's poetry as his guide. The academics scoffed. Even those who believed that Homer had existed were agreed that he had been blind – hardly the ideal guide to lead anyone to a lost city. Naturally, Schliemann found nothing.

But Schliemann would not be daunted. He went on pouring his fortune into the project, a childhood dream which had become an adult obsession.

After trying several likely spots, he succeeded. He set about excavating the site in his determined, amateur fashion, destroying parts of Troy as he went. Eventually, he came across a hoard of jewellery. To an astonished world he announced that he had discovered the treasures of King Priam. In fact, when subsequent archaeologists finally managed to piece together the heap of rubble produced by Schliemann's energetic digging, they discovered that this treasure came from an even earlier layer, pre-dating King Priam's Troy by almost 1,000 years.

Schliemann arrived back in Berlin a famous man. Society was astonished when his wife took to attending fashionable balls wearing her Trojan jewellery.

83

• *Tea house, Bergama.*

Scholars had to be helped from the room. Eventually, Schliemann was persuaded to donate the jewellery to a Berlin Museum for safe-keeping. Here it remained until the end of the Second World War, when it disappeared. Not until decades later did part of Schliemann's hoard come to light in various Russian museums.

After 'discovering' Troy, Schliemann went in search of ancient Mycenae, King Agamemnon's capital, once again using visual references in Homer's poetry – and once again the blind poet, writing 500 years after the events he was describing, led Schliemann to precisely the right spot.

After all this, the physical remains at Troy can prove a disappointment. But it need not be so. There is much to see here, and if you know what you're looking at it can stimulate original thought on several unanswered questions.

For instance, the story of the wooden horse is obviously something of a fib. The Trojans would never have been taken in by such an obvious ruse. But was this story really just a myth? The legend describes the wooden horse being dragged up a ramp leading to a gate in the walls – and this ramp is very

much a stony fact, which you can examine for yourself. You won't find any three-millennia-old scrape marks left by a wooden horse. But it is possible to detect where the gate at the top of the ramp was partly widened at one stage, and then rebuilt – just as the legend describes it was for the wooden horse. Alternatively, some scholars maintain that the walls of Troy were severely damaged in an earthquake which took place in 1275 BC. They believed that it was this which helped the Greeks overcome the city, and that afterwards the Greeks built a monument to Poseidon (the god responsible for earthquakes) in the form of a wooden horse. Take a look at the evidence on the ground, and you can decide for yourself. You can still inspect the remains of what must once have been a formidable defensive wall. And from here you can look over the coastal plain where Achilles, Hector and Paris fought it out. Did Helen stand here? And what happened when her husband Menelaus finally got her home?

Excavations have revealed that no fewer than nine cities have stood on this site, each built on the remains of its predecessor. The earliest city (imaginatively named Troy I, by those who know) appears to date from the Early Bronze

Age, around 3000 BC. The **Bouleterion** (Council Chamber), one of the better surviving ruins, dates from around the Homeric era (about 800 BC). Most of the other more interesting ruins date from the later Greek and Roman eras: these include **temples** and a **theatre**. The Romans erected the **Temple of Athena**, and in the process of digging its foundations did even more damage to the preceeding levels than the industrious Schliemann. The city continued to flourish until around 300 AD, after which it faded from history. We know that a small garrison of Turkish soldiers was billeted amongst the ruins in the 14thC, and that later the site was completely abandoned – more than 3,000 years of history gradually fading into a wilderness of mounds and stones. Until Schliemann turned up.

Nearby you can visit the modest dwelling where Schliemann and his Greek wife Sophia lived during their excavations. This has some fascinating photos dating from the period, including some of Mrs Schliemann dolled out in her finest 3,000-year-old jewellery, on permanent loan from the collection of King Priam, as well as a few of the delicate blunt instruments which Schliemann and his workers used to bludgeon their way through to their historic discovery.

Just by the car park you can also see a modern wooden horse which has what appears to be a potting shed on its back. In fact the thing looks like something out of the children's playground in a pub garden – but then the original may well have been closer to Disneyworld than the scholars would care to admit. For that authentic Greek historical experience you can climb up into the back of this horse, though some may be put off by the anatomical point of entry.

A few hundred metres from the site itself is the village of **Tevfikiye**, where you will find several restaurants and a *pansiyon*. There's also an ever-growing number of souvenir shops, many containing authentic artefacts from the Trojan Trinket Era, late 2nd millenium AD. During the high season Troy is often besieged by more people than it was in the good old days of the 13thC BC. To avoid bumping into squads of modern Achilles' armed to the teeth with video equipment, their vulnerable heels encased in bright new trainers, you're best off visiting this spot in the romantic light of late afternoon, when Helen would have looked her best.

RECOMMENDED RESTAURANTS

AYVALIK
By far the best place to eat at in this area is one of the fish restaurants along the harbour front at Ali Bey Island:

Canli Balik, L-LL; *by the harbour; no booking.*
Dining out on the terrace overlooking the sea. Try their excellent fish with a bottle of cold local white wine – very well chilled, this could be Spanish; at lesser temperatures it is definitely Turkish.

If you're staying in town, try one of the restaurants by the harbour, such as:

Sahil Restaurant, L-LL; *Gumruk Meydani*; tel. 266 311 6669.
Excellent for seafood, but not particularly quiet if you eat outside.

The restaurants down in Sarmiskali tend to be tourist traps with such enticing words as London, Paris or Novosibirsk in their titles, where you can get presented with a bill which looks as if it's been made out in 1920s Reichmarks.

BERGAMA
For Pergamon:
As you'd expect, there are plenty of restaurants for the tourists. In some of these prices tend to range from the excessive to the truly imaginative. An exception is:

Sultan Restaurant, L-LL; *Istikal Meydani; no booking.*
A leafy spot in the square of the old town. Service is genuinely friendly. My favourite dish is their tasty Paper Kebab – mildly spiced pieces of meat and vegetables cooked in a sealed paper envelope to retain the full flavour – delicious

<u>Western Turkey</u>

Between Izmir and Bodrum
Southern Aegean Coast

240 km; map GeoCenter Euro-Country, Western Turkey, 1: 800 000

The southern Aegean coastline is one of the most popular holiday destinations in Turkey. It's very hot in summer, and surprisingly warm in the spring and autumn. I've experienced 30°C and higher in late autumn. The main holiday area centres on Kuşadasi, though Bodrum is not far behind nowadays. Kuşadasi itself bears a close resemblance to Torremolinos, but nearby there are some excellent and fairly remote beaches. Also nearby are some of the finest ancient sites in Turkey. Ephesus, which is one of the country's top three tourist attractions, is the best-preserved classical city in the Mediterranean. The crown jewel is the celebrated Library of Celsus, whose façade adorns a thousand travel posters, but is none the worse for that.

Nearby Selçuk contains sights of interest from a much wider range of Turkish history, including the tomb of St John. Just down the road you can also visit the Meryemana, the house where the Virgin Mary may have lived her last years – which was discovered in mysterious fashion by a German mystic (see page 98).

If you want to travel through this region from Izmir, head south down the E87 to Selçuk. From here, as you go west towards Kuşadasi, you will see Ephesus on your left. From Kuşadasi continue to Söke. From here you can make forays west to the sites at Miletus, Priene and Didyma. From Söke Rt 525 heads south to Milas, where you turn west for Bodrum. The direct road from Izmir to Bodrum can easily be covered in a day. There's so much to see in this region – beaches, ancient sights, highly romantic places – that you could happily spend a week travelling between the two centres.

TRANSPORT
There are regular buses between all
the main towns in this region, and
dolmuşes run to within easy reach
of most of the main ancient sights.
There are international flights into
Izmir and Bodrum, but these two
are *not* linked by any internal air
service, nor is there yet a ferry
service along the coast. The easiest
way to cover the region remains
hired car.

1:2,500,000

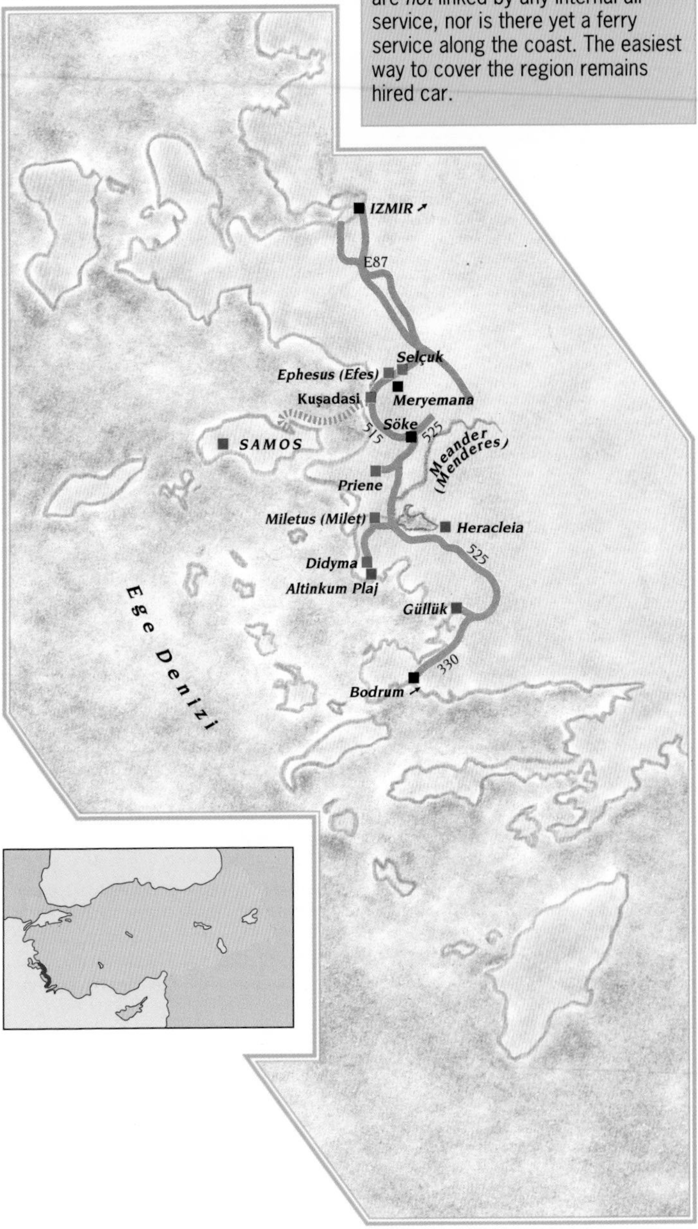

■ IZMIR ↗

E87

Selçuk

Ephesus (Efes)
Kuşadasi ■   ■ *Meryemana*
■ *Söke* 525

■ SAMOS   Meander
(Menderes)

Priene ■

Miletus (Milet) ■   ■ *Heracleia*

Didyma ■   525
Altinkum Plaj ■

Güllük ■

E g e   D e n i z i

Bodrum ↗   330

SIGHTS & PLACES OF INTEREST

ALTINKUM PLAJ ⇔ ✕
See Söke, page 101 and Recommended Hotels and Restaurants, pages 92 and 96.

BODRUM
See Turkey Overall: 4.

DIDYMA
Turn W off Rt 525 and continue 27 km S of Söke; follow signs through Akköy, then go S for 27 km. Known in Turkish as Didim, this place has been holy since time immemorial. When the early Ionian settlers arrived here in the 11thC BC, they found a shrine to a local Anatolian deity. This was eventually adapted to the worship of Apollo, and some time later priests arrived from the shrine of Apollo at Delphi to supervise the proceedings. These were, in essence, an oracle, whose pronouncements required dexterous, experienced management – if it was to gain suitably prestigious offerings.

All went well, and during the 9thC BC a vast temple with more than 100 marble columns was built on the site. This protected the holy spring and laurel tree (the plant sacred to Apollo). The fame of Didyma spread far and wide: even the King of Egypt sent a gift. In 494 BC the Persians defeated the Ionians and looted the temple, taking the cultic statue of Apollo back to Persia with them. The shrine of Apollo fell into such decline that the sacred well even dried up.

Then Alexander the Great arrived in 334 BC. This auspicious event was heralded by all kinds of omens. The priests promised Alexander that he would win a great battle, and the sacred spring even started to gush again. Alexander was so taken with all this that he ordered a new temple to be built, and when he invaded Persia he even sent back the original purloined statue of Apollo. This new temple also had more than 100 columns, and is the temple whose ruins can be seen today.

Alexander's temple was a great architectural feat for its day, and presented its builders with considerable problems. As always with builders, such problems never entirely halted the work – they just meant that it got slower and slower, and became more and more expensive. The Hellenistic age came and went, the Roman Empire rose, and then began its long decline and still the builders were at work on Didyma. By now the shrine complex even had a sacred way lined with statues and paved with marble, which led down to the sea. Then in 385 AD the Emperor Theodosius forbad all pagan rites in favour of Christianity, and finally work came to a halt.

For centuries Didyma was forgotten, except by the local Greek villagers who would sometimes filch the odd block of marble when they were building a house. (These can still be seen in some of the old houses in the nearby village.) Eventually, in 1858, the British arrived, and were so overcome by the magnificence of what they saw that they shipped as much as they could back to the British Museum. This included all the statues lining the sacred way; but the vastness of the unfinished temple defeated even these removals experts. Despite this vandalism, Didyma remains an impressive sight. The temple still sports 108 columns, you can still see the sacred well and the sacrificial shrine, and there's a magnificent head of Medusa, the goddess whose hair consisted of entwined snakes, and whose gaze could turn a man to stone. In season, this site attracts large crowds. If you want to avoid them, arrive at dusk. As the light fades around the golden columns, and the crows come in to roost, the place can be highly atmospheric.

EPHESUS (EFES) ⇔ ✕
2 km SW of Selçuk on the road to Kuşadasi. Ephesus is so famous in Turkey that the Turks have even named their major beer after it. Despite the fact that no Turks ever lived here, it comes as no surprise that modern Turkey holds this site in such cheery regard. Ephesus is one of the country's three major tourist attractions (along with the Sultanahmet district in Istanbul and Cappadocia).

It is arguably the best-preserved classical city in the world (certainly superior to Pompeii). Understandably, it attracts huge crowds, whose physical presence and attention are only partly absorbed by the vastness of the site. If you find the company of such large numbers of like-minded human beings offensive, your only hope is to arrive

• *Opposite: the Library of Celsus, Ephesus.*

here just before 8 am, when the site opens. At this hour the carpet and trinket sellers by the main gate are just opening up, but you will still doubtless be furtively approached by some beguiling seller of 'ancient coins.' (Take a good look at these: they are of coure fakes, but some of them are quite good. Similar fakes are on sale in the Museum of Anatolian Civilizations for around 100,000TL.)

Background

Ephesus has a long and distinguished history. It was traditionally founded by Androclus, the son of a king of Athens. According to the legend, before Androclus set out on his voyage to found a colony he was advised by the oracle to settle at 'the place of the fish and the wild boar.' When Androclus and his crew came ashore on the coast here they found a group of locals cooking some fish over a fire. Some sparks from the fire set alight the undergrowth, and a wild boar charged out. Androclus knew at once that he had arrived at the right spot.

There has almost certainly been a settlement of some kind here since the 2nd millennium BC. In those days there was a fine harbour, and this was at the end of one of the main trading routes from Mesopotamia and the Middle East. Ephesus quickly became a great trading city, and thus it remained for almost two thousand years – largely because it eschewed greatness in other fields.

Indeed, as everyone soon discovered, when it came to a fight the Ephesians were a push-over. Mostly, they didn't even bother to turn up for the battle: they just sent someone to hand over the keys of the city to the invading army. This tactical method obviously appealed to the victors, who seldom wreaked heavy revenge upon the inhabitants. The Ephesians went on trading, the victors took their rake-off, and everyone was happy.

On a few occasions the Ephesians became involved in intrigues with the wrong side, and on one occasion they even slaughtered all the Roman inhabitants when it looked as if the Romans were going to lose out in this part of the world. But both the Ephesians and the Romans quickly realized that this as an uncharacteristic mistake, and all was forgiven. The Romans even made the

city the capital of Asia, and lavished vast funds on fine buildings.

By now the city had a population of more than 300,000. But already it was faced with the problem which eventually led to its downfall. The harbour was silting up. This was taken so seriously that no fewer than two Roman emperors personally addressed themselves to the problem. Unexpectedly, it was Nero who came up with a plan which almost worked, whereas the masterful Hadrian's scheme was quite hopeless from the start. Ephesus had long been famous as a centre for the worship of the goddess Artemis (often known as Diana). The nearby Temple of Artemis was one of the Seven Wonders of the World, and is said to have been the largest building ever built by the ancient Greeks. The high priest lived here with his sacred virgins in attendance. In order to keep their virginity intact, one of the job requirements for the high priest was castration.

The great temple was destroyed by fire in 356 BC. This was the work of an arsonist called Erostratus, who suffered from an unfortunate condition which was rare in 4thC BC, but has reached epidemic proportions in the 20thC. Erostratus had no talents (and few wits), but he wanted to be famous. He succeeded in his aim – and was regarded with much the same pity and contempt as we today regard our own half-witted celebrities.

Christianity came early to Ephesus. St John arrived in the 1stC, and may well have written his gospel here. St Luke is supposed to have accompanied the ageing Virgin Mary to Ephesus, and later to have died here. Most notably of all, St Paul lived at Ephesus from 51 to 53 AD, his visit culminating in the stormy events described in Acts 19 verse 23 to Acts 20 v 1. Never averse to having a go at the pagans, St Paul described the followers of Artemis as idolators because they worshipped silver images of the goddess. According to Paul, gods made by human beings were not gods at all. There was an immediate slump in the sale of silver images, and the silversmiths were incensed. Their leader gave a fiery speech denouncing Paul and prophesying the economic ruin of the entire city.

• *Opposite: Library of Celsus, interior.*

A riot followed and the crowd began baying for Paul's blood. Not for the first time in his career, Paul was forced to make a hasty exit in fear of his life.

Viewing the site

There are several major sights at Ephesus. From the main gate, you enter along an avenue of trees, which makes a welcome respite from the heat. At the end of this avenue on your right you will see the **Sacred Way**, lined with columns, which once led down to the harbour. The sea has now retreated several kilometres away across the flat delta plain.

On your left at the end of the tree-lined avenue you can see the magnificent **theatre** rising on the hillside. This could once seat nearly 25,000 spectators, and was until recently used for rock concerts. But the sound equipment caused such destructive vibrations that this area is at present too dangerous to enter, and is sealed off.

From the theatre, continue southwest along **Marble Street**, and you will see the remains of a **bordello** and some **public lavatories** on your left. Just beyond here on the right you come to the **Library of Celsus**, which has one of the best-preserved classical façades still standing. Incorporated into this façade are **statues of the Four Virtues**. These have weathered the vicissitudes of time in telling fashion: Sophia (wisdom) has lost her right arm; Arete (valour) has lost her front from the waist downwards; and both Ennoia (thought) and Episteme (wisdom) have lost their heads.

There are three places of interest away from the main site. A couple of hundred metres south-west of the **Commercial (Lower) Agora**, on the hillside

---

RECOMMENDED HOTELS

ALTINKUM PLAJ

This spot gets packed during the season, making it very difficult to find a room. It's not much use booking ahead either, as in my experience these bookings aren't always honoured.

Altinkum is very much a place for a day visit, but if you want to look for a room you'll have to ask around early. Amongst the rows of pensions, try the **Gürük,** which is on small road leading up from the waterfront.

EPHESUS (EFES)

Motel Efes Tusan, LL; *corner of main road to Selçuk and road to the site; tel.* 232 892 2061.

Extremely handy for the site, but not for much else as it's in the middle of nowhere on the main road. That said, it's by far the best place to stay if you want to be sure of getting into Ephesus at opening time, 8 am. The *vast* crowds arrive soon afterwards.

GÜLLÜK

Pelit Pension, LL; *Güllük; tel.* 252 522 1205.

Friendly spot on the edge of town by the lighthouse. Often has a free room when others are booked out – or will tell you where you're likely to

find one. Great sea sunsets from your window.

KUŞADASI

This big resort offers a wide choice. Despite this, rooms are often difficult to find in season, and tend to be relatively expensive when you do find them. Out of season, despite the excellent climate, hotels are often desperate for trade. If they don't offer reductions, bargain ruthlessly.

If you feel like splashing out, try:

Club Kervansaray, LLL; 1 *Atatürk Bulvari; tel.* 256 611 4115.

Right in front of the port. This ancient Ottoman caravanserai has been completely refurbished and is now run by Club Med as a holiday hotel. The inner courtyard is highly atmospheric, complete with palm trees and fountain. Rooms are also suitably authentic – with the rigors of caravan lodging relieved by mod cons.

The courtyard runs as a nightclub at night, and can be noisy.

Less expensive, but on the seafront, is:

Günhan LL; 52 *Atatürk Bulvari; tel.* 256 610 9402.

Handy for the (rather paltry) town beach. Rooms at the front have fine

overlooking the city, is the so-called **St Paul's Tower**. This was almost certainly a watch tower which formed part of the city's defences, but according to legend St Paul was imprisoned here after a spot of bother some time prior to the silversmiths' riot.

In the south-east corner of the car park outside the *back* gate (i.e. the one close to the city's Magnesia Gate) is the so-called **Tomb of St Luke**. It's obvious that this small building surrounded by 16 Ionic columns was originally built as a pagan Roman temple, but it may well have been used later for Christian worship. The legend that St Luke was buried here appears to date from the 1stC. However, the somewhat makeshift construction in front of this building, which has been optimistically signposted as the actual grave, is certainly fraudulent.

Two hundred metres or so east of the main gate (outside the site perimeter fence) is the so-called **Cave of the Seven Sleepers**. The cave, containing some early Christian catacombs, earned its name from a quaintly implausible myth about seven Christians from Ephesus who fled the city to escape persecution during Roman times. Whilst waiting for the fury to die down, they fell asleep. They were woken by an earthquake, and set off back to town. Here they were astonished to discover that fashion and hairstyles had changed overnight. Whilst making enquiries about the new fashionable attire, the seven from the cave discovered that they had been asleep for longer than 200 years. A likely story – and one which almost certainly echoes an even earlier pre-Christian myth.

You can reach the site by regular

---

views over the bay towards the exotic liners in the harbour. Service is friendly, but somewhat laid back. Rooms are modernish, with plumbing in full working order.

The inexpensive place where all the younger travellers go is:

Rose Otel (Sammy's), LL; Arslanlar Caddesi; *tel.* 256 611 1111.
Up the hill at the end of Arslanlar Caddesi, just after the turn-off for Kibris Caddesi. Backpackers tend to treat this place affectionately as a sort of club. There are two bars (one friendly, one wild) which are excellent for meeting fellow travellers. It can even be reasonably quiet, especially when the Aussies have trekked back across Europe for the Munich Oktoberfest.

If you fancy some resort-style living, head north of town in one of the *dolmuşes* that run along the seafront to **Pine Bay Club**. There are several resorts on the way, each with all the usual facilities (beach, swimming pools, poolside bars, sports centres, discos, ideal for children). These are usually booked by package groups, and always say they're full if you ring. Try calling in personally at reception and making an LL offer to start the ball rolling. Remember, in a place like

this you must expect to take demi-pension.

SELÇUK
Across from the Otogar (where the *dolmuşes* also put in) and close to the museum is the local tourist office. This has a helpful list of accommodation, but not much information on what you actually get.
The best hotel in town is:

Pinar Hotel, LL-LLL; Sahabettin Dede Caddesi; *tel.* 232 892 2561.
Turn east off the main E24 at the Otogar, and you'll see it on the left. Rooms with all modern comforts and balcony views across to the fortified walls of the Hill of Ayasoluk. Pricey restaurant, friendly bar.

If you want to stay in the town centre, try:

Hotel Victoria, LL; 4 Cengiz Topel Caddesi; *tel.* 232 892 3203.
Despite the name, this is a modern establishment complete with lift. Prices shrink considerably in the off season. Make sure you get a room with views towards the aqueduct and the Hill of Ayasoluk. The English spoken at reception is more or less comprehensible if you listen hard.

dolmuş from Kuşadasi or Selçuk. Some of the guided tours are charmingly witty, others are merely informative.

GÜLLÜK ⊨

37 km NE of Bodrum off Rt 330. The classic case of a resort which has little to offer execpt recently developed tourist facilities. Swamped by the development is the remains of a fishing village, and a bauxite terminal which occasionally attracts the odd romantically rusted tramp steamer. Meanwhile, development extends apace to the north and the well-packaged visitors from Dortmund and Doncaster appear well tanned, well-oiled and well pleased. If you explore, you'll find some pleasant, remote beaches around the bay.

HERAKLEIA UNDER LATMOS

50 km S of Söke, off Rt 525. Herakleia is a marginally interesting site on the shores of Lake Bafa, which was formed by the meanderings of the River Meander (from which we derive the word meander). The ruins here are boring and unimpressive compared with those at such nearby sites as Miletus, Priene and Didyma. But the stories associated with this place have enticed many an erstwhile romantic (including myself) to view these lakeside ruins by the light of a full moon. The rewards are suitably stimulating – as indeed is the legend.

According to one of the sexiest of all Greek myths, the handsome young shepherd Endymion fell asleep in a cave on nearby Mount Latmos. The moon goddess Selene was so overcome by his beauty that she made love to him while he slept, apparently without waking him. However, Endymion must have been aware that something was going on, because he beseeched Zeus – who also fancied Selene – to let all this moonshine continue. And indeed it did: to such an extent that Selene eventually had more than 50 daughters by Endymion in his sleep.

The story of Endymion and Selene was to inspire both Shakespeare and the Romantic poet John Keats. The latter got so carried away that he penned the immortal lines:

> Now I begin to feel thy orby power
> Is coming fresh upon me.

Many centuries after the legendary

lunar lovers had abandoned their cave, a Christian hermit took up residence. As so often with hermits, once one has got away from it all, others soon follow. In no time the region was filled with hermits all living in splendid isolation. Of a moonlit night these hermits would sometimes find themselves pondering the legend of Endymion and his seductive moonbeams. But this stimulating line of thought merely encouraged their mystic faculties, and they interpreted the legend of Endymion in spiritual fashion. According to this reclusive retelling of the tale, Endymion was really a mystic, who spent so many years gazing at the moon and communing with the heavens that eventually he was vouchsafed the secret name of God. This version was confirmed when the hermits all congregated once a year at an ancient tomb, said to be that of Endymion. The tomb would be opened, and eerie moans would emanate from the skeleton of Endymion. The hermits would all listen hard as their deceased hero attempted in vain to communicate to them the holiest name of God.

These hermits' caves can still be seen on the slopes of Mount Latmos. The actual ruins contain some Hellenistic walls and a tumbledown theatre. But the moon over the water is as seductive as ever.

IZMIR

See Local Explorations: 2.

KUŞADASI ⊨ ✕

96 km S of Izmir on Rt E 87. When I first arrived in Kuşadasi it was a dozy little fishing village – now, in less than three decades, it's Turkey's answer to Torremolinos. At night, this is the decibel epicentre of the Aegean coast, with the uproar from Disco Altey registering on the Richter scale. Before breakfast one jogs along the seafront on tiptoe, fearful of disturbing the huge hungover-silence.

Kuşadasi literally means 'Bird Island'. Contrary to local chauvinist mythology, this name derives from the days of the Ottoman Empire, when the port was guarded by the castle on Güvercin Adasi (Pigeon Island).

The classical era is a blank where Kuşadasi is concerned. Only after the port of nearby Ephesus had completely

• *Opposite: relief of Asclepius at Ephesus.*

silted up did the settlement on this spot become of any interest. The Byzantines called the place Ania.

In the 14thC the Genoese built a castle here on Güvercin Island and rechristened the place Scala Nuova (New Steps). This castle has been drastically renovated over the past few years, much to the annoyance of the purists (a rare breed in modern Kuşadasi). But in fact this completely rebuilt castle – with its clean stone, exact lines and flawless exterior – probably looks much as it did when it was first put up. And the easy-going behaviour of the original over-heated Genoese garrison can't have been much different from that of the present-day clientèle of the castle's cafés and discos.

One of the big daytime attractions of Kuşadasi is the cruise liners which put into the port. On average at least half a dozen weird and wonderful floating gin palaces embark and disembark here each day, sporting the flags of such places as Panama, Ukraine, Bermuda, Russia, Liberia and Lebanon – but usually disgorging only genuine redskins – i.e. British or German tourists. Mostly these are whisked off to visit nearby Ephesus, seeing only fleeting glimpses of Kuşadasi beyond their coach windows. This is their loss, as there are things to see in Kuşadasi to suit every taste.

Just opposite the port is the ancient *kervansaray*, which has now been restored by Club Med as a luxury hotel. Feel free to wander in through the main gateway and look around the courtyard – unfortunately this is disfigured by a noisy and tasteless floor show in the evenings. Just inland from here is the **Kale District**, the old part of town, which

---

RECOMMENDED RESTAURANTS

DIDYMA

There's not much here except some rather ordinary restaurants which charge inflated prices. Much better to head 5 km down the road south to Altinkum Plaj, where there's a fine beach and a wide range of eating places.

EPHESUS (EFES)

There are several pricey cafés near the main entrance to the site. The best place to eat at is:

Motel Efes Tusan – for details see Recommended Hotels. It is just 1 km up the road from the site, at the corner with the main road. The dining area is under some shady trees, and the service is adequate.

KUŞADASI

There are numerous restaurants, most of which cater heavily for the tourist trade. As a result there are some nasty over-priced joints, and, surprisingly, some excellent restaurants of all kinds. This being touristiana, they serve German food, English food, and there's even a Chinese restaurant. One place I highly recommend is:

Alarga Restaurant, LL; 50 Atatürk Bulvari; *no booking*.

This is by far the most agreeable restaurant on the seafront. You dine by lamplight off smart tablecloths to classical tapes (and occasional modern Romanian Pan flute music). The service is excellent and friendly, without being intrusive. At the front of the restaurant is a fish display: if they have any sea bass, be sure to try some, with one of their very pleasant white wines.

If you want a budget restaurant, a reasonable bet is:

Öz Urfa Restaurant, L; 7 Cephane Sokak; tel. 256 611 6070.

In a small street leading off the main Barbaros Hayrettin Caddesi. As you'd expect from their name, they serve a mean Urfa kebab containing red pepper and perhaps too much onion for some. Very popular with visiting Aussies, who believe in getting value for their money and can start dinner *very* hungry.

If you want to lash out on expensive fish, the place to go is:

Toros Canli Balik, LL-LLL; at the harbour; tel. 256 611 1144.

Famous for fresh fish, which you can see on display before you dine.

has a number of steep narrow alleyways and has not yet fully succumbed to touristiana.

This last occupies the rest of the town centre, where you'll find restaurants catering for all palates (from Chinese to Irish), and all kinds of bars (except quiet ones). The shops include tat stalls, kitsch museums, some surprisingly good carpet emporiums, boutiques of brazen bodices and outfitters of outrage, and a couple of adequate foreign language bookshops.

Surprisingly for such a well-known resort, Kuşadasi has few facilities for swimming. The town beaches are a sad joke: grubby sand lapped by pallid water. But nearby there are a number of excellent beaches: the best-known is **Ladies Beach** (Kadinlar Denizi), a 2.5-km *dolmuş* ride from the town centre. Further along the coast to the north there

are a number of spectacular resort developments with swimming pools and private coves. Try **Tusan Beach**, which is 5 km from town and served by a frequent *dolmuş* service. It has all kinds of beach entertainments and water activities. Ten km north of Kuşadasi is Pamucak, which is more picturesque and tends to be a little less crowded.

Those who want something completely different can always take a day (or longer) trip across the strait to the Greek island of **Samos**. Boats leave the harbour at 8.30 am and 5 pm. Sadly, these trips are ridiculously expensive (by Turkish standards), owing to the bad relations between Greece and Turkey. A return trip will probably cost you around 650,000TL – but rumours abound that this is soon to be reduced, as a gesture towards the European Community, which Turkey is avid to join, regardless

Their *kalamar* (squid) is excellent, their mussels are a treat, and if you're feeling like lobster, this is the place to have it in Kuşadasi. (Some of the other pricier nearby restaurants, which will persistently try to entice you in, are *not* recommended.)

A pleasant place for an early evening drink out on the island at the end of the causeway is:

Ada Plaj Café, L-LL; Guvercin Adasi; no booking.
You drink on the quayside looking out over the bay and the rest of town. Below there's even a small private swimming area. You can also eat here: the menu is nothing special, but it's inexpensive.

For those who want something livelier to end the evening, the island also has a disco in the castle. The best that can be said of this spot is that it's less tacky than those in Disco Alley. (For connoisseurs of tack and tat, Disco Alley is at Barlar Sokagi in the old Kale district: earplugs essential, conversation impossible – except by explicit international hand signals. Winners of the decibel trophy: the Irish Bar.)

SELÇUK
Villa Restaurant, LL; Efes Yolu; tel. 232 892 1299.

On the road to Ephesus, just around the corner from the museum. A pleasant roadside stop where you dine in the shade beneath the vines. Good for a long lazy lunch – which is best begun late, when the traffic has died down.

Most of the restaurants are concentrated around Cengiz Topel Caddesi, which is now a pedestrian zone. Here your best bet is:

Seçkin L-LL; 22 Cengiz Topel Caddesi; tel. 232 892 1698.
It's best to eat ouside on the pavement, as inside can become noisy and hot when a coach party suddenly descends. They do an excellent fish kebab, and have a range of inexpensive dishes.

If you're looking for somewhere really inexpensive, but not too grim, try just along the street:

Bizim, L; 42, Cengiz Topel Caddesi; no booking.
Cheap and cheerful. The management tend to quiz English and German tourists on the fortunes of their various star football teams. This is no idle matter, and ignorant fibbers are soon found out. Best to admit ignorance right away, and be treated with bemused compassion. A useful place for meeting people in the evenings.

of the fact that this community includes the Greeks.

Samos is renowned for its wines (which were praised by Byron), its remote mountainous hinterland, and its resorts. It also has some interesting classical sights. Kuşadasi makes an excellent base for visiting several of the finest ancient sites in Turkey. A short *dolmuş* ride to the north-east are Ephesus (page 88) and the historic town of Selçuk. A little further to the south of town are Miletus (Milet), Priene and Didyma (see this page, and pages 88 and 100). Inland to the east lies Magnesia (see Local Explorations: 5).

MERYEMANA

5 km E of Ephesus. According to a persistent legend the Virgin Mary was brought by St John the Evangelist (some say St Paul) to Ephesus around 37 AD. She is said to have lived in this region for the last eight years or so of her life.

This story remained a historical footnote until around two centuries ago, when a German nun began having visions. Catherine Emmerich, who had never left her native land, began describing in some detail the location and dwelling where the Virgin Mary had lived for the last years of her life. Seventy years later some Lazarist fathers from Smyrna (now Izmir) set out to investigate if there was anywhere near Ephesus that matched Catherine Emmerich's visions. To their astonishment, they found just such a house as she had described. And even more astonishingly, this place had long been a local place of pilgrimage on the Feast of the Assumption, though no one really appeared to know why.

The Lazarist fathers still look after this house, which has become a great pilgrimage centre. Inevitably, a number of unexplained cures (miracles) have taken place. The spot was even visited by Pope Paul VI in 1967, who pronounced that it was indubitably the place where the Virgin Mary had lived. Recent excavations have shown that the present house, described in such detail by Catherine Emmerich, in fact dates from around the 6thC, though the foundations probably date from around the 1stC AD. As we live in a democratic age, you pay your money and come to your own conclusion. Though as the Pope rightly understood, truth has nothing whatsoever to do with democracy.

A certain amount of commercialism has inevitably taken place: commercial optimists have always been atttracted by the idea of miracles. Yet a visit can be instructive for both believers and unbelievers alike.

MILETUS (MILET)

Turn west off Rt 525 27 km S of Söke, and follow signs for 10 km through Akköy and Balat. Miletus was one of the great cities of ancient Ionia, and flourished for a thousand years. During this period (700 BC-700 AD), it established dozens of trading colonies, some as far afield as the Black Sea and Egypt. Then the harbour silted up, and Miletus fell into rapid decline.

Miletus produced far more than its fair share of famous figures. Thales, who lived in the 6thC BC, is generally credited with being the first philosopher. He came up with the idea that everything was made of water, which even at the time some of his pupils began to suspect was not the case. (But imagine if he'd got it right: that would have been the end of philosophy, and there would have been nothing left to argue about.) Thales is also remembered for saying that he was glad he was born a human being rather than an animal, a man rather than a woman, and a Greek rather than a barbarian.

Milesians were none too keen on women. The ancient historian, Herodotus, recorded that they had a law forbidding wives from sitting down at table with their husbands, or even addressing them by name. Spared the trouble of having to waste time talking to such ignorant bigots and philosophers, the women of Miletus produced several famous figures of their own. The finest of these was Aspasia, who lived in the early 5thC BC. She went to Athens, where she became a renowned courtesan. Amongst her closest friends were two of Athens' greatest men, the ruler Pericles and the philosopher Socrates, who claimed that she taught him oratory. After Aspasia's charms began to fade, she took up running a bordello; but she was still regularly visited by Socrates, who would bring along his pupils so they could hear her speak. At least, that was his story.

• *Opposite: Kuşadasi bazaar.*

Other famous Milesians include: the architect Hippodamus, who introduced the grid system as early as the 5thC BC (it was used in Miletus, found not to work, and abandoned); Anaximander, the founder of astronomy; the philosopher Anaximenes who realized that Thales was wrong about the world being made of water, anyone with half an ounce of sense could see that it was made of air; Hecateus, the world's first travel writer, whose clichés have now alas largely been lost; and Isodorus, the architect who built Aya Sofya in Istanbul.

The ruins of ancient Miletus are still visible. Most impressive is the **theatre**, which could seat up to 20,000 spectators. But not all the ruins here date from the classical period. There are the remains of an 8thC Byzantine **castle** at the head of the theatre; and the ruined **Ilyas Bey Camii** (mosque), built in 1404 incorporating various Selçuk features.

Two **stone lions** to the north of the site mark the entrance to the ancient harbour, showing how far the sea once extended.

PRIENE
3 km S of Söke, turn W off Rt 525, and follow the road until just beyond Güllübahçe. Priene may not be the most historically important site in the region, but it is by far the most beautiful. The site is on pine-covered hills with a back-drop of mountains, above the flat plain of the Meander Valley, which used to be a shallow inlet of the sea during the classical period.

The original inhabitants of Priene are thought to have arrived as colonists from Athens around the 11thC BC. The first city was founded further east, but when the shoreline began to recede in the 4thC BC, they moved to the present site. The new city was laid out by the celebrated Milesian architect Hippodamus, according to his famous new grid plan. Alexander the Great invaded just as they were in the middle of building their new Temple to Athena. He was so impressed by this temple (which is to this day reckoned to be the finest work of Ionic architecture) that he promised to pay the bill. The plaque commemorating this generous gesture is at present helpfully stored more than 2,500 km away in a basement of the British Museum.

Priene went into decline during the late Roman period, when its harbour began to silt up, and a few centuries later was abandoned and forgotten. It was rediscovered in 1765 by the celebrated early British traveller in Asia Minor, Richard Chandler (an antecedent of the 20thC British-American writer Raymond).

Much of the subsequent excavation was done by German archaeologists, who removed to Berlin any portable relics left by the British. But fortunately the mechanical resources of even the most industrious 19thC archaeologists were limited, and much of Priene still remains.

Most striking of all is the **Temple of Athinia Polias**, which now has only five of its original columns still standing, and even these are restored. Don't miss the ramshackle **stadium**, at the south-east edge of the site: this has some ancient graffiti and some of the oldest starting blocks in existence.

Across to the north from the main site is the ancient **acropolis**, which attracts those who enjoy a stiff climb. Be warned: unless you are fit, you will end up gasping for air long before you can gasp at the view.

SAMOS
See Kuşadasi, page 94.

SELÇUK ⇔ ✕
Inland 20 km from Kuşadasi. Selçuk has long been overshadowed by its neighbour Ephesus, but it has at least two sights of outstanding importance: the Basilica of St John and the Archaeological Museum, whose finds from Ephesus make it one of the finest in the land.

As you approach Selçuk, its most prominent feature is the walled defensive **citadel**. When you arrive in the city centre, its most prominent feature is the tawdry flotsam of tourism, but this is much more easily ignored than the magnificent castellated walls which still loom over the rooftops. This citadel is known as the Hill of Ayasoluk, and from below its well-preserved castellation appears for the most part to be protecting nothing much more than an enclosure of burnt grass. Closer inspection tends to confirm this view – with one exception: the **Basilica of St John**.

According to legend, St John the Evangelist left the Holy Land in the third decade of the 1stC and came to live in this region. (Some say he was accompanied by the ageing Virgin Mary. See Meryemana, page 98.) When St John died he was buried on the citadel, and a small church was built to house his tomb. This soon began attracting pilgrims from all over Christendom.

St John the Evangelist was known to the early Greek church as St John the Theologian, which was corrupted to Ayios Theologos. In time the citadel came to be known as Ayios Theologos, on account of his tomb. This is said to have been corrupted further by the Turks to Ayasoluk, its present name.

In the 6thC the Byzantine emperor Justinian decided to build a basilica on the spot where St John was buried. When completed, it was one of the greatest churches in the Eastern Empire. (Some say it was second only to the Aya Sofya in Istanbul, page 42.) After the Turkish conquest, the Basilica gradually fell into disrepair before it was effectively flattened in 1402 by Tamerlane and his invading hordes from Samarkand. For several years now it has gradually been restored with funds provided by a religious organization from Ohio – which hopes eventually to raise here a modern version of the original six-domed church, complete with marble pillars and colonnaded baptistry.

From the sacred to the secular. Selçuk's **Archaeological Museum** contains the most valuable and interesting finds from Ephesus. It is where you can see all those rude little statues that appear on the postcards. These stimulating objects of admiration can be found in the first gallery. A number of them were discovered amongst the ruins of the brothel at Ephesus, where their enormities were presumably intended to encourage the bashful, rather than intimidate those who were less cumbersomely endowed.

Visitors with a taste for sexual oddity will also be intrigued by the impressive statues of the goddess Artemis in the **Artemis Room**. Many of these may originally have resided in the celebrated Temple of Artemis, one of the Seven Wonders of the World (see Ephesus, page 88).

Artemis, the goddess of love, was the presiding goddess of Ephesus. Not long after she was originally brought to these shores by early Greek colonists, she almost certainly adopted many of the features of the indigenous Anatolian fertility goddess Cybele, who had several breasts and was attended by a eunuch high priest. Artemis became a powerful presence, and wielded great power as was only to be expected of the deity who directed the course of love in human affairs. Statues of her depict a woman with multiple breasts (or, according to some commentators, testicles). She adopted the eunuch high priest of Cybele, and some believe that her multiple testicles depict the ultimate sacrifice she demanded of her priests, rather than fonts of loving kindness. Either way, balls or breasts, Artemis was certainly a formidable influence in Ephesian society. And some of those statues of her in the Artemis Room are capable of evoking a deep echo which Dr Jung would say was more than just over-stimulated imagination.

The city derives its name from the original Selçuk Turks, who arrived in Anatolia in the 11thC and heralded the eventual Turkish take-over of Asia Minor. At the foot of Ayasoluk Hill, beneath the battlements to the west of the basilica of St John, lies **Isa Bey Camii**. This is the finest Selçuk ruin in the city, and, according to the inscription above its doorway, was constructed in 1375. An expert describes the building as 'an impure blend of late Selçuk and early Ottoman features'. In fact, it's quite interesting, and well worth going to look at.

SÖKE

15 km SE of Kuşadaşi. Prominently marked on the maps, but of no real interest. The road over the hills from Kuşadasi has some fine views. The only reason you'll want to call here is because it has useful bus and *dolmuş* services to most of the main sights in the region – including Miletus, Didyma, and Priene (see pages 88, 98 and 100). From Söke you can also reach **Altinkum Plaj** (Golden Sand Beach), which is just beyond Didyma, and offers just what its name suggests, as well as a few restaurants and pensions: an ideal spot for absorbing some live beach culture, after all that ruinous dead culture.

South-Western Turkey

Between Bodrum and Fethiye
Bodrum, Fethiye and Region

270 km; map GeoCenter Euro-Country, Western Turkey, 1: 800 000

This corner of Turkey has been transformed by the opening of the international airport at Dalaman. Its main resorts, Bodrum, Marmaris and Fethiye, have now all been ceded to International Holidayland. If you want a lively break, with some memorable night life and boat excursions to picturesque beaches, this is the area for you.

Bodrum has managed to retain much of its picturesque charm. The harbour is overlooked by a curving hillside of white cube houses and the impressive castle. It was Turkey's first resort. The nearby Gulf of Gökova has some of the finest unspoilt coastline of Turkey's Mediterranean coast. At the tip of the Gulf's lower peninsula is the spectacularly remote site of ancient Knidos, home of a famous love cult. Around the peninsula you come to Datça, a remote resort which has managed to resist the worst ravages of development. This could hardly be said of Marmaris, to the east. But here it's all the fun of the fair, and never a dull moment. The nearby Loryma Peninsula has a host of rocky coves and ancient ruins, many only accessible from the sea.

Further east is Dalyan, where you can travel by boat through the reeds to the ancient site of Kaunos. Downstream from Dalyan is Turtle Beach, habitat of the rare loggerhead turtle. This beach was recently protected from unscrupulous developers by an international outcry from conservationists. The road west from here has some superb views as it passes through the mountains and then descends towards the island-strewn Gulf of Fethiye.

The direct route between Bodrum and Fethiye, along Rts 330 and 400, is just over 270 km, much of it through spectacular mountain or shoreline scenery. It can comfortably be covered in a day, but if you want to explore, and see some of the sights, you should allow three to four days.

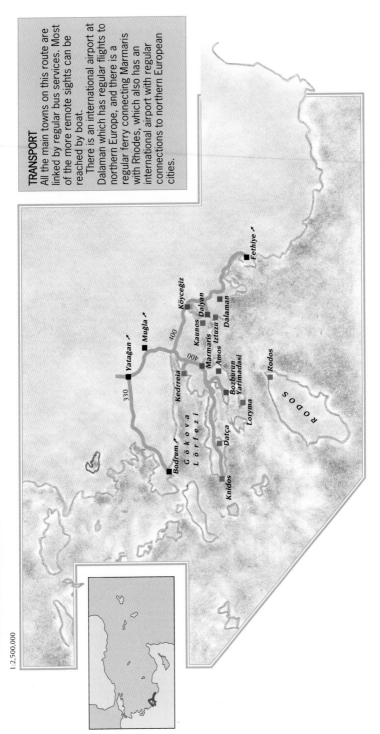

SIGHTS & PLACES OF INTEREST

AMOS
See Loryma Peninsula, page 112.

BODRUM
On the Aegean coast 141 km S of Kuşadası.
Bodrum stands on the site of the ancient Greek city of Halicarnassos, remains of which can still be seen. Halicarnassos was the home of the first historian, Herodotus, who was born here in 480 BC and likened the place to an amphitheatre. It remains so today, with its whitewashed cube houses covering the slopes of the curving hillside above the harbour.

When Xerxes the Persian Emperor invaded Greece in the 5thC BC he was supported by Queen Artemisia of Halicarnassos. She fought with conspicuous bravery alongside the Persian fleet at the Battle of Salamis. The Persians performed rather less well, and the Greeks won a resounding victory – causing Xerxes to remark: 'My men behaved like women, and my women like men.'

Another Artemisia was to bring even greater renown to Halicarnassos. Shortly after the Persians withdrew from the region, the satrap Mausolus took control of Halicarnassos in 377 BC. Mausolus greatly admired Greek culture, and during his 25-year reign he went to great pains to Hellenize this region, erecting many fine buildings and temples. So that his subjects should remember who had been responsible for these great works, Mausolus decided to build himself a vast tomb in the Hellenic style, decorated by the finest artists available. Unfortunately Mausolus died before this monument to his everlasting greatness could be completed. But the building was continued by his sister Queen Artemisia II (who also happened to be his wife). When the tomb was eventually finished, and Mausolus' corpse was lodged inside, it became known as the Mausoleum. And from this originates the word we use today. Such was the magnificence of the first mausoleum that it became one of the Seven Wonders of the World.

This 50-m-high monument to human vanity was to stand for longer than one-and-a-half millennia. Then the Crusaders arrived and began tearing it down so that they could use its stones to build a castle. This is the **Castle of St Peter**, which can still be seen guarding the entrance to the harbour. It is undoubtedly a magnificent castle – its dungeons were regarded with awe. Indeed, the town's modern name Bodrum means dungeon. However, even the most dedicated castrophile would hardly consider this 15thC castle, despite its magnificently appointed dungeons, as one of the Wonders of the World.

RECOMMENDED HOTELS

DATÇA
Hotel Dorya, LL-LLL; Iskele Mahallesi; tel. 252 712 1014.
The best hotel in town, set in well-tended gardens at the end of the peninsula. All rooms have sea views.

A less expensive option is:

Huzur Pension, L; Iskele Mahallesi; tel. 252 712 1052.
Right in the heart of town near the harbour and the beach.

MARMARIS
At the height of the summer season you may have difficulty getting a room here, so be sure to book in advance.

Karadeniz Hotel, LL-LLL; Atatürk Caddesi; tel. 252 411 1064.
Named for some reason after the Black Sea – but that's the only thing wrong with this place. It's a couple of kilometres west of the town centre on the sea, well away from the high-decibel zone. All rooms have showers, but not all have sea views. Romantic restaurant: ideal for shady lunches or moonlit dinners. Prices can reduce dramatically out of season.

Those who don't wish to spend quite so much should try:
Hotel Pina, L-LL; 6 Kemeralti Caddesi; tel. 252 411 1053.
Right in the town centre, complete with views of the yachts putting to sea and their noisier crews serenading the night.

• *The Turquoise Coast.*

Yet it is still possible to gain an idea of what the Mausoleum was used to be like. The final act of vandalism on its ruins took place in the 19thC, when the British, ever mindful of their classical heritage, tore down what little was left standing and shipped it off to the British Museum.

The Castle of St Peter now contains a **museum** of fascinating objects which have been recovered from beneath the sea. Much of the collection comes from the wreck found off Cape Gelidonya, which went down in 1200 BC. Even more exciting are the relics still being raised from the Lul Burun wreck, which went down around a century earlier, with a rich cargo of gold plate, ancient Egyptian scarabs, ivory and ostrich eggs. The scarabs have already filled certain gaps in Pharonic history, though the ostrich eggs continue to remain a mute mystery.

Bodrum was once the Turkish Siberia. Instead of sending their political exiles to shiver in the salt mines of the Gulag, the Turkish authorities banished them to the boredom of the beaches. Like Siberia, Bodrum soon became known as a colony for artists, writers and other deviants from the norm. Bohemianism flourished, and the revolution was soon forgotten amidst the endless round of jazz clubs and drag parties.

Nowadays, the jazz clubs have given way to discos and in mid-August the atmosphere can be a complete drag: temperatures soar and the little alleyways of the old town become packed with exiles from the *gulags* of Bavaria and the Home Counties. Out of season things become a little less hectic, and Bodrum regains much of its original

charm – which was considerable.

Along the quayside of the harbour you'll see rows of boats offering **trips**. As you approach, various parody nautical types will try to entice you aboard. These trips are well worth taking, but be sure to shop around for the one that suits you. Most have boards with prices, maps and photographs of your destinations. The itineraries usually include such spots as **Black Island (Kara Ada)** with its famous orange mud and cave of hot medicinal springs; some remote (but not empty) beaches around the bay; a visit to a beach-side café-restaurant for lunch (price not included, but not expensive); occasional glimpses of exotic fishes, octopi and so on. The expeditions usually begin at around 10 am and bring you back in the afternoon. Make sure that your captain speaks intelligible English, as he will often pass on various interesting items of more or less credible local lore. Much depends on the character of your captain and the attitude of your fellow passengers: choose carefully.

There is no really good place to swim in town, mainly because its two bays have been polluted by the vast number of hired boats which use the port. But

• *Opposite: marina, Fethiye.*

• *Ölüdeniz - see page* 111.

the good news is that nearby there are plenty of superb sandy beaches with crystal-clear water, ideal for snorkelling. The **Bodrum Peninsula**, which lies to the west of town, has a fine coastline of pine woods, coves and sandy beaches. Inland it is comparatively barren, but there are a number of little villages, castles and vast views out over the Aegean towards the larger Greek islands of Kos, Kalimnos and Leros. The peninsula even has its own ancient site at **Myndos**. Unfortunately parts of this area have begun to succumb to villamania, and some of the more picturesque bays are suddenly filled with yachtfuls of yahoos anchoring for the night. But it is worth exploring – there are still a few beguiling places left – especially out of season.

DALAMAN

39 km NW of Fethiye on Rt 400. This contains the region's only international airport and also an open prison. Contrary to appearances, your plane arrives at the former.

DALYAN

59 km NW of Fethiye, 5 km off Rt 400.
A sleepy spot not to be confused with Dalaman. It is located on the small river

which connects the Köyceğiz Lake with the sea. Nearby are the ruins of ancient Kaunos (see below), and down on the coast is the celebrated **Turtle Beach (Istuzu)**. The rather dozy occupants of this beach were saved from disturbance at the hands of developers by an international campaign headed by British conservationist David Bellamy. During the daytime it's pleasant for swimming, and at night you can watch the turtles coming ashore to lay their eggs in the sand. These turtles are the rare *Caretta caretta* species, whose lumbering land-bound motion aptly echoes their name.

The best way to both Turtle Beach and Kaunos is by boat from Dalyan. Boats leave the riverside at Dalyan each morning around 10 for the four-hour trip to the beach. A whole boat can be hired for around 500,000 TL, so it's worth making up a party of around a dozen. You can also hire a boat for a two-hour tour of the **Kaunos Ruins** (page 109) for 20,000TL and upwards.

DATÇA ⌂ ✕
76 km W of Marmaris at the western end of Rt 400. Datça was once an idyllic little haven at the end of the road. Now it's well on the way to becoming big business. Some may consider this an exaggeration – especially when you see what's happened to such places as Bodrum and Marmaris. Yet the fact is, the fragile atmosphere of such a tiny place is soon swamped by development.

However, the road leading to Datça is still a marvellous drive, there are still some fabulous, remote beaches nearby and the hinterland of the peninsula remains as unspoilt as ever.

Café life at Datça is lively, and the discos provide solace for those who have spent their days deprived of deafened darkness.

FETHIYE
See Turkey Overall: 5.

ISTUZU
The Turkish name for Turtle Beach - see Dalyan, page 107.

KAUNOS
Inland from the W bank of the Dalyan River. Best reached by boat from Dalyan (see

page 107). In classical times this was an important port, but its access to the sea was blocked when the Dalyan River silted up during the Byzantine era.

The first settlement here was around the 9thC BC. Despite this ancient pedigree, the city's name is a fake. Many other cities in the region were first settled by some legendary Greek hero, taking his name. Not to be left out, the inhabitants of this city invented a story that their city had been founded by Kaunos, and named it accordingly. History records that Kaunos was a grandson of Apollo who ran away from Greece to escape the amorous attentions of his twin sister. Regardless of his single unheroic deed, and the fact that he had never been near the city, the locals set up a shrine to their pseudo-founder – and the cult caught on to such an extent that it spread to several other cities.

History seems to have dealt the inhabitants of Kaunos a poor hand. They were always backing the wrong side, and they became known throughout Asia Minor as untrustworthy ruffians – as well as for their curious pallor. The latter was almost certainly due to the fact that many of them suffered from malaria, caught from the mosquitoes proliferating in the nearby swamps.

Despite all this, the site has a definite charm. Its ruins are far better than those you'd expect to be left behind by a bunch of coarse, jaundiced losers. One suspects there was more to them than has been passed down by historical gossip.

The site has a fine **theatre**, a couple of **temples** and the remains of a **Roman bath**. It's a fair climb up to the 150 m-high **acropolis**, but you're rewarded with a fine view at the top. There's not much else up there except the walls which you can see from below.

KEDREIA (SEDIR ADASI)
Small island at the head of the Gulf of Göko-va, reached by boat from the nearby fishing villages, and pre-arranged tours from Marmaris.

Kedreia contains the ruins of an ancient Greek city named after the Greek word for cedar. The ruins include a **Temple of Apollo**, a small **theatre** and the remains of strong protective **walls** with towers. The latter were not enough to save Kedreia from the wrath of the

Spartans in 405 BC, when it made the mistake of backing the Athenians in the Peleponnesian War. After the city was taken by Lysander, the Spartan leader, he had all its citizens sold into slavery.

Nearby is the legendary **Cleopatra's Beach**. Antony and Cleopatra would meet at this idyllic spot for their trysts. According to an unlikely story which Antony is said to have told Cleopatra, he went to the trouble of bringing the sand for this beach all the way from Egypt, just so that she wouldn't have to walk on stones. A recent geological survey has revealed that the sand on this beach is of a type found near the Nile Delta, so Antony might not have been fibbing after all.

KNIDOS

40 km W of Datça at the tip of the peninsula. The road from Datça to the site at Knidos begins well enough, soon becomes a track, and for the last few kilometres after the village of Yazıköy becomes a severe obstacle race, just about negotiable by an average saloon car. By far the best way to get here is by boat from Bodrum, which takes about four hours. Boats leave from the quayside daily around 10 am; the cost is 50,000TL upwards.

How on earth did such a remote spot ever become the location of a booming city? Some scholars have suggested that it guarded the important trade route from the Aegean cities of Asia Minor to Egypt. More likely is that ships plying this route were forced to put into harbour here (and pay for it) when they were caught by the notorious Meltemi wind, which could sometimes blow for days on end along this part of the coast, as it still does.

At any rate, the city prospered. In the 4thC BC it became famous for its school of medicine. The best-remembered graduate from this school is Ctesias, who became court physician to the Emperor of Persia. When Ctesias retired he wrote a 23-volume work describing the history and customs of the people of 'Persika'. The accuracy of this work has since been found to be on a par with its author's spelling.

Like any ancient city worth its salt, Knidos also produced its own philosopher: the redoubtable Eudoxus, who lived in the early 4thC BC. Eudoxus was the first person to explain the circular

TRIPS TO RHODES

In summer ferries run daily from Marmaris on the 50-km trip to the Greek island of Rhodes. Be warned: sometimes, when you least expect it, there is no ferry on Sunday. In winter there are a couple of ferries a week, except during storms.

The trip takes around $2^{1}/_{2}$ hours, and a day return ticket costs from 400,000TL. The ferries leave from the main town jetty by the castle.

What is there to see at the other end? Rhodes Town itself is even more tourist orientated than Marmaris, but it has many more interesting sights, especially in its walled old quarter, occupied by crusaders for several centuries. Prices are higher than in Turkey, but you will enjoy the novelty of experiencing the Greek way of doing things.

movement of the planets and stars (wrongly); and he was so good at geometry that he received the honour of having his works plagiarized by the great Euclid (whom many consider to have invented this subject).

Knidos was also renowned for its wine, which not only soothed the bowels but was said never to give you a hangover however much you drank. A likely story. The city was almost as famous for its vinegar and its cabbages, but despite being a great intellectual centre no one came up with the bright idea of combining these products to produce Knidian *sauerkraut*.

Yet all these achievements count as nothing beside the city's greatest possession. Praxiteles of Athens, the finest sculptor of the ancient world, made two statues of Aphrodite the goddess of love. One of these was clothed, the other nude. The latter was said to be of such breathtaking beauty that even Aphrodite wondered how Praxiteles had managed to catch her likeness in such fine detail. She might have been a little disappointed if she had discovered the truth: Praxiteles had made his mistress pose for him while taking a bath.

When these two statues of Aphrodite came up for sale in Athens, the city of

109

YACHT CHARTER

This is probably the best way to see the fabulously beautiful coastline of southern and south-western Turkey. Your best bet is to charter your yacht before you leave home. Addresses of charter firms are available from the Turkish Tourist Office, and in the classified holiday advertisements of most daily broadsheets (especially on Saturdays).

Costs vary, but chartering need not be outrageously expensive compared with conventional package holiday deals to Turkey, provided you go out of season (before May, after mid September) and if you organize a party of people to share the cost. At those times the weather is not so hot, but storms are more likely than in high summer.

Out of season, you can, with luck, pick up an eight-berth 12-m yacht for just over £1,000/$1,500 a week, excluding the skipper – i.e. you sail it yourself, 'bare boat'. In high season, expect to pay at least double this.

Before taking over your boat you will have to pay a hefty deposit (£500/$750) and at least one of the party will have to demonstrate that he or she knows how to sail a craft by producing a certificate from a credible sailing organization such as the RYA.

No certificate is needed if you hire a yacht with a skipper, but they don't

• *Above*: Üçağiz; *right*: Simena - both *Turquoise Coast.*

come cheap, have to be fed and tend to be thristy as well. You can cook on board, but there is little point in having this trouble when you can dine at so many fabulous and inexpensive beach-side restaurants.

Some companies organize 'flotilla cruising': a leader boat shepherds a group of less experienced boats, leading them to interesting anchorages. Navigation is generally not difficult in these waters, with few rocks and virtually no tide; however, some local knowledge is invaluable for making the most of your expensive charter time.

The main centres for yacht hire are Bodrum, Marmaris and Fethiye. From Bodrum you are in reach of the Gulf of Gökova with its hidden coves, classical sites and unspoilt scenery. Marmaris offers similar pleasures along its nearby coast, as well as some off-shore islands. From Fethiye your best course is to head east. If you can, make it as far as Kekova Island (Adasi), just over 100 km distant. This has a particularly beautiful safe anchorage opposite the tiny village of Uçağiz, a crusader castle at Simena, and the subterranean ruins of a Roman city off Kekova itself.

RECOMMENDED RESTAURANTS

DATÇA
Taraça Restaurant, L-LL; *at the harbour; no booking.*

As you'd expect from the name, the main feature here is the terrace, which has a romantic view of the sea.

MARMARIS
Restaurants in Marmaris tend to be more expensive than elsewhere, but luxury items are more readily available – and prepared by people who know how to cook them.

Birat Restaurant, LL; *Barbaros Caddesi; tel.* 252 411 1076.

A well-established favourite, and for my money presently the best of the restaurants on the quayside by the yacht marina. Their seafood is naturally superb, and an excellent floor show is provided by your fellow diners trying to outdo each other in *haute bourgoisie* leisure behaviour.

The budget-conscious should search out some of the newly-opening restaurants around the outer fringes of the bazaar quarter which are still trying to establish themselves.

Knidos managed to outbid all comers for the more aesthetic version. This was duly shipped to the Temple of Aphrodite at Knidos, where it was installed in a special sanctuary so that the faithful could worship their goddess from every side and angle. The statue quickly became one of the Mediterranean's first tourist attractions, with pilgrims travelling from far and wide to participate in the Aphrodisiac cult at Knidos.

The **ruins** of the Temple of Aphrodite were recently discovered by American archaeologists, who became sure they were on the right track when they began coming across inordinate numbers of pornographic pots and obscene ceramics. The ruins can be seen high on the hillside above the ancient trireme harbour. The American archaeologists also uncovered a slab of marble carved with the letters *Prax...* It seems certain that this was the plinth of Praxiteles'

famous statue. Sadly, the statue itself appears to have been destroyed by spoilsport early Christians.

The site of Knidos was rediscovered in 1749 by Lord Claremont, a young Dublin rake who had been sent on the Grand Tour by his mother in an attempt to cure him of his dissolute ways. His lordship was most impressed by the seats in the theatre which were 'shaped in a concave form for the greater convenience of sitting'. The ruins of Knidos contain two **theatres**, the most impressive of which was vandalized in the early 19thC to build a palace for the King of Egypt. The rest of the site was more comprehensively vandalized by the British throughout the same century. The results of this pillaging can now be seen in the British Museum.

The setting of this site is truly magnificent, but you may find the actual ruins less than dramatic unless you are an avid classicist. Partners accompanying the latter on a pilgrimage to Knidos should buy one of the books that describe the antics of the early Aphrodisiac pilgrims, which I promise will not disappoint. These are on sale in Marmaris.

There are now some over-priced restaurants at this site, which continue the ancient Knidian tradition of preying off visitors who arrive by boat.

KÖYCEĞIZ
86 km NW of Fethiye, just off Rt 400. A pleasant village beneath the mountains on the northern shore of Köceğiz Lake. Nothing much happens here, but you can catch a boat across the lake and down the river to Kaunos (see page 108). This trip takes you past some fine rock tombs.

LORYMA PENINSULA (BOZBURUN YARIMADASI)
Neck of land jutting S into the Aegean just W of Marmaris. The roads of this once-remote peninsula are improving, but still rudimentary. By far the best way to see it is by boat from Marmaris. Boats can be hired for around 500,000 TL per day, and there are many shorter trips available. See under Marmaris, page 113.

The shoreline is a mass of coves, beaches, and islands: ideal swimming and suntanning country. There are also many ancient ruins. **Amos**, just outside the inner bay of Marmaris, is the closest. **Loryma**, at the tip of the peninsula, is only accessible by boat from Marmaris. It hardly seems possible that in the 4thC BC a huge fleet consisting of nearly 400 ships containing over 70,000 men gathered here to invade Rhodes (unsuccessfully, as it turned out). You can still see the ruins of the ancient castle and its towers above the harbour.

MARMARIS ⊨ ✕
On the coast between Bodrum and Fethiye.
According to a persistent legend, this booming funspot was once an unspoilt little fishing village. Now it's pure holidayland, complete with rapidly spreading overnight concrete development.

Marmaris has a superb natural harbour. Both the British Admiral Nelson and Suleiman the Magnificent chose on separate occasions to anchor their entire fleets here. When Suleiman stepped ashore and noticed the appearance of the local castle, he exclaimed:"*Mimar as!*" ('Hang the architect'), and this is how the town is said to have received its name. Since then, the town has sadly not lived up to its name, and the architects of the mushrooming concrete slabs have evaded the fate they deserve.

Here you will find the largest yacht marina in Turkey, the centre of the local yacht chartering business. Chartered yacht is the perfect way to explore the remoter stretches of Turkey's exceptionally beautiful Mediterranean and Aegean coastlines: see the box on page 110.

Marmaris is still (just) a resort for everyone. Saudi princes and Turkish film stars mingle unaffectedly with western European yachties of merely middle-class origin; package tour wheeler-dealers herd their rainbow-clad prey; occasional, bewildered shepherds from the villages herd their street-wise flocks; gymnastic youths go about their business in strobe-lighted nocturnal dungeons; and a few ordinary mortals, barely recognizable for their third-degree burns, throng the alleyways of the bazaar quarter.

The main centre of Marmaris night life is by the yacht marina, which is in the harbour east of the castle. On the quay to the other side of the castle (Kordon Caddesi) you'll find the lines of

• *Seamstress, Üçağiz, Turquoise Coast.*

excursion boats. They offer tours around the bay, to nearby islands and to Loryma Peninsula, page 112, with its hidden coves and ancient sites. The boats are lined up along the waterfront and usually have a board at the foot of the gangplank giving price, starting time (usually before 10 am) and the itinerary, complete with photographs of the places you'll visit. Many of the trips include a stop at a beach-side restaurant (where you pay). Prices start at around 50,000TL. It is worth comparing what's on offer and trying to find a pleasant captain who speaks intelligible English.

In high summer, when it is extremely hot, the beaches are littered with grotesquely roasted bodies. However, in early spring and late autumn you can usually expect pleasantly warm weather, few crowds, and sometimes ridiculously low prices.

MUĞLA
See Local Explorations: 4.

YATAĞAN
See Local Explorations: 3.

<u>South-Western Turkey</u>

Between Fethiye and Kaş
Turquoise Coast, Western Stretch

107 km; map GeoCenter Euro-Country, Western Turkey, 1: 800,000

This western stretch of the Turquoise Coast is spectacularly beautiful. For once you'll find a region which lives up to the poetic name given it by optimistic developers. Tourism's arrival here was comparatively recent, and much of the area remains completely unspoilt. For those who want modern amenities, there are resort developments at Kalkan, Ölüdeniz and Kaş.

The region was once part of ancient Lycia, which featured in Homer's writings. The Lycian Federation of cities was run on democratic lines, and engaged in trade all over the eastern Mediterranean. You can visit the ruined sites of several of its most important cities – such as Xanthos and Patara. Some of these sites have particularly striking settings. See also Turkey Overall: 6.

Island lovers can take boat trips to the islands in the Gulf of Fethiye, or visit the isolated Greek island of Kastellorizo. And inland there is an entire region of superb mountain scenery which remains utterly unspoilt. The best way to explore the region is to travel along the main coast road, Route 400. As you travel east from Fethiye, the road heads inland for a stretch, and then follows the valley of the ancient River Xanthos (now the Eşen). This is overlooked by several Lycian sites, the best of which is Xanthos itself, just above the village of Kinik. At Kalkan the road rejoins the sea, with fine mountain views all the way to Kaş.

Although the distance is comparatively short, and can easily be covered in a day, it's worth allowing at least three days if you want to explore the beaches and the sites.

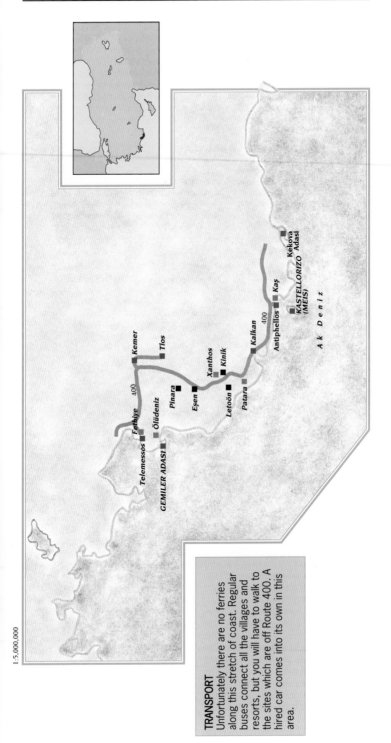

1:5,000,000

TRANSPORT

Unfortunately there are no ferries along this stretch of coast. Regular buses connect all the villages and resorts, but you will have to walk to the sites which are off Route 400. A hired car comes into its own in this area.

SIGHTS & PLACES OF INTEREST

ANTIPHELLOS
See Kaş, page 117.

FETHIYE 🚤 ✕
At the W end of the Turquoise Coast. Pronounced FEH-tea-yeh, this town of some 35,000 inhabitants is undeniably ordinary – it was completely destroyed in the 1957 earthquake which rattled the entire coastline. That said, its setting is superb; there are some excellent beaches, and neighbouring islands to explore. Fethiye also has some interesting ruins, and the town is within easy reach of more.

Fethiye itself has some colourful markets. You can still see herds of goats coming in from the hills in the mornings, and there's a fruit and vegetable market which sells delicious figs (fresh and dried) and spices at inexpensive prices (which wobble if you haggle enough).

The modern town is on the site of ancient Telemessos, ruined bits of which can still be seen. Telemessos is said to have been founded as a Minoan colony by a banished brother of the legendary King Minos of Crete.

In the 4thC BC, when Alexander the Great overran this area, another Cretan, Nearchus, played a part in the city's history. He was Alexander's governor of Telemessos, but failed to master the unruly inhabitants, who set about ejecting him. Before his departure, Nearchus asked if he could leave behind some of his slaves: a small orchestra, consisting of a few women and youths. The gullible, music-loving citzens of Telemessos agreed, not suspecting that the musicians had weapons hidden in their instrument cases. The musicians then retook the Acropolis while the citizens were asleep and invited Nearchus back.

Close to the **acropolis**, which today stands just 300 m inland from the main Atatürk Caddesi, you can see some fine rock tombs carved into the hillside. The best of these is the **Amyntas Tomb** which has columns and pediments resembling the façade of a temple.

About 500 m west of here is the ruin of a **Crusader castle** overlooking the harbour. This has sections which reflect the different stages of the town's history, it being partly built by the Lycians, ancient Greeks, Romans, Byzantines, Knights of St John (Crusaders) and the Ottomans in turn.

Fethiye stands on an inlet of a gulf which has a dozen or so small islands. Along the harbour you'll find the usual row of boats for hire. You can make a trip around the bay, along the coast or to the islands. The most popular expedition is the so-called Twelve Islands Tour, which lasts from around 9 am until 5 pm and costs around 80,000TL (haggle only if you are a group). These islands contain secluded beaches, classical ruins and the offshore rocks are good for snorkelling. Other trips are shorter and more leisurely, with options for swimming at remote beaches and picnic lunches.

Each boat has a board advertising price, departure time, usually before 10 am, and showing photographs of the destinations. It's worth shopping around, and trying to find a pleasant captain who speaks some English.

If you are interested in classical sites, there are equally exciting inland tours by minibus to the ruins at **Xanthos**, **Letoön** (pages 120 and 118), and even as far afield as **Kaunos** (see Turkey Overall: 4). If you want the best of both worlds, there are boat trips which combine beaches with ruins which can be reached from the shore. There is an excellent beach to the south of town on **Gemiler Adasi** (Gemiler Island), which has some Byzantine ruins, old Lycian tombs, and a more recent Greek Orthodox church with frescoes.

Another, more spooky, reminder of the Greek community which once thrived along this coast is the village of **Kaya**, signposted from the road to Ölüdeniz (see page 119). Kaya's houses are recognizably Aegean, but they are all deserted. This is a ghost village, uninhabited since its occupants were moved out after the exchange of Greek and Turkish populations after the Smyrna (Izmir) massacre of 1922 following Greece's ill-advised invasion of Turkey.

GEMILER ADASI (GEMILER ISLAND)
See Fethiye, above.

KALKAN 🚤 ✕
On the coast 30 km W of Kaş. Once this was an unspoilt, ramshackle hill-side

village by the sea. Now the inroads of tourism are all too visible, with holiday villas and a yacht marina in the bay. Useful as an overnight stop – the restaurants here are particularly good – or as a base for exploring nearby Xanthos and Petara (the latter has a far better beach).

KAŞ ⚓ ✕

On the coast, 110 km SE of Fethiye. The name means eyebrow in Turkish, also anything that is similarly curved. This poetically describes the town's location, hemmed in from the hinterland by 500-m cliffs.

Less than ten years ago, Kaş was a little unspoilt fishing village. Now it is a booming tourist centre, with lively nighlife, a picturesque harbour lined by tea houses, and a rash of *pansiyons* and tourist hotels.

Kaş grew up amidst the ruins of ancient **Antiphellos**, a Lycian city mentioned by the Roman historian Pliny as being famous for its sponges. You can still see relics of Antiphellos in the mod-

ern village. At night the ancient **rock tombs** in the cliffs are illuminated, adding an eerie sepulchral back-drop to your evening out.

The finest sight in town is the **Lycian Sarcophagus**, with its four lions' heads, which lies in the shade of an old tree. During the 19thC travellers noted more than a hundred such sarcophagi here, as well as a fine circular Byzantine church. All these have since vanished, their stones pillaged for use as building materials.

For no reason that I have been able to discover, the ancient Greek **amphitheatre** escaped this fate. From it you can look out over the sea towards the isolated Greek island of **Kastellorizo**. Known to the Turks as Meis, this territorial oddity is well over 100 km from the nearest Greek territory. The island is just 3 km away, and it's possible to take a day trip there. Boats leave from the harbour most mornings in season, returning in the late afternoon. Expect to pay around 100,000TL for the round trip.

RECOMMENDED HOTELS

FETHIYE
Hotel Likya, LL; *Yat Limani; tel.* 252 611 2233.

Attractive spot by the yacht harbour, set in its own garden. Rooms all have their own private shower and most have sea views. There's even a pool. Decoration is standard, adequate, Turkish style.

Otel Dedeoglu, L-LL; *Iskele Meydani; tel.* 252 611 4010.

Also down by the harbour, with sea views. Old-style local hotel with friendly lnklish-speaking staff.

KALKAN
Hotel Pirat, LL; *waterfront; tel.* 242 844 1178.

The best hotel down by the harbour. Most rooms have a private bathroom, and views out over the sea. Very much a jolly tourist hotel, despite its somewhat forbidding name.

KAŞ
Kaş Hosteli, LL; *Hastan Caddesi 15; tel.*

242 836 1271.

Seaside motel. Pleasant rooms with sea views. Also has good swimming from the rocky shore.

Toros, L; *by Üzünçarşi Caddesi; tel.* 242 836 1923.

Aptly named after the local mountain range – the proprietor used to be a mountain guide. He will arrange climbing expeditions for serious climbers, or give helpful advice to trekkers wishing to explore the Toros Mountains, which rise in the hinterland higher than 3,000 m and stretch well beyond Antalya.

ÖLÜDENIZ
There are several good hotels here, but they tend to charge a little over the odds. For a reasonable night at a reasonable price, try:

Çetin Motel, L-LL; *Belcekiz, Hisarönü; tel.* 252 616 6003.

Left off the main road from Fethiye, on the beach. The accommodation consists of a number of small bungalows, some with showers. Worth it for the location alone.

• *Lycian tomb, Kaş.*

The beaches at Kaş are laughable compared with what's on offer further along the Turquoise Coast. So go to the harbour and take a boat trip to one of the several good swimming spots nearby. I recommend the trip to **Mavi Magara** (the Blue Grotto), which lies to the west. Or try the the superb expedition to **Kekova Adasi** (Kekova Island), where you can distinguish an ancient harbour beneath the clear surface, and see the ruins of no fewer than three Lycian cities.

KASTELLORIZO
See Kaş, page 117.

KEKORA ADASI (KEKORA ISLAND)
See Kaş, page 117.

LETOÖN
SW of Rt 400 just N of Kinik. This site is named after the goddess Leto, who had a fling with Zeus. When Zeus's wife Hera heard about his, she flew into an ungoddess-like rage and banished Leto. One day Leto was wandering near here in disconsolate exile. Feeling thirsty, she asked some shepherds if they

would give her some water. They refused, and were later turned into frogs for their lack of manners. Leto's thirst was eventually quenched by the services of a friendly pack of wolves, who led her to a nearby spring. The ancient Greek name for wolf is *lykos*, and this is said to be why the region is called Lycia.

In keeping with these legends, history records that a shrine to Leto was established here, and that the spot soon became the chief sanctuary of the Lycian Federation. The Roman poet Ovid vividly describes the shrine in his *Metamorphoses* as 'an ancient altar, black with the fires of many sacrifices, surrounded with shivering reeds'. Letoön soon became the richest pilgrimage centre in Lycia, as can be seen from the ruins visible today, on which excavations only started just over 30 years ago.

There are the remains of three **temples:** one to Leto and the other two to Artemis and Apollo, the two godlets to whom Leto gave birth as a result of her affair with Zeus. Beside these temples is a ruined **Nymphaeum** (shrine to nymphs), whose waters now contain terrapins and frogs (doubtless descendants of the original discourteous shepherds). Nearby are some ancient inscriptions proclaiming the sanctuary regulations (for instance, no entry for those wearing fashionable clothes, ostentatious jewellery or bouffant hair styles).

North-east of these main ruins is an ancient Greek **theatre**, whose stage is now a field which produces a different kind of corn from that once produced by the actors.

ÖLÜDENIZ 🛏

7 km S of Fethiye. This is *the* 'beauty spot' of the Turquoise Coast. It's a lagoon, overlooked by rocky outcrops and pine forests, almost cut off from the sea. Its name means 'Dead Sea' which refers to the fact that it always stays calm, even during storms. There is a long sandy beach outside the entrance to the lagoon, and a protected area on the sandspit at its mouth, but the rest is beginning to suffer from chronic over-exploitation.

There are a number of nearby camping sites, all of which suffer from nights of a thousand guitars. The best of the

• Kaş.

bunch is the Çavuş campsite, at the head of the lagoon. Ölüdeniz is also a favourite anchorage for charter yachts. Out of season it retains its original enchantment, and you may want to linger here. In season, it's still worth a visit.

PATARA

5 km down track W off Rt 400, halfway between Kalkan and Kinik. According to legend, Patara was founded by Apollo, who used to spend the winter here after his summers on the Greek island of Delos. Apollo's oracle here was considered by some to be even better than that at Delphi. The ancient Greek historian Herodotus records that the oracle spoke in the form of dreams experienced by the priestess.

The city probably dates from the 5thC BC, but doesn't crop up in historical records until it surrendered to Alexander the Great in 333 BC. It was later a Roman city, and many of the present ruins date from this period. There are the remains of some fine **Roman baths**, which according to their inscription were built during the reign of the Emperor Vespasian, who ruled the

119

Roman Empire AD 69-79. At the site entrance there is a fine **Roman arch** which also dates from the 1stC AD. During this period St Paul and St Luke called in at the harbour, which is now silted up and some way from the sea.

In the 4thC AD Patara was the birth-place of a world-famous figure: Nicholas, Bishop of Myra, later canonized, and today known as Santa Claus. See also Demre, page 124.

The harbour was used as a vict-ualling port by medieval pilgrims on their way to the Holy Land, but when it silted up Patara's fortunes dwindled and it was soon forgotten by the outside world. The city was rediscovered in the 19thC by a British ship which was offi-cially 'surveying' the coast of southern Turkey for the Turkish government (copies of all charts were inevitably sent to the British Admiralty).

The modern village of Patara, which you reach a kilometre or so before the ruins, has some restaurants and rooms. A similar distance down the track beyond the ruins there's a long **sandy beach**, which also has some restaurants. Unfortunately this beach was recently 'discovered': first by beach-lovers, then by wandering drinks salesmen. These two interdependent species tend to be incompatible – one irritated by the commercial activity of the other, the other by lack of same in the former. Those who find themselves uninterested in this timeless human drama can retire to nurse their misan-thropy on the kilometres of empty sand further down the beach. There are now even some rooms where you can stay overnight.

PINARA

W off Rt 400, N of Eşen, down a very rough and eventually very steep track. If you are driving you may well decide to leave your car and walk the last few kilome-tres. At the top there's a reward in the form of a spring, which was safe for drinking last time I was here.

Pinara almost certainly began as a new town, built to accommodate the excess population of nearby Xanthos. However, it soon outgrew its satellite status to become one of the most important cities in the Lycian Federa-tion, even minting its own coins.

Pinara means 'round place' in ancient Lycian, and this describes the rock on

which it was originally built. The approach to the site is striking, with its **acropolis** perched on a cliff above the track. The main ruins show how the city spilled out from this original fortified spot. Amidst the sprawl of ancient stones there's a theatre and some fine tombs including the so-called **Royal Tomb**, which is decorated with some intriguing carvings.

TELMESSOS

See Fethiye, Turkey Overall: 4.

TLOS

Down the turning off Rt 400 for Kemer, 20 km E of Fethiye. From Kemer a local road leads 12 km south down the river valley to Tlos. This is one of the most ancient cities in this ancient region. Once called Tlawa, it is probably the Dlawa which was mentioned by the Hit-tites in 13thC BC. It has a spectacular setting on a promontory overlooking the river valley. There are some jum-bled ruins dating from all its historic periods, including a **Turkish fortress** on the acropolis.

XANTHOS

Just above Kinik, E off Rt 400. This was once the greatest city in Lycia. As is often the case with such places, it also suffered the greatest amount of pillag-ing, both after its defeats and during the ensuing centuries. Despite this, its ruins remain highly impressive.

Xanthos was mentioned by Homer in the *Iliad*. He implies that it was well known for its plentiful flocks, rich har-vests and fruitful orchards along the banks of the River Xanthos (now called the Eşen). It was already an important city in 540 BC when it was besieged by the Persian general Harpagus and his large army. The citizens decided that it was impossible to hold out against the Persians, but were unwilling to surren-der. Instead they made a large pyre on the acropolis, on which they burnt all their possessions – which in those polit-ically incorrect days included their wives, slaves and children. Relieved of all material cares, they then launched themselves into battle with nothing to lose – but none the less lost, not one of them surviving.

However, according to Herodotus, the city was rebuilt a few years later by a few local families who were lucky enough to be away on holiday at the time of the Persian siege. Xanthos quickly re-established itself, and when Alexander the Great arrived in 334 BC the inhabitants decided against suigenocide in favour of surrender.

Three centuries later, Xanthos fell foul of the Roman Empire, and once again the citizens resorted to their pyromaniac ways. But once again, within a few years, Xanthos had risen again in Phoenix fashion. The city continued to thrive until Byzantine times, when it became the seat of a bishop.

In the 19thC Xanthos was 'discovered' by the British explorer Charles Fellows. For two months he set about industriously pillaging the site, removing everything which was not too heavy or too firmly rooted. These spoils were then loaded on to *HMS Beacon* and shipped to the British Museum, where they remain to this day (some not even on display).

Consequently, the remains which can be seen today tend to be of the large (or unmovable) variety. You can't miss the 5thC BC **Harpy Tomb,** which is almost 8 m high. (It was even higher before Fellows removed the upper marble slabs, some of which have now been replaced by plaster replicas.) You can still see the winged figures of the Harpies themselves. Harpies were hideous female winged monsters with claws, who frequently cropped up in Greek legends as a corrective for excessively *machismo* behaviour by the gods. However, some scholars argue that the winged figures on the Harpy Tomb represent Sirens, who carried the souls of the departed to the Isles of the Dead. Also worth seeing is the Roman **Agora** (market place), north of which is a fine Roman **theatre**.

On the other side of the Agora is the so-called **Xanthian Obelisk**, the remains of a tomb which is covered with more than 200 lines of Lycian script. These have yet to be translated, as the Lycian language remains largely indecipherable. (Some years ago a professor from Belgrade achieved academic renown by claiming to have deciphered Lycian – but became so paranoid about someone stealing his secret that he carried it with him to the grave.)

Further north, across the modern road which bisects the site, is the Roman **acropolis**, on which is built a Byzantine **basilica**, which has yet to be fully excavated. This spot has spectacular views out over the ancient **walls** across the river valley, and can be particularly beautiful at sunset.

RECOMMENDED RESTAURANTS

FETHIYE
Yat, LL-LLL; *Yat Limani Karsisi; tel.* 252 611 3939.

Just opposite the entrance to the yacht harbour, hence the name. This is the smartest restaurant in town, and a great favourite with the yachting crowd. Excellent fish and *meze*.

If you're travelling *incognito* and wish to avoid the international set, try:

Tahiraga Lokantasi, L; *Çarşi Caddesi* 12; *tel.* 252 611 6308.

Cheap and cheerful Turkish cuisine as the Turks enjoy it. Good stews. Here I guarantee that your stomach will be full long before your purse is empty.

For a pleasant evening's drinking, head inland from the main Atatürk Caddesi, where you'll find a number of lively bars and cafés. One is run by a wine-drinking former 'chef' on a Turkish freighter who knows all about Liverpool – but we talked for so long that I can't remember which bar it was.

KALKAN
The best restaurants are all down by the harbour. They offer fairly standard *cuisine*, not too expensive, with little to choose between the various establishments. **Yakamoz** has never disappointed me, and **Korsan** serves good savoury pancakes (both **L-LL**).

KAŞ
Eriş, L-LL; *Cunhuriyet Meydiya (the main square); tel.* 242 836 1057.

You dine outside under the trees. It's rather smart, for Kaş, but the prices are fair. Delicious fresh fish, and a mouth-watering array of sweets on display in the refrigerated cabinet outside.

South-Western Turkey

Between Kaş and Antalya
Turquoise Coast, Eastern Stretch

200 km; map GeoCenter Euro-Country, Western Turkey, 1: 800 000

This section of the Turquoise Coast has some exceptional beaches and secluded coves, as well as all the fun of the fair at the resorts such as Kemer. There are also a number of exceptional ancient Lycian sites, of which Myra is the finest, and the most popular. For something more out of the way, try the beautifully situated Limyra, on the road to Elmali.

At Demre you can visit the church of a familiar old figure, whose historical existence in these warm parts may come as a surprise to many: none other than Father Christmas, in fact, better known here as St Nicholas, the original Santa Claus. See also Demre, page 124.

Rt 400 is the obvious key to exploring the region. Heading east from Kaş you come, in about 40 km, to Demre and the site of Myra. Some 30 km beyond here is the small yacht resort of Finike, where you can take a detour inland along Rt 635 to the picturesque market town of Elmani high in the mountains.

Beyond Finike, Rt 400 curves north with a continuous run of fine views out over the mountains and the sea. After the resort coast around Kemer you come to the beautiful and historic city of Antalya, with its palm-lined streets and ancient harbour.

It's about 200 km in all, with a 150-km round trip on the side. It can easily be driven in a day, but if you want to stop off at some of the sites and beaches, allow three days.

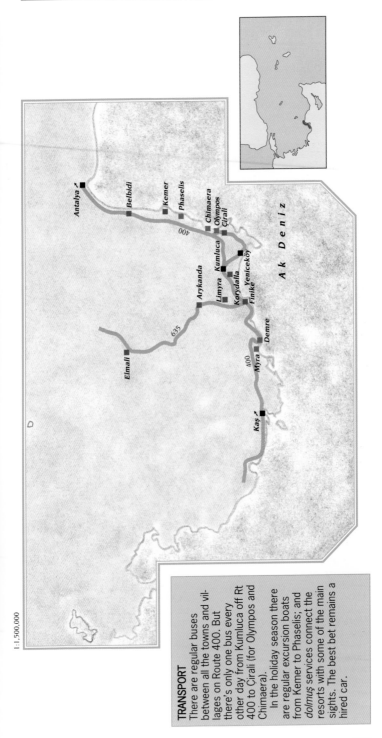

1:1,500,000

TRANSPORT

There are regular buses between all the towns and villages on Route 400. But there's only one bus every other day from Kumluca off Rt 400 to Çirali (for Olympos and Chimaera).

In the holiday season there are regular excursion boats from Kemer to Phaselis; and *dolmuş* services connect the resorts with some of the main sights. The best bet remains a hired car.

SIGHTS & PLACES OF INTEREST

ANTALYA
See Turkey Overall: 7.

BELDIBI
20 km S of Antalya, by Rt 400. Distinctly ordinary resort with stony beach. Useful as an overnight stop.

CHIMAERA
See Olympos, page 128.

ÇIRALI ⇔ ✕
See Recommended Hotels and Restaurants.

RECOMMENDED HOTELS

ÇIRALI
The village has been somewhat swamped by tourist development, with new hotels springing up all the time. At present the best bet is:

Olympos Lodge, LL; by the beach; tel. Çirali 3659.
Well-equipped bungalows amongst the citrus trees by the sea. Steepish price includes evening meal and a good breakfast.

FINIKE
Kale Pansiyon, L; central square; tel. 242 855 1457.
Basic, but in a ruined castle.

For something a little smarter (but less romantic) try the motels near the beach on the road going west out of town.

KEMER
Mostly modern, over-expensive accommodation. Try the tourist office at Limani Caddesi, 159: it has a list of recommended places to stay.
Just along the street at No. 109 there's a serviceable *pansiyon* called **Erol, L;** tel. 242 814 1755. If you want *really* friendly service try the **Otem Hotel, LL-LLL** at Yat Limani; tel. 242 814 3181. The staff here are working for their 'tourist diplomas,' and their exam results depend in part upon the quality of their service.

DEMRE ✕
50 km E of Kaş on Rt 400. A rather boring little place whose sole purpose appears to be the processing of tourists visiting the nearby site of Myra. But Demre also has a tourist site of its own. Just over 100 m west of the main square you come to the **Church of St Nicholas**. In the 4thC St Nicholas was Bishop of Myra, and is best known to us as Santa Claus.

Nicholas became Bishop of Myra by divine intervention. When the elders met to elect a new bishop, a voice from heaven told them that they were to elect the first person who walked in through the church door next morning – and guess who wandered in on his pre-breakfast stroll.

Nicholas took his new job very seriously. When he visited the Council of Nicea in 325 he was particularly needled by the behaviour of a heretic called Arius, and ended up by slapping his face so hard that his bones rattled. Nicholas appears to have had quite a presence. At the mere sight of him, demons would scatter, and once when a church collapsed on top of him he merged completely unscathed. One day he even appeared in a dream to the Emperor Constantine, ordering him to release all his prisoners who had been unjustly condemned to death.

Nicholas was, however, best known for his generosity. Anonymously he would distribute coins to the poor at night, dropping them in through the chimney when he couldn't gain access by other means. When he finally died, the good bishop was buried in his church, where he remained for more than 700 years, until he was carried off by a group of Italian merchants. These merchants seem to have been well aware of the value of St Nicholas' bones on the bullish medieval relics market. The saint's remains were enshrined in the cathedral at Bari, simultaneously placed on equally permanent exhibition in Venice, and also sold to the newly converted Russians, who adopted him as their patron saint. Not to be outdone, the locals also claimed that they still had his bones (which are now in a casket in the Antalya Museum).

It's easy to see how generous and genial old St Nicholas became the patron saint of Christmas presents,

HISTORIC LYCIA

Ancient Lycia occupied almost the entire broad peninsula which fills the coastline between Fethiye and Antalya, known today as the Turquoise Coast. Inland, the region is mountainous and was partly inaccessible in ancient times. But the coastal cities had serviceable harbours and there was fertile land along the river valleys. Lycia prospered and the people developed a distinct language, complete with its own script, which has not yet been fully deciphered – see also page 121.

The 23 cities of this region formed the democratic Lycian Federation, which elected its own officials and rulers. Each city had from one to three votes, according to its size and importance.

The Lycians also established the beginnings of a distinct culture of their own. It appears originally to have been rather savage, but soon began absorbing influences from less barbaric civilizations. The Lycians were renowned for their independence, but this didn't stop their territory from being overrun by the usual succession of powerful external empires.

• *Rock tomb, Fethiye.*

There are references to the Lycian cities in several early texts. Homer's *Iliad* mentions that the Lycians fought against Troy in the Trojan War. In the 6thC BC the Persians moved in. Then for a while the region fell under the influence of the Athenians. Alexander the Great arrived in the 4thC BC, and when he died the place became a colony of Egypt under the Ptolemies. Later the Romans took over. In the following centuries the region became an important Byzantine centre. The Arabs began to raid the coast in the 7thC, and finally the Selçuk Turks established Muslim sovereignty.

Perhaps the most intriguing and widespread relics of the Lycians are their rock tombs, which are carved into the mountainsides. These can be very elaborate, with pillars and pediments made to resemble temples; but they can also be homely, complete with murals depicting daily scenes, which give a fair indication of what life must have been like amongst the Lycians.

See also Turkey Overall: 5.

• *Tomb, Üçağız.*

though how he acquired his red uniform with white fur trimmings, and his troupe of red-nosed reindeer, remains as much a mystery as his quadruplet skeleton.

The present Church of St Nicholas is undergoing drastic restoration work, but when I was last here it still retained its cool, airy Byzantine appeal. There is also a suitably imaginative statue of old Father Christmas himself in the garden outside.

FINIKE ⌂ ✕
29 km E of Demre. The name of this small coastal town, pronounced FEE-nee-keh, hints at its earlier Lycian name, Phoenicus. The only real reason for staying here is if you need a base for exploring the nearby sites and the hinterland to Elmali.

Finike has a rather sad stony beach (not always pristine clean) and what

atmosphere the town once possessed is ruined by Route 400, which slices the place in half. The harbour is a yachting centre, with a fair amount of tourist activity. The good news is that nearby there is excellent swimming in the coves off the main road to Demre.

KAŞ
See Turkey Overall: 5.

KEMER ⌂
E off Rt 400, 40 km S of Antalya. The heartland of virtual reality, Turkish style. A spotless artificial resort with spick-and-span modern hotels, yacht marina and groups of colourful mobile robots representing tourists from many European nations. Sea, sun, sand and sin – and sitting down to eat and drink: that's about all there is to Kemer. Amidst all this epit-

ome of ordinariness just one thing stands out: the 'oriental' dancing which is staged at some of the restaurants raises tackiness to a high art form.

KORYDALLA (OR CORYDALLA)

2 km W of Kumluca, off Rt 400. This is the sight that never was. Here stood the ancient Lycian city of Korydalla. Its remains were rediscovered in the 19thC: travellers noted a wide area of ruins, including a fine theatre and even an aqueduct. Unfortunately the locals discovered them too, and immediately began moving every stone they could lift – mainly for house-building. The result? A practically bare site, and some very interesting stones incorporated into the nearby village houses. Look out for these in **Kumluca**, where one house even sports a block containing fine examples of Lycian and ancient Greek script.

Not content with this, the locals then mounted their own archaeological dig. This unearthed a fine cache of rare Byzantine plate, which immediately entered the Byzantine conduits of the international art market, before finally resurfacing, at great cost, in various American museums. Some may see this entire story as an instructive parable, in which the villains of the piece are far from being those closest at hand.

DETOUR – ELMALI

At Finike turn N off Rt 400 on to Rt 635. This leads you inland through the mountains, a breathtaking route rendered even more exciting by the lorry drivers who make their living by defying death at each corner. Drive with care.

On the way to Elmali you pass two sites that are worth a stop. The first is Limyra – turn off E at Turunçova after 7 km, and follow signs for 4 km. In the 4thC BC this out-of-the-way spot was capital of the Lycian Federation. Some 800 years later Gaius Caesar died here on his way from Armenia to Rome. The site has a **theatre**, some interesting **tombs**, and an **acropolis** which is well worth the 50-minute climb for the fine view down towards the sea. The **heroon** (mausoleum) has some decorous caryatids (supporting columns in the form of female figures).

About 30 km after leaving Finike you'll see the sign to Arykanda, directing you east off the road. The suffix -anda suggests to scholars that this city was founded in the pre-Greek era, probably some time during the second millennium BC. Its inhabitants, much like us modern visitors, were renowned locally for their indolent and spendthrift ways. In the 2ndC BC they even decided to side with invaders in the hope of wiping out their huge debts to their neighbours. This imaginative foreign policy appears to have paid off, and the rest of the city's history achieves the predictability and dullness which its citizens doubtless craved.

The site has some striking views out over the rocky hillside and the mountains. Amongst the usual clutter of rubble there's a fine **theatre**, a tall **façade to a bath-house**, and a modest **pagan temple** which may well have become one of the earliest Christian churches in the region. Inscribed in Greek on the wall is the slogan *Jesus Christ is victorious* and a cross. (This cross is unusual, as the earliest sign for Christianity was usually a fish.)

Nearly 70 km after Finike you reach **Elmali**, whose name comes from the Turkish for apple. Not surprisingly it is surrounded by gardens of fruit trees (citrus as well as apples). A peak rising to well over 2,000 m, covered in snow for much of the year, makes a fine back-drop. The town itself has some fine old wooden houses and a 400-year-old **mosque** (Ömerpaşa Camii) with some graceful inscriptions on its walls.

Recent American excavations at nearby **Semayük** have revealed hundreds of early **Bronze Age tombs**; but even more interesting is the **painted tomb** at Kizilbel, 5 km SW of town by the lake. This has wall paintings which show a number of figures from early Greek mythology – such as Gorgon and Pegasus indicating the pervasiveness of Ancient Greek culture in this region even as early as 3000-2000 BC.

KUMLUCA
See Korydalla, page 127.

MYRA
2 km N of Demre. Myra is one of the best preserved of all the Lycian city sites, and it's also the easiest to get to. This means that it's crowded in the holiday season.

The site is open 8 am-6.30 pm. Get there at opening time, or after 5, and you miss most of the crowds.

According to tradition, the city's name comes from the Greek word for myrrh, the resin used for making incense. But spoilsport modern scholars have cast doubt on this highly plausible story, citing such niggling points as the fact that Myra never actually produced any myrrh.

Myra was one of the most important cities of the Lycian Foundation, and in the 5thC even became its capital, by decree of the Byzantine Emperor Theodosius II. The city had a long, prosperous, predictable and boring history. The virtually forgotten Roman emperor Germanicus paid a visit in AD 19, but decided not to stay; and 40 years later St Paul put in here briefly, on his way to Rome as a prisoner.

Today you can see some fine **rock tombs**, many of which were designed to look like ordinary Lycian dwellings, in order to make the dead feel at home. There's also a **necropolis**, which contains the celebrated **Painted Tomb**. This has a wall painting of the family of its former occupants in happier times (i.e. before they took up residence here). One of the guides used to tell an unrepeatable story about this family, which was rendered no less amusing by its utter implausibility. I hear that he has now retired on his tips.

OLYMPOS
Leave Rt 400 4 km E of Kumluca in the direction of Yeniceköy, following signs for Olympos 20 km down disintegrating track.

Olympos is a Lycian city yet to be excavated. Its origins are something of a mystery, suggesting that unlike most other Lycian cities its inhabitants were not imaginative enough to come up with any memorable myth concerning its foundation.

In 100 BC the city was captured by the notorious pirate Xenicetes, who went into the slave business, selling his captives at markets all over the Aegean. When he was finally defeated by the Romans, he decided to set fire to himself rather than enter his own business as a marketable product.

Later Julius Caesar served here as a junior officer. One day when young Julius was sailing to Rhodes, allegedly for a philosophy lesson, he was captured by pirates – but was soon freed after the payment of a mere 50-talent ransom. Something about this incident (perhaps his low price on the ransom market) must have needled Julius, for he immediately gathered a fleet of ships, set out after the pirates, and captured them all. Then, without bothering to fix even the most humiliating ransom price, he proceeded to crucify the lot.

This site is particularly beautiful, with paths cut through the undergrowth leading to the various ruins, which include a ruined medieval **castle**, an **acropolis**, the inevitable Roman **baths**, and an intriguing **sarcophagus** with a fine, intricate carving of a ship. Those who have had a little too much of ruins may find themselves interested in the stream which runs through the site. Its clear waters are home to several species of ducks, a slightly hoarse choir of frogs, several species of little fishies, and (allegedly) turtles. You may also see kingfishers. The beach is ideal for a cooling plunge whilst waiting for the earnest, puce-faced archaeologists to return.

North along the beach from the ruins is the village of Çirali, which has some restaurants and accommodation.

Half an hour's walk above the village you come to an intriguing natural phenomenon: gas seeping from the rocks produces a number of small, perpetually burning flames known as **the Chimaera**. From historical references we know that these flames have been burning since ancient times, though scientists remain undecided about the exact explanation of this little wonder of nature – which like several similar phenomena throughout the globe is claimed as unique.

The flames are named after the mythical monster, the Chimaera, who had three animal heads that breathed fire. This schizoid beast crops up in an involved and tiresome story in Homer, describing how the Chimaera is (wrongly) accused of rape. You are expected to believe that he is then murdered by a paltry hero on a flying horse dropping lumps of lead into his mouths. Any self-respecting monster whose stomach worked on the principle of combustion could surely have dealt easily with such leaden indigestion. Anyway, this ecologically unsound monster, breathing fire and lead fumes, inhabited the surrounding mountains and bequeathed to us the word chimera – which means a nastie beastie.

PHASELIS

9 km S of Kemer. This city, with a spectacularly beautiful situation, stood on the eastern borders of Lycia. The remains are on a small headland covered with pine trees which overlook a number of bays. The water is glassy clear, and beyond the trees the peaks rise higher than 3,000 m. When I was here once in June they were still streaked with snow.

Phaselis was founded in 690 BC by colonists from Rhodes. According to legend, the site for the city was bought from a local shepherd in exchange for some dried fish. From this time on the inhabitants of Phaselis acquired a reputation for meanness, which gradually spread throughout the eastern Mediterranean as the city became an important maritime trading centre. Such was its far-flung influence that it even helped to found a colony in the Nile delta called Naucratis.

Phaselis also gained a reputation for treachery, sometimes siding with the Lycian Federation and sometimes joining its enemies. In the 4thC BC Alexander the Great took the city and spent the winter here before setting off to conquer the world.

In Roman times it was visited by the Emperor Hadrian, and you can still see the **ceremonial gate** which was erected in his honour. It stands at the end of a paved street leading to the **agora** (market place). The **theatre**, which lies east of this, could seat more than 1,500 spectators. The city had no less than three harbours, all of which are still clearly discernible today. The small **City Harbour** is particularly well sheltered, with its own beach, a little shallow nowadays, but still great for a cooling wallow.

The citizens of Phaselis were not only mean and treacherous, but according to Demosthenes they were also 'tellers of untruths'. As if all this wasn't bad enough, the distinctive Phaselian haircut, called a 'sisoe', is condemned in the Old Testament. (Scholars are of the opinion that a sisoe was a form of tonsure.) According to Leviticus (Book 19, verse 27): 'Ye shall not make a sisoe of the hair of your heads.'

Livy mentions the nearby swamp, which still exists, as being notorious for disease: probably malaria. As I once discovered to my cost, there are still vicious packs of mosquitoes here, who keep the same hours as Dracula. Nowadays, the gnats are not malarial.

Despite its bad press in history, Phaselis is now an idyllic spot. Its charms are best summed up in the words of an early 20thC traveller: 'The sleepy summer heat, the sea and the superb mountains, the contrast of the utter isolation with the living life of the ancient city, combine to leave a memory not easily effaced.'

There are several notices about the site forbidding picnicking, but the locals appear not to be able to read them. When in Rome...

RECOMMENDED RESTAURANTS

ÇIRALI
Palm Restaurant, L-LL; *by the front.*

One of the more established restaurants, which serves locally caught fresh fish.

DEMRE
The main tourist restaurants (and a few inexpensive *pansiyons*) are by St Nicholas Church. Nothing special here.

If you want something a little more up-market and distinctive, try the drive down to Demre's harbour, the site of ancient Andriake (left off Rt 400 along the river). Here you can dine at the restaurants and swim from the beach.

FINIKE
The best restaurants are around the harbour, where the yachting crowd gathers.

Between Antalya and Anamur
Mediterranean Coast:
Perge and Side

265 km; map GeoCenter EuroCountry Western Turkey, 1:800 000

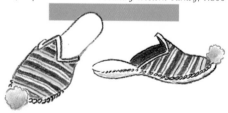

This area mixes spectacularly remote and beautiful ancient sites with the bright lights of some of Turkey's busiest resorts. Antalya is Turkey's fastest-booming city, thriving on the modern tourist trade but still managing to retain the atmosphere of bygone centuries in the narrow streets of its old quarter, with its medieval walls and the famous 700-year-old Fluted Minaret.

Inland from Antalya is Termessos, the haunting ruins of an ancient Pisidian city 1,000 m up in a superb mountain setting. On the other side of town is Perge, whose well-preserved ruins were once a leading city of the Pamphylian Federation, a group of allied cities which occupied this coast from the closing centuries of the second millennium BC. See page 134.

There are innumerable beaches to suit all tastes along this entire length of coast. As you would expect, those nearest to Antalya and the other resorts tend to be the most populated. If you want privacy, go a little extra distance and you'll find remote coves and secluded little beaches amongst the rocks.

If you decide to explore this region, you'll probably start in Antalya. Heading west along Route 400, you reach, after 17 km, the turn-off inland for Perge. In another 30 km is the sign for Aspendos, which has the best-preserved Roman theatre in the entire Mediterranean. Just over one-and-a-half millennia ago more than 14,000 people would regularly cram into this theatre to watch ancient Greek tragedies and gladiatorial displays.

Some 35 km on from Aspendos you come to Side, a pleasant, small-ish, but rapidly expanding resort. Besides some fine beaches, it has several interesting archaeological sites of its own. From here you continue along the coast road to Alanya, and then along the beautiful winding road which finally leads to Anamur.

Driving the whole stretch usually takes more than one day, even if you rush. Far better spend four or five days, allowing time to do the sites justice, as well as take a little time off for the beaches.

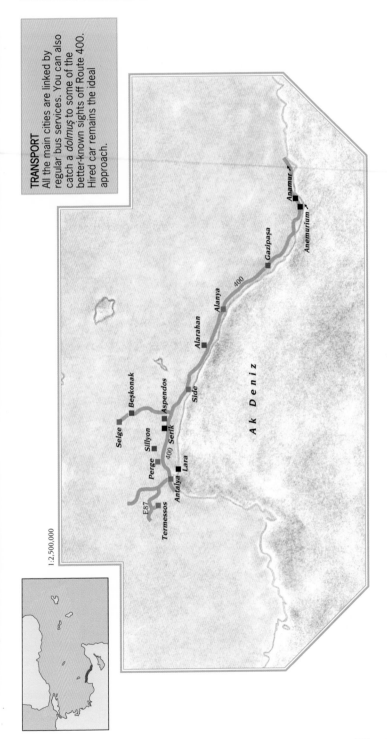

SIGHTS & PLACES OF INTEREST

ALANYA ⌨ ✕

115 km E of Antalya. Ten years ago Alanya was discovered, and since then tourism has hit this remote, sleepy spot like a hurricane. Yet, surprisingly, the place has (just) succeeded in retaining some of its old character, despite determined development. The town has a long, pristine popular **beach**, which the developers are doing their best to improve with a strip of long, pristine popular hotels.

The town itself has a striking **citadel**, which stands above the sea on its promontory. The original city was founded in the first millennium BC by Greek colonists. In 44 BC Antony made a gift of the city to his beloved Cleopatra. More than a thousand years later, when the Turks took over, the city became the main port of the unlikely but none the less powerful Sultan of Rum.

ALARA HANI

30 km E of Side, 4 km along inland turning off Rt 400. This *kervansaray* (caravanserai or wayside inn) was built in 13thC when the main trading route of the Sultanate of Rum, linking the capital Konya with the coast, ran past here. Travellers, tourists and merchants were provided with the usual amenities: somewhere to park; hay to refuel their transport; a bed for the night; somewhere to cook food and a mosque for morning and evening prayers.

The place is now derelict, but has a faded charm, and fills a long gap between sites.

ANAMUR

See Turkey Overall: 8.

ANEMURIUM

See Turkey Overall: 8.

ANTALYA ⌨ ✕

185 km E of Kaş. Antalya is Turkey's boom city, with the fastest growing population in the land. This has already begun to show in the spreading ramshackle development of the suburbs, but the old centre of the city remains strictly preserved. (Not surprisingly, since the principal reason for the boom is tourism.)

The main focus of interest is the **Kaleiçi**, which means 'inside the wall'. This is the old town, whose crumbling houses and narrow streets are gathered around the harbour, which has been in use for two millennia.

Antalya was a comparatively late starter compared with most cities in the region. It wasn't founded until the 1stC BC, by Attalus of Pergamon, after whom it was named, the present name being a mispronounced variant. In time the city became a Roman colony, and you can still see the gate put up to commemorate the visit of the Emperor Hadrian in 130 AD.

East of the harbour there's a **Roman tower** (Hidirlik Kulesi) which was originally a lighthouse. From here you can see spectacular sunsets across the

---

• *Atatürk statue, Antalya.*

water, when the blazing rays of the sun flare out behind the sharp high peaks on the other side of the bay.

During the Byzantine period Antalya was a stop for the Crusaders on their way to the Holy Land. Then in 1207 it was conquered by the Selçuk Turks. The fine **Yivli Minare** (Fluted Minaret), which was erected by Sultan Aladdin Keykubad, dates from this period. This unique minaret is built of brick in eight different grooved sections, has pieces of blue tile at its base, and is nearly 40 m high. The original mosque was destroyed, but the present construction is impressive enough, having six domes supported by Doric and Ionian capped pillars.

When the Turkish Empire was defeated in the First World War, Antalya was handed over to the Italians, but three years later they were driven out by Atatürk.

By far the most interesting thing to see in Antalya (after your obligatory walk amongst the old buildings of the Kaleiçi Quarter) is the excellent **Antalya Museum**. It is 2 km west of the city centre (regular *dolmuş* service). Some of the exhibits are laid out rather bewilderingly, but they're all clearly labelled in Turkish and English. They range from the earliest fossils found in the region, through items from the Greek and Roman periods, to modern Turkish displays. Don't miss the little **Phrygian figures** (7thC BC); the 'Gallery of the Gods' (**Room 2**), which contains Egyptian and Greek deities; and the 19thC icons in **Room 8**. The Christian collection includes the urn containing the 'only true remains' of St Nicholas of Demre – better known to us as Santa Claus. (Other 'only true remains' of Father Christmas are to be found in Bari, Venice and Russia.)

For a tourist centre, Antalya has disappointing beaches. They used to be notorious for rubbish and pollution, and these problems have been attacked with vigour. Ominously, the battle may have been won, but the war still has to go on. If you want a guaranteed pleasant and safe swim, catch a bus 10 km east along the coast to **Lara**. This is a fenced pay beach, but it's sandy – and as good as you'll get within reach of the city. Nearby are the distinctly disappointing **Düden Falls**, which had sunk to such a low state that there was practically no water to fall over them when I was last here. However, a usually reliable source claims that they are much better in spring, when the water positively gushes, and anyway you're better off seeing them on a boat trip from the Old Harbour in Antalya.

When in Antalya be sure to visit the nearby sites at Perge and Termessos (see this page and page 137). There are also boat trips which can be taken across the Gulf of Antalya to Phaselis (see Turkey Overall: 6).

ASPENDOS
5 km E of Serik, 3 km inland off Rt 400. Aspendos was almost certainly settled by Greek migrants after the fall of Troy in 1184 BC. The city's name is not Greek, which has prompted some scholars to suggest that the migrants may have taken over an already occupied site. Aspendos was to become one of the most important Pamphylian cities. Through the centuries it was occupied by the Persians, the ancient Greeks and the Romans. It was during the last occupation that the most impressive of the surviving ruins were built.

The **theatre** is one of the most spectacular ruins to be seen anywhere in the Mediterranean, indeed it is the best preserved Roman theatre in existence. Built in 2ndC AD by Zeno the architect, it is still occasionally used – for Turkish wrestling and elimination bouts prior to the Eurovision Song Contest. (Before lamenting too much this fall from grace, it's worth remembering what form the original entertainment here took: at least nowadays they only dismember the songs.) In ancient times there were awnings which used to protect the spectators from the sun. Only a few years ago, this theatre managed to accommodate 20,000 spectators for a rock concert, though in ancient times it probably seated around 15,000.

Almost as impressive is the superb **aqueduct** which brought fresh water to the city from the mountains. This arched construction still stretches nearly 900 m, and is 15 m high. Aquaphiles will be eager to study the pressure towers, pipes, friction-reducing conduits and other marvels of ancient plumbing.

BEŞKONAK
See Selge, page 136.

GAZIPAŞA
45 km E of Alanya on Rt 400. Uninspiring small town, but with inspiring beaches nearby in both directions.

LARA
See Antalya, page 132.

PERGE
Inland off Rt 400 at Aksu, 17 km E of Antalya. Perge was the greatest of all the Pamphylian cities, and its ruins are substantial.

Originally Perge was a maritime trading centre. Nowadays, the coastline has shifted, leaving the site 20 km inland – though the city was in fact never on the coast itself, but slightly inland to protect it from pirates. All merchandize was hauled from the harbour to the city.

• *Opposite: Yivli Minare, Antalya, and the old city.*

ANCIENT PAMPHYLIA
Like the neighbouring region of Lycia (page 125), this was a federation of cities run on democratic principles. It occupied the coastal region and the immediate hinterland for 100 km or so between Antalya and Alanya. But there the resemblance ends. The Pamphylians appear to have been losers from the start. The original colonists were a mixed race of people who fled from Troy after its defeat in 1184 BC. From then on they seem to have been over-run by just about everyone who came through. Yet, as with many losers, they were tenacious and ever optimistic, staying put regardless of who ruled them. In the 1stC BC Antony and Cleopatra secretly met here for trysts.

The best Pamphylian site is at Perge, above. The least visited, and in some ways the most spectacular, is away in the mountains at Selge, page 136.

The city was founded towards the end of the 2nd millennium BC and in the 2ndC BC experienced a golden age. During this period the philosopher Varus was born here. He was known as 'The Stork,' not on account of his legs, or even his ungainly philosophy, but because of his long beaky nose.

In the 2ndC AD Perge also produced the great geometer Apollonius. He remains known to this day for his celebrated classification of conic sections (into circle, ellipse, parabola and hyperbole). More than a thousand years later these were to come to the assistance of the medieval mathematician Kepler in his revolutionary theory of the solar system.

By medieval times Perge had degenerated into little more than a shepherds' settlement. It was rediscoverd by early 19thC travellers, one of whom mentions that 'the howling and barking of the jackals and wolves around my tent lasted until daybreak'. Nowadays such sounds are not heard until the daylight hours, when the site opens to the massed visitors. For peaceful contemplation, free from hyenas, try visiting at 8 am when the site opens, and the coachloads are still barking over breakfast.

Most of the present ruins date from the Roman era. They include a very fine **theatre**, a **stadium** which once seated 12,000 cheering spectators. There is also the remains of an elegant **street with colonnades**.

SIDE 🏨 ✕

90 km E of Antalya on Rt 400. A hotel owner here, who spoke excellent English and had lived in south London, once tried to persuade me that the name Side had long existed in the English language in the form of the now politically incorrect phrase 'a bit on the side.' In the face of my scepticism, he cited as his reasons that Side was the most romantic spot in Turkey (he was born here, as well as trying to fill his hotel), and also that in ancient times this was a place where Antony and Cleopatra would meet for trysts. Cleopatra's famous nose might have been put a little out of joint if Antony had referred to her as his bit on the side, but there's no denying that Side has its charms.

These are largely swamped during the summer season by swarms of visitors, but between October and May the place remains a delight – with an excellent sandy **beach**, a small but worthwhile **museum** and some interesting (mainly classical) **ruins**. All of these are in the old part of town within the **ancient walls** (the beach extends well beyond). The **theatre**, which stands at the end of a colonnaded street leading to the old harbour, could once seat 20,000 coughing spectators, and remains highly

---

DETOUR – SELGE

About 10 km E of Serik turn inland off Rt 400, following the sign 'Milli Parki' (National Park) and Selge. The road degenerates after Beşkonak (just over 20 km), after which you come in 5 km to the **Kanyon Restaurant**, built in the trees above the river. Here they serve excellent fresh trout (purportedly from the river, but in fact from a nearby fish farm). Just beyond you come to **Oluk Bridge**, which spans the deep gorge and dates from Roman times. You then continue on the spectacular 13-km drive up to Selge, with views out over the forests and mountains.

The ruins themselves are in fact somewhat thin on the ground (though of course *well* worth it after all your effort). But to be honest the most inspiring feature is the view of the snow-streaked peaks all around, rising to nearly 2,500 m.

The best things to see among the ruins are a **theatre** whose stage was struck by a thunderbolt nearly two millennia too late to enliven a performance; the **agora**, with its truly panoramic setting; and the Byzantine **church** which *looks* as if it was struck by a thunderbolt.

Why people ever chose to live in such a remote spot remains a mystery. History records little of this early community of misanthropes. An aqueduct helped support a population of more than 20,000. Alexander the Great didn't even bother to conquer them, and the Romans didn't pay them much more notice. The citizens went about their business in peace, until one day the aqueduct collapsed – and that was the end of Selge.

impressive.

Other points of interest include the **agora**, whose slave market was mentioned by the ancient geographer Strabo, the remains of a fine Byzantine **basilica**, and several **temples**.

It's chastening to learn that most of these impressive constructions were financed by piracy and the slave trade. Scholars remain undecided as to how this city received its unusual name, but suggest that it might have been the word for pomegranate in a lost Anatolian language, which sounds even less likely than the hotel manager's theory.

SILLYON

26 km E of Antalya, turn inland off Rt 400 to Asra Koyu. Here ask for Sillyon and you'll be directed to the unsignposted track which leads to the site. These are the ruins of a Pamphylian city which was founded at the end of the second millennium BC. Owing to its easily defensible location, it even managed to repulse Alexander the Great. The site has a Greek **gymnasium**, which a later unathletic Byzantine bishop used as his palace. Another Greek building, which still has its upper windows, was used by the Selçuk Turks as a **castle**.

Just north-east of this is the only known inscription in the Pamphylian language, 37 lines long. Despite Pamphylian being a dialect of ancient Greek, scholars have only been able to decipher a few stray words, so the inscription's content remains a mystery. Later inhabitants hacked a doorway through the lower part of the inscription, which has hardly helped would-be decipherers.

TERMESSOS

35 km NW of Antalya off Rt 350. The site is 9 km from the car park, at the end of a long track climbing through the woods This spectacular site almost 1,000 m above sea level was founded in the 1st millennium BC by a war-like tribe called the Pisidians, who originated from the mountains. The surrounding land was so barren that the citizens were forced to live on olives and the occasional goat, a diet which provoked them into fierce onslaughts on their better-fed neighbours. However, no one bothered to attack them in their mountain fastness. Even Alexander the Great evaded the challenge, and the Romans decided to confer on them the status of 'allies'. This meant that Termessos never effectively became part of the Roman Empire. The city issued coins which didn't display the emperor's head, and instead bore the inscription 'autonomous'.

The site itself is overgrown with shrubbery, but there are many things worth seeing. Besides the usual (but no less interesting) **city walls, temple** and **agora**, there are two fascinating remnants, both sadly pillaged by vandals. By the outer wall in the gateway of the look-out tower there used to be a famous **dice oracle**. It gave such counsel as:

'Three fours and two sixes. This is the gods' advice: Stay at home and do not go elsewhere, lest the destructive Beast and avenging Fury come upon you.'

One feature not to be missed is the **necropolis**, a 3-km walk up the valley from the agora. It contains a litter of tombs and toppled sarcophagi in a breathtaking location. Just above, on the hillside, there's an even better view of the mountains, the valley and the city below.

RECOMMENDED RESTAURANTS

ALANYA

To eat adequately, without spending over the odds, try the restaurants on the main seafront, Gazi Pasa Caddesi, or one of the smaller streets leading off it. **Mepheri, LL**, on the front, serves swordfish; better value, but not so much choice, can be had at **Toros, L**, on Iskele Caddesi, the street that runs parallel to the sea.

ANTALYA

Hisar, LL-LLL; *Cumhuriyet Meydani; tel.* 3111 5281.

Above the yacht harbour in the Kaleiçi quarter (the old city), incorporated into the walls of an ancient castle. Renowned for its *meze* and fresh fish.

SIDE

Afrodite, LL; *end of main street on beach front; tel.* 3213 1171.

Fine romantic location overlooking the sea. Try their bountiful *meze* with a bottle of cool white wine, and you may require nothing more for your dreams to come true.

Southern Turkey

Between Anamur and Adana
Eastern Mediterranean Coast

300 km; map Kümmerley + Frey, 1: 1,000,000

This easternmost stretch of Turkey's Mediterranean coast ends close to the Syrian border. You'll find an increasingly Middle Eastern influence, especially in the food.

The coastline has experienced all kinds of influences, from Armenian kings to the Crusaders, from the Jews to the ancient Romans. As you press eastwards, you enter increasingly remote country, beyond the reach of the package tours, with miles of unspoilt beaches. The resorts are less hectic, tending to attract a higher proportion of locals.

There are several exceptional sights, ranging from the finest medieval castle in Turkey (Mamure Kalesi) to the celebrated Caves of Heaven and Hell (Cennet ve Cehennem), a region of limestone caverns filled with spooky delights for speliologists. You can take a trip inland into the mountains to visit Uzuncaburç, which has been settled since Hittite times and came into its own in the classical period. If you feel like voyaging even further afield, you can always take the ferry over to northern Cyprus, just 70 km across the water.

The 300 km between Anamur and Adana takes at least a couple of days by road, but the sights deserve your attention and to do the region justice you need at least five days.

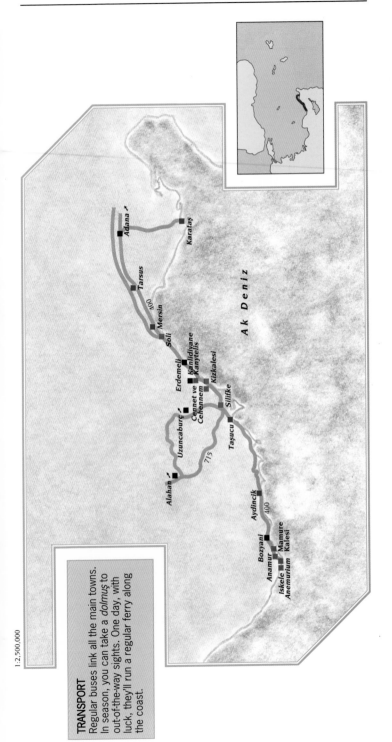

TRANSPORT
Regular buses link all the main towns.
In season, you can take a *dolmuş* to
out-of-the-way sights. One day, with
luck, they'll run a regular ferry along
the coast.

1:2,500,000

SIGHTS & PLACES OF INTEREST

ADANA
See Turkey Overall: 9.

ALAHAN
See Local Explorations: 6.

ANAMUR ⊭ ✕
60 km E of Alanya. A rather sleepy spot with its own rather sleepy (but not for long) resort at **Iskele,** 5 km to the south. This is in fact the southernmost part of the Turkish mainland – on approximately the same latitude as Tehran, Tokyo and San Francisco. The name Anamur derives from the Greek word *anemos,* which means spirit or wind; indeed the city is fanned by more or less constant breezes. Despite this, there is still a mosquito problem from the nearby swamps. Take appropriate precautions.

Several years ago the government promised Anamur a museum – but that seems to be still in the post. There's not much to see in town, but it's useful as a base for exploring the many excellent nearby sights. These include the ancient city of **Anemourion** (below), the castle of **Mamure Kalesi,** page 141, and some wonderful beaches, especially between Silifke and Mersin.

ANEMOURION
8 km SW of Anamur. Anemourion is now a deserted Byzantine city. The original settlement was almost certainly founded by the Phoenicians, and it crops up in historical records from the 4thC BC onwards. The Romans colonized the city, but it wasn't until the 3rdC BC that it experienced its golden age. When the city became Christian its inhabitants entered into the swing of things so imaginatively that they were soon practising heretics – adhering to the Mono-physite heresy, a popular deviation here and in the African churches. This claimed that Christ had not been human as he was possessed of a singe divine nature. (The African churches were never cured of this heresy, which is maintained to this day in the Coptic and Ethiopian churches.)

The city was finally overrun by Arab raiders in the 7thC, and has remained unoccupied ever since. This means that much of the city is in comparatively good repair. (Centuries of earthquakes tend to do less harm than centuries of human habitation.) Many of the buildings are virtually intact apart from the roofs.

The site itself is in an attractive set-

RECOMMENDED HOTELS

ANAMUR
Eser Pension, L; *at Iskele, on the sea; tel. 757 2322.*

Friendly atmosphere, clean rooms, right by the beach. Be sure to book ahead in the high season.

KIZKALESI
There are innumerable places where you can stay here, with a wide range of choice near the sea. The snag: in summer it's packed, and in my experience phone booking can be unreliable. Best just to arrive, walk around and ask.

If you don't want the noise of the front, try **Set Motel, L-LL,** *tel. 7584 1314,* which makes up for being away from the sea by having its own pool.

MERSIN
Otel Edge, L-LL; *Istiklal Caddesi, 33 Sokat No 24; tel. 741 21419.*

A small hotel which really does have the edge over the others. The bonus is the decoration, incorporating local ethnic craftware. All rooms have private shower. Near city centre, but requires patience and patient questioning to locate.

SILIFKE
Çadir, L-LL; *Atatürk Caddesi 8; tel. 759 11244.*

In the centre of town close by the river and the tourist office. The smartest hotel in a not particularly smart spot, but the rooms all have showers and balconies.

TAŞUCU
It's only worth staying overnight here if you're stuck and waiting for the ferry. If you fit into this luckless category and can't make it to a nearby resort, try the fairly basic **Otel Işik, L,** *by the harbour; tel. 759 31026.*

ting, on a hillside overlooking a stony beach. As always, the **necropolis** is worth a visit. Several of the tombs here have murals inside – the best of which depicts Hermes (in his Christian re-incarnation) guiding the souls of the dead to the next world.

Try climbing to the acropolis: this is the southernmost tip of the Turkish mainland, and I'm assured by a clear-sighted informant that on certain days 'when the atmosphere thins just before rain' it is possible to see the island of Cyprus 70 km away.

Recent excavations by Canadians have unearthed many interesting finds, which are on display at the small museum in Iskele.

AYDINCIK

53 km E of Anamur. Unspoilt small town, with not much to spoil, but there is a sandy beach.

CENNET VE CEHENNEM

25 km E of Silifke, inland off Rt 400. These are the so-called Caves of Heaven and Hell. In fact there are not two but several caves, of varying interest. The biggest is the Cave of Heaven (Cennet Deresi). It is a large, dank limestone hole in the ground, leading to the Cave of Typhon. This you may find a little claustrophobic, as did the ancient geographer Strabo, who ventured in convinced that he had discovered his own entrance to the Underworld. Typhon was a mythical triple-headed scaly dragon, and when I visited the cave it smelt as if its former resident had only just moved out.

Just north is the Cave of Hell (Cehennem Deresi), which plunges sheer and dark into the earth, with no apparent way out (or in). Those who insisted upon inspecting their future permanent accommodation used to be able to descend by a ladder.

There are several other nearby caves of diminishing magnitude, spookiness and interest.

ISKELE

See Anamur, page 140.

KARATAŞ

45 km S of Adana, at the tip of the delta. This little hideaway has a pleasant beach and is usually empty, even in the summer – unless you arrive as I once did on a public holiday, when the entire population of Adana descends.

KANYTELIS (KANLIDIVANE)

Inland off Rt 400, 13 km W of Erdemli, following sign for 3 km to Kanlidivane, the Turkish name for this spot. The modern Turkish name means 'wild place filled with blood', and refers to the ancient inhabitants' custom of tossing criminals into the chasm to be devoured by wild beasts.

The site of ancient Kanyletis has yet to be excavated, and its hillside location retains an air of mystery (some say, of menace). Steps descend into the chasm, at the bottom of which you can see a number of carved figures and Greek inscriptions. The city itself lies in ruins all around the chasm. There are some **temples**, a fine Greek **tower**, and a few tumbledown Byzantine **basilicas**.

The chief attraction remains the atmosphere, which is best experienced towards dusk, when the silence becomes quite eerie – and you can feel yourself far removed from the grim reality of the present to an even grimmer past.

KIZKALESI ⌫

27 km E of Silifke on coast off Rt 400. An attractive little resort with a sandy beach and a couple of romantic castles. One of these is on its own island a hundred metres offshore (only strong swimmers should try to reach it). This stronghold is also known as Kizkalesi, which means Maiden's Castle. It has the usual tragi-pathetic story about a maiden who was locked away in order to evade her foretold death by snake-bite. (The snake eventually slipped in amongst some figs and had his venomous way, unaware that he was only meant to be a Freudian symbol.)

There are interesting nearby **rock tombs** and a **necropolis**.

MAMURE KALESI

8 km E of Anamur on the sea shore off Rt 400. This is perhaps the best preserved of all the medieval castles in Turkey, superbly situated right on the sea. It has castellated battlements, many towers of different shapes and sizes, and even a (rather clogged) moat – just like all real castles should have.

The original fortress on this spot dates from the 3rdC AD, but the pre-

• *Street market, Mersin.*

sent meticulously magnified plaything was built by the Crusaders as an outpost of the Kingdom of Cyprus. Over the centuries it fell into decay, but was re-used during the First World War as a coastal defence. (The Turks suspected that the British might invade from Cyprus, but overestimated British military intelligence.) Nowadays the inside is peacefully derelict, but you can still walk the battlements and look down on the waves breaking below.

In my earlier troubador incarnation I once spent an evening playing my guitar on the beach beneath the walls under a full moon, while my audience rendered this romantic experience endurable by drinking her way through a bottle of wine.

Castrophiles and would-be troubadors should also try visiting the nearby Crusader castle of **Softa Kalesi** (take road inland off Rt 400 further east at Bozyazi and follow signs). Softa Kalesi is a forbidding ruin atop an outcrop of rock, its name meaning Castle of the Fanatics. This was for a time a pirate stronghold, but the present structure is largely Byzantine. It's quite a climb if you want to get up to the castle – and

• *Opposite: sherbet seller, Adana.*

there's not much to see when you get there. Best viewed from a distance.

MERSIN ⛴ ✕
A modern port city, with regular ferries to northern Cyprus and Syria. An enchanting spot for those who enjoy watching maritime activity in a moderately busy harbour, but of no interest otherwise.

SILIFKE ⛴ ✕
140 km E *of Anamur on* Rt 400. Fairly pleasant, rather ordinary town: Turkey beyond the tourist façade, with life slowed down to a leisurely pace. It is a useful base for exploring the many excellent nearby sites, including **Uzuncaburç** and **Cennet Ve Cehennem**, pages 145 and 141. Or it can be used as an overnight stop before catching the ferry at Taşucu – see page 145.

Despite its ordinariness the town has an interesting history. It was founded by Seleuceia, one of Alexander the Great's generals. It became capital of the Seleuceian Empire and was named after its founder, who so liked naming cities after members of his family that he called no fewer than 16 cities

143

Antioch after his father.

In 1190 the Emperor Frederick Barbarossa arrived here from Germany with his great army on the Third Crusade to the Holy Land. Unfortunately he went for a swim in the river and drowned (some say because he insisted upon wearing his armour as a bathing costume). And that was the end of the Third Crusade.

The town **museum** is worth a brief visit: its coin collection is genuinely interesting. From the walls of the medieval **castle** there are fine views out over the town and the surrounding countryside.

SOLI

At Viranşehir, just W of Mersin's outskirts. Unlike the claim which was made to me by the hotel-owner in Side (see page 136) this city's name actually has entered the English language. In ancient times its inhabitants were notorious for speaking such bad Greek that the word *solekismos* was coined to describe their speech. This has come down to us as the word solecism, meaning a verbal blunder.

The city was founded by colonists

• *Metal workshop, Antakya.*

from the island of Rhodes in the early 7thC BC. Six centuries later it was conquered by the Armenian king, Tigranes the Great, who moved the entire population to his new capital on the River Tigris (a city which he modestly named Tigranocerta). Soli flourished during Roman times, when it too suffered from a spell of nomenclatic immodesty – being named Pompeiopolis after Pompey. At its height the city contained more than a quarter of a million inhabitants, but now it is just a ruin.

The most interesting sight is the grand **ceremonial roadway**, once lined with 200 columns, of which almost a fifth are still standing. The Turks called the place Viranşehir, meaning city of ruins – an apt description.

The nearby village of the same name has an uninviting mud beach lapped by polluted waters from nearby Mersin. Plunge at your peril.

TARSUS

31 km NE of Mersin on Rt 400. Several events of importance happened at Tarsus, but there's not much of interest here nowadays. The main commercial activity is dependent upon the surrounding cotton harvests – yes, this is the Turkish Deep South.

That said, the faintly ramshackle old houses and equally ramshackle streets (axles beware) do have a distinct charm. They are best explored on foot. In fact, the oldest remains of Tarsus are beneath a large mound, which can be seen as you drive in on the western edge of the city. Recent excavations have revealed no fewer than 23 layers of habitation: down, down, down through the rubbish heaps and razings of history to the origins of time – which in this case is around 6300 BC. (According to an Islamic legend, the city was founded by Seth, a son of Adam and Eve.)

Early Greek settlers arrived here in 1100 BC. When Alexander the Great conquered the city in 333 BC he caught a bad chill after a swim in the river, but unfortunately for the rest of the world he recovered in time to set out on his megalomaniac expedition. By the 2ndC BC the city had a sizeable Jewish population. Then in 41 BC Cleopatra arrived for her celebrated meeting with Mark Antony. According to Shakespeare (who plagiarized Plutarch, who plagiarized even earlier sources):

the barge she sat in, like a burnished throne
burn'd on the water: the poop was
beaten gold,
purple the sails, and so perfumed that
the winds were love-sick with them.

All this was too much for Mark Antony, who was soon behaving like the wind in a perfumed purple sail himself. Nowadays you can see the Roman ruin of what used to be called Cleopatra's gate, which with ungallant hindsight the Turks now call Kancik Kapisi (The Gate of the Bitch).

Around 5 AD Saul of Tarsus was born here, one of the large Jewish community. After the experience on the road to Damascus which led to his name transplant, St Paul energetically travelled this entire region rallying the faithful to the Christian cause and laying down the law on church dogma. Heretics and disbelievers crossed swords with him at their peril, much like the Christians before he had seen the light.

TAŞUCU 🛏

11 *km S of Silifke on* Rt 400. This port has little to recommend it, apart from the regular ferry and hydrofoil service which runs to Cyprus – but only to the Turkish northern half. Services leave most days for Kyrenia, now called Girne.

UZUNCABURÇ

See *Local Explorations: 6.*

If *you want to see Alahan as well, see also* Local Explorations: 6.

RECOMMENDED RESTAURANTS

TURKISH DELIGHTS
The eastern Mediterranean coast of Turkey is justly renowned for its fish, much of it freshly caught on the day you eat it. Try *buglama* (the local variant of *bouillabaisse*) a rich fish stew with that spicy Turkish extra. For another novelty, try *hamsi*: fresh anchovies fried in batter. My favourite is *hiliç* – swordfish kebab, usually with peppers and tomatoes. But make sure that the swordfish is fresh and not dry, as then it can become chewy.

ANAMUR
There's nothing I'd particularly recommend in town. Your best bet is to head 5 km down the road to the beach resort of Iskele, where there are a number of cheap and cheerful holiday restaurants.

MERSIN
If by this stage you're feeling like a little gastronomic reassurance, you can always try the coffee shop in the **Hilton** at Adnan Menderes Bulvari 3310. Otherwise you're best off at one of the restaurants down near the port on Ismet İnönü Bulvari.

SILIFKE
Kale Restaurant, L-LL; *by the castle; tel.* 7591 1521.

An attractive spot with reasonable prices, and a fine view out over the city. Some of the waiters speak comprehensible English; all of them are polite and welcoming.

<u>Central Turkey</u>

Between Adana and Kayseri
Taurus Mountains and Southern Cappadocia

320 km; map Kümmerly + Frey, 1:1,000,000

This region stretches from the eastern shores of the Mediterranean up across the Taurus, or Toros, Mountains (Orta Toroslar) and into one of the most historic parts of Turkey. It contains some superb mountain scenery; the vastnesses of the inland steppe; and three historic cities – Adana, Niğde and Kayseri.

Adana is the fourth largest city in Turkey, mentioned in the Old Testament. Niğde is a virtually unspoilt provincial city which has been guarding the mountain passes since Hittite times well over three millennia ago. At the northern edge of the region is the historic city of Kayseri. The central citadel here, and the nearby mosques, form one of the best unspoilt traditional city centres you'll find in the land. If you have time, explore the city streets, searching out the dozens of ancient mausoleums which crop up everywhere from the walls of a bath-house to the middle of a roundabout.

Other attractions of this section include my suggested detour to the mysterious underground cities of Derinkuyu and Kaymakli; and the important wetland bird sanctuary at Sultansazligi. Just north of here is one of Turkey's ski resorts at Mount Erciyes, also a fine walking area in the summer months.

Travelling through the whole region makes a comparatively long journey. You could cover it in a couple of days, but if you want to have time to see a selection of sights, allow four to five days.

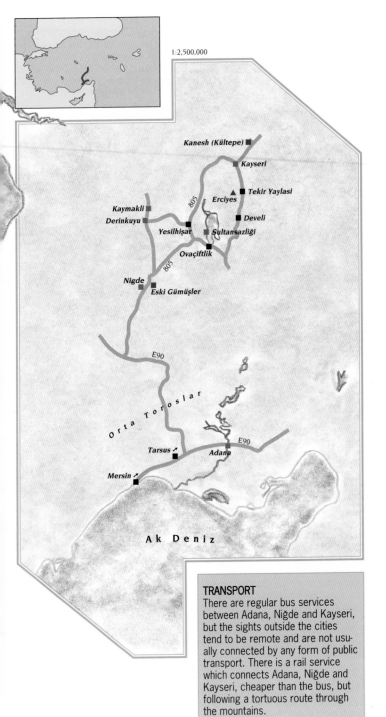

1:2,500,000

Kanesh (Kültepe)

Kayseri

Erciyes ▲ Tekir Yaylasi

Kaymakli
Derinkuyu
Yesilhisar ■ Sultansazliği
Develi

Ovaçiftlik

805

Niğde
Eski Gümüşler

E90

O r t a   T o r o s l a r

E90

Tarsus
Adana

Mersin

A k   D e n i z

TRANSPORT

There are regular bus services between Adana, Niğde and Kayseri, but the sights outside the cities tend to be remote and are not usually connected by any form of public transport. There is a rail service which connects Adana, Niğde and Kayseri, cheaper than the bus, but following a tortuous route through the mountains.

• *Ulu Camii (the Great Mosque), Adana.*

SIGHTS & PLACES OF INTEREST

ADANA ⚑ ✕

69 km NE of Mersin on Rt 400. After Istanbul, Ankara and Izmir, Adana is the largest city in Turkey, with a population of more than one million. It can get oppressively hot here in the summer, but the city has a number of gardens and a pleasant river-side park which can go some way towards alleviating the high-decibel oven effect of a mid-summer day's nightmare.

This is the main city of the Cilician plains, and its geographical position has contributed both to its importance and even on several occasions to its downfall.

According to legend the city was founded by Adanos, the son of the Greek god Uranus. There is a reference in the Old Testament to King Solomon

buying horses from here. In the early centuries BC the city was sometimes a Greek colony, and at other times fell to the Persian Empire.

More permanent prosperity came when the Romans took over. In 2ndC AD, during the reign of the Emperor Hadrian, a bridge was built over the river. This still stands and remains in use.

After the Roman era Adana became a fortified city at the edge of the Byzantine Empire, but in the following centuries its exposed position meant that it was overrun by a succession of conquerors – including the Selçuks, Arabs and the Armenians. In the early 16thC the city was finally occupied by the forces of Selim I and became part of the Ottoman Empire.

When this empire eventually collapsed after its defeat in the First World War, Adana was occupied for a couple of years by the French. The city now owes its prosperity to the cotton market, also to gold trading.

Adana has several interesting sights. The best is **Taş Köprü**, the Roman stone bridge which spans the River Seyhan. This has 21 arches (three now filled in) and was built by a local engineer called Auxentius between 117 and 138 AD. This work rate – one arch per year – suggests that either Auxentius was building for posterity, or wanted to eke out the contract. Until a dam was built upstream, the river was navigable as far as this bridge.

Between Taş Köprü and the Bazaar lies Ulu Camii (the Great Mosque), built in the early 16thC in the Syrian style with black and white marble. Inside there are some fine tombs and mosaics.

The nearby park contains the **tomb** of the great Turkish poet **Ziya Paşa,** author of the timeless lines:

*The needle of my passion
sews your name into my heart.*

The local **Archaeological Museum** near the river is the usual tired collection of provincial relics, or a fascinating treasure trove of great architectural finds, depending upon your tolerance level, and the heat. Their collection of Hittite seals from Tarsus, and the gold collection, both fall into the latter class for me – though I confess to finding the rest a little less fascinating.

There is also an **Ethnographic Museum**, housed in a building that was once a Christian church. This has some fine Koranic texts (calligraphy at its finest) and a discouraging example of a nomadic tent.

If the heat becomes too much, try a drive up to the artificial **lake** created by the damming of the river. Just over 10 km north of town you come to a number of swimming places. They're admittedly pretty grim – but it's either the lake or the oven air.

ESKİ GÜMÜŞLER
See Niğde, page 152.

KANESH (KÜLTEPE)
NW off Rt 300 15 km NE of Kayseri. This site was occupied from earliest times. The experts have reason to believe that it was first settled around 4000 BC in the early Copper era. Then came the Assyrians. The Hittite civilization came into being here around the start of the 2nd millennium BC and flourished for more than 700 years. This late Bronze Age culture centred on Kanesh. Thousands of clay tablets were found here, giving us a detailed record of this civilization.

Many superb finds from the site are on display in the Archaeological Museum in Kayseri. These include a mysterious Sphinx Head and several cuneiform tablets. Unfortunately the most valuable finds have been hijacked by the Anatolian Museum in Ankara.

KAYAKEVI
See Mount Erciyes, page 152.

KAYSERI ⊨ ✕
280 km SE of Ankara. This city is traditionally the capital of Cappadocia, and believes in living up to its past. It has an uncompromisingly eastern air: Muslim standards of dress are increasingly expected. On the other hand, the people also maintain a traditional hospitality towards strangers.

The setting is magnificent, with rising forests and meadows beyond the domes and minarets, and to the south the distant snows of Mount Erciyes rising to almost 4,000 m. Modern building has begun to blight (or to bring into 20thC) this ancient city, but much of its fine past remains.

This entire region was a centre of the Hittite civilization in the late Bronze Age of the 2nd millennium BC. The Hittites almost certainly had a settlement here, but the earliest remains are mainly from ancient Greek times. The city saw a golden era during the Roman occupation, and during the reign of Tiberius it was named Caeserea after him. During the Byzantine Empire it was the birthplace of St Basil, who beame the local bishop, and played a formative role in

---

RECOMMENDED HOTELS

ADANA
Otel Ipek Palas, L-LL; *Inonu Caddesi 103, tel. Adana 010 60.*

Centrally situated. Moderately spartan rooms with private showers at economic rates. Helpful service in eccentric English. Fan-conditioning and public TV (binoculars necessary during important football matches).

KAYSERI ⊨ ✕
There are two types of hotel in Kayseri: the modern (rare), and the prehistoric (more than enough to delight entire teams of archaeologists.) The former:

Hotel Titiz, LL; *Maarif Caddesi 7; tel. 351 7197.*

Modern hotel with TV and bath in every room. Welcoming staff of smiling inscrutability (i.e. little English).

For the historian:

Hotel Turan, LL-LLL; *27 Mayis Caddesi; tel. 351 1968.*

A traditional hotel, which presumably gained its two official stars by sheer persistence. Here you will find that character is not necessarily a synonym for awfulness. I stay here by choice. Excellent restaurant on the roof (a godsend in the heat).

NIGDE
Otel Evim, L; *Hirkumet Meydani; tel. 483 11860.*

Central hotel right by Atatürk Square. The usual monastic decoration, but showers in each room. Boasts a lift, but purely for decoration when I was last here.

DETOUR – **DERINKUYU AND KAYMAKLI, UNDERGROUND CITIES**
17 km N of Niğde turn N off Rt 350 on to Rt 765 in direction of Derinkuyu, reached in 30 km. (For other interesting sights which can covered in conjuction with this trip, see Turkey Overall: 10.)

Until you actually see these undergound cities, it's difficult to comprehend precisely how amazing they are. The original underground settlements were dug into the rock in 2nd millennium BC, but were extended through later periods of occupation until some of them could hold as many as 20,000 occupants. Almost certainly, the dwellings were first constructed by the Hittites, and were probably extended when they came under threat from the eastern spread of the Greeks after the fall of Troy in the 12thC BC. Later they were used by early Christians.

Their complexity is astonishing. Even more astonishing is how the inhabitants managed to accommodate all that was necessary to survive – everything from living quarters to grain stores, cattle compounds to public drinking pools.

If you drive north along Route 765 from Niğde, you come first to the

• *Market above underground city, Derinkuyu.*

village of **Derinkuyu**. This takes its name from the underground city, whose name means 'deep well'. The city has still not yet been fully excavated, and you'll see why when you descend into the underground passages. They are now lit, but remain distinctly claustrophobic in places. A few facts will give you an idea (but only an idea) of the sheer scale of the place. Derinkuyu is now known to have at least eight levels, descending more than 50 m into the ground. Already, barely 2,000 square metres have been mapped out, but the archaeologists are well aware that much, much more remains to be explored.

The guided tour takes you through parts of the top two floors. Of particular interest are the **rock chapel**, the individual **burial chambers** and the **prison**. Perhaps the greatest feat of all is the ventilation system, whose shafts ensured that fresh air circulated even at the lowest levels. Those who wish to see more should drive on the further 10 km to **Kaymakli**, where there is another similar monument to troglodyte perversity.

the establishment of the eastern monasteries.

For a few years at the end of 11thC the city was ruled by the Crusaders, who had become side-tracked from their eponymous task in the Holy Land. Just over 150 years later the Mongol Hordes of Genghis Khan arrived. After having pillaged and plundered their way across over 7,000 km of Asia, the little men on their ponies were beginning to lose interest in foreign travel by the time they arrived in Kayseri. After customarily slaughtering the entire population and razing most of the city to the ground, they found that they rather liked the place and decided to settle.

The Mongols ruled for almost a century before the local governor decided to declare himself independent of Ulan Bator. He set himself up as the ruler of his own private emirate, but this independent outpost of Mongolia was to last for less than half a century.

In the ensuing complex struggles the place briefly became part of Egypt before the Ottoman Turks took over on a more permanent basis in 1515 under the forbidding figure of Selim the Grim. There are numerous sights worth seeing, mainly centred on the historic heart. The very centre of this is occupied by İç Kale, the ancient citadel. The walls were built in local black vol-

• *In a Kayseri carpet bazaar.*

canic stone. Inside it is now a shopping precinct, but there are still a few stairways which climb to the ramparts, where you have a view over the city.

Just west of here are the old **covered markets**, three in all. The oldest, Bedesten, dates from the late 15thC and is now the main carpet market. The local carpets are of the highest quality, but don't expect to come away with any amazing bargains. The Kayseris are well aware of the value of their product, and are renowned throughout this hard-bargaining land for their hard bargaining. The nearby Vezirhani market was built in 1727. This also sells carpets, but you can find leather goods and clothes here as well. The later Covered Bazaar (built in 1859) is said to contain more than 500 shops, whose proprietors are all desperate to practise their bargaining tecnique on innocent foreigners.

Kayseri has several fine mosques. The **Hunat Hatun** complex, which stands to the east of the citadel, was built in 1228 by Sultan Alladin Keykubat for his favourite wife, whose tomb it contains. The mosque itself is one of the finest examples of Selçuk architecture still standing. The religious seminary in the complex has been turned

• *Adana kebab.*

into the local **Ethnographic Museum**. Like me, you may find the building a little more interesting than its somewhat mundane contents, which consist mainly of domestic utensils of more or less primitive provenance, some tatty old costumes and a few swords.

Other interesting mosques include **Ulu Camii** (the Great Mosque) which took more than 100 years to build and was completed in the 13thC, and Kurşunlu Camii which is famous for its lead dome.

The **Archaeological Museum**, southeast of the city centre on Kisla Caddesi, is especially interesting. It has some superb Hittite finds from the Bronze Age settlement at Kanesh (see page 149) as well as relics from the classical period.

Kayseri is also famous for its ornate **tombs**, which are scattered at odd spots throughout the city. The most ornate, the 13thC **Doner Cumbet**, is in the middle of a roundabout near the Archaeological Museum. Its Turkish name means 'Revolving Tomb', which was originally supposed to be a reference to its miraculous properties, but now only applies to the traffic.

MERSIN
See Turkey Overall: 8.

MOUNT ERCIYES
25 km S of Kayseri, on the road to Develi. This mountain is in fact an extinct volcano. It rises to over 3,900 m and dominates the southern skyline of Kayseri. You can drive to it in less than half an hour. (Buses only go as far as Hisarak, leaving you with 15 km to hitch or walk – usually the latter, alas.)

At **Tekir Yaylasi** (on the road, over 2,000 m up) there's a ski lodge (Kayakevi). In the winter season (Dec–Apr) people ski here, witness the chairlift. In summer there's hiking: it's demanding terrain, unsuitable for beginners and the not-terribly-fit.

NIĞDE 🚤 ✕
106 km S of Kayseri on Rt 805. A strategically important town astride the main route between Cappodocia and Cilicia, guarding the pass which runs through the mountains.

This rather ordinary spot has witnessed the usual comings and goings of great armies, which invariably left the place a heap of rubble. Under the name of Nakida it crops up in early Hittite records, and didn't become Turkish until the Selçuks overran it in the late 11thC. But just over two centuries later when it was visited by Ibn Battutah, the great Arab traveller who roamed widely through this region in 14thC, the place was once again in ruins. This time it was the result of a visit by the Mongol hordes of Genghis Khan, who must have found that the pillaging here failed to live up to their expectations, because they didn't bother to press on much further into the region.

There's not much to see, though if this is as far north as you get, be sure to visit **Eski Gümüşler**, north-east of town off the main Rt 805 to Kayseri. This is a monastery compound which remains in surprisingly good repair, and attracts surprisingly few visitors. There are some fine murals in the 10thC chapel, and the monastery itself is carved into the rock. It used to be the sort of place you could regard as your own secret: a spiritual sanctuary to remember when the pagan world of home became too much.

OVAÇIFTLIĞI

See Sultansazlığı, below.

TARSUS

See Turkey Overall: 8.

SULTANSAZLIĞI

Wetlands lying 45 km S of Kayseri, between Yeşilhisar on Rt 805 and Develi S of Mount Erciyes. Sultansazlığı means The Sultan's Marshes. The region consists of several salt lakes, fresh water marshes and miles of dried and drying mud flats. This makes for one of the most spectacular bird sanctuaries you're likely to see outside Africa. The site happens to be on the main migration routes of a large variety of birds. In fact it's a crossroads, where migrants from Africa turn left for Eastern Europe or right for southern Russia – and no matter how tired they are, or how far they've come, they never mistake the turning.

As well as storks and waders of many kinds you may well catch sight of pelicans and flamingos. The surrounding mountains and steppes also harbour eagles – including golden eagles. It is claimed that over 300 bird species have now been recorded in this area, (though sadly no parrots, which don't willingly migrate).

The best place to start is Ovaçiftliği, the small village to the south of the wetlands, south-east of Yeşilhisar off Rt 805. Here there's a viewing tower; guided tours and boat trips (water levels permitting). The best times to visit

are the main migration seasons, spring and early autumn. In summer some parts become rather parched, but there's still plenty to see. Sultansazlığı really is something different.

RECOMMENDED RESTAURANTS

ADANA

The city is famous for its Adana kebab, which is made from packed lamb mince and fiery peppers. If you're not impressed by this, try pot luck with one of the Syrian dishes which are served in many of the restaurants. They can be exquisitely spicy.

Yeni Onbasilar Restorant, L-LL; *Ataturk Caddesi; tel. Adana 11 41 78.*

Best reasonably priced menu in town. Handily situated (up some stairs) across the street from the tourist office.

KAYSERI

Kayseri is famous for its time-honoured spicy sausage, called Sucuk.

My favourite eating place here is the roof-top restaurant of the Hotel Turan (see page 149).

Otherwise you can eat well in the centre of town at:

Iskender Kebap Salonu, L-LL; 27 *Mayis Caddesi 5; tel 351 2769*

You dine upstairs looking down on the sweltering hordes thronging from the nearby citadel. Across the way is the Hunat Hatum Mosque. Those who want the full oriental experience should venture up another flight of stairs to the smarter Aile Salonu (Family Saloon) where one of the waiters will chivalrously present your female companion with a flower, but not a menu, which is for your eyes only.

NIDĞE
Aile Pastenesi L-LL; *Atatürk Meydani; no booking.*

Relaxed provincial restaurant in the main square by the statue of Atatürk. Great for a long lunch of meze and cold white wine in the shade.

Between Kayseri and Ankara
The Heart of Cappadocia

360 km; map GeoCenter Euro-Country, Western Turkey, 1:800 000

Here you will find the most bizarre sight in Turkey: the cave dwellings of Cappadocia. There are other places in the world where people dwell in caves, but these are unique, both visually and historically. Their setting, amongst volcanic rocks eroded by centuries of rain and wind into 'fairy chimneys', must have been spectacular long before human occupants honeycombed the rocks with caves, tunnels and churches. The religious community here produced such celebrated Byzantine figures as Basil the Great and Nikos Monopthalmos (One-eyed Nick). Leading lights from Cappadocia were to do the theological homework on the knotty Christian doctrine of the Holy Trinity.

If you start from Ankara your journey takes you south across the barren steppe of central Anatolia, past the 100 km-long salt lake of Tuz Gölü, to the oasis town of Aksaray. Nearby is the Ihlara Valley, a beautiful gorge with numerous cave churches. From Aksaray it's just over 60 km to the heart of Cappadocia. The main sights here lie in the triangle of Nevşehir, Ürgüp and Avanos, with the most spectacular (and most popular) being at Göreme.

South of Nevşehir you can take a side-trip to the underground cities at Derinkuyu and Kaymanli (see Turkey Overall: 9). And north of Nevşehir lies Hacibektaş where the 13thC Sufi philosopher Haci Bektaş founded his powerful order of dervishes, the Bektarşi.

From the Cappadocian sights you can continue east to the ancient city of Kayseri, set beneath the snow-capped peak of Erciyes Daği, which is almost 4,000 metres high.

This 360-km journey can be covered in a day, but that means you miss some of the most exciting sights you can see anywhere in the world. It's best to allow three days.

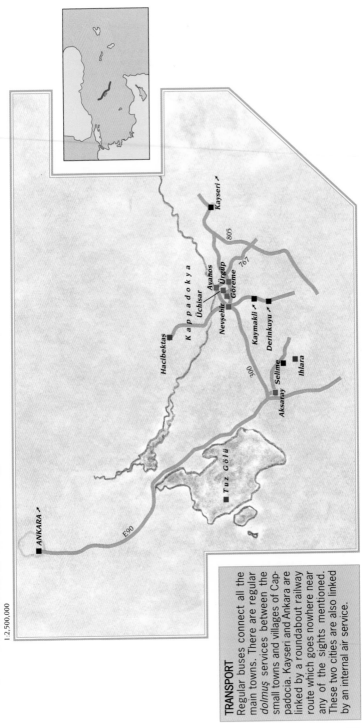

1:2,500,000

Kayseri

805

767

K a p p a d o k y a

Avanos
Üçhisar
Ürgüp
Göreme

Nevşehir

Kaymaklı
Derinkuyu

Hacıbektaş

300

Selime
Ihlara

Aksaray

T u z   G ö l ü

ANKARA

E90

TRANSPORT

Regular buses connect all the main towns. There are regular *dolmuş* services between the small towns and villages of Cappadocia. Kayseri and Ankara are linked by a roundabout railway route which goes nowhere near any of the sights mentioned. These two cities are also linked by an internal air service.

SIGHTS & PLACES OF INTEREST

AKSARAY 🛏 ✕

Largish market town 225 km S of Ankara on Rt E90. When the 14thC Arab traveller Ibn Battuta passed through Aksaray, the surrounding countryside was green, filled with gardens and trees, and irrigated by rushing rivulets. Nowadays the town is very much an oasis in the wilderness. Until the 11thC this was the Byzantine city of Achelais, but its exposed location meant that it was overrun and destroyed by the Mongols in the 13thC. After Constantinople (modern Istanbul) fell to Mehmet the Conqueror in 1453, many of the inhabitants of Aksaray were transported to help repopulate the new Ottoman capital. The district where they lived is known to this day as Aksaray.

For centuries Aksaray has been a **carpet-making** centre, and this is a good place to buy your souvenir. Aksaray has one unusual sight – Turkey's answer to the Leaning Tower of Pisa. This is the **leaning red-brick minaret** of the 14thC **Nakkasi Mosque**, in the old part of town. Also worth seeing is the **Zinciriye Medresesi**, a former Islamic theological seminary which was built by the Selçuks in 1336. This has an atmospheric courtyard, and today houses the somnolent silence of the town Archaeological Museum, a haven of calm which houses little of interest to other than the expert or the perverse.

ANKARA
See Turkey Overall: 11.

CAPPADOCIA (KAPPADOKYA)
Today the name Cappadocia refers just to the region with the caves; formerly it described a large area of central and northern Turkey. Once upon a time this region was invaded by a king and his army. The desperate unarmed locals prayed to Allah to save them, and He was so moved by their pleas that He turned the king and his army into stone. This is the mythological explanation for the region's fantastic appearance.

Cappadocia is unique. It is a region of soft volcanic rock sculpted into fabulous shapes by the erosion of wind and rain through the millennia. These rocks are described by the locals as 'fairy chimneys', but this is only half the story. The rocks are pitted with thousands of man-made caves. When you stand in the midst of this landscape you can detect all kinds of shapes amongst the rocks, but most of all human heads: bleached skulls, ghosts, agonized faces. (However this Rorschach test may well produce different results for someone with a sunnier temperament.) Towering above all this are the snow-capped peaks of the dormant volcanoes which thousands of years ago produced this vast spill of volcanic rock.

RECOMMENDED HOTELS

AKSARAY
Otel Ihlara, L-LL; *Eski Sanyi Caddesi; tel.* 481 11842.

Near the city centre, signposted off main street. Most rooms have bath or shower. The reception desk will recommend a particularly good stomach remedy for 'Atatürk's Revenge'.

GÖREME
Melek Motel, LL; *Göreme Village; tel.* 485 71463.

A deservedly popular spot run by a cheery Dutch exile, who does everything except carve out further rooms from the rocks. Some of the rooms here are authentic cave dwellings, ideal for those who feel nostalgic for those golden pre-historic days.

ÜRGÜP
Hotel Eyfel, L-LL; *Elgin Sokak 8; tel.* 486 1325.

Superb little spot, with a superb little swimming pool (and I mean little). There's also a shower in every room, for those who wish to conduct their aquatic pursuits in private.

One night I enquired about the unusual name of this road – Elgin Sokak – in the *Harem* disco down the road, and was informed by a knowledgeable schoolmaster from Munich that it was named after Lord Elgin, the Scottish aristocrat who stole the marbles from the Acropolis in Athens. In his words: 'Any man who harms the Greeks is a hero in Turkey.'

• *Easy riders, Cappadocia.*

But not all the rock is the same, and you'll find as you travel about that the fairy chimneys and skulls give way to sheer canyons, unexpected plateaux, balancing rocks and lines of sinister Ku-Klux-Klansmen.

The earliest people to settle here in significant numbers were the Hittites, an Indo-European people who came from beyond the Caucasus in the 2nd millennium BC. Cappadocia was consequently defeated by the usual succession of Lydians, Persians, Alexander the Great, the Romans and so forth – yet owing to its geographical inaccessibility it retained a quasi-independent way of life. Christian hermits first began living here in the 4thC, and were soon joined by families of anchorites (who usually brought along their wives, children, goats, donkeys and chickens). Each family would carve out its home in the tufa – the soft volcanic rock. Contrary to first appearances, this is a surprisingly fertile region. The volcanic ash is rich in potassium, and the locals also used pigeon droppings as fertilizer. (Productive pigeons were kept in coops carved in the stone.) Crops were grown to support the cave-dwellers (or troglodytes), and they even grew their own grapes. Indeed, it is said that the local wine of Cappadocia has been produced by the same method since Hittite times more than 3,000 years ago. Be sure to try some, just for the experience. It is just as you would expect a wine produced by Hittite troglodytes to taste, and the hangover is genuinely pre-historic.

The early Christian communities here carved out hundreds of underground churches, many decorated with exceptional frescoes. These depict religious scenes of compelling simplicity and spirituality. This is not great art, but the simple expression of a profoundly religious way of life. It is no accident that Christianity's innermost concept – that of the Trinity – was in part developed by theologians living here. According to their thinking, the Holy Trinity was God in a single essence manifest in three forms: The Father, the Son and the Holy Ghost. Echoing the religion of this region, the idea was both profound and simple.

When Cappadocia was conquered by the Selçuk Turks in the 11thC, the local communities came to something of an accommodation with their rulers. And when things went wrong, they simply retired to inaccessible places and dug out further cave homes in secret. Many of these (and their churches) have yet to be discovered.

Christianity continued to flourish in Cappadocia even after the Ottoman takeover. The local Christians – mainly Greeks and Armenians – were able to live without too much interference in the midst of Muslim Turkey. Then came the horrors of the First World War and its aftermath – the Armenian Massacre of 1915-16 and the Smyrna Massacre of 1922. The population exchange took place and the Christians were forced to leave – after continuously occupying the area for longer than 1,500 years. They left behind them more than a thousand churches built over a period of a thousand years. Today, just over one hundred of these churches still contain their original frescoes, while many others are crumbling into disrepair (or in a few cases have simply not yet been discovered).

Most of the best sights in this region exist in the triangle between **Avanos**, **Nevşehir** and **Ürgüp**. It's only just over

20 km between Nevşehir and Ürgüp, which means that all are within easy reach. Of all these sights, the **Göreme Valley** is the best: don't miss it if you only have time to visit one location.

Places to visit in Cappadocia:

Avanos

20 km NE of Nevşehir. Avanos is famous for its earthenware pottery, which you can see being made. Nearby at **Özkon-ak** there is an underground city. This was discovered by the local *muezzin* in his garden. (A *muezzin* is a Muslim official, whose duties include calling the faithful to prayer from the top of the minaret, usually nowadays through a loudspeaker; often, the voice is taped.) As underground cities go, Avanos is something of a disappointment, especially compared with those of southern Cappodocia – for the latter see below.

Göreme ⋈ ✕

12 km E of Nevşehir. Small town consisting almost entirely of weird troglodytes who never come out into the sun except for a few weeks of the year. These strange people emerge from

• *Avanos.*

their picturesque coloured transport wearing special glasses to protect their weak eyes from the glare of day, and are immediately led off to be relieved of their currency by kindly locals willing to exchange it for carpets or useless trinkets.

The so-called **Open Air Museum** 2 km south-east of town is in fact an excuse for charging you to visit the best of the churches and cave dwellings in the entire region. It's well worth it. This valley has several superb churches, including **Yilanli Kilise** (Church of the Snake), the **New Church** (which contains some superb paintings), and the **Columned Churches** (which mimic above-ground Byzantine churches, complete with domes and pillars).

The big snag here is your fellow troglodytes, who blunder about blindly in groups. Try to position yourself between the progressing groups, so that you can have a look at these churches before the trogs come and completely block the doorway – and thus the light. It's worth bringing a torch as well, if you're planning to explore – either here, or at the other sights.

Nevşehir

71 km E of Aksaray on Rt 300. Nevşehir literally means 'new town'. Three hundred years ago a young man called Ibrahim set out from the local village of Muşkara to seek his fortune in Istanbul. This he found in no uncertain fashion: he eventually became the Sultan's grand vizier (virtually equivalent to prime minister) and married the boss's daughter. In order to improve his background image he decided to build an entirely new home town – Nevşehir – beside his old home village (which can still be seen on the edge of town).

The most important feature of this 300-year-old new town is the **mosque of Damat Ibrahim Paşa**, which was built in 1726. This, together with its outbuildings, stands below the citadel, which has some ruined Byzantine walls and a fine view from the top.

The town also has an **Archaeological Museum** with some interesting local

• *Right and below: Cappadocia rockscapes.*

finds. Best are the early Byzantine relics from the caves, and some rather odd 3rdC stone coffins.

Southern Cappadocia
For the underground cities of **Derinkuyu** and **Kaymakli**, *see Turkey Overall: 9.*

Üçhisar
14 *km E of Nevşehir.* The village here is overlooked by a 50 m-high rock honeycombed with caves and passages. From the top you get a fine view out over a large part of the surrounding region.

Ürgüp 🍴 ✕
21 *km E of Nevşehir.* An avid tourist trap, but none the worse for that. The locals seem to enjoy their predatory way of life. Ürgüp is in the heart of Cappadocia's geological Disneyworld. Above the town many of the caves are still lived in, mainly by donkeys, whose enthusiastic ee-aws compete with the *muezzin's* call to early prayer. In the old part of town you can see some caves which have been adapted for modern human use (glass windows, TV, troglodyte goldfish). The main street has a tourist-generated concentration of carpet, trinket and relic sellers. Look closely (if you are able to put up with the pestering): there are sometimes bargains to be had here.

HACIBEKTAŞ
At *the end of a magnificent drive 46 km N of Nevşehir.* This is the birthplace of the great Anatolian theologian and mystic Haci Bektaş Veli, who founded an important order of dervishes in 13thC. The teachings of this sect were a blend of Sunni and Shiite Muslim teachings and Orthodox Christianity, and were widely adopted at the time. This paved the way for the advance of Islam and the Turkish language into Asia Minor.

The dervishes of the Bektaşi sect were to achieve great political power, mainly through their influence over the Janissaries (the élite corps of the Sultan's army). Unlike many such sects, the Bektaşi were in some respects surprisingly liberal. According to Haci Bektaş himself: 'Society will always remain backward as long as the women are not educated.' He advocated the abandonment of the veil (seven centuries before it was banned by Atatürk)

though as you will see, this repressive garment is now returning – with a vengeance – in some parts. Haci Bektaş also advocated purity, modesty and above all consistency (particularly between public and private behaviour). In pursuit of this, the Bektaşi were to advocate the drinking of wine, and also the eating of food during daytime in Ramadan.

Several Bektaşi customs had Christian echoes – such as baptism with holy water and ritual communion meals.

The Bektaşi were eventually outlawed by Atatürk, along with all other dervish sects. (Their political power base, the Janissaries, were also disbanded at the same time.) But the teachings of the sect and its founder still exert considerable influence in Turkey. Each August, there is a pilgrimage to Haci Bektaşi's tomb here.

You can visit the large 14thC monastery where Haci Bektaş is buried. It has a museum devoted to relics of the sect. In one of the monastery courtyards there is a Lion Fountain which was brought from Egypt in 19thC. But most important of all is the **Rose Courtyard** which has the *türbe* (tomb) of Haci Bektaş. Nearby is his small cell. Don't miss the sacred *Karakazan* (Black Cauldron) which the Janissaries used for their ritual communal meals.

IHLARA VALLEY (PERISTREMA)
20 *km SE of Aksaray on rough road.* This idyllic spot isn't exactly undiscovered, but it attracts far less crowds than the other Cappadocian sights, and out of season you can sometimes find yourself alone here.

The valley itself is really a gorge, with 150-m cliff walls rising from the little river, along whose green banks grow poplar trees and wild olives. In the walls of the gorge there are more than a thousand caves, and at least a hundred churches, some of which are still particularly well preserved. High above the valley to the south rises the 3,200-m peak of **Hasan Dagi**, a dormant volcano whose cone still emits a ribbon of smoke. (It last erupted over 2,000 years ago, just as the classical historian Strabo happened to be passing through the region.)

There are several ways you can see this valley. The ambitious and energetic will choose to walk the 6 km from

Selime in the north down through its entire length to Ihlara at the southern end. (I can assure you from grim experience that this will take you much longer than its length would suggest, and there's much to see on the way.) Those who wish to browse, rather than take part in an endurance test which may keep them in bed for the entire day afterwards, should stop at the **Valley Restaurant**, on the road halfway between the village of Belisirma and Ihlara. Here you can descend the 285 steps down the rock into the gorge. There's also a plan of the gorge here.

Many of the best churches have been given fairytale names by the locals. **Yilanli Kilise** (The Church of the Snakes) contains my favourite murals. These depict in insouciant pre-Freudian style the torments of the damned in Hell – women entwined with writhing snakes (one even having her nipple bitten by a serpent, allegedly because she didn't breast-feed her child). These are pre-Hieronymus, but the Bosch is the same. Other churches which shouldn't be missed are **Pürenli Seki Kilise** (The Church with the Terrace of Pine Needles); and **Sümbüllü Kilise** which translates touchingly but inappropriately as The Church of the Hyacinths.

These three are close to the foot of the steps. Further upstream is **St George's Church**, high on the western cliffs just below Belisirma. This not only has a fine fresco of St George, but is dedicated to the tolerance of the Selçuk Turks. It was founded by a Greek-Christian Emir called Basil. The further you walk from the steps, the more you enter the sanctity and solitude of this highly atmospheric spot.

KAYSERI
See Turkey Overall: 9.

TUZ GÖLÜ
SW *of Rt E90 on the way to Aksaray.* The road runs alongside the edge of this huge salt lake for about 60 km. At certain points you can stop and walk along the salt crust which forms the edge.

The rarity-interest of this hot, shimmering vision soon wears off. My most memorable experience here was seeing a mirage of a string of camels.

RECOMMENDED RESTAURANTS

AKSARAY
The most reliable restaurants in town are in the hotels. For a decent inexpensive meal try **Otel Ihlara, LL** – details in Recommended Hotels, page 156.

For the best restaurant in town, head out to the main road, where you'll find:

Orhan Ağaçli Turistik Tesisleri, L-LL; *Ankara-Adana Asfalti (road); tel.* 481 14910.

North of town at the turn-off for Nevşehir. Smart hotel with smart restaurant, but underneath the veneer the waiters are particularly friendly. Out of season, they are bored and keen to sharpen their linguistic skills with some witty cut-and-thrust. The food is sharp and spicy too. The bill can on occasions be humorously halved.

GÖREME
Mehmet Paşa, LL; *Kayseri Caddesi; tel.* 485 72310.

This restaurant is in a former merchant's house, decorated in traditional style with carpets on the walls. The menu is not particularly imaginative, but what they do produce is superb. Part of the dining area is carved into the rock, to make visiting troglodytes feel at home.

ÜRGÜP
Han Cirgan Restaurant, L-LL; *Cumhuriyet Meydani; tel.* 486 1169.

Here you dine in the leafy courtyard of a former *kervansaray* (traditional caravan inn). Good local dishes, and they even have their own-label bottles of local wine (which still doesn't improve the contents).

Central Turkey

Between Ankara and Istanbul
Ankara and Western Anatolia

420 km; map GeoCenter Euro-Country, Western Turkey, 1:800 000

Istanbul was the capital of three empires, an imperial feat matched by no other city; but for Turkey's new age, starting after the First World War, Atatürk chose Ankara as the capital. Much of the city was built at his behest. It is largely modern, but there are a few sights worth your attention (including a museum worthy of any capital city); and it's a good place to get to know the Turks and what their country is all about.

If you're in Istanbul and want to reach Ankara quickly, the obvious route is the motorway via Düzce. It can suffer from heavy lorry traffic, but the distance is easily covered in a day. If you want to cover the ground quickly in order to explore eastern Turkey, this is the obvious choice.

With time to spare, the southern route via Eskişehir takes you first along the Marmara coast, with a chance to stop off at Termal, an old spa resort; then it's a short drive to the lakeside city of Iznik, ancient Nicaea, once briefly the capital of the Byzantine Empire. Down the road from Eskişehir you can take a detour to historic Kütahya, which was founded by the Phrygians, and on to the superb Roman ruins at Aizanoi, both covered in Local Explorations: 5.

Continuing from Eskişehir down the E90, you can detour north just before Polatli for Gordion, the mysterious Phrygian capital, once home of the fabulous King Midas.

This option means covering around 470 km, and if you're stopping to take in the sights you should allow three to four days.

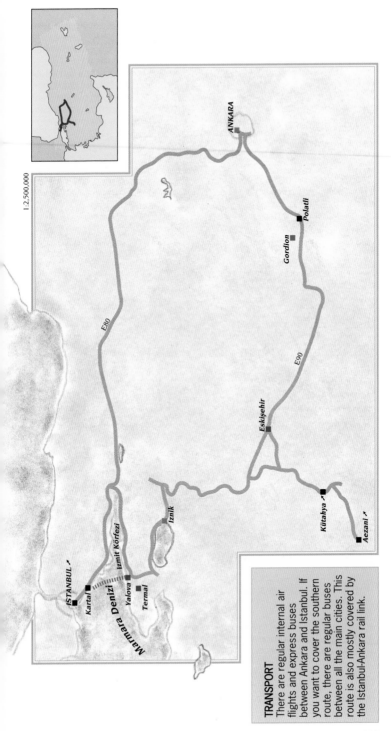

1:2,500,000

TRANSPORT
There are regular internal air flights and express buses between Ankara and Istanbul. If you want to cover the southern route, there are regular buses between all the main cities. This route is also mostly covered by the Istanbul-Ankara rail link.

163

SIGHTS & PLACES OF INTEREST

AIZANOI
See Local Explorations: 5.

ANKARA 🚩 ✕
Some 425 km E of Istanbul. When you get to Istanbul, you feel you've finally reached the East. When you get to Ankara, you find a modern, western-style city, with an international feel. The foreign embassies are here, and this is the centre of Turkey's awesome bureaucracy.

You'll experience some curious juxtapositions. Ankara is busy, yet often nothing actually gets done. It prides itself on being efficient, yet you're always coming across things that don't work. Buildings are constantly being built, but not always finished. Its air of modernity is everywhere, yet it's not long before you discover that this is sometimes only skin deep.

A few facts:
An early variant of the city's name gave us the word Angora, the name of the famous mohair goat wool which comes from this region of Anatolia.

Seventy years ago Ankara had a population of 30,000. Now its population is 3 million. An expansion of a hundredfold in less than a century – an expansion still unrivalled by any modern capital.

Ankara is almost 850 m above sea level. In winter the temperature can be below zero for as long as three months; in summer it's sweltering, but with a low humidity, which makes the heat dry and relatively bearable.

Before the recent introduction of gas fuel, the city burned soft coal. Result: smogs worthy of Dickensian London.

Ever since Ankara became the capital of Turkey, it has been famous for its modernity and its chaos. A mayor complained to its citizens: 'You're always demanding new roads, then you com-

---

RECOMMENDED HOTELS

ANKARA
The best choice of inexpensive hotels in Ankara is around Ulus, the old part of the city just north of the centre. This is also handy for many of the sights. Some of the cheaper hotels can be distinctly tatty and flea-ridden, but this is not the case with:

Otel Akman, L-LL; *Itfaiye Meydani, Tavus Sokak 6; tel. 4 342 4140.*

All rooms have shower or bath, and there is a restaurant next door. For what you get – including laughing liveried staff – this is real value.

If the Akman is full, try the slightly more expensive:

Hotel Sultan, LL; *Bayindir Sokak 35; tel. 4 131 5980.*

Just east of downtown Kizilay, a couple of km south of Roman Ankara. All rooms with shower, and friendly staff (some English spoken).

Luxury hotels in Ankara are not expensive compared with luxury hotels in most other capital cities, so you might like to try:

Buyuk Ankara Oteli, LLL; *Atatürk Bulvari 183; tel. 4 125 6655.*

The swankiest spot in town, right opposite the parliament building. You'll enjoy the swimming pool and the air conditioning. Clientèle often includes a surprisingly broad cross-section. (For example, two archaeology PhDs from Illinois, a Norwegian apprentice orchestra conductor and an Argentinian polo player – all on one night when I was drinking at the bar with an out-of-work London politician.)

IZNIK
Camlik Motel, L; *Gol Kenari; tel. 252 71631.*

Very good value, right by the lake. Good restaurant. All rooms boast a shower which actually works.

TERMAL
Turban Yalova Termal Hotel, LL-LLL; *Termal; tel. 1931 4905.*

Spa resort hotel which, like all such, appears to have survived from a previous era. This one dates from 1930s, is right by the baths, and has a fine view. (Front rooms are more expensive because of this.)

plain about the dust.'

In order to improve the transport, it was decided to dig a subway system. Result: traffic snarl-ups greater than ever before.

The present mayor has promised that he is planning for the 21stC – and indeed, it is possible that by the 21stC all cities will look like this.

Everyone complains that Ankara has no soul, yet the few residents I know all agree that they would prefer to live here rather than anywhere else in Turkey. As one explained to me: 'This is a city with nothing to hold it back. It's a place with no history.'

Actually, there has been a city on this spot for well over two and a half millennia. According to legend it was founded in the 7thC BC by King Midas of Phrygia. This was the mythical King Midas, and everything he touched turned to gold – except, seemingly, the city he founded. In the 4thC BC Ankara was overrun by Alexander the Great, and later became part of the Roman Empire. During this latter period the Romans minted coins here, and the currency of Ankara became a laughing stock because its coins always had an anchor on the back – despite the fact that the city was more than 200 km from the sea. (The Romans had used an anchor as an emblem for the city, mistaking its name for the Greek word for an anchor.)

During the early Christian era St Paul visited the city, which was then in the Roman province of Galatia. He founded a church here, but as soon as he left the church began developing its own ideas. As a result St Paul wrote its members a furious letter telling them to mend their ways. This appears in the Bible as the Epistle to the Galatians.

Later Ankara became a great Byzantine stronghold, and the city was fortified using recycled stones from the Roman ruins. It was spared the wrath of the Mongols, who fortunately decided that they'd had enough of pillaging Asia by the time they got this far. But Tamerlane of Samarkand made up for this by besieging the city at the start of the 15thC. The Ottoman army which came to relieve the siege was defeated at the Battle of Ankara. The Ottoman Sultan Bayezit I was taken prisoner and later exhibited in a cage, where according to one source he died of shame.

After this Ankara returned to being a sleepy provincial backwater. Its 10,000 inhabitants were mainly involved in herding the goats which produced the famous Angora wool. In winter the inhabitants would wrap up against the bitter cold in their mohair skins, and in summer they would flee the mosquitoes from the nearby swamp – taking to the vineyards and grazing grounds in the hills.

Soon after the Turkish defeat in the First World War, Atatürk launched the War of Independence. Owing to the city's central location, he chose Ankara as his headquarters. In October 1923 the victorious Atatürk declared the Turkish Republic and named Ankara as his capital.

At this time Ankara had a population of less than 30,000. Its streets had no pavements or lighting, and there were no below-ground sewers anywhere in the city. Enthusiastic Turks came from all over the land to help build their new capital.

Choosing Ankara as the capital in place of Istanbul was a symbolic break with the old and discredited Ottoman past. The city was also more easily defended than Istanbul, should the great powers decide to intervene in the new republic's affairs. Significantly, it is claimed that Atatürk never even visited Istanbul from the start of the War of Independence until 1927. To begin with the new city was designed in neo-Ottoman style, but Atatürk soon called in modern architects. Hermann Jansen, the architect of Berlin, was commissioned to lay out a system of boulevards, and the new German Bauhaus style of stark modern architecture was employed for many public buildings. Thus Ankara became the vast building site which in many ways it still is.

If you are here for a few days there are a handful of things definitely worth seeing:

Anadolu Medeniyetleri Muzesi (The Museum of Anatolian Civilizations)

Just SW of the citadel. The collection here is the finest of its kind in the world, and is also very well laid out, with exhibits labelled in English and German. Some of the guides (who offer their services on a freelance basis) are exceptionally well informed – whilst a few others are so ill-informed as to render a visit one

• Modern housing, Ankara.

of the hilarious high-spots of your holiday. Take your pick, depending upon your frame of mind: it's fairly obvious which is which, after the briefest of job interviews. Some are freelance schoolmasters making up their pay; others are freelance freeloaders making up as they go along. (For example: 'This plate once belonged to the god Apollo, but he dropped it in a rage when his wife ran away with another god.') The plate in question was quite clearly labelled Roman, and at this point the performance became too much for one of my companions, who had to be assisted from the scene.

The museum is housed in the buildings of a former bazaar and warehouse, which date from the 15thC. The exhibits become more fascinating the more you know about them, so if you don't take a guide at least buy one of the booklets. The finds from Catal Höyük (see Local Explorations: 6) may not look much at first glance, but when you realize that they come from what is possibly the oldest settlement yet discovered anywhere on the planet, they appear in an entirely different light. The section devoted to finds from the Assyrian trading settlement at Kültepe, and the Urartian sections are also of exceptional interest. As are the Hittite exhibits.

Anit Kabir (The Atatürk Mausoleum)
SW of city centre in a park atop a hill. An

• Opposite: the Ankara Sheraton.

essential sight in the city of Atatürk – or at any rate for those who are interested in the tombs of great leaders. As you'd expect, everything is suitably monumental and reverential. Yet the whole place is surprisingly free of bad taste – unlike most such grandiosities.

The Mausoleum is a neo-Modernistic-Hellenistic etcetera, with an austere marble interior, goose-stepping guards, and other less threatening guards who will tell you to put on your shirt or take off your hat. Atatürk was the man who built the modern Turkish nation, though elements of his legacy remain very much in question to this day. Again, the more you know about this remarkable man and his achievements (and what is happening to them today), the more this place will take on meaning.

Roman Ankara
North of the city centre. Here you'll find the rather sparse remains of the **Roman Baths**, the **Temple of Augustus and Rome**, the **Column of Julian** and a few other remnants, all within 300 m or so of each other. Beside the remaining wall of the Temple is the 14thC **Hacibayram Camii**, a mosque dating from the end of the 13thC, built by Haci Bayram Veli, a Muslim saint who founded an order of dervishes. This spot is now revered by pilgrims.

BURSA
See Local Explorations: 1.

ESKIŞEHIR

151 km E of Bursa on Rt 200. An apparently ordinary commercial city – with a surprise. Some 20 km outside town are the world-famous Meerschaum quarries, and in the centre of town you can see shops selling all kinds of Meerschaum *bric à brac*. The pipes, with their bowls carved into all kinds of weird and wonderful heads, are obviously the main attraction, and the best display of these is at Işik Pipo on Satarya Caddesi.

GORDION

96 km SW of Ankara off the E90. Ancient Phrygian capital of King Midas, who features in the Greek myths. (It was he who was granted the 'Midas touch', which turned everything into gold.)

The Phrygians are thought to have come originally from the northern Greek mainland. They crop up in Homer, who refers to their territory here in Anatolia as 'the country of vineyards.' Their capital was named after one of their early kings, Gordios.

The city was destroyed by the Persians in the 6thC BC, then again in the following century by an earthquake, and finally by Alexander the Great in 333 BC. According to legend, it was here that Alexander untied the famous Gordian knot, a puzzle which no one had managed to solve for four centuries. In fact, he cheated – simply slicing the knot in two with his sword – but in doing so still won the prediction of a great destiny.

The site itself is not immediately spectacular, but contains several intriguing features. The precise details of Phrygian culture are still unknown to us, and much of the site remains a mystery. What, for instance, is the secret of the Great Tumulus here? Who was the 60-year-old man whose body lay within it, undisturbed for more than two and a half millennia? Could this have been King Midas himself? The scholars

---

RECOMMENDED RESTAURANTS

ANKARA

The best cheap restaurants tend to be around Ulus.

Yavuz Lokantasi, L; *Konya Sokak 13/F; tel.* 4 311 8508.
    Value for money, friendly service.

Or, if you want simply a snack and a few beers, try:

Santral Kefiterya, L; *Cankiri Caddesi; no booking.*
    Lives up to the individualistic promise of its name. Stays open late; popular with young travellers.

A useful area for reasonably priced eating is around Kizilay. The best place here by far is:

Korfez Lokantasi, L-LL; *Bayindir Sokak 24; tel.* 4 131 1459.
    Surprisingly, for a city such as Ankara, this is a respectable seafood restaurant. You can eat outside in summer on the terrace (but make sure you're in the shade or you'll be roasted before your kebab is even half done).

Those who want something more up-market should try next door:

Washington Restaurant, LL-LLL; *Bayindir 22; tel.* 4 131 2219.
    The Washington has a deserved reputation with locals and foreign residents (so much so that one forbad me from mentioning it). This is Turkish *cuisine* at its best, though without the fancy prices that often accompany such accolades in other international cities.

IZNIK

By far the best choices are down by the lake. The one which will immediately catch your eye is:

Dallas Restaurant, LL; *Gol Kenari; no booking.*
    Fortunately this place bears little relation to the TV series after which it was named. In fact, it's just the spot for a long romantic evening, gazing rapturously at your companion while pretending to listen to all the amazing episodes which you missed. Great local dishes, good fish, and suitably soapy service.

are still arguing. Take a look inside this amazing ancient construction and decide for yourself.

From Roman times onwards this site was derelict. But history returned once again to this area during the first half of the 20thC, when the Turkish army of Atatürk halted the Greek invasion force on the banks of the nearby Sakarya River in 1921. There is a suitably glorious monument to this victory above the nearby town of Polatli.

ISTANBUL

See pages 38-61.

IZNIK ⌘ ✕

77 km NE of Bursa, at E end of Iznik Gölü (Lake Iznit). Nowadays Iznik is little more than a small market town, but at least twice in its history this apparently insignificant spot was the most important place in Christendom.

The city was probably founded around 1000 BC. In the 4thC BC one of Alexander the Great's generals, Lysimachus, named it after his wife Nikaea. Its surrounding walls were heavily strengthened during the Roman era, when Pliny the Younger resided here as governor of the surrounding province.

The first great ecumenical council was held at Nicaea in 325 under the auspices of Constantine the Great. This resulted in the condemnation of the Arian heresy (whose adherents maintained that Christ was not divine) and the formulation of the Nicaean Creed, which laid down the law concerning Christian orthodoxy. (This creed is still strictly enforced by the Orthodox Church.)

A later council was held here in 787 under the Empress Irene, when a pronouncement was made concerning the correct attitude towards icons. (They could be revered but not worshipped.) After the armies of the Fourth Crusade sacked Constantinople (Istanbul) in 1204, Nicaea became a capital city of the displaced Byzantine Empire (along with two rivals – one at Epirus in Greece, and one at Trebizond (modern Trabzon: see Turkey Overall: 13). Two centuries later Tamerlane of Samarkand attempted to raze the place to the ground, but fortunately in his zeal he missed a few buildings. These are now some of the main attractions of the place.

Try a walk along the ancient walls, which once had more than 100 towers. The most interesting remnant of the glorious Byzantine era is the ruined **Church of Sancta Sophia**. This has some mosaics and frescoes, some of which are nearly 1,500 years old. When the Ottomans took Nicaea in the 14thC they turned Sancta Sophia into a mosque. (If it is locked, you can apply for the key at the **museum**, which is a moderate walk away east off the main Kiliçaslan Caddesi.) The museum is housed in Nilüfer Hatun Imareti – a 14thC soup kitchen founded by the daughter of a Byzantine emperor who was married off to the Muslim leader Orhan Gazi. Inside its impressive pillared entrance you'll find a wide range of relics relating to almost the entire history of Iznik. But best of all is the garden, where you can see a fascinating jumble of ancient tombs, inscriptions and column heads.

Just opposite is **Yeşil Camii** (The Green Mosque), a beautifully tiled building in the Persian style which dates from the 15thC. This is generally regarded as the finest of its kind in the land.

KÜTAHYA

See Local Explorations: 5.

TERMAL ⌘

12 km SW of Yalova, inland from Marmara coast. As the name suggests, this is a hot springs spa resort. Many of the buildings are in the 'Ottoman Baroque' style and date from the turn of the century, when partaking of such lukewarm lightly radioactive fluids (both internally and externally) was considered a panacea. Atatürk was a great believer in taking the waters, and built himself a small villa here. This town will be instantly recognizable to all who know Baden Baden or Bath – right down to the small orchestra of aged musicians playing old favourites as you sip your tea.

YALOVA

On the coast 40 km SE of Istanbul across the Sea of Marmara. Pleasant market town and port which can be reached by ferry from Kartal just east of Istanbul, or via Rt 130 around the Gulf of Izmit. Handy for Termal.

<u>Northern Turkey</u>

Between Istanbul and Samsun
Black Sea Coast, West of Samsun

650 km; map GeoCenter Euro-Country, Western Turkey, 1:800 000

This section covers largely unspoilt and infrequently visited territory. If you're heading east from Istanbul, going via the Black Sea coast is a slow but rewarding alternative to the E80. Jason and the Argonauts sailed this coast on the way to find the Golden Fleece, and the unspoiled stretches remain much as they were then.

The large industrial port of Samsun is not particularly interesting to visitors, though you may well be glad of its creature comforts after a few days of hard travelling through remote country. Sinop, north-west of Samsun on Rt 010, is another matter: it has the best natural harbour on the Black Sea, some fine beaches and a fascinating history. West of here the coastline, with its string of small seaside towns and miles of empty beaches, is rarely visited by foreigners.

From Inebolu you can detour inland along a beautiful mountain drive to the historic city of Kastamonu. Further west along the coast on Rt 010 you eventually come to Amasra, another historic city in a superb setting. This was once a Byzantine outpost, and on one of its picturesque twin bays you can see a small medieval lighthouse.

The road turns inland from here. On your way south along Rt 755, be sure to turn off and see Eski Safranbolu, a town of old wooden houses in a gulley beneath cliffs. South of here you can join the E80, the main link between Ankara and Istanbul – see Turkey Overall: 11.

To cover the whole stretch, allow three days minimum. If you want to explore, and enjoy the beaches, at least a week.

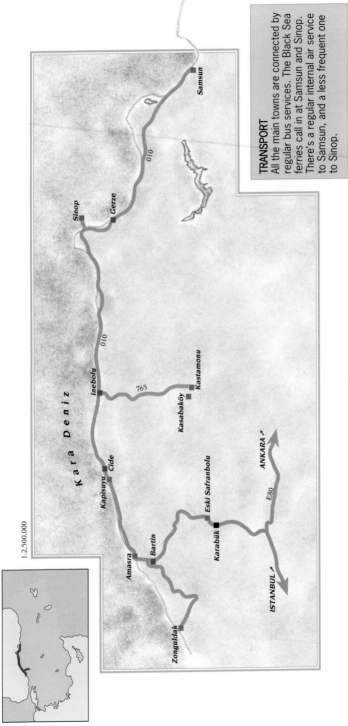

TRANSPORT
All the main towns are connected by regular bus services. The Black Sea ferries call in at Samsun and Sinop. There's a regular internal air service to Samsun, and a less frequent one to Sinop.

1:2,500,000

SIGHTS & PLACES OF INTEREST

AMASRA ⌂ ✕

230 km W of Sinop, on Black Sea Coast, on Rt 010. This picturesque spot was once a Byzantine stronghold. The old town is situated on a rocky promontory between two bays, complete with an attractive harbour and a small cen-turies-old Genoese lighthouse.

The town is said to derive its name from Amastris, a nephew of the Persian king Darius who invaded ancient Greece. The Genoese Empire (see Turkey Overall: 13) held out here against Mehmet the Conqueror until 1459. You can still see the ancient **city walls**, **towers** and **gates**. Some of these still sport the coat of arms of the City of Genoa, 500 years ago the greatest maritime power in the region.

The main Byzantine church is now a mosque, and another smaller church is rapidly crumbling away (despite being in use until 70 years ago). There is also a town museum, which contains little of interest other than some fine sculp-tures dating from classical times.

Unfortunately the beaches here have recently suffered from filth and jellyfish. I'm told these problems have now been resolved.

BARTIN

10 km inland from Amasra, just off Rt 010. Worth a stop for a stroll amongst the ramshackle old wooden houses. The bazaar has a few geniune items which are worth bargaining over – brassware

RECOMMENDED HOTELS

AMASRA
Nur Turistik Pansiyon, L; *Western Bay; tel.* 395 1015.
Close to the museum. A friendly family-run spot.

CIDE
Basin Mocamp, L-LL; *on the front.*
Belies its unpromising name. Ideal for sun, sand and sea. No telephone number available at time of going to press, but there's usually a room avail-able, even in mid summer.

ESKI SAFRANBOLU
If you want to spend the night here you'll have to stay in modern Safran-bolu at:

Hotel Uz, LL; *Mahallesi Kiranköy; tel.* 464 21086.
A functional modern hotel, all rooms with private bath or shower. You may have to use sign language if you want anything out of the ordinary. (But be sure to embark upon this with caution in order to avoid grotesque misunderstandings. Many years ago, after several weeks of travel in Turkey, I had a delicate stomach and wanted to order a lightly boiled egg. My skilfully executed signals failed to deliver an egg. Instead, the hotel man-ager's face clouded over, I was slammed against the wall, and the police were called. I never did discov-er what I'd done wrong – but by the time it was all cleared up, and the boiled egg finally appeared amidst many smiles of reconciliation, I was far too ill to eat it.)

SAMSUN
There's a wide range of hotels around central Cumhuriyet Meydani. The best in town is:

Turban Büyük Samsun, LLL; *Sahil Cad-desi; tel.* 3611 10750.
This has a fine garden, very restful after the decibel-rich rigours of the city streets; and, best of all, a won-derful cooling pool.

Those who require atmosphere will seek out:

Vidinli Oteli, LL; *Kasim Paşa Caddesi 46; tel.* 3611 51141.
Pleasingly old; decaying without the grandeur. The service is of another era, and not likely to arrive until then – but they're delightfully friendly.

SINOP
Hotel 117, LL; *Rihtim Caddesi 1; tel.* 3761 5117.
Ask for one of the rooms overlook-ing the harbour (more expensive, but still **LL**). The sort of place you dream of hiding out in for the winter.

• *Traditional timber house,* Eski Safranbolu.

especially – as distinct from the tat on offer up the road in Amasra.

A reliable express bus from Ankara arrives here, if you're planning to cover the coastal stretch of this route west to east by public transport.

CIDE

72 km E of Amasra. Another rather boring small inland town, but a couple of kilometres away at the sea there's a long, long stony beach with a few hotels and restaurants.

ESKI SAFRANBOLU

10 km NE of Karabük off Rt 755. Not to be mistaken for modern Safranbolu, the forlorn outcrop of concrete nearby. This is an enchanting small town of Ottoman wooden houses set below the cliffs of a ravine. It was 'discovered' only a few years ago, and has not yet been spoilt – though there is a tourist bazaar, to remind you of the civilization you hoped you'd left behind. Walk the streets and soak up the atmosphere. There are some intriguing courtyards and a crumbling *kervansary* (traditional inn) which is threatened with hotelification.

GERZE

35 km S of Sinop. Pleasant if unremarkable resort on main coastal Rt 010. Attractive beaches.

INEBOLU

158 km W of Sinop on coastal Rt 010. Small seaside town whose very ordinariness is its main attraction. (Ordinariness here is not quite the same as in Doncaster or Dortmund.) There are winding little streets, a river, a stony beach and a lone fisherman who will assure you that he catches huge tuna fish, but not when you're watching.

KAPISUYU

20 km W of Cide on the Rt 010. If you want to stop at one of the many little resorts along the coastal stretch between Amasra and Sinop, try this village. It is by the mouth of a tree-lined little river, has a sandy beach, and a small restaurant where you can also arrange to stay overnight. No phone booking unfortunately, so it's pot luck in the high season, when this spot attracts quite a few locals. If there's no room here, try the beach settlement on the coast outside Cide, just 20 minutes' drive away.

KARABÜK

81 km S down Rt 755 from Bartin. If you're visiting Eski Safranbolu you'll probably have to pass through here (changing buses, if you're on public transport). A choking spot, covered with a delicate dew of grime from the nearby steel complex – showing that anything Magnetogorsk can produce, the Free World can do equally well.

KASABAKÖY

See Kastamonu, page 174.

KASTAMONU ×

94 km inland from Inebolu on Rt 765 at the end of a magnificent drive through the mountains. The town lies beneath a ruined 12thC **castle** built by the fearsome Tamerlane of Samarkand when he stopped by to raze the rest of the place to the ground. Perched on a rock above the river is the **Ismailbey Camii,** a 500-year-old mosque with two domes. Just 5 km outside town to the north-west you come to the village of **Kasabaköy,** which has a delightful mosque built of wood that dates from medieval times. The interior is said to be the finest of its kind anywhere.

SAMSUN ⛴ ×

On Black Sea Coast 320 km NE of Ankara. Modern Samsun is a large industrial port with a population of over a third of a million, making it the largest city on the Turkish Black Sea coast. Its commercial life is centred around the tobacco industry. There's not much to see, but it's useful for the ferry and a few of those urban luxuries which you may have missed whilst travelling the countryside.

That said, the city has had an eventful history. It was founded in the 7thC BC by colonists from the ancient Greek city of Miletus on the Ionian coast of south-western Turkey (see Turkey Overall: 3). During the following centuries it

• *The port, Samsun.*

was taken by the usual run of conquerors – including the Persians, the Kings of the Pontus, and the Romans. By the 15thC it had become an important trading centre for the Genoese, at the time the leading Mediterranean maritime power. But in 1425 the Ottoman Turks took over. In a fit of pique before abandoning the city, the Genoese burnt it to the ground and the entire population fled.

This attack of pyromania put an end to Samsun's importance as an international port shipping goods all over the Mediterranean. For years the city was little more than a fishing village amongst the blackened ruins, and only gradually did it swell to become a sleepy provincial backwater. History passed it by as the Ottoman Empire rose to greatness, and afterwards began its long decline. Then in 1919, just after the Turkish defeat in the First World War and the final collapse of the Ottoman Empire, history once again arrived in Samsun. This time in the form of Turkey's modern saviour, Kemal Atatürk.

Atatürk had been despatched from Istanbul to disarm the Turkish groups that had been harassing the Greeks who lived in the region. In the event, he did precisely the opposite. He orga-

• *Figs for sale, Samsun old quarter.*

nized these guerrillas and irregulars into a formidable Turkish army, then embarked upon the Turkish War of Independence. Four years later, having defeated the invading Greeks, Kemal Atatürk brought the war of Independence to a successful close when he declared the Turkish Republic.

In order to avoid further massacre and inter-racial bloodshed, the Greek populations living in Turkey and the Turkish populations living in Greece were exchanged. This resulted in considerable disruption and distress – except in Samsun. Here the upheavals were mitigated by a neat transfer. The Turkish tobacco workers who lived in Kavalla (in northern Greece) were imported, and the Greek tobacco workers of Samsun were shipped to Kavalla. If you find yourself with time on your hands in Samsun visit the **museum**, which has a number of interesting Roman relics, as well as the inevitable Atatürk exhibits. Those who find that one of the great joys in life is watching ships in a harbour where nothing much appears to be happening will be rewarded by a visit to the port, where nothing much can happen for hour after fascinating hour, as you sit on your bollard meditating upon equally exotic ports across the Black Sea. During the 19thC this was the main port which linked Europe to Baghdad, and became even

more important strategically when the famous Berlin-Baghdad railway had its terminus here (the Romania-Turkey stretch was accomplished by boat across the Black Sea). However, this importance remained largely strategic and nothing much was ever actually transported along this link, owing to certain difficulties with prehistoric rolling stock in Romania and the antediluvian equipment used by the Ottoman railway system. The rails alone were German-built.

SINOP ⚓ ✕

172 km W of Samsun. The place on the Black Sea coast: it has beaches, a fascinating history, a harbour with some good bars, and several interesting sights.

Sinop has the finest natural harbour in the entire Black Sea, rivalled only by that at Odessa. This geographical wonder is rendered superfluous by the fact that there's virtually no need for a harbour here. The small port area is now largely devoted to fishing boats and motionless locals.

The city is named after the Amazon queen Sinope. When she took the fancy of Zeus, the lusty patriarch of the gods, he promised her whatever she wanted in exchange for a night of heavenly bliss

175

• *Lottery ticket seller, Sinop.*

back at his homely heaven. Sinope took him at his word and asked for eternal virginity. Fortunately for Sinope this was the pre-philosophic era and Zeus was unable to call upon logical analysis to solve the conundrum, which eventually defeated both his logical faculties and his ardour.

Sinop's strategic position – on an isthmus connected to a peninsula – has made it popular since earliest times. It was already occupied by the time the Ionians arrived in the 8thC BC and turned it into a Greek colony.

In the classical era Sinop produced two notable figures. The philosopher Diogenes the Cynic was born here in 412 BC. Diogenes cared so little for the world and its ways that he lived stripped to his loincloth in a barrel. When Alexander the Great came to see this philosophic marvel *in situ*, he was so impressed that he offered Diogenes whatever he wished. To which Diogenes replied: 'Could you stand aside, you're blocking the sun.'

Sinop's second famous son was an altogether different type called Mithradates Eupator, a Pontic king who lived at the end of the 2ndC BC. He ascended the throne by deposing his mother and keeping her locked up in a dungeon. After wreaking untold psychological damage on his psyche by this ungrateful act, the *angst*-ridden Mithra-

dates became convinced that his subjects were scheming to poison him. (This was not a mere delusion: Mithradates was a cunning psychopath, not a paranoid.) In order to overcome his *angst* and his enemies Mithradates secretly took to consuming ever-larger doses of poison, which he hoped would immunize him against his subjects' regular attempts on his life. Having established the sort of tyranny you would expect from a poisonous psychopath (accompanied by the customary vicious and sensuous excesses), Mithradates then decided to take on the Roman Empire. As an opening shot, just to get the enemy in the mood, he slaughtered all 80,000 Roman and Italian citizens living in his empire, which now extended over large areas of central and western Turkey. The Romans duly took the bait, Mithradates blackmailed the Greeks into joining his side, and the Pontic wars began. To the surprise of many historians (but few psychologists) the Romans encountered stiff opposition from Mithradates. Indeed, it took them decades before they finally triumphed. With defeat staring him in the face, Mithradates decided to commit suicide rather than endure the ignominy of being confined for his own good. He tried to poison himself – but to his irritation this didn't work. So instead he ordered a nearby mercenary to run him through with a sword, and thus died around 50 years too late.

For the next millennium or so, Sinop continued spinning in the revolving doors of history, as one conqueror after another barged through. But things had calmed down by the 14thC when the great Syrian intellectual al-Umari paid a visit and lovingly described the city as: 'a mountain more beautiful than the buttocks of the *houris* of paradise, and adjoining it is an isthmus more graceful than the slenderest of loins.'

Most of the locals appeared not to have minded having their city likened to an unnatural act, but one of them at least was determined to defend it against further foreign encroachment and blue-purple prose stylists. At the sight of hostile ships entering the harbour the local hero Gazi Celebi would fortify himself with hashish, dive into the sea, and drill holes beneath the enemy waterline. Unfortunately one day he must have overdone his preparations, for he ended up sinking a number of his own ships. And that was the end of the Turkish navy's first frogman, whose tomb can still be seen at the entrance of the Alaiye Medresesi, which stands beside the rather tumbledown **Allaedin Camii**, the oldest mosque in town.

In 1853 the Russians went one step further than Gazi Celebi, and destroyed the entire Turkish fleet at Sinop – the act which started the Crimean War. Sinop is the closest point in Turkey to the Crimea, which is only 300 km away. This fact accounts for the forest of radio masts and sophisticated listening devices on the citadel – all part of NATO's priceless defence against a massive invasion by the bankrupt Republic of the Ukraine.

Another (less farcical) establishment on the citadel is the local prison, a chilling reminder to any holidaymakers on the nearby beaches who might be tempted to use Gazi Celebi's training methods, that this is the land of *Midnight Express*.

Be sure to visit the town **museum**, which has a number of finds from local digs and an (exceedingly rare) exhibition of icons pillaged from the local churches after the Greek exodus. There is an **ancient Greek temple** in the museum gardens, where a Mask of Serapis was found. (This is on display in the museum.)

ZONGULDAK

At *the W end of the coast, where* Rt 010 *rejoins the coast after a brief sortie inland W of* Amasra. A distinctly nondescript town in the heart of a coal mining region. The only reason you'll want to come here is because it has good bus connections with Ankara and Istanbul.

RECOMMENDED RESTAURANTS

AMASRA
Canli Balik, L-LL; Küçük Liman Caddesi 12; *no booking.*
Atmospheric location by the sea on the East Bay. Superb fresh fish and reasonable wines.

KASTAMONU
Ulag Pide ve Kebap Salonu, L-LL; Cumhuriyet Cadesi; *no booking.*
As its name suggests, this is a slightly more up-market than the others you'll see in town. It may not be *cordon bleu*, but it is in just such ordinary eating places that you realize the genuine wealth of Turkish provincial *cuisine*.

SAMSUN
If you're stuck here it's worth taking advantage of what the big city has to offer, so for a real treat try the roof garden restaurant at:

Hotel Yafeya, LL-LLL; Cumhuriyet Meydani; *tel.* 3611 51131.
Imaginative, genuine *cuisine*. Try their fresh fish *brochettes*.

SINOP
There's a wide range of restaurants by the harbour and along the southern seafront. My favourite in this district is:

Saray Restoran, L-LL; Iskele Caddesi 14; *no booking.*
This is popular with the locals and has a deservedly high reputation for seafood. I once met a man here who claimed that at least a quarter of the population of Sinop were descended from the 2ndC BC tyrant Mithradates Eupator (see page 176), though they were not aware of this fact.

<u>Northern Turkey</u>

Between Samsun and Trabzon
Black Sea Coast, East of Samsun

330 km; map GeoCenter EuroCountry, Eastern Turkey, 1:800 000

This stretch of Black Sea Coast is one of the unexpected delights of Turkey. It's not so suffocatingly hot in summer as the south coast – and as it often rains the countryside is pleasantly green. The beaches are visited by Turkish holidaymakers, but foreign tourists are comparatively rare.

Route 010 runs along the coast most of the way between Samsun and Trabzon. Much of the scenery is dramatic, with mountains shelving sharply down to the sea. This was the often forbidding coastline seen by Jason and the Argonauts, and the scene of many of their legendary adventures.

East of Samsun lies the pleasant resort of Ünye. Further east is Giresun, the city which gave its name to the cherry. A nearby island was the home of the legendary female warriors, the Amazons, and is still the venue of a strange pagan ritual each spring.

At the eastern end of Route 010 lies Trabzon, which 700 years ago became the capital of the Trebizondite Empire. In the mountain hinterland south of Trabzon there are some spectacular, remote monasteries well worth exploring.

With your own transport you can cover the coast in two days, but if you want to detour inland you should allow at least four days.

Warning: the road between Samsun and Giresun was destroyed by floods several years ago and parts are still in the process of being remade.

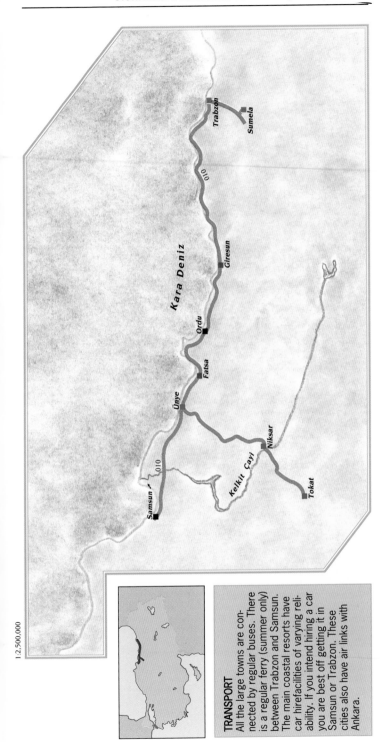

1:2,500,000

TRANSPORT

All the large towns are connected by regular buses. There is a regular ferry (summer only) between Trabzon and Samsun. The main coastal resorts have car hirefacilities of varying reliability. If you intend hiring a car you are best off getting it in Samsun or Trabzon. These cities also have air links with Ankara.

SIGHTS & PLACES OF INTEREST

FATSA

21 km E of Ünye on the coastal Rt 010. A grubby spot by some grubby beaches. The local population belong to a religious sect related to the Sufis. Fifteen years ago they decided to put their communalist principles into practice and voted in a Marxist-style town council run by Terzi Selim, a local tailor. This innocent social experiment was savagely crushed by army tanks in 1980, with many locals killed and Terzi Selim dying in jail. Nobody here wishes to talk about this now, however, it is essential to know of such events – or what is history for?

GIRESUN ⊨ ✕

120 km W of Trabzon on coast. The ancient name of this spot was Cerasus. When the Romans arrived in the 1stC BC they discovered that the locals were fond of a luscious little stone-filled fruit which hung in twin lobes from the trees. The Romans immediately began exporting the fruit, naming it after Cerasus – the origin of the word cherry.

There's not much to see in modern Giresun. You can visit the usual ruined medieval **castle**, and an Orthodox church that has been converted into the local **Ethnographic Museum**, fascinating, but only if you're keen on small provincial ethnographic museums. Giresun also has a pleasantly busy small port, where you will notice (in season) vast quantities of walnuts being shipped out to an eagerly awaiting world. Yes, Giresun is the world's walnut capital.

Just 6 km east of town the island of **Giresun Adasi** lies a couple of kilometres offshore, opposite the mouth of the Aksu Kayi (White River). In prehistoric times this island was known as Aretias – home of the Amazons (see page 181). Jason and the Argonauts boldly put in here on their journey in search of the Golden Fleece, encountered the fearsome females, and lived to tell the tale.

After being an all-female stronghold, the island later went to the other extreme when the Byzantine Monastery of St Phocas was established. Its ruins are still visible.

On May 20th each year Giresun Adasi is the focus of an obscure rite, which almost certainly derives from pagan times. The locals circle the island three times, and then place a stone in the cleft of a rock whilst making a silent wish. This done, they proceed to get gloriously drunk.

NIKSAR

105 km inland from Ünye on Rt 850, at the end of a picturesque drive through the mountains. Former capital of the Kings of Pontus, who lost their territory to Julius Caesar after a four-hour scrap in 47 BC – see Tokat, below.

A short stay reveals a sleepy, unspoilt provincial spot, which occasionally erupts when the local football team does better than usual.

ORDU 🛏

On the Black Sea coast 45 km W of Giresun. The ferry occasionally puts in at Ordu, then sails off again. This is all you need to know about this grey spot on the Black Sea.

Poetasters of tedium should be sure to step ashore for a numbing visit to the local Ethnographic Museum. In ancient times this city was called Kotyora, and surviving historical records indicate that it had a similar atmosphere to that of today. (No one visited, except Xenophon, on the expedition that ruined his career.)

SAMSUN

See Turkey Overall: 12.

SUMELA

See Turkey Overall: 14.

TOKAT ✕

55 km SW of Niksar on Rt 850. This small, unimpressive town is famous as the spot where Julius Caesar made his famous remark: 'Veni, vidi, vici.' (I came, I saw, I conquered.) He did so in 47 BC after he had conquered Pharnaces II, King of Pontus, in a nearby battle. This had apparently lasted just four hours, ending in an easy away win for the European champions.

Tokat is way off the beaten track, and if you see any other tourists you may well wonder what on earth they are doing here. The city's old quarter has winding streets of fine wooden houses, amongst which you will find several centuries-old mosques and bath houses. Above is the town's ruined castle. It was here that the Emperor of Trebizond, Romanus Diogenes, received the dispiriting news that he had been deposed, and that the Turks were after him. He only made it 100 km down the road before they caught up with him, and blinded him.

The main sight in town is **Göl Medrese** (the Sky Seminary), so named because when it was built in 1275 it

THE AMAZONS

A tribe of fierce women who lived along the north coast of the Black Sea in Homeric times. Some say they originally came from the Caucasus, others that they migrated from as far afield as India.

The Amazons lived together in a strictly female community. Once a year they would descend upon some nearby tribe of innocent, unsuspecting men and force them to indulge in wanton behaviour, before departing as abruptly as they had arrived. The resulting children would be divided according to sex. The females were kept and brought up as war-like Amazons. The despised males were sent back to their fathers, so that they could be raised as mild-mannered shepherds and perhaps be raped once a year.

According to ancient Greek sources, the Amazons cut off one breast so that this didn't get in the way of their archery or javelin throwing.

One day Theseus, King of the Athenians, managed to lay his hands on the Amazon Queen Hippolyte. He then sailed off to Athens with her as his captive. The outraged Amazons set off in pursuit. Eventually, after devastating all who dared to stand in their path, they reached Athens. But alas, Hippolyte had already given birth to a little Hippolytus. So they left her behind and returned home.

Misogynist classical scholars have claimed that the Amazons were just a myth. Indeed, a recent psychologist has gone so far as to suggest that these fierce women were simply a fantasy induced when the ancient Greek male psyche felt itself under threat on account of the rampant Dionysiac revels conducted by their womenfolk. But these paranoid scholars have yet to explain certain Amazon relics and ruins which are known to have existed in classical times on the very route taken by the Amazons on the trail of their sister-queen.

was covered in blue tiles. You can still see a few remnants on the walls. The seminary was once a hospital, but is now a museum containing the usual odds and ends. If you're feeling in the mood to browse, it's ideal – with everything from prehistoric remains to mementoes of the city's once-flourishing Armenian and Greek communities. In the garden there's an exhibit commemorating a British missionary who died here on his way home after having survived several years trying to convert fire worshippers in Persia.

Don't miss the **Tarihi Ali Pasa Hamami,** a fine old Turkish baths with an intriguing multi-domed roof. The town also has a clock tower, which was erected in 1909 by frightened local subscription to honour 25 years of the reign of the paranoid despot Sultan Abdulhamit II. No sooner had this been erected than the joyous news came through that Abdulhamit had been deposed.

TRABZON ⊨ ✕

310 km E of Samsun on Rt 010. In bygone times Trebizond (the old Greek name for the place) was regarded as one of the most romantic destinations in the East. And justly so. The city's fabulous wealth, its palaces with their shimmering halls of mosaics, its Byzantine intrigues, profligacy and esoteric vices all contributed to the legend which inspired writers from Marco Polo to Rose Macauley, author of the marvellous novel, *The Towers of Trebizond.*

Trabzon was founded in 746 BC by colonists from the ancient Greek city of Miletus (whose ruins are just south of Kuşadasi in south-western Turkey). The city's name comes from the Greek word *trapeza*, meaning table, refering to the promontory which served as the city's first acropolis.

During Roman times the city flourished as a terminus of the Silk Road – the fabled route which extended all the way to China, bringing silk, spices and other oriental novelties to the West.

Yet it wasn't until the early 13thC that Trebizond came into its own. In 1204 the soldiers of the Fourth Crusade seized and sacked Constantinople (now Istanbul), the capital of the Byzantine Empire. The Ottoman nobility fled the city in disarray, and a leading member of the Comnenus branch of the imperial family ended up at Trebizond, where he re-established the Byzantine court and had himself crowned emperor. Meanwhile, in customary Byzantine fashion, two rival emperors were crowned, one at Epirus and the other at Nicaea.

The Trapezuntine Empire soon began to flourish. Intrigue came second nature to the Byzantines, whose name has entered our language as a byword for devious intricacy. The new emperors in Trebizond proved themselves pastmasters of the art. They succeeded in playing off the two powerful European maritime powers, the Genoese and the Venetians, against each other; and at the same time used this European influence to buttress them against encroachments from the powerful Selçuk Turks and the Mongols in the east, whom they also played off against each other.

However, it remains debatable whether all this intrigue was really necessary. The city would have been very difficult to take: its port is easily defensible, and the hinterland consists of barely penetrable mountains. Also, it was in almost everyone's interest for the merchandise of the Silk Route to pass through an independent Trebizond. So merchandise continued to flow through from Samarkand, China and Persia, and was heavily taxed before being shipped out by the Venetians and the Genoese.

According to several reputable historians the culture of 14thC Trebizond rivalled that of the Renaissance cities of Italy. This is indisputably true in terms of sheer wealth and diversity – but bunk where artisitic merit is concerned. Trebizond produced nothing of originality: it was a melting pot of cultural influences which evaporated to leave nothing but stereotyped golden dregs.

Inevitably, it wasn't long before things began to fall apart amidst this welter of intrigue. In 1341 fighting broke out and the city succeeded in sacking itself. Yet still no outside power could be bothered to upset the apple cart, Trebizond rose again, and this time the decline proved even more gloriously decadent. Historians of the period avidly describe of scenes of unrivalled voluptuousness and cruelty (a combination which according to one noted philosopher is the lowest form of

• *Carpet weaving, Trabzon.*

decadence). In order to keep the outside predators at bay, the ruling family took to marrying off its daughters to Turkish and Mongol chieftans, who much prized their dimpled, light-skinned beauty.

Eventually, in 1461, the Ottoman Mehmet the Conqueror marched on Trebizond. The party was over: the Emperor went into 'negotiations' with Mehmet, which allowed his Turkish troops to enter the city unopposed. The future Sultan Selim the Grim was appointed governor, and later his more famous son Suleiman the Magnificent was born here.

Trebizond was to remain part of the Turkish Empire until the First World War, when the Russians took the city. After the Russians left there was a power vaccum, and the local Greeks and Armenians briefly proclaimed the so-called Republic of Trebizond, but this was soon crushed by the Turks.

At first sight you may find modern Trabzon a disappointment. Nowadays the city is a busy commercial port, crammed between the mountains and

183

• *Tea-house, Ünye.*

the sea. But you don't have to look far to find remnants of the glorious past.

The centre of town is **Atatürk Alani** (sometimes known as the Meydan) on the sight of the classical **agora** (market place). It was in this square that the emperors of Trebizond would conduct their grand ceremonial each Easter, when diplomats from all over Europe would be presented to the court.

At the corner of this square there used to be camel stables, where Muslim pilgrims would set out on the first leg of their pilgrimage to Mecca. Now they leave from the bus station, in a convoy of specially equipped buses, for the 2,500-km journey across mountain and desert. The square has a statue of Turkey's great leader Atatürk, who brought the country into the 20thC after the collapse of the old Ottoman Empire at the end of the First World War. Atatürk's impressive white villa, **Atatürk Köşkü,** can be reached by bus from this square. It stands above the town, and contains memorabilia of the great man. It was here, on one of his rare holidays, that he wrote his will, bequeathing all he had to the nation.

As you'd expect, Trabzon has many

historic churches. Its oldest is **Küçük Ayvasil Kilisesi** (the Basilica of St Anne) which was built some 1,300 years ago. Nearby you'll find the **church of Panaghia Chrysoskephalos**, which was for many years the city's most important place of worship. It was to be superceded in the 13thC by **Aya Sofya Kilisesi** (Church of the Holy Wisdom) which is on the hillside overlooking the coast. Centuries previously this site had been occupied by a pagan temple. The church has a 15thC tower, and inside you can see some fine frescoes and mosaics which were only restored some 30 years ago after centuries of neglect. Originally there was a monastery here as well, but this has disappeared.

Near here is the stadium of Trabzonspor, the local football team, which receives fanatical support. A recent suggestion by an archaeologist that its pitch should be dug up to see if anything remained of the 500-year-old imperial polo grounds met with predictable lack of enthusiasm; the archaeologist has now left town to practise his profession elsewhere.

While you are in Trabzon be sure to take a walk around the **old town**, which contains a variety of churches, mosques and castles. This is on the ancient acropolis after which the city is named. The **bazaar** area is north-west of the Meydan, and here you can still pick up old Czarist Russian banknotes, dating from the occupation more than 70 years ago.

If you have time, be sure to visit the monastery out at **Sumela** (see Turkey Overall: 14), some 50 km south of town. This is one of the main sights in the land – though in my view it is most notable for its spectacular location.

ÜNYE ✏

74 km W of Ordu on the Black Sea coast. What Giresun is to walnuts (page 180), Ünye is to hazelnuts. In fact, they produce so many hazelnuts here that in the season their shells are used as fuel instead of wood.

Ünye is also a fine modern resort, the best of its kind you'll find along the entire Turkish Black Sea coast. There are pleasant beaches (the best lying west of town) and an increasing number of modern hotels line the tree-fringed promenade. Those who consider there is more to life than the usual resort pleasures of sunburn, hangovers and rabitting will want to drive 5 km inland and brave the climb up to **Çaleoğlu Kalesi**, a ruined medieval castle with fine views out over the countryside and the coast.

RECOMMENDED RESTAURANTS

GIRESUN

The best place to eat at in the centre of town is the **Giresun Oteli** (see Recommended Hotels, page 180). Here they have all the usual favourites, and a few mouth-watering regional specialities.

If you want to go further afield, try:

Kale, LL; *in the park on the acropolis; no tel; only open May-Sept.*
Run by the most celebrated chef on Turkey's north coast, Mr D.A.Tekbas.

Out opposite Giresun Adasi (the island) you'll find **Cerkez, LL-LLL**, a smart spot on the riverbank looking towards the legendary island. Renowned for its fresh fish.

TOKAT

Belediye Lokantasi, L-LL; *Meydan Carsisi; tel. 475 19924.*
Excellent value unpretentious spot, close to the Gok Medrese.

TRABZON

Kibris Restaurant, L-LL; *Atatürk Alani 17; tel. 031 17679.*
The best menu in this price range anywhere in town. It's pleasantly plain downstairs, but upstairs you'll find the standard designers' nightmare. The food is excellent. Try asking one of the waiters about their fresh fish dishes: be daring, they're superb.

If you want pie in the sky, try the roof-top restaurant at:

Otel Trabzon, LL; *Atatürk Alani; tel. 031 12788.*
A good menu of local dishes, as well as the usual favourites. Very friendly service with egstraspezial inklish ant Cherman.

Eastern Turkey

Between Trabzon and Van
The Far North-East

700 km; map GeoCenter Euro-Country, Eastern Turkey, 1:800 000

This region contains some of the most remote and spectacular terrain in Turkey. Here you're well off the tourist trail and into adventure travel country. Among the high, barren mountain ranges (many of whose peaks rise higher than 3,000 m) you'll feel far from 'civilization'. The scenery is often hauntingly beautiful, and you can travel for mile upon mile without meeting a soul. In the primitive villages the people appear distinctly Asiatic, and are usually most hospitable. Marking the northern end of the region is Trabzon, the legendary port on the Black Sea – see Turkey Overall: 13. The influence of the Greek Orthodox Church is still noticeable here, with a legacy of all-but-forgotten monasteries hidden in the mountains inland, the best of which is at Sumelas.

Heading out of Trabzon on the E97 you climb into the mountains on the long drive to Erzurum. Nowadays this is a large garrison city, but through its long history it has been subjected to invasions by tribesmen of all kinds – the last being in the 60s when waves of hippies passed through on their way to India.

From here Rt E80 leads east through the passes. (The rivers from this point drain into the Caspian Sea.) At Ağri you turn south along the winding Rt 965. This brings you eventually to the shores of Lake Van. Here you can detour west to visit Adilcevaz, which lies by the lakeshore beneath Turkey's third highest mountain, and then on to the historic Muslim graveyard at Ahlat, before continuing to the end of the trail at Van, one of the most exotic locations in the land.

The road is almost 700 km long, and will take you at least a week if you wish to stop and explore.

Warning: The road between Trabzon and Erzurum was destroyed by floods several years ago. Parts of it are still being remade despite the work being 'completely finished last year.'

TRANSPORT

All the main cities are connected by regular bus services, but some of these journeys are a very long haul. Erzurum and Van both have railway stations, but they are not linked in any meaningful sense. You really need your own transport to travel this part of Turkey.

SERIOUS WARNING

Because various Kurdish separatist groups operate in this region, it can be dangerous. Travellers have been kidnapped and buses blown up: your life could well be at risk. Be sure to contact the police before undertaking *any* travel in this section. If you want to explore the region, it's essential to find out about the situation *before* leaving for Turkey: contact your Turkish Tourist & Information Office, or the embassy.

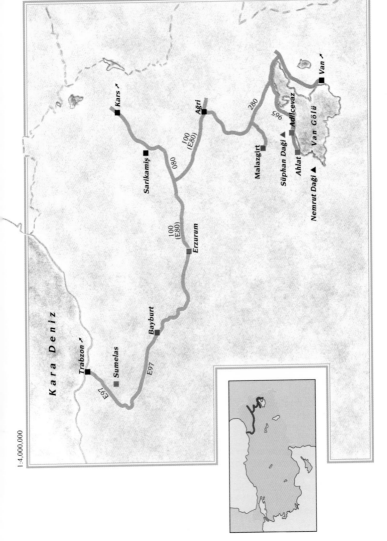

1:4,000,000

SIGHTS & PLACES OF INTEREST

ADILCEVAZ

N *shore of Lake Van on Rt E99, 20 km E of Ahlat.* Small town on a strip of fertile land beside the lake. On the western side of town, by the shore, there's a rather strange little dark-stone **mosque** which dates from the 13thC and is said to have been in continuous use ever since. Above the town is **Kef Kalesi**, an old Selçuk castle.

To the north of the lake rises **Süphan Daği**, the third highest mountain in Turkey, rising to over 4,000 m.

AHLAT

50 km N of Tatvan on Rt E99 beside N shore of Lake Van. Modern Ahlat is a decidedly drab spot in a splendid setting between high mountains and the green waters of the lake. But history has left its mark here in picturesque fashion.

To the west of town, in a field by the shore, you can see the **Ulu Kümbet** (Great Tomb). This is the mausoleum of the magnificently named Shadi Aǧa, a Mongol lord who died here in 1273, more than 7,000 km from home.

Nearby is the main sight in town, the large **graveyard** (covering over 2 square km) which is littered with Muslim gravestones. These are anything from 200 to 700 years old. Time, earthquake and weather have reduced the upright monuments to a lurching,

RECOMMENDED HOTELS

BAYBURT

There's not much to see here except the castle, but you may well find yourself in need of a hotel on the long drive between Trabzon and Erzurum.

Saracoglu, L; *Cumhuriyet Caddesi 13; tel. 0291 1217.*

Basic provincial accommodation, in the spartan Turkish style. All rooms have their own showers.

ERZURUM

Büyük Erzurum Oteli, LL; *Ali Ravi Caddesi 5; tel. 011 16528.*

Old-style hotel on the main road that leads south out of the city centre (Menderes Caddesi leads into it). All of the staff appear to understand English, some of them actually do – and they're courteously friendly too. Avoid the front rooms, which can be noisy. There are more than 40 rooms, all with shower.

Hitit Hotel, L; *Kazim Karabekir Caddesi 26; tel. 011 11024.*

Budget travellers should not miss this once celebrated spot. Alas, it has been refurbished since the good old days – though you may not notice, as this epoch-making event took place some time ago. In the late 60s the walls of the rooms were decorated with murals (and other rudimentary inscriptions) by hippies passing through on the way to India. The management didn't object to this practice (which would have incurred a raid from the porn squad in most countries) as these exotica saved unnecessary decoration costs.

Today this is sadly a much more modern spot, and dutifully clean. But it remains enlivened by a highly enthusiastic old lobbyman (who may or may not actually be a member of the staff: I couldn't tell). Whether you're here for reasons of nostalgia or economy, whether your waist-length hair is now cropped or vanished, this lively old man will invariably claim to remember you from the old days. 'Crazy, man!' A historic hotel which once lived up to its quasi-prehistoric name. Newsflash: it appears that this character has departed on 'a holiday away.'

SARIKAMIǦ

Turistik Hotel, LL; *Halk Caddesi 64; tel. 0229 1176.*

Serviceable spot on the main street in the centre of town. All rooms have private baths.

If you're coming up here in the skiing season, head for:

Sartur Moteli, LL; *on the hillside above town close to the lift; no booking.*

This *is* the ski resort – there being no other facilities besides the ski lift. All 30 rooms have their own shower, and the Turkish skiers (often military families) can be a very jolly lot.

leaning field of stones. Many are inscribed with intricately ornate carvings. Here lie the conquerors of Ahlat, many from far-off lands, who never made it home – Persians, Turkomen, Kurds and even some Mongols. A fine place to meditate on the folly of human endeavour. There are also a number of *kumbets* here and around. The traditional shape of these mausoleums is said to derive from that of a nomad's tent.

Ahlat was originally an Armenian city, and for a brief period in the 11thC it became part of the Byzantine Empire. But it was too remote, and soon began falling to a succession of conquerors. Finally, in 1548, it was taken by Suleiman the Magnificent, who incorporated it into the Ottoman Empire.

The ruined **castle** to the east of town by the lake shore was built by the Ottomans in the 16thC.

BAYBURT ⌫ ✕
H*alf way between* E*rzurum and* T*rabzon, just N of* R*t* E97. A nondescript spot which happens to boast the largest **castle** in the land. It was built in the 6thC and for centuries afterwards armies would come from far and wide for the sheer pleasure of attacking it, besieging it, setting fire to it or bombarding it. Curiously, the castle walls are still standing, but not much else. Worth only a passing glance – as you knowledgeably pass on the above information to your companions.

ERZURUM ⌫ ✕
O*n* R*t* E97. A large drab city in the middle of a wilderness fringed by distant barren peaks. If this isn't exactly Nowhere, it certainly feels like it. At weekends hundreds of scruffy dispirited conscripts come from the huge military camps nearby to amble aimlessly up and down the streets. The few women pass by veiled to the eyeballs, and the chilling wind whistles in from Siberia (which in spirit is just down the road). In summer, this same wind roasts you, or dies so that you swelter in a leaden stillness. All over Turkey you will encounter men whose eyes glaze over at the mere mention of Erzurum. They will have spent their military service here, in transports of boredom, defending their country against the Soviet threat from the Caucasus.

RECOMMENDED RESTAURANTS

BAYBURT
If you need to stop here for a meal on the long drive between Trabzon and Erzurum, try

Coruh Lokantasi, L-LL, by the river. Standard provincial fare at very reasonable prices.

ERZURUM
The best choice of restaurants is to be found on and around the main Cumhuriyet Caddesi. If you're not too hungry, try a stroll around the neighbourhood before making your choice. Keep your eye open for the onomatopoeiacally descriptive **Güzelyurt** (L and licensed); also the **Melunruz Kebap Salonu (LL)** which is named after a famous Parisian nightspot (those who can, can guess).

For slightly more up-market dining try:

Salon Asya, LL; C*umhuriyet* C*addesi* 21; *tel.* 011 21243.
   This comparatively smart spot has a range of local and regional dishes. (Their Adana Kebap is superb and exotically spicy, just as it should be.) If you're feeling adventurous, try asking one of the helpful waiters to explain some of their more esoteric dishes, though don't expect him to do this when the place is full.

Just across the street from here is **Kafe Kandil**, the main meeting place in town. It is a useful spot in which to encounter students who will tell you stories about the *real* Turkey, and their views on what should be done about this. A few of the conscripts you'll see here will also have had a university education. When speaking of literature, mention Nazim Hikmet, the great Turkish pre-war poet who ended up living in exile in Moscow (for obvious reasons). Opinions will gush forth.

189

• *South of Trabzon.*

Surprisingly, there are a number of things worth seeing here. The city has an interesting history which makes its present air of stultifying tedium seem a considerable cultural advance.

There has been a city here since earliest times. The Hittites had already occupied the site for a millennium when the Armenians arrived around the 6thC BC. In those days the place was known by the enticing name of Karin. Not until the 4thC AD did the city fall from grace, nominally speaking. This happened when the Byzantine Emperor Theodosius – possibly wreaking some obscure unconscious revenge, or maybe he'd just been jilted by someone called Karin – mellifluously renamed the city Theodosiopolis.

Not surprisingly, this proved too much of a tongue-twister for its multiracial inhabitants, and the place ended up as Erzurum, the sort of name you'd expect from a multi-lingual committee. In the early 14thC the Mongols moved in, putting into practice their usual pacification policy (raze the place to the ground and slaughter all the inhabitants). Later it was briefly held by Tamerlane of Samarkand.

The city finally became part of the Ottoman Empire in 1515, when it fell to Selim the Grim, who must have felt quite at home here. All went well until the 19thC, when the Russians began moving in, and out, and in again. Their final occupation ended in 1918, when the invading troops decided that they wanted to get home for the Revolution. (If only all history was like this.)

You can still see remnants of the Russian occupation if you visit the cas-

tle, **Erzurum Kalesi**, where there are several Russian cannons. The structure dates from the 5thC, originally built by the vengeful Theodosius. When it was captured by the Turks they added a minaret, which was later turned into a clock tower. In 1897 the Russian army pinched the clock. The British were so distressed at the prospect of a garrison town which couldn't tell the time for early morning parade that they presented the Turks with a new one.

The city's main sight is **Çifte Minareli Medrese**, a 13thC religious seminary which has two minarets. At the back you can see the **kumbet** (tomb) of Hudavend Hatun, who was the daughter of a sultan called Alladin and founded the seminary.

In a small park just south of here you can see three more tombs, the so-called **Üç Kümbetler**. The earliest of these dates from the 12thC and houses the mortal remains of Emir Sultan Turbesi. It has windows that are said to exhibit Georgian influence (but you can't see the sultan inside).

The scattered **bazaar district** is fairly ordinary as bazaars go. ·The big attraction here is to be found in the **jewellery bazaar** (on the right up the street leading north-west from Tebriz Kepi, just where it bends slightly). Here numerous merchants are just dying to sell you ornaments decorated with the Erzurum Taşi, a shiny black semi-precious stone· which is found locally. Another good bazaar is Rüstem Paşa Bedesteni at Menderes Caddesi.

South-west of the centre is the city's

190

Ethnographic Museum. Entry costs very little and there's very little to see. On the other hand, it is well worth trying to get in to the **Halicilik Enstitüsü** (Institute of Carpet Makers), which you'll find west off Paşalar Caddesi.

As you drive in to Erzurum from the west you may notice on the outskirts the barracks with a clock standing by its gate. I have visited Erzurum three times: once the clock was running four-and-a-half hours late; another time it had stopped. But when I first came here, immediately after the massive 1966 earthquake which rattled the entire city, the clock was keeping perfect time.

KARS
See Turkey Overall: 16.

MALAZGIRT
On Rt 280, which runs parallel to and about 40 km N of the N shore of Lake Van. This spot is miles out of the way, and is of no possible interest to visitors. But it witnessed an event as important in Turkish history as the Battle of Hastings is to the British. In 1071 (just five years after the Battle of Hastings) the Selçuk Turkish leader Sultan Alp Arslan routed the army of the Byzantines under the Emperor Romanus Diogenes, who suffered the further indignity of being taken prisoner. From then on began the Turkish migrations into Anatolia; the Sultan of Rum established himself at Konya; and the Turkomen tribes began occupying the north. After 1071, the land we now know as Turkey started to become Turkish.

NEMRUT DAĞI
Off Rt E99 8 km N of Tatvan. (Not to be mistaken for the other Nemrut Daği that has the statues at its summit, and is 300 km east of here.)

It's possible to climb this 2,900-m mountain quite easily in four hours (or use the driveable track which ends near the summit). This mountain was a volcano, and in the large crater left by its most recent eruption more than 500 years ago you'll find a deep, dark blue lake. It's possible to swim in these eerie waters, and many years ago they provided me with the highest and most blood-curdling dip I have ever (very briefly) experienced. Those who have no wish to become involved in such

lunacy can pretend to be much more interested in the little hot springs, solidified lava flows and Cinemascope view. As you gaze through your binoculars, far below you will see the miniscule ferry inching its way across the lake, appearing to move just as slowly as it did when you were on board.

SÜPHAN DAĞI
See Adilcevaz, page 188.

TRABZON
See Turkey Overall: 13.

VAN
See Turkey Overall: 15.

DETOUR – SARIKAMIŞ
83 km E of Erzurum turn NE on Rt 080; 45 km up this winding valley road, turn N for a magnificent drive through the mountains to Sarikamiş. This is said to be the coldest spot in Turkey. The town nestles amongst the pine-covered hills. Unusually, it has some Russian houses dating from the occupation during Czarist times. The surrounding mountains rise to almost 3,000 m and are snow-capped for most of the year.

In 1916 this spot witnessed one of the most hideous military blunders of the First World War. News came through that the Russians were advancing up the valley from Kars. Immediately Turkish commander Enver Paşa rushed the ill-clad and ill-equipped Turkish Third Army to Sarikamiş to meet them. In the ensuing *débâcle* it is estimated that more than 75,000 Turkish soldiers were either frozen to death or mown down by the Russians, who then moved on to take Erzurum. There is a monument to those who died on the eastern edge of town.

Sarikamiş is now a lumbering centre. In the hills above there is a pleasant little ski resort, with a lift going up the mountain. In summer you can hike up through the woods.

From here it's only 60 km down the valley road (E 80) to Kars. See Turkey Overall: 16.

DETOUR – SUMELAS

28 km S of Trabzon on Rt E97 turn E for Sumelas, which you reach after 17 km down an awful road, following the signs for Meryam Ana Monastiri (Mother Mary Monastery). From the car park here it's a 40-minute steepish hike up the trail through the woods and upland meadows, ascending nearly 300 m, to the monastery itself.

This superbly situated monastery is one of dozens which existed in the mountains behind Trabzon when such communities flourished during the Byzantine period. According to the well-worn legend, this one was founded in 385 by a Greek monk called Barabas. He is said to have tramped all the way from southern Turkey, bringing with him his only possession, an icon of the Virgin painted by St Luke. As was often the case in those days, he claimed that he'd experienced a vision – and was searching for

the exact earthly location which matched his heaven-sent picture. This he found in a cave on a ledge high in the mountains, which he proceeded to make into a home for his worldly possession.

The inevitable miracles soon followed, and by the 6thC a monastery had been built on the spot. Eventually it achieved such prestige that the rulers of Trabzon would come here to be crowned. Even after the Turks took over, a sultan would occasionally call in on a pilgrimage to bestow gifts. By now St Luke's icon of the Virgin was working miracles at a greater rate than any other icon in the Hellenic world. Soon the Monastery of the Virgin of the Black Rock, as it was called, gained such renown that it was considered the Greek Orthodox Church's third most holy spot, after Mount Athos and Mount Sinai.

Later came the complete break-

• *Above and opposite: the monastery, Sumelas.*

down of Greco-Turkish relations which followed the First World War. As a result, all the Greeks in Turkey were shipped back to their motherland (which many had never even seen). No exception was made for the monks at the Monastery of the Virgin of the Black Rock, who were forced to depart without even being allowed to take their precious icon with them.

A few years after this, a fire broke out at the deserted monastery. Some Greeks have claimed that this was deliberate, but it was more likely to have been caused by shepherds sheltering for the night. Then in 1931 one of the monks managed to sneak back, disguised as an odiferous goatherd. With the aid of his secret diagram (X marks the spot), he began searching for the place where the monastery's treasures had secretly been buried. This he eventually found, and under cover of darkness began digging. He found that the miraculous icon of the Virgin had survived, but the priceless Byzantine texts had disintegrated. The monk then made his way back to Greece with the icon, which can now be seen in the Benaki Museum in Athens.

Unfortunately the present state of the monastery is a disgrace. The frescoes are all but rotted away, or are defaced by graffiti. However, it's still possible to distinguish a few figures on the roof of the original cave including an unlikely one of Jonas in the belly of the whale. Some of these frescoes date from the 14thC, but most of them have been so 'improved' by artists during subsequent centuries that further vandalism is superfluous. Now a new form of vandalism has arrived in the form of 'restorers,' who have begun a comprehensive programme which has reduced the entire place to a building site.

Your best course is to be content with the view – and try, if you can, to imagine what life must have been like up here for the monks. This is a holy spot, and despite centuries of 'improvement' and desecration, it remains one. Regardless of my objections, this remains (justly) one of the most popular sights in eastern Turkey.

There are many other monasteries in these mountains, all in a far worse state of decay and in places that are equally inaccessible. **St George Peristereota** at Kustul and **St John the Baptist** at Vazelon are the best. The exact location of some of the other monasteries is no longer known. Enterprising Byzantine scholars please note.

<u>Eastern Turkey</u>

Between Lake Van and Adana
Westwards from Van

850 km; map GeoCenter Euro-Country, Eastern Turkey, 1:800 000

If you manage to travel between Van and Adana (see the warning on page 195), you'll be undertaking the longest, indeed the most epic journey in this guide. It takes you from Lake Van in the heart of eastern Turkey, across the upper Tigris-Euphrates basin and along the Syrian border, through Turkey's ancient oriental cities, down to the shores of the eastern Mediterranean.

The green waters of Lake Van, surrounded by barren snow-streaked mountains which rise higher than 4,000 m, have long been one of the wonders of the Levant. It is possible to cross Lake Van on the fine old ferry (it carries cars) which plies between Van and Tatvan on the southwestern shore. For details on Lake Van and Van the town, see Turkey Overall: 16.

Going south-west from Tatvan along Rt E99 you negotiate the steep pass which takes you down to the wilderness plains. Here you pass through Diyarbakir, the traditional capital of the region, and then Şanli Urfa, 'the city of the prophets' where Abraham and Job once lived, before reaching the Mediterranean hinterland and Adana. *En route* you can take a detour to the summit of Nemrut Daği, to see one of the forgotten wonders of the ancient world.

With your own transport, you should allow at least a week to cover this route, even if you intend doing some hard driving.

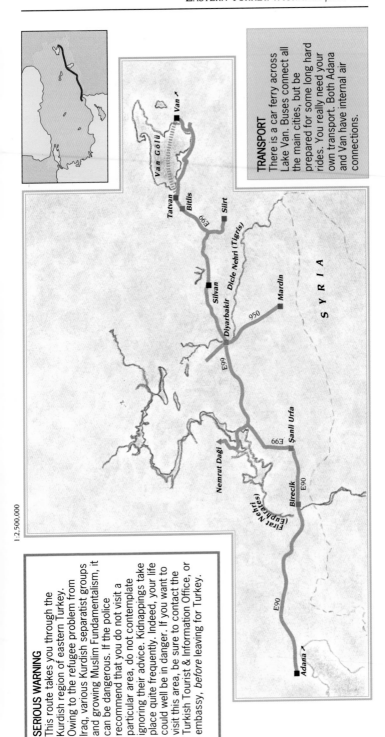

1:2,500,000

TRANSPORT
There is a car ferry across Lake Van. Buses connect all the main cities, but be prepared for some long hard rides. You really need your own transport. Both Adana and Van have internal air connections.

SERIOUS WARNING
This route takes you through the Kurdish region of eastern Turkey. Owing to the refugee problem from Iraq, various Kurdish separatist groups and growing Muslim Fundamentalism, it can be dangerous. If the police recommend that you do not visit a particular area, do not contemplate ignoring their advice. Kidnappings take place quite frequently. Indeed, your life could well be in danger. If you want to visit this area, be sure to contact the Turkish Tourist & Information Office, or embassy, *before* leaving for Turkey.

SIGHTS & PLACES OF INTEREST

ADANA
See Turkey Overall: 9.

BIRECIK
80 km W of Şanli Urfa. Wild East frontier town with a ruined crusader castle and well known among wildlife enthusiasts for being the habitat of the bald ibis.

BITLIS 🛏
Kurdish city 25 km SW of Tatvan. This gloomy, ramshackle spot lies deep in the valley of a mountain stream which eventually flows into the Tigris. It has an old **curved bridge**, an uninteresting **castle** and a rather odd **mosque** which dates from 1126 and is said to be built in the Artukid style. For some reason its main street is named NATO Caddesi. According to local legend, Bitlis was founded by Alexander the Great. For centuries the city was the fiefdom of various semi-autonomous bad-tempered rulers, whose hobbies included collecting wives and chucking miscreants from the castle walls. Then in 1847 it became part of the Ottoman Empire. The population was half Armenian before the First World War and the Armenian 'movement of population' (i.e. massacre). Several of the older houses still contain Armenian inscriptions.

The town is a centre of the tobacco industry, and has nearby groves of walnut trees, whose products are sold by young boys on the streets. Sometimes you can see the black tents of nomads camped up in the valley above the town, which lies on the old caravan route between Lake Van and the Euphrates basin.

DIYARBAKIR 🛏 ✕
230 km W of Tatvan on Rt E99. This is the ancient capital of this ancient region, which covers the upper reaches of Mesopotamia. It is Turkey's most Middle Eastern city – a volatile mixture of ancient and modern, race and outlook. Until recently, Syrian, Iraqi, Iranian, Kurdish, Armenian and Turkish traders all did business here, and doubtless will again when history takes its course.

Diyarbakir could possibly be the oldest inhabited city on earth, and there has certainly been a settlement here since the Stone Age. The city takes its name from Beni Bakr, the Arab clan which overran it in 639 – the name literally means 'Place of the Bakirs'.

Its strategic position ensured that it was successively overrun by all the powers who have ruled the region. The Persians, Alexander the Great, the Romans, the Turcomen, even the Mongols, have all left their distinctive mark. The Romans bequeathed a wall, the Arabs a religion, and the Mongols succeeded in destroying the complex irrigation network which had watered the surrounding land for millennia. (It is still semi-desert as a result.)

Diyarbakir's most famous feature is its **wall**, enclosing the old city. It was built of black basalt, and 67 of its original 72 **towers** are still standing. The original structure was Roman, dating from the 4thC BC, with improvements and breaches by many since.

The city's layout is characteristically simplistic: a child's pattern of a city before the use of imagination comes into play. There are four gates, which point north, south, east and west. Two straight roads cross at the centre, dividing the city into four quarters. Outside the ancient walls there is now a modern city, whose concrete tawdriness speaks of a more contemporary, and more drastic lack of imagination.

Inside the old city you'll find an atmosphere distinct from anywhere else in Turkey. Water-carriers and fruit juice sellers wail as they pass through the throngs of baggy-trousered men; there are Kurds in their distinctive headresses and muffled peasant women in brightly coloured garb. Pitiful beggars lie outside the mosques and irritating groups of street urchins pull at your clothes and jeer, while their elder brothers courteously attempt to conduct you on a guided tour which ends in the bazaar. Here you are obliged to have a glass of tea with their rapacious, hard-bargaining boss, who tries to convince you that life is not worth living without one of his larger carpets that would do nicely for the ballroom at home. Meanwhile the passing perfume sellers assault your nostrils and the choir of watermelon sellers continues with its requiem for the undead.

Diyabakir can claim to be the watermelon capital of the world: the surrounding wilderness is capable of producing little else. Holes are dug in the earth so that the melon roots can reach the water level and the plant is liberally fertilized with the local bird droppings. The result is whopping watermelons. In the old days, according to local sources of the usual reliability, the watermelons of Diyabakir would grow so large that some weighed more than 100 kg and had to be carried on camels. In order to split them open, swords were needed (wielded no doubt by Baron von Munchausen). Nowadays they even have a regular watermelon festival, held at the end of September. The prize watermelon at this event regularly tops a massive 50 kg – but alas its contents remain the same tasteless pip-filled mush as any other watermelon. Yet you would be surprised how this pippy pulp becomes a positive delight when the temperature soars into the 40s.

In fact, modern-day Diyabakir is more than just a picturesque spot. Amongst its citizens is an explosive mix of brash DM-rich returned *gastarbeiter*, puritan Muslim Fundamentalists, left-wing students, U.S. soldiers from the nearby NATO base, and separatist-minded Kurds.

The city, in the heart of the Turkey's Kurdish region, witnessed an uprising in 1925. The history of subsequent events has remained deliberately obscure – but it is likely that more than 100,000 Kurds were massacred. More recently, this has been the main distribution centre for aid to the Kurdish refugees forced out of nearby Iraq by Saddam Hussein, many of whom are still housed in primitive camps in the mountains. Neither a happy, nor a stable part of the world.

There are a number of things worth seeing in Diyabakir. First, of course, the walls and the gates. (The best overall view of the city and the surrounding Tigris valley is from the hill a couple of kilometres south of the Mardin Gate.) The **Ulu Camii** (Great Mosque) dating from 1091 was built by the Persian Sultan Malik Shah. Incorporated into this mosque are the remains of a Christian church which pre-dates the 7thC. My favourite mosque is **Safa Camii**, built in the 16thC in the delightful Persian style. Off the main road to the eastern gate is **Surp Giragos Kilisesi**, a curious old Armenian church that has an equally curious old janitor.

Unfortunately the town's historic **acropolis,** which occupies the northeastern corner of the old city, has been taken over by the Turkish Army. They are none too keen on tourists gazing in awe at their military methods, which they prefer to conduct in private. According to a student I once met here (secretly a militant Marxist, but for economic reasons a mosque-going assisant in his uncle's carpet business) this forbidden acropolis contains an early Christian church which is now

RECOMMENDED HOTELS

BITLIS
Adventure seekers should try the optimistically and ambitiously named **Turistik Palas Otel**. This is by the town monument and costs practically nothing.

Those who actually want to sleep should try **Hotel Hanedan, L;** NATO *Caddesi*.

DIYARBAKIR
Otel Büyük Kervansaray, LLL; *Gazi Caddesi; tel.* 831 43003.

In the old city near the South Gate. Expensive, but worth it. Housed in a refurbished 400-year old traditional inn. The fine swimming-pool is a priceless bonus.

If on a budget, and prepared to swelter, try the pool-less **Touristik Oteli, LL;** *Ziya Gölkalp Bulvari; tel.* 831 12662, by the North Gate outside the old city.

ŞANLI URFA
Hotel Harran, LLL; *Atatürk Bulvari; tel.* 871 34918.

Worth paying extra for the air conditioning alone, despite occasional Stockhausen effects. Rooms also have fridge and TV (fascinating, if incomprehensible – the comic shows are unintentionally hilarious, the deadly serious soaps can do serious damage to your laughterworks).

TATVAN
Whatever you do, spend the night elsewhere. Try Van, across the lake, or Bitlis, 25 km down the main road west.

197

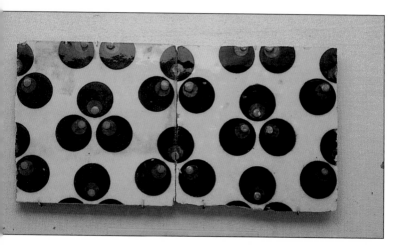

• 16thC tiles, Mardin.

used as a dungeon for military malefactors, its ancient frescoes defaced with despairing inscriptions by its present penitents.

MARDIN

96 km S of Diyarbakir, off the road to the Syrian border. This city is built on a rock overlooking the surrounding wilderness. It has a number of old Arabic houses which are worth seeing, but their old (and young) Arabic inhabitants aren't particularly interested in seeing you. Mardin has recently become a hotbed of Fundamentalism and is best avoided for the time being.

NEMRUT DAĞI

220 km N of Şanli Urfa on zig-zag route and dirt track roads via Atatürk Dam, Adiyaman and Kâhta. This 2,000-m mountain boasts the most amazing sight in Eastern Turkey: a series of enormous carved stone heads standing in remote splendour on a solitary peak.

The best approach is from Kâhta, which is 170 km E of Diyarbakir on Rt 360, or 70 km N of Şanli Urfa off Rt E99. From Kâhta it is 70 km to the summit – a two-and-a-half drive all the way to the top along ragged mountain roads which are often impassable out of season (October to April) owing to snowfalls. There are some basic restaurants in the villages along the way, and there's a café at the summit (drink, but little food). You can also stay overnight in dormitory accommodation (don't be

tempted to sleep out as the temperature *plummets* overnight).

This high-altitude marvel owes its existence to the delusions of grandeur of an all-but-forgotten king, Antiochus I Epiphanes, who during the 1stC BC ruled over an all-but-forgotten kingdom, the Commagene Empire. During the course of his reign, Antiochus' delusions of grandeur gradually took on manic proportions. First he decided that he was descended from Darius, the great Persian emperor, and Alexander the Great; then he decided that he was a god; and finally he decided to challenge the Roman Empire.

But before taking the last step, he took the precaution of building himself the massive tomb-temple complex on the top of this mountain. After Antiochus' defeat by the Romans, the site was forgotten, and soon became lost to history. It was only rediscovered by the German engineer Karl Puchstein in 1881, and was not properly surveyed until 1953.

The main objects of interest here are the famous **stone heads.** They represent the gods (such as Apollo, Zeus and Helios) whom Antiochus claimed as his ancestors. There's also one of Antiochus himself. Don't miss the huge **altar** (intended for the worship of Antiochus) and the ruined **temple** (purpose ditto). Also worth seeing are the row of **headless statues** and the **lion** carved with astrological symbols which acted as a horoscope.

The best time to visit is at first light, to watch the dawn – these days a pop-

• *Cutlery bazaar.*

ular pastime, unfortunately.

ŞANLI URFA  ×

182 *km* SW *of Diyarbakir on the* E99. The name means 'Glorious Urfa', and its history certainly lives up to this. In prehistoric times Abraham was born here, and Job also lived here for a while before taking his torments elsewhere. The Garden of Eden is said to have been near here. (Our word paradise

comes from the ancient Semitic word *pardes*, meaning garden.)

Şanli Urfa, or Urfa as it is known ingloriously by the locals, is another mixed-population city with a large Kurdish element. It is very much a Middle Eastern city, with men wearing baggy trousers and an increasing proportion of veiled women. Notorious as one of

199

the main centres of Muslim Fundamentalism in Turkey, Şanli Urfa is referred to as 'the City of the Prophets.' This, and the Kurdish problem, have caused considerable conflict with the authorities. (In the late 80s the mayor was arrested for allegedly encouraging Fundamentalism.)

However, ancient Urfa is due to undergo a transformation during the 90s. Upriver there is a massive dam, the third largest of its type in the world. It is intended to irrigate the surrounding barren region and transform it into a fertile plain – as it was in Biblical times.

The city is mentioned in the Bible, and also by the Babylonians. Later it was occupied by the Hurrites, then the Hittites, then the Assyrians. Alexander the Great arrived in the 4thC BC and renamed it Edessa (after a town back home in Macedonia). Christianity came early to Urfa/Edessa, arriving in 200 AD. The locals worshipped Christ in the language which he himself had spoken, Aramaic (the language still used by the Syrian Orthodox Church). Unfortunately they soon strayed into heretical ways and became Nestorians.

True righteousness came on the scene in 1098 in the form of Count Baldwin of Boulogne, who established an independent Crusader principality in the region, with Edessa/Urfa as its capital. When this fell half a century later, it precipitated the disastrous Second Crusade.

There's plenty to see in Urfa. Most of the sights are half a kilometre south of the city centre. Here you can see **Abraham's Cave**, which is considered a holy spot by the locals. (Abraham is also revered as a patriarch in the Islamic faith.) According to legend, Abraham was not only born in this cave, but forced to hide out here for his first ten years because of a decree by King Nimrod that all children should be put to death. This early advocate of population control was to cross swords with Abraham at a later date, ordering him to be burnt at the stake. But Jehovah caused a spring to gush forth which put out the fire. Sceptics can still see this spring near the cave. Its waters now feed a number of pools filled with shoals of aged carp, who are all said to be descended from one original pair which lived centuries ago. (The ancient Greek writer Xenophon records that in

the 4thC BC the locals worshipped these fish as gods.) This pool complex is called **Balikli Göl** (which means fish pond) and has a number of gardens and mosques.

The **bazaar** in Urfa is one of the finest (and most authentically 'oriental') you'll find in Turkey. You're only 50 km from the Syrian border here, and the influence of Damascus permeates the atmosphere.

On the ancient citadel you can see the two **Corinthian columns** which form the so-called 'Throne of Nimrod'. The ruined **castle** here dates from the Crusader period of Count Baldwin. It provides fine views out over the old sector of the city.

All melancholics and *aficionados* of misery should be sure to visit **Eyüp**, the sacred cave 2 km S of the city. This was where Eyüp (Job) endured seven years of his trials and tribulations. Mothers now bring their children here, in the hope that they will be blessed with patience.

A further 50 km south of the city is the settlement of **Harran**. Here you can see a village of mud-built beehive dwellings where Abraham is said to have lived for a while. It doesn't look as if it has changed much since his day. The modern occupants are nomads, who make a living smuggling flocks across the border with Syria.

SIIRT

Midway between Silvan and Tatvan on Rt E90, turn S on Rt 370 for 30 km. This brings you to the Selçuk city of Siirt. You may find this spot better to read about than to visit, owing to the present political climate. As recently as the end of the 1980s the local security forces were responsible for a massacre, which has only partly been admitted. The city's close proximity to the Iraqi border (just 80 km as the crow flies) makes it an uneasy spot, where Turko-Kurdish relations are not seen at their best.

The city of Siirt was founded by the ancient Babylonians and has remained very much oriented towards the east. It experienced a golden era under the Arabs, which continued when the Selçuks took over 700 years ago. Many of the grander buildings date from this period. Among these is the **Ulu Camii** (Great Mosque) whose patterned square brick minaret is not such an acquired taste as you might imagine.

In the little streets to the back of the mosque there is said to be a quarter of houses built in the mud-brick fashion which dates from Biblical times, though I have not yet found it.

TATVAN ✕

On SW *shore of Lake Van*. The initial impression is of a distinctly end-of-the-line spot, and this hardly changes on closer acquaintance. The place seems to consist mainly of sad Turkish army conscripts and sadder factories. It has little to offer, apart from the setting beneath bare, snow-capped mountains beside the mysterious green waters of Lake Van. But it is the terminus of one of the world's great ferry rides. Two superb rust-buckets maintain an exceptional service across the 80 km of open water between here and the town of Van. The ambitious timetable (printed far away) announces four regular sailings a day. In practice, with a supreme effort, one day is usually managed – though not without heavy altercations between the land- and sea-based admirals in charge of this operation. The service contrives to leave at least two hours later than even the most knowledgeable quayside experts can predict, so missing the boat here is something of an achievement, which I can proudly claim. Once on board, you're at the mercy of the crew, who have decreed an inflexible no-food policy, except for biscuits and essential fluids, which are dispensed at surprisingly reasonable rates considering the captive status of the customers.

Anyone who gets as far as Tatvan and does not venture to take this trip is far better off back at home watching the world go by on TV.

It is possible to take a side trip from Tatvan along the northern shores of Lake Van to Nemrut Daği (*not* the famous one described on page 198), Ahlat and Adilcevaz – see Turkey Overall: 14.

VAN

See *Turkey Overall*: 16.

<hr>

RECOMMENDED RESTAURANTS

DIYARBAKIR
The old city abounds in cheap eateries where you can gnaw your kebab outside as a kind of personal advertisement for the place. The snag is that practically everywhere in town is dry. If need alcohol, you must go up-market and eat in a hotel restaurant.

The local speciality of this region is *kaburga*, which if cooked properly is said to take up to 12 hours to prepare. It consists of well-basted lamb ribs stuffed with a rich rice concoction, and tastes delicious.

The most famous *kaburga* restaurant in Diyarbakir is **Selim Amca Sofra Salonu, LLL**; *tel.* 831 21616, where they serve nothing else and you have to reserve at least a day in advance. This restaurant is said to be unique, but it's worth paying attention to their unique accounting methods when perusing the bill.

ŞANLI URFA
The city is justly renowned for its kebabs, and also for its Middle Eastern dishes which often have more than a hint of oriental spice. As I know from painful experience, these can wreak havoc with the digestive tract if taken wholesale and without caution.

The same applies here as for Diyarbakir, where booze and cheap eating are concerned. The best place to eat in town is:

Hotel Harran (see hotels, page 197). The restaurant here is on the roof terrace, which is comparatively cool, as is the beer.

TATVAN
Van Gölü Denizcilik Kurumu Oteli, LL; *Gol Sahili*; *tel.* 8497 1777.

A reasonable hotel restaurant on the lake front away from the main port activities. Get there early and insist on being served straight away, as sometimes they're swamped by the sudden arrival of the entire population of Gothenburg.

Eastern Turkey

Between Van and Kars
The Far North-East: Van and Ararat

500 km; map GeoCenter Euro-Country, Eastern Turkey, 1:800 000

This terrain is some of the most remote you can experience in Eastern Turkey: the outback of the outback. It forms an extension to the trail around the east of the country formed by Turkey Overall: 12 to 15, and it takes you north-east from Van towards the Turkish frontier with Armenia and Iran.

You can visit the ancient sites of several all-but-forgotten cultures, travel to a holy island on a lake one and a half times the size of Luxembourg, and visit a medieval ghost town which until recently stood in the very shadow of the Iron Curtain.

The historic city of Van began as a capital of the ancient Urartians, who thrived in this region more than 3,000 years ago. Just down the road you can visit the island of Akdamar, where an Armenian king set up his palace. The mountains nearby, ranging towards the Iranian border, rise to over 3,500 metres. Up a spectacularly beautiful and remote valley here you can visit the remains of an Urartian palace built in the 8thC BC, and the fairytale castle of a Kurdish king built more than two thousand years later.

Drive further north still and you come to Mount Ararat, the 5,000-m peak where according to the Bible Noah's ark came to rest after the flood. North-west of here along the Armenian border you come to Kars, a historic staging point on the way to Ani, the deserted Armenian city which is one of Turkey's finest sights.

If you cover the entire route, you'll have to travel more than 500 km – at least a week.

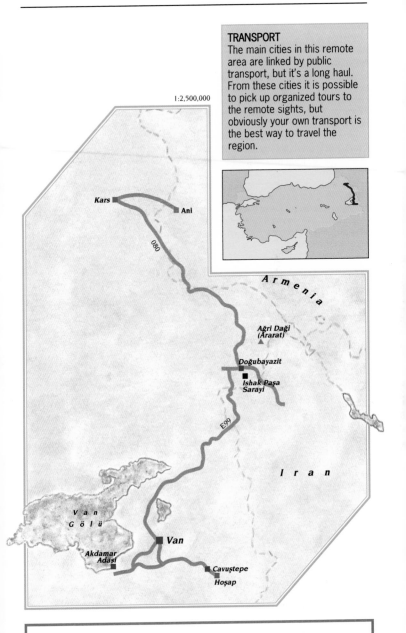

1:2,500,000

Kars

Ani

080

A r m e n i a

Ağri Daği
(Ararat)

Doğubayazit

Ishak Paşa
Sarayi

E99

I r a n

V a n
G ö l ü

Van

Akdamar
Adasi

Çavuştepe

Hoşap

SERIOUS WARNING
The region around Van is largely Kurdish. The present political situation is volatile and 'freedom groups' are known to operate in the mountains. Check the current situation with your Turkish Tourist & Information Office, or the Turkish embassy, before leaving for Turkey. Don't think of entering a remote area without contacting the local police. If they advise against travelling to your chosen destination, don't ignore their advice. If you do, you'll be lucky if you're only kidnapped.

SIGHTS & PLACES OF INTEREST

AKDAMAR ADASI

Island off SW shore of Lake Van. Boat leaves for the island from quay 5 km W of Gevaş every half hour in season. The island of Akdamar contains the **Church of the Holy Cross**, one of the finest examples of Armenian ecclesiastical architecture. It was built in the 10thC by the Armenian king Gagik Artzruni who wished to get away from the cares of his court and people continually mispronouncing his name. He also built a palace and a monastery here, but these have not survived. What has survived is a small but intriguing building whose walls are covered with some marvellous **reliefs**. These depict versions of Adam and Eve; David and Goliath; and Jonah being swallowed by the whale, which looks just as you'd expect a whale to look, depicted by a 10thC Armenian who had never seen a whale – it even has ears.

The inside of the church is a distinct disappointment, with the faded remains of a few murals.

Be sure to bring along your own picnic as there's nothing to eat on the island. Unfortunately, this spot can get crowded with tour parties at the height of the season. However, it's usually possible to find a corner where you can take in the early Christian atmosphere without being disturbed.

ANI

48 km E of Kars on the Armenian border. Permit required – see end of this entry. This is one of the most spectacular sights in Turkey, as well as being one of the most remote. It is situated on a promontory between two ravines. The stream at the bottom of the ravine to the south forms the border with Armenia. Across the gorge you can still see the old watchtowers of the former Iron Curtain, where grim guards would scrutinize the tourist groups through their binoculars for

---

RECOMMENDED HOTELS

DOĞUBAYAZIT

Once upon a time this spot had several picturesque *pansiyons* where you would find tribes of hippies girding up their loins in preparation for the migration to the East, mingling with the forlorn figures of those who had actually made it back. Alas, such adventurous souls are now a thing of the past.

Hotel Tahran, L; *Büyük Ağrı Caddesi 86; tel. 0278 2223.*

A serviceable hotel for those who expect little and are willing to accept less. But they're very friendly here, and the price is low for what you get.

KARS

The hotel situation in Kars is fairly basic. The best you'll find is:

Yilmaz Oteli, LL; *Kuçuk Kazimbey Caddesi 24; tel. 021 11074.*

A fairly basic spot, run by a fairly basic crew. They've cornered the market, so they don't have to be pleasant – but there's no accounting for human nature, and sometimes they actually are agreeable. Most rooms have private water sprinkling apparatus.

VAN

Büyük Urartu Oteli, LLL; *Hastane Caddesi 60; tel. 061 20660.*

The best hotel in town. You will find the little expensive comforts here a small price to pay when the outside temperature starts matching that in the Empty Quarter of Arabia. As you might expect from the name, the decoration is on an Urartian theme, and even the manager here used to be a professional archaeologist – presumably until he discovered that unearthing tourists was more profitable. The waiters in the excellent restaurant are friendly and speak rare dialects of both English and German.

For those who believe in sweltering the pounds out of themselves rather than their wallets, there's always the nearby:

Otel Çağ, L; *Hastane Caddesi 2; tel. 061 12717.*

Fairly basic accommodation, but it's clean. Some rooms have contraptions which squirt water in unexpected places, or not at all. Others have showers. Be sure to check first. You're guaranteed a friendly welcome at the desk.

spies and potential invaders.

Ani has a history going back to Urartian times, at the start of the first millennium BC, but it only rose to prominence some 2,000 years later. In the 10thC AD the city became the Armenian capital. Afterwards, it was overrun by a succession of conquerors, including the Persians, the Selçuks and finally the Mongols, who fortunately did much less damage than usual, though its inhabitants were despatched with the customary thoroughness and fervour. The city and its many churches were then left derelict for centuries, only suffering damage from earthquakes and the ravages of time.

The city had its golden age during the Armenian era (935-1045), and the most impressive churches and ruins all date from this period. You can still see the fine protective **walls**, an impressive entry **gate** (Alp Arslan Kapisi) and a Selçuk **mosque** which is claimed as the first of its kind in Anatolia. The **cathedral**, still largely intact, was built at the turn of the 11thC and was once the finest in all Armenia. Several other churches have murals and external reliefs depicting biblical scenes.

As you stand amongst the grassy ruins here it is difficult to imagine that this remote spot was once the glorious capital of an empire – a regional rival to Baghdad, with a population of more than 1,000,000. For more information on the Armenian Empire, see Van, page 208.

Because of Ani's politically sensitive location, you need a permit to visit. This is obtained in Kars: see last paragraph of Kars entry, page 207.

AGRI DAĞI (MOUNT ARARAT)

By the Turkish-Iranian-Armenian border. This superb, isolated snow-capped mountain towers above the surrounding plains. An extinct volcano with an impressive cone shape, it has two summits, the highest, Büyük Ağri, over 5,000 metres. According to the Bible, this is the spot where Noah's ark came to rest after the flood. This was usually accepted as something of a fable – but some people had second thoughts when in 1951 an expedition climbing the mountain came across some pieces of ancient wood frozen in the permanent ice near the peak. (I have seen a rather blurred photograph of this 'find', which

looks like a large frozen portion of bangers and mash.)

Despite regular organized searches (one of which included the U.S. astronaut James Irwin) no one else has yet managed to locate these elusive remains. In the old days of the Iron Curtain, this is the spot where the British double agent Kim Philby would secretly slip across to the U.S.S.R. to meet his Soviet controller. As an act of bravado, Philby always kept a photo of Mount Ararat in his office – which he would freely admit to having taken himself. But what no one realized was that he had taken this photo from the Soviet side of the mountain.

South of the mountain, 5 km west of the Iranian border, N of Rt 100, there is a large **meteor crater**. If you've never seen a large meteorite crater before, except in aerial photos, this is your chance to be disappointed by the real thing. Even so, its sheer size will make you reflect that the impact must have produced quite a bang. (Despite the demise of the Iron Curtain, this remains a sensitive military area highly sensitive to big bangs. Contact the police in Doğubayazit before you set off down any side tracks.)

CAVUŞTEPE

50 km SW of Van on Rt 975 to Hakkari. This site has the remains of an Urartian hill-top town which was built by King Sardur II in the 8thC BC. You can see a **temple**, complete with inscriptions; a sacrificial **altar stone** (according to my guide, who proved a little untrustworthy in other spheres, this was used for human sacrifice); and the remains of the **royal palace**. The latter's chief marvel is the sewage system, complete with ducts, and even the remains of the royal lavatory.

DOĞUBAYAZIT ⇌ ✕

On Rt E80 35 km from the Iranian border. This town is little more than a stop-off for lorry-drivers on the long-distance run from Europe to Iran. You may find yourself staying here on your way to Ararat or Kars. If so, be sure to allow time for a drive out to **Ishak Paşa Sarayi**, which is on a 2,000-m plateau 5 km SE of town.

This huge fortified palace was started in 1685 by a local Kurdish ruler called Çolak Abdi Paşa, and was eventually finished 99 years later by his son Ishak

• *Light relief, Kars.*

Paşa. The palace originally had a room for every day of the year (with an extra one added for leap years). Its architectural style appears to have been conceived in similar whimsical fashion. Persian, Russian and Turkish influences are blended like chalk, cheese and cherries. Nothing mixes, but it doesn't matter, this is a delight. You can still wander through some of the salons and inspect the 200-year-old central heating and sewage systems – which no longer work, but appear to be in much better order than many local hotel systems whose owners insist that they do. The entrance to the palace once had large golden doors, but these were pillaged by the Russians during the First World War. (They are now on display in the Hermitage Museum at St Petersburg.)

Below here you can see the remains of Eski Bayazit ('Old Bayazit'), an Urartian city which flourished in 1000 BC.

HOŞAB

10 km beyond Cavuştepe on Rt 975 to Hakkari. The mountains around here and towards the Iranian border are spectacularly beautiful and remote, with lofty snow-capped peaks rising to over 3,500 m. At sunrise the valleys are filled with an eerie stillness, which is gently broken by the sound of unseen waterfalls, and the haunting, echoing cries of the goatherds calling to one another across the ravines.

Hoşab is a fairytale castle built in 1643 by the great Kurdish leader Sari Suleyman. The castle's name means 'beautiful water' in Kurdish, and it stands in a fine setting above a stream and the village of Güzelsu. Sari Suleyman was so pleased with the design of his castle that when his architect had finished the work he ordered his hands to be cut off so that he could never build another one like it. Parts of the castle are still virtually intact, including its crenellated wall, its entry tunnel and several inscriptions carved into the stone.

ISHAK PAŞA SARAYI
See Doğubayazit, page 205.

KARS 🛏 ✕
50 km W of Armenian border on Rt 957. Kars is a rather grim spot with a long grim history. The only reason for com-

ing here is because it is so remote, and also because it's on the way to Ani (see page 204).

The city was founded in the 8thC BC by the Urartians. The usual alternation of slaughter and slumber persisted through the following centuries. Then in the 10thC AD the Armenian king Abas made it his capital. This was a golden era: Armenian culture flourished as never before (and seldom since). Then at the start of the 13thC it was back to business as usual. Kars was taken in a cloud of dust by the Georgian cavalry. Next came the Mongols, who reduced the city to a cloud of dust. Some 150 years later Tamerlane of Samarkand staged an encore, but then thought better of it and rebuilt the place. By the middle of the 17thC Kars was once again flourishing; according to historical records it contained more than 50 mosques. Then in 1664 it was flattened by an earthquake. And so it went on. During the 19thC the Russians invaded, and invaded, and invaded – finally deciding to stay and turn the place into something of an Armenian colony, ejecting the local Turks and Kurds in large numbers. In 1918, after signing away Kars at the Treaty of Brest-Litovsk the Russians decamped, and the Armenians wisely decided to accompany them. But the Soviets still looked upon Kars as part of the Russian Empire, and Stalin asked for it to be returned in 1945. The Turks refused, and at once took the precaution of forming a strong alliance with the United States.

You can still see the Russian influence in Kars. If you look closely, you'll find several old **Czarist buildings**, which the Turks have cunningly put to modern use. The Russian Orthodox cathedral is now a gymnasium, and another church has been turned into a power station.

There's not much to see here. You can take a stroll on the **citadel**, which now has a park, and you can also visit the **museum**, which has a few oddments from Ani.

To obtain your pass to visit Ani, call at the tourist information office in Ali Bey Caddesi, fill in the form, and take it to be stamped at the Security Police just over 100 m around the corner on Faik Bey Caddesi. You should allow an hour for this process.

CLIMBING ARARAT

Philby, and other Soviet spies, may have flitted back and forth here with comparative ease; however, you will find it much, much more difficult to climb Mount Ararat. It is now illegal to go on the mountain without written permission from the authorities in Ankara, plus a recognized guide. None the less, Ararat is for many people an attractive challenge: a big mountain that can be conquered without any Alpine-style rock climbing.

Parties can be arranged through your local Turkish Embassy, or Trek Travel, Aydele Caddesi 10, 80090 Taksim, Istanbul; tel. 1 155 1642. You must apply at least three months before you wish to climb, and be prepared for a constant uphill battle against a mountain of bureaucracy – after which the 5,000-m peak will seem straightforward.

The lower slopes are essentially easy (but hot) hill walking. Nowadays, organized expeditions make two overnight stops in tents before the assault on the summit (it can be done with one). The upper slopes are paved by vast boulder fields and scree slopes giving way to the snow-and-ice cap. All water has to be carried – the meltwater from the snow cap is not safe to drink. There is no rock climbing of any severity, but you need a head for heights and there is plenty of scrambling. It's a gruelling ordeal. You spend a relatively long time at a high altitude and despite acclimatizing slowly overnight at the camps you'll need to take precautions against the body changes caused by altitude: heed your party-leader's advice – the changes are extremely uncomfortable and potentially fatal. Organized expeditions will have oxygen equipment and crampons for the snow/ice at the top, though the mountain has often been climbed without. Those who make it to the summit – including the British publisher of this guide, who did it without oxygen or crampons, and wearing ludicrously inadequate slip-on shoes – describe it as an unforgettable experience.

VAN GÖLÜ (LAKE VAN)

Some 100 km W of the Iranian border. Covering more than 3,700 square km, this lake – better described as an inland sea – is almost as large as Luxembourg. It used to be a large valley, but this was blocked by a lava flow from the nearby volcano Nemrut Daği. Now rivers flow into it, but it has no outlet. This means that the level of the lake has been known to fluctuate by up to 3 m over the years. In the 19thC it rose and flooded the town of Erciş on its northern shore, so that the entire place had to be completely rebuilt on a higher level. As the only loss of water is through evaporation, the lake has a high concentration of salts, particularly sodium. This means that you can wash your clothes in it without using soap. It's safe enough to swim, but make sure that you don't have any open cuts or these will sting badly. The water near Van itself has a tendency to be polluted, and the best safe swimming beach is a few kilometres south of Edremit.

Curiously, a species of fish still manages to live in the lake. This is locally called *darek,* and is a form of carp. In medieval times the fish was considered a great delicacy throughout the Middle East – one traveller even mentions coming across salted *darek* in Afghanistan.

VAN 🛏 ✕

On the E shore of Lake Van some 100 km W of the Iranian border. This is the largest city in Turkey's 'Far East', with a population of nearly 150,000. Here it's either freeze or fry – winter temperatures drop to minus 30˚C, and summer temperatures often rise above 35˚C.

Van is the home of the famous Van cats, which have distinctive fur and eyes of different colours. They are reputed to be very fond of swimming, but I have never come across any taking a dip in the lake. Van is now also a tourist centre, with numerous carpet shops selling all kinds of exotic floor coverings (some so exotic you're only meant to hang them on the wall). Keep your eyes open for genuine Kurdish kilims, some to be had at bargain prices. Otherwise there's not much to say about modern Van, which is really rather uninteresting. **Old Van**, on the other hand, is another matter.

Old Van has played host to an intriguing mix of peoples. There's been a settlement here since the 13thC BC, when the Hurrites arrived, followed soon after by the Hittites. Then came the Urartians (who sound as if they came from a different planet, and probably looked like it to the locals in those days). They took over in the 8thC BC and established a large empire which stretched well into the modern Iran, Iraq and Syria. The Urartian Empire (referred to as Ararat in the Bible) produced beautiful jewellery and even engineered a canal almost 80 km long to bring fresh water from the mountains. Part of this is still used for irrigation.

As the Urartian Empire declined, tribes began moving in from the west. These were named by the Persians 'Armenians' (what this name actually means is disputed). In time the Armenians took over, but were then overrun by the comings and goings of empires (Persian, Alexandrian, Roman and so on) until finally they decided to set up an empire of their own. At the end of 3rdC AD this became the first state to adopt Christianity as its official religion.

In the 11thC the Turks took over, but Van remained a flourishing Armenian centre. This state of affairs came to a tragic end only during the 20thC. In the First World War the Russians encouraged the Christian Armenians to rebel against the Muslim Turks with the aim of gaining independence. Fighting broke out, and numbers of Turks and Kurds living in the region were killed. The Turkish response was as immediate as it was horrific: genocide. Armenians living throughout Turkey were slaughtered – estimates vary, but the death toll was certainly more than a million. This was to be the second major moral blot on the 20thC: following the exterminations in the Congo by the Belgians and preceding the Nazi Holocaust.

Van itself suffered an upheaval worse than anywhere else in Turkey during the Massacre of the Armenians. Prior to the outbreak of the First World War it had been a city of around 70,000 inhabitants; afterwards it contained less than a tenth of this figure. As a result, a new city was built, 5 km inland from the lake, and nowadays Old Van is but a ruin.

The citadel of the old city was the **Rock of Van**, a striking outcrop which stands between the new city and the lake shore. This is just 3 km from the city centre – a short inexpensive *dolmuş* ride. The pathway to the top of the citadel is at the north-western end of the rock. To reach this you pass a ruined **Urartian temple**, a **mosque** and the **tomb of a Muslim saint** which attracts pilgrims from all over the region. The top of the rock also has several Urartian ruins and relics. My favourite is the Ozymandias-like boast to be found inscribed in cuneiform on the remains of the 8thC BC ramparts: 'I, Sardur, the glorious king, the mighty king, king of all the lands in the world, king of the universe, a king without equal, I built these walls.' You can also see the tomb of the great Urartian king Argistis, who ruled in the 8thC BC. This also has some cuneiform inscriptions, but unfortunately these are in a dialect of Urartian which I have yet to master. Beside this tomb is the so-called imprint of the Devil's foot.

If you find yourself wandering about up here in the late afternoon, as the shadows lengthen and the temperature dips to a mere 30°C, hang on for a while: the sunsets over the distant mountains and Lake Van are far more exotic than any cocktail that could possibly be waiting for you back at your hotel.

South of the Rock of Van is the site of **Old Van**. This now consists of little more than stones amongst the grass, though there are a couple of remaining mosques dating from the 16thC. On the face of the rock here there is a large inscription in ancient Persian, Babylonian and Medean extolling the virtues of King Xerxes of Persia, who reigned in the 5thC BC and passed through here on his way to take on the ancient Greeks. At the edge of Old Van is the site of **Tushpa**, the ancient capital of the Urartian Empire, a hive of activity all of two and a half millennia ago.

In modern Van, one block east of the main Cumhuriyet Caddesi, you'll find the **museum**, one of the best provincial collections in Turkey. Here you can see some rock carvings found in the region which are said to date from 8000 BC. But best of all is the Urartian jewellery, breastplates and coloured glass – which give you just an inkling of what it must have been like so long ago in this all-but-forgotten civilization. Upstairs there is an ethnographic section which contains a dispiriting and repugnant exhibition that attempts to pass off the entire Armenian Massacre as a non-event.

RECOMMENDED RESTAURANTS

DOĞUBAYAZIT

Eating here can be quite a problem if you want something above the basic level. Your best bet is to try a hotel restaurant. The best of these is at:

Hotel Isfahan, LL; *Emniyet Caddesi 26; tel.* 0278 1138.

Hotel with a pleasant bar and a viewing room on the fourth floor that looks out towards Mount Ararat – which I have seen turn blood-red, with an eerie luminescent pink snowcap, in an autumn sunset.

KARS

The only place to eat at if you want to survive this grim spot is the restaurant at the **Yilmaz Oteli, LL**, see Recommended Hotels. This has some surprisingly imaginative local fare on the menu, though not always in the kitchen. But it does serve alcohol to soften the blow.

VAN

Your best plan is to eat at one of the tourist hotels: the stress of exotic temperature and exotic diet makes for a heavy fall-out rate, so it's best to minimize the risk of upset stomach. In any case, there aren't many good restaurants here. For the hotel option:

Büyük Urartu Oteli L-LL-LLL; details, *see Recommended Hotels.*

A reassuring menu, with enough to tempt the heat-jaded palate.

More adventurous souls should try:

Safak Lokantasi, L; *Kazim Karabekir Caddesi 16; tel.* 061 1192.

Unpretentious spot which serves several good local dishes, including the celebrated Otlu Peynir cheese. Can be something of a madhouse at lunchtime, but okay in the evenings.

<u>Western Turkey</u>

South of the Sea of Marmara

530 km; map GeoCenter EuroCountry, Western Turkey, 1:800 000

This part of Turkey is often overlooked, yet there are many places of interest. These include Bursa, the first capital of the Ottoman Empire; the historic city of Iznik (ancient Nicaea); and the picturesque Marmara Islands, long a favourite with the Turks but seldom visited by foreigners. If you want to explore this region, your best – and most likely starting point is Istanbul. In order to save the tiresome drive out of Istanbul and along the northern shore of the Gulf of Izmit, you can take a car ferry from Kartal to Yalova. From here it's just a short drive to the lakeside town of Iznik. Beyond Iznik you come to Bursa, set on a hillside overlooking the Nilüfer Valley. Here you can see some of the finest mosques in the country, as well as several royal tombs. From a southern suburb of Bursa you can catch a cable car up Mount Uludağ – which has a winter ski resort as well as a National Park with some pleasant summer hiking trails through the woods.

West of Bursa you pass Kuş Gölü, the famous 'Bird Lake', which has one of the oldest bird sanctuaries in Europe. North of here is the Kapidaği Peninsula, whose eastern shore is a disgrace but whose western shore is a delight. Even better, however, are the Marmara Islands, which can be reached by ferry from the port of Erdek, at the foot of the Kapidaği Peninsula.

West from here you come to the Dardanelles (known in Turkish as Çanakkale Boğazi), the narrow strait through which the Sea of Marmara drains into the Aegean. Towards the southern end of the Dardanelles is the town of Çanakkale, which for centuries has stood watch over the sea lanes to Istanbul and the Black Sea.

Driving from Istanbul to Çanakkale (not including detours) takes a day or so; allow at least three days if you want to stop and see some of the sights.

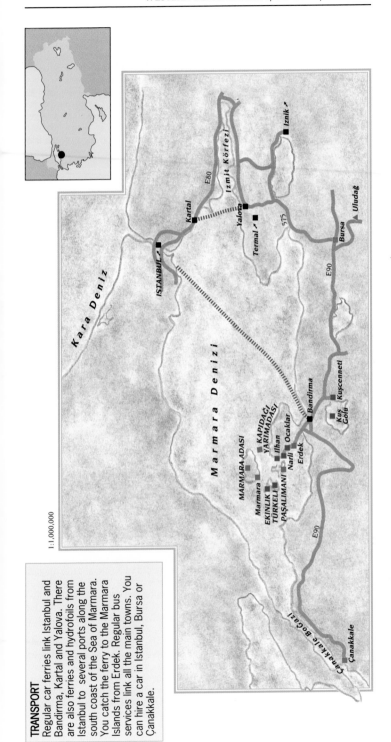

1:1.000.000

TRANSPORT

Regular car ferries link Istanbul and Bandirma, Kartal and Yalova. There are also ferries and hydrofoils from Istanbul to several ports along the south coast of the Sea of Marmara. You catch the ferry to the Marmara Islands from Erdek. Regular bus services link all the main towns. You can hire a car in Istanbul, Bursa or Çanakkale.

SIGHTS & PLACES OF INTEREST

BURSA ⌖ ×

A modern industrial city which has many fine sights: it was the first capital of the Ottoman Empire.

The city was founded at the end of the 3rdC BC by King Prusias of Bithynia, who modestly named it after himself. (According to legend it was Hannibal, the great Carthaginian general, who chose the site for him.) The Bithynians were a wild tribe from Thrace in northern Greece who were renowned for dressing themselves in fox skins. The name Prusias soon degenerated into Bursa, and during the Roman Empire the city rose to prominence on two counts. Hot springs were discovered here, and the bath-loving Romans would come from far and wide for a warm wallow.

More interesting, around this time some Nestorian Christians cracked the Chinese monopoly on the silk trade. They succeeded in smuggling some silk worms out of China inside their hollow walking canes, bringing them 8,000 km down the Silk Road to the West. Bursa quickly acquired some silk worms and established itself as a centre for silk production, which it remains to this day. The main silk market is held here in April, when the villagers come in to buy their silk worms. The best place to see the market is at the eastern end of the Bedesten (covered market), at the Koz Han *caravanserai*.

After the Roman era Bursa had a succession of overlords. It was taken and re-taken by the Crusaders, the Byzantines and the Selçuk Turks. Finally a group of nomadic Turks under their chieftan Osman laid siege to the city. The citizens of Bursa were well-prepared for a long siege, but Osman was a patient man – and after almost a decade the somewhat reduced inhabitants decided to call it a day. In 1326 Osman moved in, promoted himself to the rank of sultan, and declared Bursa the capital of his new empire. This became known as the Osmanli Empire, which Europeans usually call the Ottoman Empire. When Osman died he was succeeded by Sultan Orhan, who set out to conquer all of central Anatolia and Thrace. He was eventually succeeded by Sultan Beyazit I ('The Thun-

derbolt'), who expanded the Ottoman Empire as far as Bosnia and Hungary. In order to oversee these operations, Beyazit moved the capital 300 km north-east to Edirne in Thrace.

But the Ottomans never forgot their first capital, and Bursa retained an honoured place in the expanding empire. This was the burial place of both Osman and Orhan. Even after the final collapse of the Ottoman Empire following its defeat in the First World War, Bursa remaind a spiritual centre with a special place in Turkish history. Then in the 1960s it became a boom town when the car industry arrived – making Renault, Murat (Turkish Fiat) and Anadol (Turkish) cars.

Bursa has a wide range of sights, some of which are as fine as you'll see anywhere in the land. My favourite is **Yeşil Camii** (the Green Mosque) which was completed in 1419 by Mehmet I. It is built in the Eastern style (Persian, with other influences from as far east as Samarkand). Its exterior is justly renowned, with some exquisite marble carving around the main door. Inside, just above this, were the sultan's apartments. Unusually for a mosque, these contain not only his living quarters, but also quarters for those whom no self-respecting sultan could do without – such as his bathroom attendant, his ministers and a choice selection from his harem. This mosque was reduced to a shattered birthday cake by the great earthquake of 1855, but within a decade had been completely restored to its original grandeur.

Across the way from here is the **Yeşil Türbe** (Green Tomb) of Mehmet I. This is a suitable monument to the builder of the Yeşil Camii, and one of the finest of its kind in Turkey (a country with no mean record when it comes to magnificent tombs). Alas, when this tomb was rebuilt after the earthquake the restorers must have been colour-blind, for despite its name the tiles which now decorate it are blue.

Just east of here there are some cafés where you can sit and look down over the city.

In fact there are several mosques worth visiting in Bursa. Don't miss **Yildirim Beyazit Camii**, built by Beyazit the Thunderbolt during a rare constructive period at the end of 14thC. It contains his tomb. The **Ulu Camii** (Great

Mosque) was completed in 1396. The sultan who built it promised Allah that if He gave him victory in battle he would build a mosque 20 times the size of a normal mosque. After gaining his victory the sultan remained as good as his word, and Ulu Camii has no less than 20 domes. Also worth a visit is the **Emir Sultan Camii**, which stands on a hillside overlooking the city, and is built in a style aptly described as Ottoman Rococo. Nearby is a large Muslim **cemetery**. Try visiting this, as I once did, with someone who can decipher the inscriptions – some of them give touching glimpses into a distant age of a distant empire.

The **Muradiye Külliyese** dates from medieval times and contains ten royal tombs. The life histories of the occupants of these tombs are *extremely* interesting. To whet your appetite: two were poisoned 'for their own good' by Selim the Grim; and Cem, the son of

Mehmet I, was a devout Muslim and prolific poet who almost led one of the Crusades and was eventually poisoned by the Pope.

The **Museum of Turkish and Islamic Art** contains a number of gems, which also well illustrate the history of the Ottoman Empire.

The best of the city's famous baths is **Yeni Kaplica**, built in the 16thC on the site of the original baths erected by the Roman emperor Justinian.

The best places for wandering about are in **Bat Pazani**, the labyrinthine old market quarter where about the only thing you won't find on sale is a bat (in fact, *bat* means goose in Turkish).

Also not to missed is **Hisar**, a well-preserved district of old Bursa.

The **Archaeological Museum** has everything from Roman glass to Byzantine skulls, as well as a fabulous collection of early coins from all over this region.

RECOMMENDED HOTELS

BURSA
The traffic along central Atatürk Caddesi is an orchestrated bedlam both day and night – so avoid any hotels in this district unless you're a modernist composer seeking inspiration. Centrally situated, but quiet, is:

Hotel Dikmen, LL; *Fevzi Çakmak Caddesi 78; tel. 24 214 995.*
Modern hotel with English- and German-speaking staff. There's a pleasant garden with a plashing fountain at the back. Can suddenly fill up with pre-booked tour groups, so be sure to ring ahead.

Termal Hotel, LLL; *Gönlü Murat Caddesi 24; tel. 24 362 700.*
For luxury at not too luxurious a price try this spot, perched above the Nilüfer Valley, out at Çekirge, the eastern suburb which contains the thermal baths. Classy metropolitan *ambience*, complete with visiting Middle-Eastern potentates.

ÇANAKKALE
A word of warning. Unless you book well ahead, it is almost impossible to get a room here in mid-August, on

account of the Çanakkale-Troy festival. At other times of the year you should have little problem. Try:

Otel Anafartalar, LL-LLL; *Iskele Meydani; tel. 196 14 454.*
Two-star hotel right by the ferry docks looking over the Dardanelles. The higher rooms have the best views.

Dardanelles views at a slightly less expensive rate can be had at:

Hotel Bakir, LL; *Rihtim Caddesi 12; tel. 196 12 908.*
More than 30 rooms, all with bath or shower, overlooking the harbour by the clocktower.

ERDEK
Ümit Hotel, L; *Balikhani Sokak; tel. 1989 1092.*
In town and close to the ferry jetty.

If you want to stay by the beach, try:
Kafkas Motel, L-LL; *on the seafront north of town; tel. 1989 1256.*

MARMARA ADASI (MARMARA ISLAND)
Marmara Otel, L-LL; *Marmara village; tel. 1984 1185.*
On the seafront; most rooms have private shower or bath.

• Çanakkale welcome.

BANDIRMA

A grotesque spot close to a NATO base. It has a car ferry link with Istanbul, which is the only reason you'll find yourself here if you have any sense. Perverse travellers who have ignored this advice out of curiosity should try heading for Erdek, 15 km up the road, the port for the Marmara Islands. Or head 18 km south to the bird sanctuary at Kuş Gölü. For both, see separate entries.

ÇANAKKALE 🛏 ✕

Makes an ideal base for visiting Gallipoli and Troy – see Turkey Overall: 1 and 2.

Çanakkale guards the entrance to the Dardanelles, the channel which links the Aegean with the Sea of Marmara (and hence with Istanbul, the Bosphorus and the Black Sea). The Dardanelles, which divide Europe from Asia and are only just over a kilometre wide at this point, have always been of great strategic importance.

The channel was initially called the Hellespont, after the unlucky goddess Helle who fell from the back of her flying sheep and drowned in its waters. Its later name comes from Dardanus, who was once king of the city now known

• Clock tower, Çanakkale.

• Çanakkale bakery.

as Çanakkale.

In 480 BC the Persian king Xerxes built a bridge of boats across this stretch of water to enable his huge army to pass on its way to Greece.

In the 14thC the Ottoman sultan Mehmet the Conqueror fortified the city and built a castle on the opposite shore of the Dardanelles, thus cutting off the sea route to Constantinople (Istanbul), the capital of the tottering Byzantine Empire. Mehmet called this new castle Kilitbehir, which means 'the lock which closes the sea'). It lived up to its name, and Constantinople fell to Mehmet soon afterwards.

In 1915, during the First World War, Churchill came up with an ambitious scheme 'to knock out Turkey and join up with the Russians'. This characteristically gung-ho notion involved the Allied fleet sailing up the Dardanelles to shell Istanbul into submission. The fleet was stopped by the Turkish guns at Çanakkale (a setback which led to the even more disastrously misconceived Gallipoli campaign – see Turkey Overall: 1). Today you can see the remains of these **guns** – including a spectacularly exploded cannon and a suitably lurid wall-painting depicting the Allied ships under fire – at a **memorial** south-west of the town centre.

Also worth a visit is the nearby **Army and Navy Museum** on the seafront. The prize exhibit here is Atatürk's battered pocket watch, which was hit by shrapnel during the Gallipoli campaign and saved his life.

The **Archaeological Museum**, which is south of town on the road to Troy, contains various relics unearthed at Troy (which become much more interesting after you have visited Troy) as well as all kinds of ancient junk.

EKINLIK
See Erdek and the Marmara Adasi, below.

ERDEK AND THE MARMARA ADASI (MARMARA ISLANDS)

There's a beach north of town, but you'll probably be here to catch one of the ferries across to the islands. (These all tend to leave around 3 pm, when the sleepy port wakes up with a vengeance.)

The Maramara Islands were inhabited almost exclusively by Greeks until the enforced exchange of populations in the 1920s. They're the nearest in atmosphere you'll get to the Greek islands in Turkey. This said, don't expect anything too spectacular. They are fairly well developed as local tourist resorts.

Only the four larger islands are inhabited. **Marmara** used to be called Elafonisos by the Greeks, and was first colonized by the Ionian city of Miletus (see

215

Turkey Overall: 3, on the south-western Turkish mainland. Its present name derives from the Greek word *marmara*, meaning marble, on account of the island's marble quarries. Its inland mountain, **Ilyasdaği**, rises to 700 m, and it's possible to follow trails over its barren flanks into the interior. The little beaches are okay for swimming but not much more. The main village (also

ENTELLEKTÜEL RESTAURANT

RECOMMENDED RESTAURANTS

BURSA

Once upon a time a local chef called Iskender (the Turkish for Alexander) decided to invent a new form of kebab. It contained lamb doner, tomato and yoghurt sauce, and melted butter. This was called the Iskender kebab, or alternatively, Bursa kebab. You'll see it all over Turkey, but this is its home. The city is also renowned for the variety of its fruit juices.

The restaurants here are mostly of a high standard, and inexpensive. The exceptions are those out at Çekirge, which can be very dear.

Kebapci Iskender, L-LL; *Atatürk Caddesi 60;* No *booking.*

This is *the* place to have your authentic Iskender kebab – it's said to have been invented here. Can get very crowded at midday.

For a more relaxed meal, try:

Inegöl Kofteçi, L-LL; *Atatürk Caddesi 42; no booking.*

Down a side street off busy Atatürk Caddesi. This spot is named after another regional speciality, *Inegöl kofte* (lamb meatballs). Friendly service and value for money.

ÇANAKKALE

By far the best place to eat here is at one of the restaurants looking out over the Dardanelles, where you can dine in the open air and watch all kinds of craft passing along one of the busiest shipping lanes in the world. (Tankers and rusty freighters, smart liners and battleships, plying from Odessa and Istanbul to every port in the world – a sight to gladden the heart of anyone with but a spark of imagination.) Those perverse intellectuals who wish to pay atention to the food as well as this captivating sight, should try:

Yeni Entellektüel, LL; *on the waterfront; no booking.*

Literally 'the new intellectuals' restaurant, it is fortunately free of this dangerous species. Those of us with a rather broader-based learning will enjoy their excellent fish.

Hardened philistines who can't stomach anything even remotely intellectual should try:

Yavlova Liman Restaurant, L-LL; *on the waterfront; no booking*

You eat on a third-floor terrace which looks out over the Dardanelles towards Kilitbahir. Their salads and side dishes are particularly good. (Though even here you'll find that you're not entirely free from intellectual interference. Across the strait on the hillside are large letters depicting the first verse of a poem by an unfortunate highbrow called Onan.)

called **Marmara**) has steep little streets retaining a distinctly Greek feel.

The nearby island of **Türkeli** has the most immediately appealing scenery (long sandy beaches and pleasant swimming), but this has also appealed to a large section of the population of Istanbul. Next door **Ekinlik** is too small and too near to be unspoilt. Your best choice is **Paşalimani,** which has several little seaside villages and is hearteningly difficult to get to. Life here is friendly and spartan, but with few beaches.

ISTANBUL
See pages 38-61.

IZNIK
See Turkey Overall: 11.

KAPIDAĞI YARIMADASI
(YARIMADASI PENINSULA)
Owing to its proximity to the Istanbul ferry and Bandirma, the eastern side of the Kapidaği Peninsula is a tatty mess of caravans, military refuse tips, fuel dumps, booming factories devoted exclusively to the production of pollutants and the like. Only bathe here if you are suffering from a rare fungal infection of the skin which has failed to respond to all other chemical treatment.

The western shore is different. Here you'll find the pleasant little port of **Erdek** (see page 215). Some 5 km north of here is the seaside village of **Ocaklar** which has a pleasant beach. If you press on up to the villages of **Narli** and **Ilhan** you can sometimes get a small boat across to the islands. Both these spots remain pleasant enough, though they can get a little crowded in the high season. These are almost exclusively Turkish holiday resorts, and remain semi-developed after their own fashion.

KUŞ GÖLÜ
The main point of interest of the celebrated 'Bird Lake' is the famous **Kuşcenneti Bird Sanctuary,** which is 18 km south of Bandirma. Kuşcenneti literally means 'bird paradise', which apparently is just what this place once was when established more than 50 years ago. It's on important migration routes and literally millions of birds pass through every year. They claim that some 200 species have been spotted.

Unfortunately the lake is at present suffering from shrinkage because its water is being pumped out for irrigation. This has left the 'bird paradise' somewhat dry – the best wildlife I saw when I last visited were the stuffed exhibits at the **visitors' centre**.

During the migration season (October especially) I'm assured that the site is 'a marvel of the ecology world,' to quote a warden. It's worth making enquiries before you visit – apparently Kuşcenneti really was a marvel some years ago (and may well become so again when the real meaning of the word ecology sinks in).

PAŞALIMANI
See Erdek and the Marmara Adasi, page 215.

TERMAL
See Turkey Overall: 11.

TÜRKELI
See Erdek and the Marmara Adasi, page 215.

ULUDAĞ
2,500-m mountain rising SE of Bursa. This was named the 'Olympos of Mysia' by the Greeks who used to live here. Interestingly, scholars now believe that the ancient Greek word Olympus was not originally Greek at all. Some say it arrived in this region with the early Germanic migrations, others that it is Phoenician – though all are agreed that it meant mountain.

In winter Uludağ is a ski resort, and in summer there's excellent hiking through the woods to the lakes. But it is most spectacular in spring, when the slopes are covered with a myriad of multi-coloured flowers.

The best way to get here is by the cable car from Teferüç on the outskirts of Bursa, reached by taking the 'Teleferit' *dolmuş* from Atatürk Caddesi 100 m E of the tourist office.

Izmir, Çeşme and Region

100 km; map GeoCenter EuroCountry, Western Turkey, 1:800 000

I zmir – the ancient port of Smyrna – is the third largest city in Turkey, with a glorious and sometimes tragic history. It rose to prominence after being re-founded by Alexander the Great and later became the gem of the Roman Empire, considered by some to be the most beautiful city in the ancient world.

Izmir's setting remains beautiful, though the modern city itself could hardly be so described. Despite this, there are many sights worth visiting. The bazaar quarter is second only to Istanbul's, the museums are interesting and the ruined castle of Kadifekale provides one of the finest cityscapes in Turkey.

West of Izmir Rt 300 leads you towards the Karaburun Peninsula, where you'll find several remote villages and beaches (as well as some outbreaks of villamania). At the end of Rt 300 you come to Çeşme, the ferry port for the Greek island of Chios which lies just across the water. There are some pleasant beaches north of here, and some ancient ruins. A few of the beaches to the south of Çeşme are exceptional, and one or two remain almost completely unspoilt.

By far the best way to get to Izmir is to take the ferry from Istanbul. This sets off in the afternoon, takes you through the Sea of Marmara (with the superb sight of Istanbul and its great minarets receding on the horizon), along the Aegean coast past the islands, and arrives at Izmir next morning. Be sure to book well ahead (at any TML agent), as this route is very popular.

TRANSPORT
Izmir is connected to Ankara and Istanbul by rail, regular bus services and internal flights. There is also a regular ferry service between Istanbul and Izmir. Çeşme is connected to Izmir by a regular bus service.

1:1,500,000

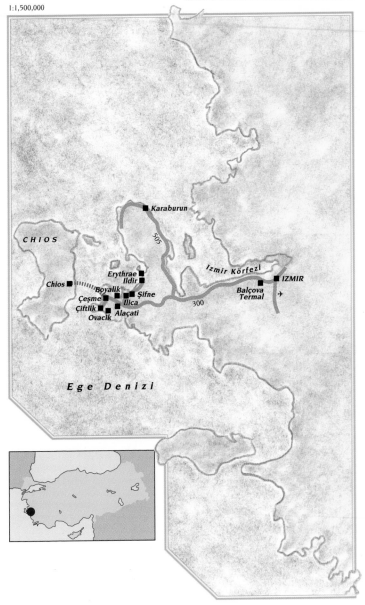

CHIOS

Karaburun

505

Erythrae
Ildir

Chios

Boyalik
Şifne
Çeşme   Ilica
Çiftlik   Alaçati
Ovacik

Izmir Körfezi

Balçova
Termal

IZMIR

300

Ege Denizi

• Bus station, Izmir.

SIGHTS & PLACES OF INTEREST

BOYALIK
Also Chios, Ilica, Şifne and other places west of Izmir the neighbourhood of Çeşme, see Çeşme, below.

ÇEŞME 🛏
This ancient town is named after its drinking fountains (Çeşme means fountain) and you can still see some of them on its streets, though few are now in working order.

Çeşme is dominated by its Genoese fortress, which rises in the centre of town and overlooks the harbour. It was largely rebuilt by Sultan Beyazit I in the early 15thC. A self-appointed local historian who once latched on to me here claimed that when Beyazit relaid the foundations of the castle he crushed a crusader, a pirate, a Christian priest and a disloyal eunuch beneath its towers 'to warn his enemies'. (I have been unable to confirm this tale from any other source.) The town has some pleasant old houses and mosques, but has recently undergone something of a boom. This is partly owing to tourism, partly owing to its new terminal for the ferry to Venice, and largely owing to the new multi-lane highway direct from Izmir. Some summer weekends it seems that every vehicle that can move in Izmir, and many that can't, are on this highway to the cool clear air of Çeşme.

Çeşme is at the end of the barren peninsula which juts out to form the southern coast of the Gulf of Izmir. It has a regular ferry service across the 10-km channel to the Greek island of **Chios**. This makes a pleasant day trip. Even better is to take a trip around the peninsula, which has some fine beaches.

The beaches on the north of the peninsula are sandy and popular, but not always clean. Closest is **Boyalik**, just north-east of town. Far better is **Ilica**, where there is a long beach 4 km from town. The spa resort of **Şifne,** just beyond here, is a dump.

But 11 km further along the coast you come to **Ildir**, which has the ruins of **ancient Erythrae**. This spot has a long and tedious history stretching back over almost three millennia – consisting of the usual slaughter and havoc wreaked by the stars of history whom we have mistakenly been taught to admire. The site itself has the remains of a theatre, a villa and bits of temples. These may not sound much – but there's a fine view looking out from the acropolis over a blue bay studded with tiny islands.

South of Çeşme the coastline is even better. Inland you can wander around the little old streets of **Alaçati,** which was once Greek, as were most of the villages in this region. Several of them have remained half deserted since

1922. Beach lovers should take one of the two roads south from Çeşme. The road beyond **Ovacik** leads to a fine beach with its own little café. The other leads along the west coast beyond **Çiftlik** to a string of lovely small beaches, only a few of which have succumbed to villamania. The others are all you could wish for: an enchanting secret which will not remain unknown for much longer, even without me spilling the beans.

IZMIR ⇌ ✕

The ferries disembark at Alsancak Terminal, which is 2 km up the waterfront from the city centre. The bus station is 2 km NE of the city centre. Both have a regular dolmuş service into town. There is also a regular bus service from the airport. The city centre is around Konak Meydani (Government House Square), inland to the bazaar quarter, and south to the smart district containing the State Opera House.

As a port, Izmir is second only to Istanbul. It is superbly situated, on hillsides overlooking a long gulf, complete with islands. Two millennia ago the classical geographer and historian Strabo described the city as the most beautiful he had seen in all the world; and when it was destroyed by an earthquake the Roman Emperor is said to have wept.

The fine setting remains, but there's no getting away from the fact that modern Izmir is a large, pulsating, high-decibel, overheated, odiferous mess. Accept these facts (taking precautions accordingly), and you may well be surprised to discover that the city has much to offer. I usually enjoy my visits to Izmir, which I consider to be one of the world's unjustly neglected seaports (much like Antwerp). Not least of Izmir's charms is its people, who are easygoing and friendly. Listen to them, and you'll learn much more about Turkey than you can ever find in a book.

That said, there are of course certain indispensable snippets of information which you could *only* get from a book (such as the one you are at present reading). For instance, you're unlikely learn from the locals whether the city was established in 2nd millennium BC by the Hittites, or was in fact founded even earlier by those legendary female warriors the Amazons. Or, as has been suggested by some modern professor who ought to know better, whether the

---

RECOMMENDED HOTELS

ÇEŞME
Ertan Oteli, LL; *Cumhuriyet Meydani 12; tel.* 549 26795.

Tall white building on the front. Some rooms have views out over the sea. With almost 70 rooms, it usually has a bed even when the rest of town is booked out. Somewhat expensive, but that's Çeşme.

IZMIR
The best area for reasonably priced hotels in town is around the Basmane Station, just south-east of 9 Eylul Meydani. If you want somewhere closer to the front, try:

Ankara Palas, L-LL; *Kanak; tel.* 511 42850.

Large hotel that has reasonably equipped rooms – most with shower or bath. Owing to its size and turnover, this often has rooms when others are full.

For those who must have a pool, and are willing to pay for it, try:

Büyük Efes Oteli, LL-LLL; *Gazi Osman Paşa 1; tel.* 511 44300.

Just by Cumhuriyet Meydani. This is a genuine oasis of calm in the maelstrom. It has cool, pleasant grounds, a cool, even more pleasant pool, and some rooms with views of the gulf. Prices vary considerably, and out of season in a room with only a street view you can get exceptional value.

For a cheaper option with pool, you'll have to head out to the airport:

Dal-Pet Motel, LL; *Kisikköy; tel.* 546 11449.

South-east of the city just a couple of miles from the airport on the main Rt E87 to Aydin. (Watch out for the BP petrol station.) This is by the main road, but doesn't feel so claustrophobic as some of the hotels in town.

grubby pre-historic Hittites and the superb, awesome Amazons might even have been the same people. A likely story. (Is nothing sacred?) Either way, the ancient city was at Bayrakli, which is now at the very head of the gulf, some way north of the modern city centre. The city's early name, Smyrna, is said to derive from its Hittite name, Tisurma.

In the 9thC BC the city was occupied by Ionian Greeks, who had established several cities along the Aegean coastline of Asia Minor. Smyrna prospered, though it never became one of the major Ionian cities (some of which had colonies as far afield as ancient Egypt, the south of France and the Black Sea). By the 4thC BC earthquakes and invaders had left the city virtually derelict. Then one day Alexander the Great went hunting on nearby Mount Pagus (now known as Kadifekale, the mountain which overlooks the city centre). While Alexander was resting from his exertions he fell asleep and had a dream in which one of the gods told him to found a city here. Alexander consulted a local oracle, which confirmed this dream, and the city was re-founded, with Mount Pagus as its acropolis.

During the following centuries the city once again prospered, its popula-

tion growing to more than 100,000. It was the wide paved streets and fine buildings laid out during this era which impressed the historian Strabo more than any other he had seen on his long travels, and caused the Emperor Marcus Aurelius to weep when he heard that it had been destroyed in the 178 AD earthquake.

The city's geography makes it the obvious port for the Anatolian hinterland. This has been its role through centuries of prosperity and conquest, prosperity again, and conquest again. The Romans, the Byzantines, the Selçuks, the Crusaders, the Venetians, and even Tamerlane of Samarkand all took Izmir, and lost it.

Meanwhile the city attracted traders of all kinds. By the end of the 16thC Izmir had a thriving Armenian quarter, a community of Sephardic Jews (from Spain) as well as resident groups of peoples from various parts of the Mediterranean litoral. It was known to the Ottoman Turks as 'Gavur Izmir' (Infidel Izmir) – but continued to be known to the rest of the world by the name favoured by its majority Greek community: Smyrna.

And in 1922 it was to be the scene of a catastrophe which shook the world, one of the great horrors of the

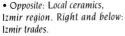

• *Opposite: Local ceramics, Izmir region. Right and below: Izmir trades.*

early 20thC. The story is complex, and no one involved in it emerges without blame.

Briefly, after Turkey's defeat in the First World War, the Greeks (and nominally the other allies) were given control of Smyrna and the immediate hinterland. The Ottoman Empire collapsed and Turkey plunged into the War of Independence. The country was falling apart, and the Greeks decided to invade the Anatolian hinterland, while the Allies turned a blind eye. The Greek army, led by a commander who suffered from the delusion that his feet

were made of glass, advanced towards Ankara committing widespread atrocities amongst the local Turks. But in the summer of 1922 the Greeks were confronted by the forces of Mustafa Kemal, later to be known as Atatürk. The Greeks suffered a crushing defeat.

The remnants of their army retreated in disarray towards Smyrna, joined by the local Greek peasantry who feared reprisals from the advancing Turks. By the first week in September 1922 there were over 150,000 Greeks camped out on the waterfront at Smyrna, desperate to get out, with the vengeful

223

Turkish army advancing into the suburbs. Despite pleas from the Greeks, the British and Italian ships anchored in the gulf refused to interfere and to ship out the refugees. As the Turkish army took possession of the city, a fire broke out amongst the old wooden houses in the Armenian quarter. For three days the unquenchable flames raged through the city. Panic and slaughter were widespread. By the time the fire had been put out, at least 30,000 (mainly Greeks) had lost their lives, and the city was almost completely burnt to the ground. The Sephardic Jewish quarter, the old Armenian quarter, the ancient Frankish houses and thousands of years of history had been reduced to a smouldering ruin.

In order to avoid further massacres more than 100,000 Greeks living in Turkey had to be uprooted in exchange for a similar number of Turks living in Greece. Communities which had lived for centuries in the same spot were transported wholesale, to become refugees in a 'motherland' they barely knew. To this day you can still encounter people in Greece who refer to themselves as 'Smyrna Greeks'; and many of the 'repatriated' Turks didn't even speak Turkish.

The continuing antagonism between Greece and Turkey, most recently over Cyprus, and over oil drilling rights in the eastern Aegean, has to be seen against this background of a long and difficult history marred by appalling horrors such as the Smyrna Massacre. As many Greeks and Turks are coming to realize, apportioning blame is now futile – attempted reconciliation is the only answer.

Sights

Inevitably, Izmir is now largely a modern city. However, you can still see parts of the **Ancient Agora**. This is half a kilometre inland from the waterfront, east of the bazaar quarter. There was a market here during ancient Greek times, but most of the remaining ruins are Roman. You can see the columns of the 2ndC AD **Stoa** (colonnade) and a jumble of ancient relics, including a rather tumbledown Ottoman graveyard. Although there's not all that much to see here, it's worth a look before you visit the **Archaeological Museum** (1 km south-west), which contains a number

of the best relics from the Agora. It also has exhibits ranging from relics dating from 3000BC found elsewhere in the province to exhibits from the Byzantine era, which came to an end here seven centuries ago. But best of all is the superb collection of **classical statues and reliefs** on the ground floor. Look particularly at the little statue of Eros asleep, which comes from Pergamon. There are also several excellent finds from the major sites along Turkey's Aegean coast.

For once, the local **Ethnographic Museum** (opposite the Archaeological Museum) has something of interest to other than carpetologists and costumophiles. Those who dare should enter the Circumcision Room. Others should see the display devoted to camel wrestling. This unlikely sport still has a large following. Do not mistakenly assume, as I once did, that this involves a human being wrestling with a camel. Camel wrestling really does involve one camel wrestling with another camel. One contestant attempts to entwine its neck around the other's – until the loser is forced to its knees in submission.

Some 200 m east is the **Painting and Sculpture Museum**, which houses travelling exhibits of painting and sculpture. Try this one, without any great expectations, and you may be pleasantly surprised. The shows vary considerably in quality – from the unutterably bad to the unevenly interesting. (Turkey has no great tradition in the respresentational arts owing to the Islamic taboo on idolatry.) Even so, the art shows at this museum can sometimes give you a deep insight into contemporary Turkey: its *angsts*, its aspirations, and how it sees itself.

The **Kültür Park**, which stretches north of the main 9 Eylül Meydani (9th September Square) houses the annual International Trade Fair, which is probably not why you have come to visit Izmir. This is held from the third week in August until the second week in September, and is an excuse for all hoteliers to double their prices. (To be fair, there are often few rooms available at this time anyway.) Likewise, don't be fooled by all those advertisements for the International Izmir Festival, which runs from mid-June until July. This is certainly international, and often features faded or up-and-coming international stars. But there's only one snag: it hardly takes place in Izmir at all – most of the events are held at out-of-town spots such as Çeşme or Ephesus. One spot in Izmir which you should not miss is **Kadifekale** (ancient Mount Pagus). From here you have a superb view out over the city, its bay, its ships and its islands. There's a ruined castle up here, whose earliest foundations were laid by Alexander the Great, and there's an open air café. You can walk up (heading south-east for just over 0.5 km from the Agora, uphill), or you can take a *dolmuş*. By far the best time to go is late afternoon, when you can watch the sun set beyond the bay and the light fading over the city below. Kadifekale means Velvet Castle, which aptly describes how this castle appears in the dusky twilight.

Also worth a visit is the city's **bazaar quarter**, which is centred around Ana-fartalar Caddesi. This leads off Konak Meydani, the square which is the hub of the city. In the bazaar it's all the fun of the fair, with a thousand dealers all itching to sell you anything from that leather gun holster you've always wanted to a live chicken or a single sprocket. Best buys here – for quality and price – are to be found in the leather-ware section. Don't bother with the carpets – you'll find much better elsewhere in the country.

Warning: it may get very hot, but don't even consider swimming in the Gulf of Izmir. Pollution ranges from the exotic to the lethal. When it gets really hot (which it certainly does in high summer) and you're desperate to immerse yourself in water, head for **Balçova Termal**, 8 km south-west of central Izmir. Here you can take a dip in the famous **Baths of Agamemnon**. According to legend, this is where the great warrior himself would come to clean up after the rigours of battle at Troy – though it seems rather a long way to come for a bath, even a legendary one. An expert on literary hygiene once pointed out to me that at no point does Homer indicate Agamemnon ever took a bath during the entire ten-year siege of Troy. Either way, the thermal springs here are slightly warm and pleasantly tingling. Otherwise, if you want a dip you'll have to stay at one of the few hotels in town which has a pool (see Recommended Hotels).

KARABURUN AND PENINSULA

Until just a few years ago this rocky peninsula was almost entirely deserted, with small villages and remote beaches. Now it has suffered from a rash of Izmir holiday homes, but still retains an element of its old self.

The best stretch is just before **Karaburun**, where there are several mountainside villages. Beyond here the beaches become inaccessible, unless you're willing to walk and scramble – when you will be rewarded for your troubles accordingly.

RECOMMMENDED RESTAURANTS

IZMIR 🍴 ✕

Izmir is justly renowned for its seafood. The *kalamar* (fried squid) is as good as you'll get anywhere, though be wary of the mussels, which can suffer from an unfortunately high strike rate.

Cheap eateries proliferate around the Basmane Station, and also in the bazaar quarter. If you fancy something a little more up-market, try the restaurants along Birinci Kordon (Atatürk Caddesi), the main waterfront, just north of Cumhuriyet Meydani, where you can dine in the open air with a view of the busy harbour.

North of the main Talvat Paşa Bulvari turn-off (beyond the NATO headquarters), there is a lively café scene along the waterfront.

Mangal Restaurant, L-LL; *Atatürk Caddesi (Birinci Kordon)* 110; *tel.* 512 52860.

This is the best place in town for reasonably priced seafood. Only one snag: you'll have to get here early if you want to eat outside – it's that popular.

Another good place along here is:

Sirena, L-LL; *Atatürk Caddesi (Birinci Kordon)* 94; *no booking.*

North of the NATO building. Attracts a lively young clientèle. You can just drink beer if you want, but they also serve kebabs and seafood.

<u>Western Turkey</u>

Aegean Coast Hinterland

180 km; map GeoCenter EuroCountry, Western Turkey, 1:800 000

This area is often overlooked, but has a charm of its own, making an interesting contrast to the more obvious pleasures of the adjacent coastline.

East of Izmir, at the head of the Küçük Menderes Valley, are the remote villages of the Boz Dağlari Mountains, where rural life has changed little since Ottoman times.

South of the Aydin Dağlari range lies the Büyük Menderes Valley. Here, on a mountainside amidst the olive groves, lie the ruins of ancient Nyssa. This was one of the chief cultural centres of Asia Minor during the Roman era, the city where the classical historian and geographer Strabo was educated. The Çine River is a tributary of the Büyük Menderes, and flows from the mountains to the south. The gorge at the head of the Çine Valley was the scene of the legendary contest between Apollo and the ill-fated Marsyas. Above this gorge lies the mysterious site of Gerga.

South of here, just outside Yatağan, you can see the shrine of Lagina where the malign Hecate, Goddess of the Underworld, was worshipped. If you have time, be sure to head east up into the mountains above Yatağan for a visit to Kavaklidere and its Dickensian copper foundry, where the copper beaters turn out traditional coffee pots, cauldrons and plates.

The inland route shown on the map opposite from Izmir to Bodrum via Aydin along Rt 550 is just 180 km, but if you want to make a few detours you could find yourself covering almost double this distance. Allow two or three days for this region.

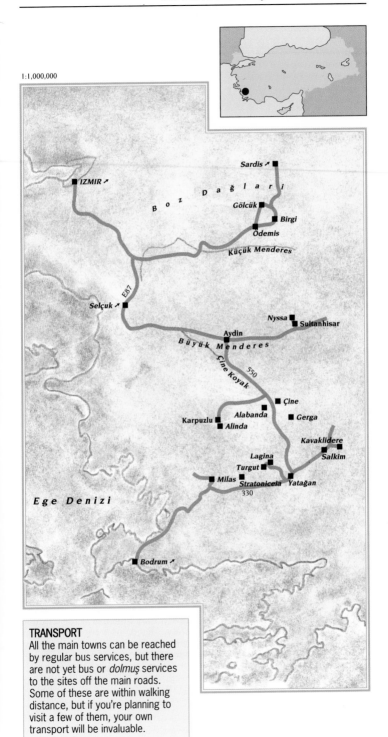

1:1,000,000

Sardis ↗

IZMIR ↗

B o z   D a ğ l a r i

Gölcük

Birgi

Ödemis

Küçük Menderes

E87

Selçuk ↗

Nyssa

Sultanhisar

Aydin

B ü y ü k   M e n d e r e s

Çine Koyak

550

Çine

Alabanda

Gerga

Karpuzlu

Alinda

Kavaklidere

Lagina

Salkim

Turgut

Milas

Stratoniceia

Yatağan

330

E g e   D e n i z i

Bodrum ↗

TRANSPORT
All the main towns can be reached
by regular bus services, but there
are not yet bus or *dolmuş* services
to the sites off the main roads.
Some of these are within walking
distance, but if you're planning to
visit a few of them, your own
transport will be invaluable.

227

SIGHTS & PLACES OF INTEREST

AYDIN 🏨
An undistinguished provincial town in the valley of the River Menderes (the ancient Meander), which according to the classical historian Strabo was founded by barbarians from Thrace (northern Greece). Its subsequent history is as boring as you'd expect of a place occupied by civilized barbarians. There is little of interest here, but it makes a useful base for visiting the ruins of ancient Nyssa and the villages of the Çine Valley – see the separate entries.

BIRGI
Also Gölcük and Sardis, see Boz Dağlari Villages, below.

BODRUM
See Turkey Overall: 4.

BOZ DAĞLARI VILLAGES 🏨 ✕
On Rt 310, which leads up the valley of the Küçük Menderes River. These largely unspoilt, remote villages are in the valleys of the Boz Dağlari mountains, whose peaks rise above 2,000 m. They have old wooden houses, and a few interesting mosques.

At **Birgi** many of the old houses are in a rather ramshackle state, but some of the more impressive ones have recently been restored. The main mosque here (**Aydinoğlu Mehmet Bey Camii**) is well over 500 years old, and incorporates a number of Roman pillars in its construction. Further up the road near **Gölcük** is a picturesque little lake by the woods, where there's a recommendable fish restaurant and a hotel where you can stay overnight – see pages 229 and 233.

Further north across the mountain, the main road leads down to the ruins of Sardis, home of the legendary King Croesus: see Local Explorations: 5.

ÇINE KOYAK (ÇINE VALLEY)
On Rt 550 S of Aydin. The Çine River, which runs down this valley, is the ancient Marsyas, named after the legendary figure who fell foul of Apollo. Marsyas was wandering by the river and found a deer-bone flute which had been discarded by the goddess Athena, who had placed a curse on it. Marsyas was so enchanted by the music he played on the flute that he challenged Apollo to a music contest. Apollo agreed, on condition that the winner could choose his own punishment for the loser. Marsyas narrowly lost the contest, and the vengeful Apollo tied him to a plane tree and flayed him alive. According to local legend, the river was first formed by Marsyas' blood. Those who prefer to ignore their rich classical heritage will find the upper stretch of this river flows through a delightful gorge.

There are three sites in this area:

Alabanda
8 km W of Çine on a minor road. The ruins stand in and around the village of Aphisar. Alabanda was always considered a remote spot, even in classical times. It would fall nominally under the power of whichever empire happened to hold sway in the area, but in fact continued to go about its quasi-independent democratic ways. It produced nothing startling, did nothing startling, and is referred to by Strabo as being notorious for scorpions and debauchery. (He makes reference to 'lots of girls who play the harp.')

The ruins include a rather shaggy **theatre**, a **Temple of Apollo** (no longer, alas, decorated with its original frieze depicting a battle between Greeks and Amazons), and a few scatterings of stones marking the agora and the baths. Such sites may not compare with their better-known peers, but they often have far more atmosphere.

Alinda
8 km N of Çine turn W off Rt 550, follow minor road 25 km to village of Karpuzlu, which means Land of the Water Melons. This is the best of the sites, and most of its ruins date from the Hellenistic era. Surprisingly little is known about Alinda, apart from one rather touching story. This dates from the 4thC BC and concerns Ada, a sister of Mausolus of Halikarnassos (modern Bodrum). She was deposed by her younger brother and banished to Alinda. But when Alexander the Great arrived here on his great expedition of conquest, Ada saw her chance. She sent a message to Alexander offering to surrender Alinda to his forces if he

• *Inland from Bodrum.*

would reinstate her as Queen of Halikarnassos. Alexander agreed, and when the two of them met they became so enamoured of each other that Ada insisted upon adopting Alexander as her son. Alexander must have been taken with this idea, for he often later referred to the reinstated Queen of Halikarnassos as his mother. Ada, for her part, re-named Alinda Alexander-by-Latmus, but the name didn't stick.

The site stands above the edge of the modern village of Watermelonland (though this modernity is of a suitably fairytale quality). The most interesting ruin is that of the huge **market building**. In its prime over 2,000 years ago this was almost 100 m long and three stories high – and enough of it remains standing to give an impressive idea of what it must have been like when its columned halls were filled with bawling stallholders and canny buyers haggling over the water melons.

The ruined **theatre** has fine views across the nearby valley. Higher up the hill on the acropolis is a two-storey **tower** which was built to keep watch over the approaches to the city. Near here is a so-called secret tunnel, which was meant to enable citizens under siege to escape from the acropolis to the theatre, but may well have been used in the opposite direction when the local drama company was playing yet another great tragic revival.

Gerga

In *the hills* SE *of* Çine. It's usually said that this site is only of interest to specialists. I disagree. It may be difficult to reach, but there are few experiences more rewarding after a longish walk through remote countryside than arriv-

---

RECOMMENDED HOTELS

AYDIN

The town isn't over-endowed with recommendable hotels. I usually stay at:

Hotel Kabaçam, L-LL; 11 *Hükümet Bulvari Sokak* 2/B; *tel.* 631 12794.

One of the desk staff speaks serviceable English and can help with transport difficulties, the other is in the Manuel class (and may well have his own sit-com by now). A jolly spot, despite attempts to give the place an air of restrained impersonality.

GÖLCÜK

Gölcük Motel, LL; *Gölcük; tel.* 545 43503.

An ideal hide-away with all mod cons, but little in the way of unnecessary luxury. The service, like the region, is remote but pleasing.

• *Kavaklidere.*

ing at your own classical site.

To reach Gerga, start from the old Ottoman bridge in the Çine gorge. Cross it and follow the track up to the village of Incekemer Mahalle, where they'll direct you to the track you need to take up the valley. Follow their instructions closely, especially concerning the last bit where you turn left at the top of the valley. (A few years ago there were moves afoot to have all this properly signposted, but such things take time.) You'll need walking boots and stamina sufficient for a one-and-a-half-hour walk uphill. The return takes less time, but make sure you're not overtaken by darkness as I once was.

Some hospitable villagers allowed me to spend the night in what appeared by lantern-light to be a store-room of some kind. The little friends I picked up during the course of my sleepless night ensured that I emerged next morning down at the old bridge burrowing under my armpits with gorilla-like enthusiasm. The ruins of Gerga have the attraction of being something of a mystery. Prac-

tically nothing is known about them for certain, and scholars even argue over whether they date from the ancient Greek or the ancient Roman era. It has also been suggested that the place wasn't a city at all, but a sanctuary. This is reinforced by the main ruin, which is a temple. Above the entrance is inscribed the word 'Gergas' in ancient Greek, which according to some experts is the not the name of the settlement but that of the God worshipped here. (The fact that this inscription is written in ancient Greek is naturally dismissed as irrelevant by those who favour the Roman theory.) Nearby lies a huge headless statue. There's also what appears to be a fountain, which is also inscribed with the word 'Gergas'. There are the remains of a number of houses and *stelae* (upright carved stones) littered over the hillside.

Those who are interested in this site may be intrigued to know the result of my own researches. When I first visited I took a pebble away with me as a souvenir. This I later placed in the hands of a man from Galway who claimed to be clairvoyant. After clutching the stone and closing his eyes for a suitably dramatic period, he announced that my stone from Gergas came from a place where long ago people had worshipped fire.

IZMIR
See Local Explorations: 2.

KARPUZLU ✕
See Recommended Restaurants, page 233.

KAVAKLIDERE
Turn E off Rt 550 4 km N of Yatağan. Continue down minor road through the mountains for 25 km, and turn E at fork just beyond Salkim. I was taken to this small, remote town high in the mountains by an Ottoman princess, a Muslim whose first name is Christian (this is true, and she probably won't forgive my untoward name-dropping). The reason for our visit was to see the town's remarkable old copper foundry. They melt down scrap copper, which barefoot workers beat into traditional pots, cauldrons, and coffee pots of great beauty.

The factory itself is like something

• *Opposite: working the copper barefoot, Kavaklidere.*

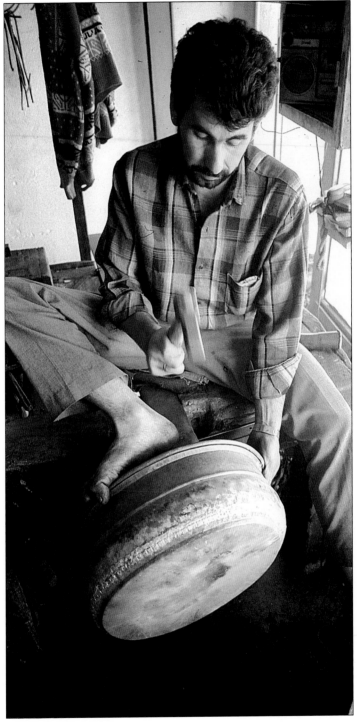

• *Olive grove, Büyük Menderes valley.*

out of the early Industrial Revolution, but the workers are very proud to show you around. Across the street you can see the beaters at their craft. (They are only barefoot because this makes it easier to hold the metal with their feet.) If you want authentic copperware, buy it here. The only tourists who ever come here are those brought by the princess – whose interest in this foundry appears to have done much to aid its survival.

LAGINA
See Yatağan, page 233.

MILAS
This is the site of ancient Mylasa, whose famous marble quarries provided the material for the Mausoleum of Halikarnassos (modern Bodrum, see Turkey Overall: 4), one of the Seven Wonders of the World. Indeed, the town's most distinguished ruin, a classical tomb known as **Gümüşkesen** (the Silver Purse) is thought to have been modelled on the original mausoleum. This is on the hillside to the west of town, just north of the road beneath Hidirlik Tepe (Hill). Note the hole where mourners could pour libations of wine down into the burial chamber. The Gümüşkesen was probably built in the 2ndC BC, but as to whose tomb it is – this remains a mystery. When it was 'rediscovered' in the 18thC by the British traveller Richard Chandler it was being used to house cows.

There's not really much else to see in town, though the bazaar is worth a visit if you have some time to spare.

NYSSA
A beautifully situated site amongst olive groves on the hillside above the wide valley of the Büyük Menderes River.

The city was probably called Nyssa in the 2ndC BC after the wife of the local ruler. The original settlement was almost certainly founded more than three centuries earlier by Spartan colonists, and is thought to be the amalgamation of three separate settlements founded by three Spartan brothers. This, at least, is the claim of the classical historian Strabo, who should have known what he was talking about – he studied here in the 1stC BC. At this time Nyssa was a renowned centre of culture, so much so that it even had its own school of philosophy. One of its leading lights was Aristodemus, who managed to believe simultaneously that the world is rational through and through, yet that its workings are directed by Fate. He pronounced himself a lifelong Stoic, though one can't help feeling that this stoicism may have been developed in the face of his pupils' derision.

There are just a few items of interest at this site. The **theatre** is becoming delightfully overgrown with olive trees. Just east of it you can descend into the gorge which divided the ancient city into two. Here there is a 150 m-long **Roman tunnel** which was used for diverting the waters of the mountain stream when it became a torrent during spring.

The ancient **agora** (market place) and virtually intact stonework of the **bouleterion** (council chamber) lie on the other side of the gorge, which in Roman times was spanned by two bridges (whose remains are still visible). There are the remains of a large stadium, and also the rather disappointing heap of stones which is all that remains of the **library**, in its time the third greatest in the world (after those at Alexandria and Pergamon).

There are no good eating places near here, so it's best to bring your own food and picnic under the olive trees. You'll also need a torch if you want to explore the tunnel.

SELÇUK
See Turkey Overall: 3.

STRATONICEIA
Ancient city founded in the 3rdC BC, which had its golden age during the Roman era. It came under the protection of the extremely powerful god Zeus Chrysaoreus (Zeus with his sword of gold), but he was sadly unable to protect the site from the local mining industry, whose vast eyesore of a lignite quarry nearby has blighted the entire site with dust and noise.

Stratoniceia has a sacred way leading to the nearby shrine to Hecate at Lagina (see Yatağan, below).

TURGUT
See Yatağan, below.

YATAĞAN
A boring little spot. But if you do find yourself here, it's worth making the detour across to the village of **Turgut**, which lies 8 km west.

Just outside Turgut is the **shrine of Lagina**, which was dedicated to the most chilling of all goddesses, Hecate. She is not part of the original Olympian pantheon, but is reckoned to have been a local goddess from this part of the world. Hecate held the keys of Hades (Hell) and ruled over the dead. She was the goddess of witches and sorcerers, and was only worshipped by night at deserted crossroads, where dogs were sacrificed in order to appease her. She is usually depicted as a fearsome woman with three heads. It has been

suggested that she was a distant echo of the female deity who became the Indian goddess Siva, and that she was brought to this part of the world by the original Indo-European settlers. (You can see a statue of her in the museum at Bodrum.)

The shrine at Lagina stood at a crossroads, just as it does today. You can still see the vast temple precinct where visitors came to witness the 'mysteries'. A jumble of broken columns marks the site of **Hecate's Temple** in the centre of this precinct. The ruined structure just east of the temple is thought to have been an altar.

Many years ago I was once bold enough to camp out here overnight with a couple of German students. We took turns telling suitably chilling horror stories, and then fell asleep. In the early hours I woke with a start to the sound of a nearby rustling. As I sat up petrified, I was aware of a low gasping sound. The German boy then woke and became hysterical, whereupon his girlfriend began slapping his face and shouting at him. In the middle of all this a local cur emerged from the undergrowth wagging his tail. He later curled up beside my sleeping bag and went to sleep.

RECOMMENDED RESTAURANTS

AYDIN
This town is famous for its figs, which are best around July and August. There are no restaurants of merit or interest.

GÖLCÜK
Rihtim Restaurant, L-LL; *by the lake; no booking.*

This delightful spot looks out over the lake. You can eat delicious fresh trout, at a price that adds savour to your dish as much as a *cordon bleu* sauce, which alas is not available.

KARPUZLU
Fortunately in this remote spot near the Alinda site (page 228) there are several restaurants, though none of them particularly stands out.

Surprisingly, given the town's name (see page 228), I have had difficulty getting water melon here.

<u>Western Turkey</u>

Denizli, Aphrodisias and Pamukkale

260 km; map GeoCenter Euro-Country, Western Turkey, 1:800 000

Inland from Bodrum – Turkey's original Aegean resort, and despite being a funspot its most attractive (see Turkey Overall: 4) – you find another world. Climbing into the remote mountains of the hinterland you come upon Muğla, the region's provincial capital, with one of the most picturesque weekly markets in the country. Further inland the peaks rise to over 2,500 m, beneath which are many unspoilt, timeless mountain villages.

The city of Denizli makes a useful base for exploring the nearby major sights of Pamukkale and Aphrodisias. The salt springs and glistening white pools of Pamukkale look like a mirage of snow as you ascend its hot, winding valley. Beside these pools are the ruins of the Roman city of Hierapolis, which has a remarkable necropolis.

Aphrodisias lies east of Denizli, and is one of my favourite ancient sites in Turkey. Its remoteness means that out of season you're not disturbed by huge crowds of daytrippers – as at Ephesus or Troy. Aphrodisias was one of the great cultural centres of the Roman Empire, famous for its sculptors and philosophers. Its magnificent stadium is one of the finest you can see anywhere, and there are the impressive remains of the Temple of Aphrodite which gave the city its name.

You can easily cover the country between Bodrum and Denizli in a day, but if you want to spend some time at the sights as well, allow two or three days.

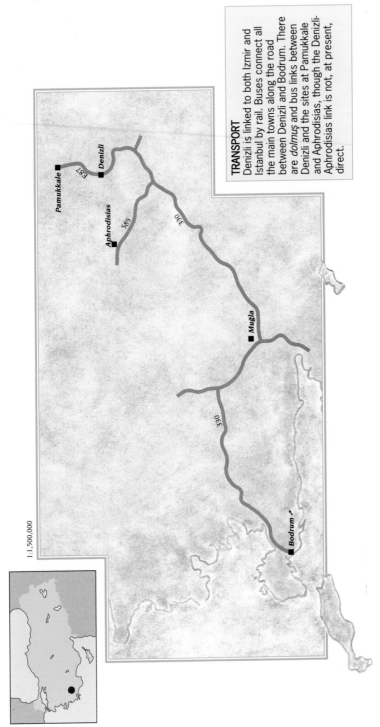

TRANSPORT
Denizli is linked to both Izmir and Istanbul by rail. Buses connect all the main towns along the road between Denizli and Bodrum. There are *dolmuş* and bus links between Denizli and the sites at Pamukkale and Aphrodisias, though the Denizli-Aphrodisias link is not, at present, direct.

Pamukkale

E87

Denizli

Aphrodisias

585

330

Muğla

330

Bodrum

1:1,500,000

SIGHTS & PLACES OF INTEREST

APHRODISIAS

I was once assured by an unscrupulous tour operator in Kuşadasi that the ancient city of Aphrodisias was famous for the production of aphrodisiacs, which were exported throughout the Roman Empire. Sadly, the truth is a little more prosaic; even so, Aphrodisias remains one of the most exciting sights in Turkey. Its ruins rival those at Ephesus, and except during the height of the season their remoteness means that they are not completely overrun by visitors.

The city was named after its magnificent **Temple to Aphrodite**, whose ruins can still be seen. This attracted pilgrims from far and wide, and was responsible for the city's prosperity.

It seems probable that this spot was the centre of some kind of fertility cult from pre-historic times. Worship of the Great Mother gave way to the worship of Ishtar, who eventually became the Aphrodite of the ancient Greeks (more familiar to us in her Roman guise as Venus the goddess of love).

The city achieved its golden age under the Romans. Gifts were lavished upon it by Sulla, Julius Caesar and Augustus, in recognition of its allegiance to Rome, and during this period Aphrodisias became one of the great cultural centres of the Roman Empire. Its sculptors were famous throughout the Mediterranean, and their work was much sought after in Rome. The renowned physician Xenocrates taught here; and the first Greek novel *Chaereas and Callirhoe* was composed by one of its citizens, Chariton. (Indeed, some stern critics consider that the modern novel is still essentially of the same genre as this founding work: an aphrodisiac love story.)

Aphrodisias even produced two philosophers: Alexander, who claimed that immortal souls are completely ignorant; and Asklepiodotus whose teachings were even more obscure, to the extent that debate still rages as to what exactly they were, let alone how true they were.

Among the extensive ruins of Aphrodisias it is still possible to see the distinctive blue-marble pillars of the **School of Philosophy** were these two giants of

RECOMMENDED HOTELS

DENIZLI
Halley Hotel, LL-LLL; 30 *Istasyon Caddesi; tel.* 621 19544.

On the main street that leads south-west from the railway station, which is close by the *otogar* (bus station) and *dolmuş* terminal. By far the best (and most expensive) hotel in town – but if your budget allows, a boon in the high summer heat. Prices dip to bargain levels in the low season. On my last visit here a Turkish guest insisted that the place was named after Halley's Comet, but I wasn't able to extract any plausible reason for this.

If feeling budget conscious try:

Ero Pansiyon, L; *Atatürk Caddesi; tel.* 621 35536.

Downhill from the city centre, half a kilometre off the main route to Aphrodisias. Moderate accommodation, popular with discriminating French backpackers.

PAMUKKALE
Pamukkale Motel, LLL; *by the main car park opposite the museum; tel.* 621 81024.

Undeniably expensive, but it has one of the most unusual swimming pools you'll find anywhere: the ancient Sacred Pool, whose floor is littered with fallen ancient columns. The palm-shaded waters are as clear as a mountain stream, yet you wade into a chemical-rich mix as warm as washing up water. Enjoy the pool early before the crowds arrive, or after they've left.

A cheap alternative is:

Ali's Pansiyon, L; *Pamukkale village; tel.* 621 81065.

A short walk down from the main area of tourist activity. Used to be a great favourite with the hippies, who came to groove the far-out view. But, like many of them, it has now smartened up its act. Though the view remains as groovy as ever.

the intellect baffled their pupils. Near-by are the magnificent remains of the Temple of Aphrodite, beside which, in a simple tomb, is buried the body of Professor Kenan Erim who made it his life work to excavate this site.

Unfortunately, large-scale archaeological work is still continuing at Aphrodisias. This means that extensive areas of the site are fenced off by the archaeologists, who after all 'created' the site, in order to protect it from ignorant visitors such as us whose entrance fee helps finance their work. This *impasse* has reached new heights with the barring of photography of these no-go areas, which is as ludicrous as it is unenforcable. The archaeologists here seem to be aspiring to turn their craft into an art form – by becoming as mindful of their audience as all other dedicated modern artists.

Luckily, Aphrodisias is a very large site, which means that we are still allowed in to see a wide range of amazing ruins. The **theatre** is magnificently situated, and could hold more than 8,000. Even more impressive is the **stadium**, which lies several hundred metres north of the main site. It could seat 30,000 spectators and is one of the finest classical *stadia* in existence. Its apparent simplicity of construction is deceptive. If you look closely, you can see how the long rows of the straight sections at each side curve slightly, so that people in all seats could see what was going on at the other end of the stadium. I find it particularly atmospheric: take a seat here, and with a little imagination you can can visualize the clamour of the crowds and the tension of the hard-fought events.

Aphrodisias staged its own version of the Olympic Games, with running races, boxing and wrestling matches, music and marathon poetry competitions, which presumably helped to clear the stadium at the end of the day.

Also not to be missed is the delightful **odeum**, which demonstrates that the ancients could also achieve great architecture on the small scale. This was where the city council met. It was also a venue for lectures, debates, concerts and small-scale poetry readings where the author could detect which of his friends slipped out.

The **museum**, which stands outside the main gate, contains a large if rather jumbled assembly of the sculptures for which Aphrodisias was famous. My favourites here are the nasty-looking **Pugilist**, and a superb fragmentary **Head of Athena.** Be sure to see the recently discovered **Shield Portraits of the Philosophers**, which for some reason also include two of the ancient Greek philosophers' most notorious pupils: a chinless Alexander the Great and an appropriately headless image of the headless Alcibiades. There are some attractive postcards of the museums' exhibits, so that you can stimulate your friends back home with a bit of Aphrodisiac culture.

RECOMMENDED RESTAURANTS

APHRODISIAS
If you're going to be at Aphrodisias over the lunch period you're best off bringing a picnic. There are a few ordinary restaurants west down the road between Geyre and Karacasu, which are really only interested in large pre-booked coach parties.

DENIZLI
There are plenty of cheap eateries and kebab joints in the district by the railway station and the *otogar* (bus station). The best place for a more substantial and relaxing meal is at the smart Halley Hotel – see Recommended Hotels, page 236.

MUĞLA
Santral, L; 19 İnönü; *no booking.*

As its name suggests, this is in the centre of town. Big bonus: it serves alcohol. You can't expect anything too fancy in Muğla.

PAMUKKALE
Koru Motel, LL-LLL; *west of main car park;* tel. 6218 1429.

This caters mainly for tour groups, but has a huge pool, and a terrace.

For a cheaper meal down in the village, try:

Gürsoy Restaurant; *Pamukkale village;* tel. 6218 4151.

A delightful shady spot overlooking the main square, justly renowned for its grilled meat dishes.

BODRUM
See Turkey Overall: 4.

DENIZLI ⊯ ✕
Denizli makes a useful base for visiting Aphrodisias (see page 236) and Pamukkale (see page 239). There's not really much to see here, but it's linked by train to both Izmir and Istanbul, and has *dolmuş* and/or bus services to the above-mentioned sights.

In the old days, when the summer heat became unbearable, the inhabi-

• *Aphrodisias.*

tants would remove themselves to the surrounding fields and orchards where they lived for months on end. A 19thC traveller noted that during the summer the bazaar was deserted, apart from a few stray dogs.

A friend of mine once pointed out to me here the only Irish mosque in Turkey. This is on the outskirts on the south side of the road leading out of town towards Pamukkale. Its minaret is toppped with a distinctive cap of orange, white and green glass which precisely mirrors the Irish flag.

MUĞLA ✕

Every Thursday Muğla has one of the finest local markets you will see in Turkey. Here the traditionally dressed peasants from the hinterland squat before their piles of peppers and spices; enticing characters will sell you perfumes which smell of anything from delicate rose petals to pungent candy floss; and you can buy a similar range of exotic teas. There are also clothes stalls which seem to specialize exclusively in items for blind giants and aesthetically disadvantaged midgets. But the shoes here are a particularly good buy.

To the north of the town centre there is an interesting **bazaar**, and beyond this the alleyways lead you through districts of old wooden Ottoman houses. Also some newer ones; there's even a new wooden mosque, complete with varnished clapboard minaret.

PAMUKKALE 🛏 ✕

It's difficult to know what to say about Pamukkale. This is undoubtedly one of the geological wonders of Turkey, yet the authorities seem to be doing their best to eliminate the very thing which makes the place interesting.

The warm calcium salt springs bubbling from the mountainside have created a series of chalk pools. These fan out down the hillside, spilling one into the other, like a landscape in some lunar fantasy. The warm calcium-saturated water has been flowing for around 15,000 years, the calcium slowly solidifying to form the blinding salt flats and white rims of the pools.

Unfortunately, the last time I was here this 15,000-year-old process seemed to have come to an end. The pools were drying up into rather ordinary salt pans with remnant puddles of salty water, and the spilling cascades shown by the postcards were nowhere to be seen.

When I expressed my disappointment, I was told that this was just the unfortunate effect of a long hot summer drying up the springs. Later I learned that in fact the water had been diverted to fill the swimming pools of the local motels which have sprung up to cater for the tourists. Obviously a potentially disastrous financial short-circuit is going to take place soon unless something is done about this absurd situation.

That said, there are a number of other things worth seeing here. The **sacred pool** now encircled by the rather expensive Pamukkale Motel is well worth a visit. Here you can swim in the warm palm-shaded waters amongst the fallen ancient pillars, much as visitors have done since classical times. These radio-active waters are said to be a cure for gout, though I cannot personally comment on their efficacy in this department.

The nearby **museum** contains a frankly disappointing collection of bits and pieces unearthed from the ruins of nearby **Hierapolis**. But the ruins themselves *are* interesting. There's a fine **Roman theatre**, and a **Temple of Apollo**. Beyond the city walls to the east is the 5thC **martyrium**, which is said to mark the spot where St Philip was stoned to death.

In Roman times the waters here were renowned throughout Asia Minor for their healing powers. People came from miles around to take the cure, contributing greatly to the affluence of Hierapolis. As always with such health-cure spots there is a big **necropolis**, said to be the largest in all Asia Minor, which doesn't seem to have discouraged trade too much. The necropolis contains some historically interesting 2ndC AD **tumuli**, and all kinds of grandiose **Roman tombs** which would have been the envy of any Victorian graveyard.

From the necropolis there is also a spectacular view out over the vast plain far below. The lurid sunsets over this plain produce long, billious blendings of cherry, lilac, custard, blackcurrant jam, egg yolk and almond ice cream, powerful enough to render even the most dedicated romantic a little queasy. To ease the strain, head for the Koru Motel where you can sit on the veranda and take in this aesthetic hotchpotch with a similarly coloured cocktail to ease the digestion.

<u>Central Turkey</u>

The Hinterland West from Ankara

600 km; map GeoCenter Euro-Country, Western Turkey, 1:800 000

This is a large slice of Turkey, from the Anatolian plains west of Ankara, across the mountains, to the fertile river valleys and the Aegean coast. For the most part, it attracts few visitors, yet there is much to see, from faraway archaeological sites to historic capitals of great bygone emperors.

The territory was once occupied by the ancient Phrygians and the Lydians. In pre-classical times they were both, in their different ways, the golden people of Asia Minor. Legend has it that King Midas of the Phrygians turned everything he touched into gold; and King Croesus of the Lydians was once the richest man in the world.

You can visit King Midas' capital, and the city named after him. You can also visit Croesus' capital Sardes, whose empire once stretched from the Aegean to Persia.

Sultan Selim I invaded Persia and brought back with him its famous tile makers, setting them up in Kütahya. Once the delicately hued tiles made here were the envy of Europe, and the city remains to this day famous for its ceramics. From here you can visit the remote Roman site of Aizanoi, whose Temple of Jupiter is the finest of its kind in Asia Minor.

Another feature is Afyon, Turkey's 'Opium City' – nowadays, however, better known for its clotted cream.

Travelling through this region takes a couple of days. Allow at least double this time if you wish to spend time exploring the sites, some of which are well off the beaten track.

1:3,000,000

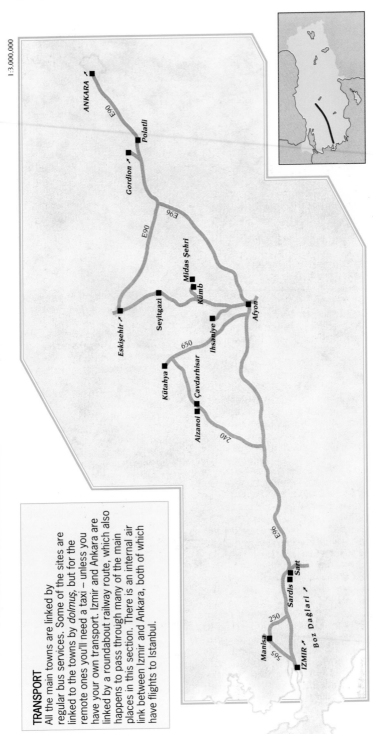

ANKARA

E90

Polatlı

Gordion

E90

E96

Midas Şehri

Kümb

Eskişehir

Seyitgazi

Afyon

İhsaniye

Kütahya

650

Çavdarhisar

Aizanoi

240

E96

Sart

Sardis

250

Manisa

İZMIR

Boz Dağları

505

TRANSPORT

All the main towns are linked by regular bus services. Some of the sites are linked to the towns by *dolmuş*, but for the remote ones you'll need a taxi – unless you have your own transport. Izmir and Ankara are linked by a roundabout railway route, which also happens to pass through many of the main places in this section. There is an internal air link between Izmir and Ankara, both of which have flights to Istanbul.

SIGHTS & PLACES OF INTEREST

AFYON 🚩 ✕

Once upon a time Afyon was known as Afyonkarahisar, which means 'The Black Castle of Opium'. This sounds as if it's straight out of Arabian Nights, and at first sight modern Afyon all but lives up to its ancient name.

The city lies beneath the rock of its **citadel**. This is the rock upon which the Black Castle (Kara Hisar) was built, and there's said to have been a fortress here since Hittite times well over 3,000 years ago. You can walk to the citadel from the town, up a stairway which has more than 700 steps. Near the top you may well notice coloured strips of cloth tied to various branches. This is an ancient quasi-religious custom (almost certainly pre-dating Islam, but now incorporated into it) by which the worshipper makes a secret prayer: for the health of a family member; for a marriage partner; and so on. The castle is now a ruin, but still has some battlements which give a fine view out over the city.

Just 200 years ago some Napoleonic French soldiers found themselves enjoying this view for longer than they'd bargained. They were imprisoned in the fortress after being captured in Egypt. I once met a French exchange teacher in Afyon who maintained that amongst these prisoners was the grandfather of the poet Arthur Rimbaud.

The town's main **monument** is to a

• *Afyon.*

comparatively recent event: the defeat of the invading Greek army nearby in 1922.

Try walking about the town and you will come across several streets of **old wooden houses** with picturesque balconies in the Ottoman style (particularly in the quarter directly below the citadel). The town also has several old mosques, an Archaeological Museum and a museum devoted to the Mevlevi Cult, a Muslim mystic order of dervishes which once thrived in the city.

Opium is still a major product of Afyon (whose truncated name simply means opium). But the opium den quarter is now a thing of the past. All opium produced here is for medicinal purposes, and the poppy pod harvest is closely inspected by the police to ensure that all the seed pods make it intact from the fields to the processing factory. Only a quarter of a century ago this region produced no less than 50 per cent of the world's opium supply. Indeed, in the late 60s it became a popular resort for connoisseurs and other colourful characters wishing to take a holiday from reality.

Nowadays the city is better known for its clotted cream, called *kaymak*. This is said to be unusually rich because the cows that produce it become unusually contented after graz-

• *Opposite: Kütahya.*

ing in the opium fields.

North of town is a region famous for its mineral waters and hot springs. About 23 km north-east of town at **Gazligöl Termal** there are some hot springs which have been in use for over three millennia, and are said to be particularly effective for the curing of opium withdrawal symptoms. The exchange teacher who told me about Rimbaud's grandfather said that he had once tried taking these waters for a hangover, but they hadn't worked. I later tried some in bottled form for the same complaint, and found that it didn't work internally either.

AIZANOI

The remains of a Roman city high in the mountains beyond Kütahya. There's a scattering of ruins beneath the **Murat Daği** range, whose peaks rise above 2,000 m and remain snow-capped for much of the year. You can see a couple of **Roman bridges**, both still in use, a **theatre**, and part of the old **agora**. Carved on the wall of the agora is the famous edict issued by the Emperor Diocletian in 301 AD which fixed the prices for all market produce throughout the Roman Empire. (Inevitably, these quickly bore as much relation to the actual price you paid as your bill does to the menu in many a restaurant today.)

But outshining all is the **Temple of Jupiter** dating from the time of the Emperor Hadrian, who reigned between 117 and 138 AD. Much of the walls and many of its Ionian columns are still standing, complete with the original frieze. It is the finest Roman temple in Turkey, and was a centre for the worship of Zeus (the earlier Greek name for Jupiter). It was probably also a centre for the worship of Cybele, who was the mother of the gods in Near-Eastern mythology. Beneath the Temple you can see a smaller, vaulted **chapel** dedicated to the worship of Cybele.

This site suffered badly during the 1970 earthquake, but the temple remains a superb monument to Roman architecture and building technique.

ANKARA
See Turkey Overall: 11.

BOZ DAĞLARI MOUNTAINS
See Local Explorations: 3.

ESKIŞEHIR
See Turkey Overall: 11.

GORDION
See Turkey Overall: 11.

IZMIR
See Local Explorations: 2.

KÜTAHYA ⇄ ✕
This famous ceramic city is almost 1,000 m above sea level. It was known in classical times as Cotyaeum, and was probably founded by the Phrygians some time during the early centuries of the first millennium BC. It claims to be the birthplace of Aesop, who wrote the fables – but this too is unfortunately a fable. Christianity arrived here early, and St Menas is reliably reported to have preached here in 267.

Kütahya's central Anatolian location guaranteed that it was conquered at one time or another by everyone who was passing into or out of the Near East. This included the usual roll call of

---

historical golden oldies: Alexander the Great, the Romans, the Byzantines, the Crusaders, Tamerlane and eventually the Ottoman Turks, to name but a few. When Selim I captured Tabriz in western Persia in 1514, he brought back with him all the local tile makers, who were responsible for the beautiful tiled Persian mosques of the period. These involuntary immigrants were resettled at Kütahya, which soon became a centre of the ceramic industry. Its renown spread far and wide, eliciting orders from as far afield as western Europe and Jerusalem.

It remains a centre of the ceramic industry: there are more than 30 factories in the city, where you can see the production of pottery as well as look over (and have a chance to purchase) the full range of wares. Many of the city's buildings are covered in the local tiles. You can buy the tiles and the local ceramicware in the **bazaar**. Here you will also see **Kavalflar Pazani**, a fine 16thC market building.

The **Ulu Camii** (Grand Mosque) dates from 1411. Nearby is a district of old houses. From behind the Ulu Camii you can climb up to the **citadel** which dominates the city. Here you can see the ruined **battlements**, and inside these the remains of a **Byzantine basilica**.

Back in town you'll find a rather mediocre **Archaeological Museum** and an oddity, the **Kossuth Evi**. This old house was for a few years the home of the great Hungarian patriot Lajos Kossuth, who led the 1848 popular uprising in his country, but then had to flee for his life after it was suppressed. (He later lived in the Notting Hill district of London.)

MANISA (ANCIENT MAGNESIA) ⌦ ✕

This city makes a useful base for exploring the nearby ruins at **Sardis** (see below), and also has a few interesting sights in its own right.

The modern city of Manisa is the site of Ancient Magnesia, which has the main claims to fame: the element magnesium was named after it. And in preclassical times it was ruled by the legendary King Tantalus, who tried to eat one of his sons. Tantalus was punished for this by being sent to Hades (Hell), where he had laid out before him an enticing meal of fruit and wine, but which always remained just beyond his reach: the origin of the word tantalize.

The main sight in modern Manisa is the **Sultan Camii** mosque. This was built in 1522 by Ayşe Hafize Hatun, mother of Suleiman the Magnificent, after she was miraculously cured of a mysterious near-fatal illness by eating *mesir macunu*. This sickly spicy paste (said to contain more than three dozen separate spices) can still be sampled by those who feel as if they might be suffering from a similar complaint. The Sultan Camii has some unusual paintings on its exterior walls, but inside it is somewhat plain.

More interesting is the **Archaeological Museum**, which contains a wide range of intriguing relics from ancient Sardes (see below) as well as exhibits from other Lydian sites.

For centuries this city was renowned for its Ottoman buildings, but most were destroyed in 1922 by the retreating Greek army after its defeat by Atatürk. Today you can still see sufficient of these to give you an idea of what the city must have been like in all its Ottoman glory.

MIDAS SEHRI

The name means city of Midas. Midas was the Phrygian king who was granted by the gods the original 'Midas touch,' which turned everything into gold. The best way to get here is to go to Afyon, then take the minor road north in the direction of Eskişehir. Here you follow the signs for Ihsaniye, then Kümb. Along the way you will pass a number of Phrygian rock tombs and other monuments which date from around 600 BC.

Little is known of the Phrygians, a mysterious people. Yet as you will find for yourself at Midas Sehri, which is just by Kümb, theirs was a considerable culture. You can see a number of **tombs**, **temples**, and the so-called **Midas Mounument** which dominates the city's ruins. This large religious sculpture is named after Midas because his name is the only word which posterity has been able to decipher among its carved Phrygian inscriptions. A particularly atmospheric spot.

SARDES

These ruins are of the capital city once ruled by Croesus, the richest man in the world. Sardis was probably founded early in the 1st millennia BC by the Lydi-

• *Anatolian market.*

RECOMMENDED RESTAURANTS

AFYON
Oruçoğlu Oteli, L-LL; *Bankalar Caddesi; tel.* 491 20120.

Hotel dining room which looks up towards the citadel. Local specialities, including the famous *kaymak* (clotted cream), which is best sampled on top of *kadayif* (pancake soaked with syrup). Those who wish to do themselves proud can try their *kaymak* with Turkish Delight.

KÜTAHYA
The best restaurants here tend to be in the hotels. Try:

Otel Cumhuriyet, L-LL; *Belediye Meydani; tel.* 2311 13502.

A range of provincial dishes and old favourites, all at reasonable prices.

MANISA
Hardly a culinary centre, but round the corner from the Otel Arma (page 244) you'll find:

Safak Kebap Salonu, L; *Cumhuriyet Caddesi; tel.* 551 12760.

Simple fare at simple prices, but none the worse for that.

ans, by all accounts a curious people.

According to Herodotus, Lydian fathers would send out their daughters as prostitutes in order to earn their dowries. In fact many stories concerning the Lydians have a salacious element. Queen Omphale is said to have bought Hercules as a slave. But Hercules' legendary strength gave him energy to spare at the end of the day, and he ended up fathering Queen Omphale's children and founding a new dynasty, which ruled Sardes.

In the early 7thC BC King Candaules was so proud of his wife Nyssia's beauty that he couldn't help secretly showing her off to his great friend Gyge while she was bathing naked. When Nyssia heard of this loutish behaviour she was furious and confronted Gyge. In order to restore her honour, he would have to be executed – either that, or he would have to kill her husband and marry her. This was a come-on Gyge found himself unable to refuse – so he gallantly despatched King Candaules and busily set about founding a new dynasty.

Sardes now became so powerful that it conquered Troy, and its empire eventually stretched all the way from the Aegean to Persia.

The city gained its wealth from its gold, panned from the local River Pactolus by laying out sheepskins on the river bed. Tiny particles of gold washed down from the lodes in the mountains would be trapped in the fleece of the skins. It has been suggested that this was the origin of the word to 'fleece' someone of their gold – but such an explanation was surely the idea of some sheltered scholar who has never taken a hand at a fixed poker game and ended up resembling a sheep after the shearing season. (The idea of the Golden Fleece which was sought by Jason is thought to originate from a garbled description of this ancient method of gold extraction, which may well have been common in the territories by the Black Sea, where Jason ended his quest.)

The fabulously rich King Croesus ruled from 563 to 456 BC. By now Sardes had so much gold that its citizens needed a handy method of distributing it and dealing in it: so they invented coinage. When the great Athenian law-maker Solon visited Croesus, the King proudly showed him around his great capital, asking if any man could be happier than he. Solon was unimpressed, and replied: 'No man can be called happy before his death.' These words impressed Croesus, and he was later to recall them at a most opportune moment.

Meanwhile, Croesus' wealth was beginning to attract envy on all sides – and particularly from the powerful neighbouring Persian Empire. Croesus wasn't sure what to do, so he consulted the Delphic Oracle, which told him that if he went to war 'he would destroy a great empire'. Croesus immediately launched an attack on the Persians, but was defeated. Only then did he realize that the great empire to be destroyed was his own.

King Cyrus of Persia captured Sardes and took Croesus prisoner. As part of the customary victory celebrations, Croesus was to be burned at the stake, but as the flames leapt about him he suddenly recalled Solon's words and called out to to the gloating Cyrus: 'No man can be called happy before his death.' This evidently struck a philosophic chord in Cyrus, for he immediately ordered the flames to be doused. There are two separate sites at Sardes. Just to the east of the village you can see the ruins of the **Marble Way**, which dates from the Roman era. This was

built on top of a section of the even more ancient **Royal Road**, which was built by the Persians and ran from their homeland to the Aegean (the route for their advancing armies on the way to Greece). At the edge of the Marble Way you can see the remains of various **Byzantine shops**, a **restaurant**, and a **public lavatory**. Nearby is the **synagogue**, which has some excellent reconstructed mosaics. There was a Jewish community here in Sardes from the 6thC BC, when the region was a province of the Persian Empire known as Sfarda. Hence the Jews from here came to be known as Sephardic Jews. (This is but one of several suggested origins of the name.)

The other site is above the village of Sart. It contains the beautiful **Temple of Artemis**, which was begun in the 3rdC BC and not completed until the end of the 2ndC BC. The **acropolis** is an energetic 45-minute walk up the hillside, and has some Byzantine ruins.

Around Sardes there are numerous **tumuli**, some of which are believed to have been Lycian royal tombs. The thought of finding the original man who was as rich as Croesus buried in one of these proved too much for tomb robbers through the centuries. However, their erudite successors, the archaeologists, are still hoping that their earlier colleagues might have missed one.

SEYITGAZI

Tomb complex of the mythical hero Seyit Gazi, who features in the great Turkish epic *Battalname*. This recounts the legendary deeds of Seyit Battal Gazi, who fought for the Arabs against the Byzantine Empire around the start of the 8thC. A typical tale involves Seyit Gazi on the run from a Byzantine general. He arrives at a Byzantine convent, where he gains entry by subterfuge and is hidden by the abbess. Later he tracks down the general, and kills him. He then returns to the convent, marries the abbess, and takes all the nuns with him as well.

The **tomb-memorial** here is highly impressive, as befits the hero. It dates from the 16thC, contains several other tombs, a soup kitchen, and a former lodging house for dervishes. During medieval times this was a great pilgrimage centre.

<u>Central Turkey</u>

Anamur's Hinterland – Konya and Region

400 km; map GeoCenter Euro-Country, Western Turkey, 1:800 000

Inland from Anamur there's some truly spectacular mountain scenery, with peaks rising to well over 2,000 metres. North of this mountain range, around Konya, you're on the rich Anatolian plateau; west of Konya is Turkey's own lake district.

The region has been inhabited since earliest times, and boasts many fine historical sites dating from a great span of history. The recently discovered remains at Çatal Hüyük are still yielding fascinating insights into the Neolithic way of life.

Near Beyşehir, on the banks of a lake littered with tiny islands, is a curious and rather mysterious Hittite temple. If you're more interested in classical sites, try Uzuncaburç. Here, in the mountains above Silifke, you can see some of the finest Hellenistic remains in the country.

But the indisputable gem is Konya, one of the holy places of Islam, and the home of the Order of Whirling Dervishes. Visit the Mevlana Museum and you can learn more about this fascinating Islamic order, founded by the Sufic poet and mystic Celalladin Rumi in the 13thC.

The coastline between Anamur and Silifke remains for the most part very beautiful and unspoilt, and it has one of the finest seaside castles you'll see anywhere: Mamure Kalesi – see Turkey Overall: 8.

If you want to drive up to Konya, you'll probably start from the coast. Route 715 north-west from Silifke has some superb mountain scenery. From it you can make detours to visit the sites at Uzuncaburç and Alahan. It's just under 400 km all the way from Anamur, via Silifke, to Konya. Allow three days if you want to see a few of the sights. However, you could easily spend a week covering this region.

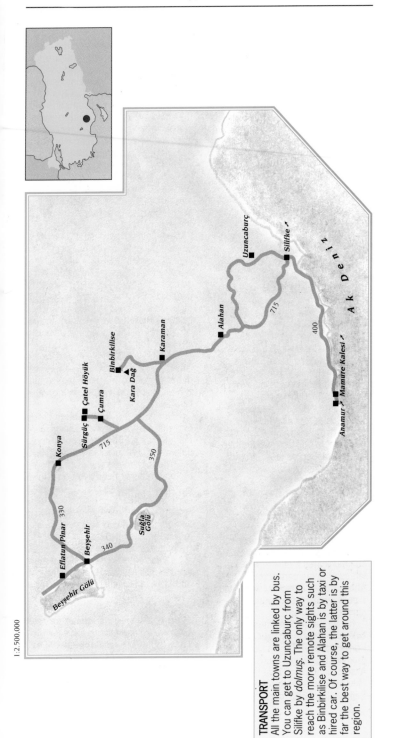

1:2.500.000

TRANSPORT

All the main towns are linked by bus. You can get to Uzuncaburç from Silifke by *dolmuş*. The only way to reach the more remote sights such as Binbirkilise and Alahan is by taxi or hired car. Of course, the latter is by far the best way to get around this region.

SIGHTS & PLACES OF INTEREST

ALAHAN

8 km N of Mut on Rt 715, turn E up sign-posted track, continuing 2 km. It's well worth making the detour to this remote Byzantine monastery standing high above the River Göksu. Among the ruins there are two **churches**, one of which dates from the late 5thC. This has some fine carvings. Search amongst the ruins and you will find the monks' cells carved into the rock.

The mountain scenery on this part of the main road (Rt 715) is particularly spectacular.

ANAMUR

See Turkey Overall: 8.

THE WHIRLING DERVISH CEREMONY

The ritual dance performed by the Whirling Dervishes depicts an attempt at union with God. As they whirl, the dancers free themselves from bondage to earthly things.

The costumes which the dancers wear, and all their actions, are symbolic. The black cloak represents the tomb, and when the dancer sheds this it symbolizes his escape from the tomb and the ties of the flesh. The long white robes of the dancers are their shrouds, and their strange conical hats are their tombstones.

The music of the dance represents that of the heavenly spheres. Each movement made during the dance is also symbolic. The upturned right palm recounts the blessings of Heaven, which are communicated by the downward left palm to the earthly realm. Afterwards, the dancers kneel and a passage from the Koran is chanted over them.

For further information and tickets to the ceremony call at the Konya Kültür ve Turizm Derneği (Konya Culture and Tourism Association), which is at the end of Mevlana Caddesi opposite the Selimye Camii mosque.

BEYŞEHIR 🛏

This ancient town stands on the banks of a 30-km-long lake, and there are several other large lakes west and south of here amongst the mountains. Indeed, this is sometimes called Turkey's 'Lake District'. Forget all comparisons with the windy wastes of water where Wordsworth wandered – these Asian lakes and their surrounding mountains have a rugged charm of their own.

Beyşehir remains unspoilt by tourism. You arrive, as if in a time warp – and it comes as quite a shock to see a picture of Atatürk on a café wall. (His dress code has largely been ignored in this remote spot.) Beyşehir was a city to be reckoned with almost seven centuries ago, and many of its finest buildings date from the early 14thC. This includes the intriguing **Eşrefoğlu**, said to be one of the finest wooden mosques in the country. (In fact, it's only partly built of wood.) Nearby there are various buildings from the same period, including a tomb, a sweat shop and a *hamam* (Turkish bath).

Hire a boat and set out to explore the islands on the nearby lake. There are more than two dozen of these, and their number increases when the water level falls.

Halfway up the north-eastern shore of the lake is the so-called **Eflatun Pinar** (Violet Spring). This is a rock temple dating from Hittite times – about 1300 BC. The rocks are carved with ancient figures, monsters and symbols. Down at the water's edge there are statues of gods and goddesses. Even if you know nothing about Hittite culture, there is something profoundly mysterious and moving about this place.

Eflatun Pinar can be visited by boat, but it's easier to take Rt 695 north-east towards Yalvaç. The site is signposted off this road to the left, after 20 km.

BINBIRKILISE

41 km N of Karaman, beyond the village of Kilbasan, and then Madenşehir on the north side of 2,300-m Kara Dağ (Black Mountain). The final part of the journey is down a pitifully pitted track which tests the suspension of vehicle and passengers alike.

This remote hidden valley is filled with the remains of early Christian churches. Indeed, its very name means A Thousand and One Churches. Most of

• *The Mevlana Museum, Konya.*

these date from the 9th to the 11thC, and include a number of monasteries. Archaeologists have discovered that there was a settlement in this valley from ancient Greek times. It remained occupied through the Roman and Byzantine eras until the 7thC and the period of the Arab raids. Only after the Arabs withdrew two centuries later did the settlers return.

ÇATAL HÜYÜK

Another remote site, (signposted at Sürgüç) this time on the vast Anatolian plateau. It was only discovered in 1958 by the British archaeologist James Mellaart, who just happened to be passing by and discovered what has turned out to be the most significant Neolithic site in Turkey. Thirteen levels of occupation have so far been excavated, the earliest dating from 6800 BC.

Excavations have revealed large clusters of dwellings, and the first evidence of town planning. Unfortunately, as is often the case with town planners (and not just from Neolithic times), one essential factor was overlooked at the blueprint stage. No allowance was made for streets or alleyways between the houses, so people had to climb over the rooftops and descend through ladders into their homes.

A vast amount has been learned about Neolithic civilization from this site, including the fact that they liked to have pictures of dancing girls and musicians on their walls. Such primitive habits die hard. Also discovered were terracotta statuettes of the Neolithic Mother Goddess, who is thought to be a forerunner of the Anatolian goddess

Cybele and the ancient Greek goddess Artemis (Diana).

Sadly, these historically interesting sites are sometimes the least interesting to visit, and Çatal Hüyük is no exception. Come here well armed with an architectural guide and you can spend a fascinating day. Otherwise a lengthy period spent plodding amongst the mounds will soon induce Stone Age tedium. The inhabitants themselves appear to have suffered from a similar complaint, for the site was abandoned in 5500 BC and never reoccupied.

EFLATUN PINAR
See Beyşehir, page 250.

KONYA ⌨ ✕
Konya is the celebrated City of the Whirling Dervishes, and one of the holy places of Islam. It was here in the 13thC that the poet and Sufic mystic Celalledin Rumi, better known now as Mevlana (meaning master), founded the Order of Whirling Dervishes, so-called for their gyrating ritual dance. Atatürk disbanded them in the 1920s – but they now appear to have made a comeback, if only for the pilgrims and tourists. See below.

But Konya's history long pre-dates the Whirling Dervishes, and is one of the longest in all Turkey. According to an ancient Phrygian legend, this was the first city to be established after the Flood had subsided. Indeed, Konya's long history is littered with doubtful tales. The Arab historian Al-Harawi, passing through the city in the 12thC, recorded how he visited 'the tomb of Plato in the church near the great mosque'. Two centuries later the great traveller Ibn Battuta visited Konya and recorded that 'this city was built by Alexander.'

In fact, the site of the city was almost certainly first occupied in the 3rd millennium BC. Later the Hittites moved in, followed by the Phyrgians. In the early Greek period the citizens erected an image of Perseus – in thanks to him for having slain the fearsome Gorgon Medusa, who wore a wig of writhing snakes and whose gaze was so aweful it turned men to stone. Because of this image of Perseus the city came to be called Ikonium (*ikon* means image in Greek). Its modern name is a corruption of this classical title.

Ikonium thrived during the classical period, despite never being visited by Plato (alive or dead). It was, however, visited by St Paul on no less than three occasions during the mid 1stC. The Acts of the Apostles records how on one occasion St Paul, accompanied by St Barnabas, had to make a hasty exit from the city to avoid being stoned.

Konya achieved its golden age under the Selçuks, who made it their capital of Anatolia from the end of the 11thC until they were overrun by the Mongols two centuries later. At the height of its power the city walls had no fewer than a dozen grand castellated gates, while its sultan's palace was renowned as a centre of culture and learning, attracting poets and philosophers from far and wide. One of these was Celalladin Rumi (Mevlana), who was to found the Order of Whirling Dervishes.

Mevlana's tomb can be seen at the **Mevlana Museum**. To describe this as a museum is something of a misnomer. In fact, it's far more than this: a place of pilgrimage and a repository for the holy relics of the Whirling Dervishes. These still perform their rite once a year, around the middle of December. This intriguing ceremony takes place rather inappropriately in the Spor Salonu (Sports Hall). See box on page 250.

Also not to be missed is the **Ince**

RECOMMENDED HOTELS

BEYŞEHIR
Hotel Bulvari, L-LL; *42 Atatürk Caddesi; tel. 3411 4535.*

The best you can expect in such an out-of-the-way place. The shower in my room worked perfectly, but others report otherwise.

KONYA
The main hotels are around Mevlana Caddesi, which runs west from the Mevlana Museum. These tend to be more expensive than normal. My choice is:

Hotel Tur, LL; *Mevlana Caddesi, Eşarizade Sokak 13; tel. 3311 9825.*

Down a side street close to the Mevlana Museum; quiet and friendly.

Minare Museum. This was once a mosque dating from the 13thC, and still has a ruined minaret (struck by lightning in 1901). The museum contains all kinds of salvaged bits and pieces from destroyed buildings of the city's great Selçuk period.

SILIFKE
See *Turkey Overall: 8.*

UZUNCABURÇ ✕
The village is on a minor road which leads through some spectacular mountain scenery and the odd fairytale remote mountain village, the sort of place you dream of living in until you actually live there.

The present village of Uzuncaburç stands on the site of the town which the Romans knew as Diocaesarea, and before that the Greeks knew as Olba. Before that the Hittites lived here, but had sufficient foresight not to confuse matters by giving it a name.

This is an ideal site to visit in the middle of summer. While the coast far below fries in the heat, up here, at over 1,000 m, you're cooled by soft mountain breezes, (which only rarely give way to thunderbolts, flashes of lightning and torrential rain, such as I experienced on my first exhilarating visit.)

This remote spot contains what to my taste are some of the finest ruins in the land. Unlike those at Ephesus and the major sites, everything here is rather ramshackle and on a smaller, more human, scale. Even the crowds of visitors die away to a comparative trickle out of season. This makes it much easier to imagine what it was actually like to live here around 2,000 years ago. The Hittites, who occupied the site more than 1,000 years earlier than that, stood by their policy of anonymity right to the end and left nothing behind. The city's original Greek name, Olba, is said to be derived from the Greek word *olbos*, meaning happy. Why its inhabitants were happier than those in neighbouring cities remains a mystery. Around the beginning of the 3rdC BC the Greek ruler of this part of Turkey, Seleucus I (formerly one of Alexander the Great's generals), built a temple to Zeus here. The remains of the **temple** are still standing, and contain the earliest known examples of Corinthian pillars yet found outside Greece.

Over near the modern village is a 22-m-high **Hellenistic tower**, whose plain features are impressive only on account of their age. An ancient Greek inscription by the entrance indicates that the first repair work on the tower was carried out in the 3rdC AD. But unless some more repair work is carried out very soon, all this early work will have been in vain, as the tower is now in a dangerously sagging state. The tower was the symbol of the ancient city, and appeared on its coins; it has also lent its name to the modern village, whose Turkish name means High Tower.

It's worth wandering about, for there are plenty of things to see – including a rather scruffy **Roman theatre**, the remains of a **monumental arch** and a **paved way**. The village itself is also rather pleasant: you can buy leather goods and the local speciality, *kenger kahvesi*, a sort of coffee made from the fruit of acanthus: an ideal gift for your tasteless know-all friend back home.

These fine ruins owe their preservation largely to their remoteness, and to the fact that during the Byzantine era the locals craftily converted their magnificent pagan temples into churches.

RECOMMENDED RESTAURANTS

KONYA
The snag is that many of the restaurants don't serve alocohol, but there is no problem at:

Restaurant Damla, L-LL; 32 Mevlana Caddesi; *no booking.*

Just off the main street, and has a particularly mouthwatering local speciality made of spiced meat and peppers. I have not yet been able to discover the name of this dish, because you just have to point to it in the kitchen. When I did ask its name, the result was a long discussion between the waiter and the chef, who each gave it a different name.

UZUNCABURÇ
There's a basic restaurant in the village called Burç, where you should be sure to have your first and last taste of the local delight, *kenger kahvesi* – acanthus coffee.

Central Turkey

Northern Anatolia

420 km; map GeoCenter Euro-Country, Eastern Turkey, 1:800 000

This section explores the territory between the busy industrial port of Samsun on the Black Sea, down through northern Anatolia to Ankara. Amasya, one of my favourite Anatolian cities, is a highlight: not only does it have a striking setting, on a river between cliffs, but there's plenty to see and it's still not on the main tourist trail. This was the capital of the kings of the Pontus, who ruled this region until the 1stC AD.

Beyond Amasya, travelling south along Route 785, you come to the Hittite sites. The Hittite Empire was one of the forgotten civilizations of history, and it's only during the 20thC that we have begun to discover much about these people. Yet in their time they conquered Babylon and rivalled ancient Egypt. You can visit the vast ruins of their capital at Hattuşaş, and see reliefs depicting just some of their many gods at their religious centre, Yazilikaya. Just north of here there's a further Hittite site at Alacahöyük. Those who want to see more of this intriguing civilization should visit Kanesh, just outside Kayseri see Turkey Overall: 9.

Most of the best finds from these sights can now be seen at the superb Museum of Anatolian Civilizations in Ankara, but it is worth visiting the sites themselves first: you get a background to the exhibits, in all senses, and it helps you to appreciate the Hittite civilization.

You can cover the route marked on the map in two days, but if you want to do justice to the sights, allow double.

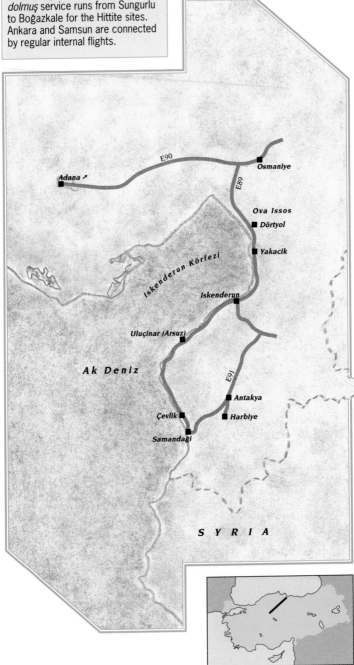

TRANSPORT
There are regular bus services connecting the main towns. A *dolmuş* service runs from Sungurlu to Boğazkale for the Hittite sites. Ankara and Samsun are connected by regular internal flights.

1:1,500,000

E90

Adana

Osmaniye

E89

Ova Issos

Dörtyol

Yakacik

İskenderun Körfezi

İskenderun

Uluçinar (Arsuz)

Ak Deniz

E91

Antakya

Çevlik

Harbiye

Samandagi

S Y R I A

• *Yeşil Irmak (The Green River), Amasya.*

SIGHTS & PLACES OF INTEREST

AMASYA 🛏 ✕

A remote town nearly 400 m up in the moutains on the banks of the Yeşil Irmak (Green River) beneath steep cliffs. It has a ruined castle, notable mosques and a quarter of old wooden buildings. It's as picturesque as it sounds, almost a self-contained little kingdom, with its own nearby pastures amidst the high hinterland wilderness.

According to an unlikely legend (and the locally born historian, Strabo, who ought to have known better), the city was founded by an Amazon queen called Amasis. However, tediously factual sources suggest that it was probably founded by the Hittites. In the 3rdC BC Mithradates set up here as King of the Pontus. This dynasty lasted until the 1stC AD when the casebook psychopath Mithradates Eupator took over as ruler. Being one of his relatives was a rare distinction, and being a surviving relative was even rarer. After mur-

HITTITE CIVILIZATION

Until the turn of the 20thC the Hittites remained a mysterious, forgotten people. All that was known of them were references found in ancient Egyptian records, and a few mentions in the Bible. Abraham's grandson is recorded as having two Hittite wives, and the luckless Uriah the Hittite was disposed of by David when he lusted after Uriah's delectable wife Bathsheba.

But in 1834 a French architect, Charles Texier, stumbled across some ancient ruins near Boğazkale. Texier claimed that he had found the remains of a vast forgotten empire, but was ignored by all serious historians on the grounds that such a civilization wasn't possible. As the historians patiently pointed out to Texier, there simply wasn't room for such a civilization at that point in history.

Then in 1905 a German team began digging at Boğazkale, and further impossible evidence was unearthed, including large caches of cuneiform tablets which appeared to document the history of this unhistorical civilization. Within a few decades the cuneiform script began to be deciphered. It became clear that this was the earliest Indo-European text yet known.

Gradually, an astonishing picture began to form. This picture remains incomplete, but as new finds are made, new astonishing facts continue to emerge. What we know so far appears to be as follows:

The Hittites migrated into Asia Minor from somewhere the other side of the Black Sea. When they arrived in central Anatolia, they found that the region was already occupied by the Hatti. (Scholars disagree about precisely who or what these people were.) According to the historians, the Hittites appear originally to have been nameless, and to have incorporated the Hatti, taking on a version of their name. A century or so after this merger, the Hittites took over the Hatti capital of Hattuşaş. However, they didn't bother to rename it Hittuşaş, which might have helped archaeologists in millennia to come. On the other hand, the first Hittite king who took up residence here called himself Hattusilis (rather than the much more logical Hittusilis).

The Hittite Empire soon began to expand all over Anatolia. Such was its power that in 1594 BC the Hittites even conquered Babylon. In the following centuries they began to compete with the ancient Egyptians. A clash between these two world powers seemed inevitable. In an attempt to patch up these difficulties, the widow of Tutankhamon even wrote to the Hittite king asking if she could marry one of his sons.

Eventually the two empires clashed at the great Battle of Kadesh in 1288 BC. This was the first conflict between two superpowers, and in a tradition maintained to this day both sides claimed victory. Some modern historians maintain that this was in fact a narrow win for the Egyptians, but most remain convinced that it was a draw. Yet before a replay could be arranged the Egyptians and the Hittites signed the world's first peace treaty – which is still recorded in the Temple of Amun at Karnak in Egypt. It was sealed with a marriage – and as a result Ramases II was delighted (or forced) to marry the eldest daughter of Hattusilis III, whose feelings on this matter have not yet been deciphered.

Hittite civilization differed from that of ancient Egypt or Babylon in that it was not centred on the fertile plain of a great river. These were a hardy highland people. The empire was apparently run on a feudal basis. Hittite religion was of the liberal polytheistic persuasion so sadly out of fashion today. Instead of being bound by fanatic monotheism, the Hittites had a wide choice of gods including dead kings, local deities, mythical figures they had brought with them from their ancestral homelands and even deceased relatives.

Society was governed by 200 laws. These consisted of a familiar blend of what some would like to see happen today, and what actually happens today. Rape, opposition to the state or conducting a deep and meaningful relationship with one of your farm animals was punishable by death (for the animals too, apparently, even if they weren't consenting parties). But less hardened criminals, such as murderers and armed robbers, went unpunished – on condition they paid back their victims and promised to behave better in future.

The usual First Great Empire was followed by the inevitable Second Great Empire. This then degenerated into a series of protracted dynastic squabbles of soap opera proportions, both in banality and implausibility. Then all of a sudden the Hittite empire mysteriously came to an end. Unfortunately, scholars haven't yet reached this chapter in the translation of the cuneiform tablets. Some scholars have even gone so far as to suggest that the final chapter may be missing. All we know is that the end took place at around the same time as the fall of Troy and of the migration of the equally mysterious Sea People into ancient Egypt. So the epic empire collapsed, leaving the remaining Hittites with nothing to do except pop up at obscure points in Egyptian records and in the Old Testament.

eral altars, a number of characteristic carvings and storerooms capable of housing grain mountains and wine lakes of EC proportions. Vast ritual ceremonies were held in this temple.

Beyond the temple there's a circular road around the site. Following this in an anticlockwise direction you come to a ruined **fortress** and the **Lion Gate (Aslanlikapi).** Beyond here the road follows a restored section of the ancient walls, then you come to another gate and a 70-m **tunnel** beneath the walls.

After this you come to the **Great Fortress (Büyükale),** where the royal family lived. It was here that German archaeologists discovered the vast trove of cuneiform tablets containing the annals of the Hittite Empire.

THE HITTITE SIGHTS

Boğazkale ⌧

This is the village for two of the main Hittite sites. It was near here that the French archaeologist Charles Texier stumbled across the ruins of the Hittite civilization in 1834. Today Boğazkale is a one-horse place with a few restaurants on the square and the main street, which sports a modest Welcome to Boğazkale arch. It also has a somewhat second-class **museum:** all the first-class finds – and they *are* first class – are in the superb Museum of Anatolian Civilizations at Ankara. But it's worth a quick visit to this museum, if only to see their few Hittite finds and to peruse the diagrams of the sites.

The road to Hattuşaş leads out east from the main square.

Hattuşaş

This was originally the capital of the Hatti, and became the great capital of the Hittite Empire from 1375 BC until 1200 BC. The site's size is immediately impressive: the walls stretch for more than 6 km. The road around the site runs alongside the walls for much of their length.

The road to the site leads east from Boğazkale. In 400 km you come to the **Great Temple of the Storm God (Büyük Mabet),** which dates from 1400 BC and appears to have been destroyed some 200 years later. The huge temple complex contains sev-

Yazilikaya ⌧ ✕

The name of this site means 'inscribed rock'. This appears to have been the religious centre of the Hittite Empire, and contains ruins of a large **temple.** In one of the temple galleries you can see carvings which represent a large procession of Hittite gods and goddesses marching towards one another. (In all the Hittites had more than 1,000 deities, to cover every conceivable exigency. However, only 63 of them have made it into this particular Hall of Fame.) The gods of the underworld are to be seen in the next gallery, which is where the royal funerals were held.

Alacahöyük

This is some distance from the other sites, but it is worth visiting, even if it's not quite so impressive. You can see the fine **Sphinx Gate,** also a **relief** depicting a royal religious procession with musicians and tumblers, and a **secret tunnel,** probably an escape route (but for whom?). There's also a small **museum** with an absorbable number of exhibits, including a **Hittite bath** that was probably much more comfortable than the one in your hotel.

• *Amasya.*

dering his mother, he married his sister and then murdered his sons (and later his sister-wife); finally he murdered all his concubines for good measure. Alas, Dr Freud was not around to counsel him, so he took on the Roman Empire instead, and lost. For further details, see Sinop in Turkey Overall: 12.

When the Romans took over they named this region Asia Minor. The name has stuck, but people often overlook the fact that for the Romans the real Asia – Asia Major – was *west* of here.

Around this time the great early historian and geographer Strabo was born at Amasya. Luckily for us he spent many of his 85 years travelling through Europe, north Africa and Asia, record-

ing his experiences. He wrote more than 60 books, but most of these are now lost. Fortunately Strabo achieved the supreme accolade: his work was widely plagiarized – by authors whose work *has* come down to us. Alas, Strabo has little to say of Amasya beyond: 'My native city is situated in the large deep valley of the River Iris...' He continues in similar prosaic vein without aspiring to a single travel writer's cliché, despite the fact that even in his day this must surely have been a city of contrasts, steeped in history, with a unique atmosphere of its own.

After the Roman era the city was overrun by the Byzantines and the

Selçuks. Then came the Mongol hordes, followed by some even uglier intruders called the Ilkhanids and the Uygurs. For some reason the Mongols departed from their usual even-handed policy of slaughtering all the inhabitants and razing the place to the ground. Instead, they built a madhouse – see below.

Later, Amasya became part of the Ottoman Empire. Its location, near the edge of the empire, was a little too close to the Persians for comfort. As a result, Ottoman sultans were in the habit of despatching their heirs apparent here as governors to gain experience of international relations at the sharp end.

From the 17thC onwards Amasya became renowned as a great religious and intellectual centre. Poets, theology students, expert calligraphers and illiterate flautists thronged the streets, jostling with the visiting travel writers of the period who vied with each other for the ultimate descriptive cliché to describe Amasya, which they labelled variously as 'the Baghdad of Anatolia', 'the Oxford of Anatolia' and 'the Athens of Asia Minor' (but curiously, never as the Left Bank of the Levant).

The best-known sight here is the **Kral Kaya Mezarli (Rock Tombs)**. To reach them, take the path up the cliff which towers over the north of town. First you come to the remains of the so-called **Palace of the Maidens**. This was ineptly named, it seems, since this was where they kept their harems. Above here you come to the tombs themselves. These are no mean structures, and some of them date back to the early 3rdC BC. There are a dozen or so in all, a couple are particularly elaborate, and there are also some tunnels deep into the rocks. From here you

---

RECOMMENDED HOTELS

AMASYA

Turban Amasya Oteli, LL; *Emniyet Caddesi 20; tel. 3781 4054.*

Pleasant modern hotel at a very reasonable rate. Be sure to ask for a room overlooking the river. Popular with groups, so it's best to book well ahead.

Rather less expensive, but highly atmospheric, is:

Ilk Pansiyon, L; *Hittit Sokak 1; tel. 3781 1689.*

A refurbished old house which once belonged to an Armenian merchant. For centuries there was a large Armenian community in Amasya, but it vanished after the Armenian Massacre in 1915. This pension only has half a dozen rooms, so be sure to book ahead during the season.

BOĞAZKALE

If you're planning to stay overnight be sure to book into a room before visiting the site, as the accommodation can suddenly be swamped by groups.

Asikoğlu Touristik Moteli, L-LL; *main street; tel. 4554 1004.*

You can't miss this one, it's by the arch. An American friend once described it as cute; others might find it a little monastic in its simplicity. Prices tend to be settled by whimsy and haggle. As with all other accommodation in town, it's closed in winter – which begins in Octorber and ends in April.

SUNGURLU

Some way from the Hittite sites (just 27 km), but this is where you'll have to come if everything is booked in Boğazkale and you want to spend the night in the vicinity. Sungurlu itself is nothing to write home about, but fortunately it has a gem of a hotel where you can even buy postcards to write home about it.

Hitit Motel, LL-LLL; *on Rt 795 to Corum at E edge of town; tel. 4557 1042.*

The bonus here is the grounds and the pool – just the place to cool off in after a hard, hot Hittite day. They even have a shop where you can buy ingredients for a picnic. No need to stray further afield if you want to eat in, either. The restaurant here is fine for dinner, or even if you're just passing through for lunch. (You're not meant to use the pool if you're just having a meal, but...)

YAZILIKAYA

See Recommended Restaurants, page 261.

have a fine view down over the town.

Higher up you can see the **castle** on the citadel, which has an even better view – though its ruins are nothing special. You can't get to it by the path. Instead, drive left off the Samsun road after the bridge by Büyük Ağa Medresesi. This was completed in 1485 as a religious centre and welfare complex for those who lacked the necessities of life. It was built on the orders of the Chief Eunuch of the sultan, who must have experienced great empathy with those who lacked the necessities of life.

Across the river from here is the **Beyazit Paşa Camii,** which was completed some 65 years earlier, and was one of the finest Ottoman mosques in its day. Also, be sure to visit the **museum**, which has a fine *türbe* (tomb) in its garden. This contains the mummified remains of two Mongol governors, which were discovered beneath the **Burmali Minare Camii** (the Mosque with the Twisted Minaret), so-called because of the spiral effect on its minaret.

The **Bimarhane** (Mogul Madhouse), 300 m north of the main Atatürk Square, is now a ruin, but has the remains of a pleasant garden inside.

In 1919, at the start of the War of Independence, Atatürk had a clandestine meeting in Amasya at which he worked out the principles for the 'new Turkey'. There is a **statue** commemorating this event off Atatürk Caddesi towards the river.

If you are lucky enough, as I once was, to arrive here during Ramadan, you can lie on your bed watching as beyond your balcony the light slowly fades over the city. The swallows skim above the rooftops beneath the minarets while the dusk thickens: a vision of utter peace, which is suddenly shattered by the firing of a large cannon – its boom reverberating between the cliffs – to announce the end of the daily fast. Dinner is served – for the deaf and the deafened alike.

ANKARA
See Turkey Overall: 11.

ÇORUM
Known in ancient times as Niconia, Çorum has a couple of interesting mosques. The best is the **Ulu Camii**

(Great Mosque) which dates from the 13thC but was heavily restored during the 19thC after an earthquake.

HAVZA
This town played an important role during the War of Independence (1919-23), which was led by Atatürk. The house where he stayed is now a **museum** containing momentos of this period. There are some **cave tombs** nearby at Kapu Kaya and by the river.

SAMSUN
See Turkey Overall: 12.

SUNGURLU ⌫ ✕
See Recommended Hotels, page 260.

RECOMMENDED RESTAURANTS

AMASYA
By far the best eating place in town is the local Municipal Club, which welcomes non-members, and is in a building that looks out over the river:

Belediye Şehir Külübu Dernegi, LL; *Karişiyaka Mahallesi* 1; *no booking.*

This is one of those spots where you begin to appreciate the sheer wealth and variety of Turkish regional cuisine. It is *the* place to eat at in the city, and is justifiably renowned beyond its borders – even if it doesn't look exeptional.

Otherwise, try the restaurant at the **Turban Amasya Oteli, LL,** details under Recommended Hotels, page 260. This has a range of dishes which you can order separately, but I particularly recommend its *tabldot,* a meal which is by no means as garbled as its name suggests.

SUNGURLU
See Recommended Hotels, page 260.

YAZILIKAYA
Başkent Restoran Pansiyon ve Campink, L; *on the road between Yazilikaya and Boğuzkale; tel.* 4554 1037.

Pleasant unpretentious restaurant with hill-top view out over the ruins. They also have a few rooms, which can be amazingly cheap out of season. All of these have showers.

Eastern Turkey

The Hatay

220 km; map GeoCenter Euro-Country, Eastern Turkey, 1:800 000

The finger of Turkish territory known as The Hatay stretches down the eastern Mediterranean coastline south of Osmaniye into Syria. Its atmosphere is distinctly Middle Eastern, with Arabic frequently spoken on the streets and many Arabic dishes served in the restaurants. The region has long been popular as a holiday area with visitors from all over the Arab world.

Though small (just 50 km wide by 100 km long), The Hatay has seen more than its share of world-class events. One of ancient history's most important battles was fought here near Yakacik, when Alexander the Great defeated the Persian King Darius in the 4thC BC. To celebrate his victory, Alexander founded the port of Alexandretta, now known as Iskenderun. South-east of here along the coast are some fine beaches.

Directly south of Iskenderun on Rt E91 you come to Antakya, ancient Antioch. In its day, this city was the third greatest in the Roman Empire, outstripped only by Rome and Alexandria. It had a population of nearly half a million and was the western caravan terminus of the Silk Road, which brought merchandise and spices all the way from China. Here you can still see the church where St Peter preached, and for my taste the Archaeological Museum has the finest collection of Roman mosaics in the world. South of Antakya is the hillside resort of Harbiye, whose woods and groves are steeped in myth. The citizens of Antakya have been coming to this cool mountain valley to relax amongst the pools and tumbling waterfalls since before the Roman era.

It's just 220 km from Adana to Antakya, which means that you can easily drive there and back in a day. But if you want to stop off and see a few of the sights you should allow three days for this region.

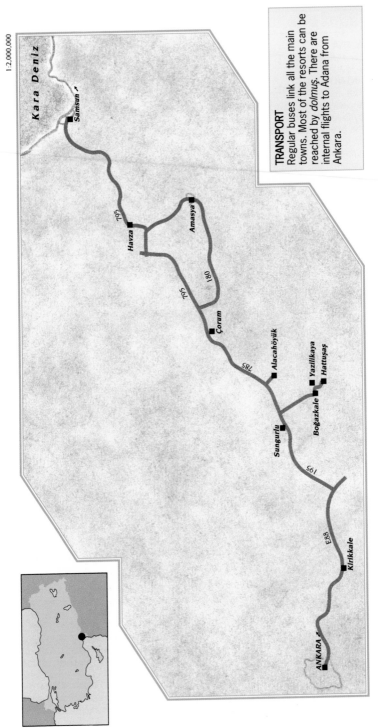

1:2,000,000

Kara Deniz

Samsun

795

Havza

Amasya

795

180

Çorum

785

Alacahöyük

Yazılıkaya

Hattuşaş

Sungurlu

Boğazkale

561

Kırıkkale

E88

ANKARA

TRANSPORT
Regular buses link all the main towns. Most of the resorts can be reached by *dolmuş*. There are internal flights to Adana from Ankara.

SIGHTS & PLACES OF INTEREST

ADANA
See Turkey Overall: 9.

ANTAKYA ⊯ ✕
The main city of The Hatay: this was ancient Antioch, founded in the 4thC BC by Seleucos Nicator, one of Alexander the Great's four generals who divided up his empire after his death. Seleucos named the city after his father, and it became the capital of his far-flung domain, the Seleucid Empire, which stretched from Macedonia to the borders of India.

By the 2ndC BC Antioch had become one of the greatest cities in the world, with a population of nearly half a million. In the Roman era it became capital of Syria. The city derived much of its wealth and importance from being the main western caravan terminal of the Silk Road, which had recently opened up trade with China. Camels would arrive here bearing spice, silk and other exotic merchandise from beyond the Himalayas. By this time Antioch was the third city of the Roman Empire, after Rome and Alexandria. It gained a reputation as a great intellectual centre, and as is often the case with such places it soon became notorious for the licentious behaviour of its inhabitants.

In order to combat these public displays of heedless hedonism and happiness, St Peter founded one of the first Christian churches here, but this only resulted in further exotic behaviour. Saint Simeon Stylites found himself so outraged by the down-to-earth excesses of his fellow citizens that he withdrew from the world and took to living at the top of a pillar. In all, he was to spend 25 years up the pole. (Some etymologists claim that Simeon Stylites' life-style was the origin of this useful phrase.) At intervals Simeon would deliver long sermons to the gathered earthbound mortals below, viciously castigating their low behaviour. This method of gaining the moral high ground soon became all the rage among local Christians with aspirations to sainthood, and according to contemporary records the city soon boasted over over 200 Stylites. (This word comes from the Greek word *stylos* which means a pillar, and like its practitioners has nothing whatsoever to do with style.)

Antioch was a haven for Jewish refugees from Judea, and many of them converted to Christianity, as well as large numbers of Gentiles who had grown tired of enjoying themselves amongst the local intellectuals. As a result of this heterogeneous mix, Christianity became more than a purely Jewish faith. The idea of a universal Christian church was conceived, and soon the first missionaries were being sent from Antioch to convert the heathens.

Later the city was to fall foul of these converted heathens, who took to interpreting the rules very strictly. Antioch developed the Arian heresy, which denied the divinity of Christ and claimed that he was purely human. This erronoeus thinking was roundly condemned at the Council of Nicaea in 325. Later the citizens embraced more orthodox

THE HATAY
Many of the local people are Arabic-speaking and indeed the region only became part of modern Turkey in 1939, having previously been under French control as part of Syria.

When the Ottoman Empire collapsed after its defeat in the First World War, the Allies took control of various Turkish territories. Italy was given Rhodes and the other Dodecanese islands, plus part of the mainland around Antalya. The Greeks inherited Thrace and the other Aegean islands, while France took over Syria, including The Hatay. This territory was used as a bargaining tool by the French to keep Turkey out of the Second World War. A plebiscite was held, and as most of the voters appeared to want to become Turkish, The Hatay once again became part of Turkey.

Recently there has been some agitation for the territory to be returned to Syria, both by the locals and by the Syrians. During the past decade there has been serious unrest in Antakya, and the Syrians have shot down a Turkish plane. However, at present the region is quiet.

beliefs and Antioch became a pillar of the Byzantine church.

In the 6thC Antioch was destroyed by an earthquake, which is said to have killed more than 200,000 people. (If this was in fact so, as several historians claim, it means that the Antioch earthquake was probably the greatest localized disaster ever – three times as awful as Hiroshima.)

By now the city had begun its long decline. The further reaches of the Silk Road had become impassable owing to warring kingdoms along its route, thus cutting off trade from the Orient. Also, the city's river, the Orontes (now known as the Asi), was gradually silting up.

In 1098 the city was captured by the Crusaders, who set up a Frankish Christian kingdom in the region which lasted for more than 150 years.

In 1516 the city had the distinction of being captured by Selim the Sot, after which things rapidly declined to the point where even the resident intellectuals moved to greener pastures. By the 17thC Antioch consisted of little more than peasants camping out amongst the ruins of what had once been a metropolis of world renown.

After the First World War and the collapse of the Ottoman Empire, the city fell under the French mandate as part of Syria. The city's fortunes revived, and the French laid out the street plan of the modern city, in part following the old Roman design. (The city's main street, Kurtuluş Caddesi, which runs from its south-western outskirts to the north-west, was formerly the Roman road through the city, which once had grand triumphal arches at each end.)

Modern Antioch is a bit of a mess, but it still has a few rewarding glimpses of its glorious past. The **Rana Köprüsü** (Old Bridge) which crosses the Asi River at the city centre was originally built by the Romans during the 3rdC AD, though it has been rebuilt several times since.

East from here is the **old quarter** of the city, which has a warren of streets beneath the cliffs. Look closely as you lose your way here, and you will catch glimpses of a number of delightful 'secret' courtyards. What you see as you wander these hot, narrow crowded streets is only the public face of the city – elsewhere, the citizens themselves are often enjoying inner gardens

RECOMMENDED HOTELS

ANTAKYA

Büyük Antakya Oteli, LL-LLL; *Atatürk Caddesi 8; tel.* 891 35860.

Undoubtedly the best hotel in Antakya: a large white building on the west bank in the modern section of town. It's worth the price for the air-conditioning alone – summer temperatures soar here.

HARBIYE

Çağlayan Hotel, LL; *Ürgen Caddesi 6; tel.* 8983 10111.

Pleasant spot for a night, or as a cool base for exploring hot Antakya and its surroundings. Nothing fancy, but the staff are helpful and it has a pleasant atmosphere.

ISKENDERUN

If possible, you're better off staying at Uluçinar (Arsuz), but if you have to stay in town try:

Kavalaki Pansiyon, L; *Şehit Pamir Caddesi 52; tel.* 880 14606.

Modest inexpensive spot, away from the front.

If you want something up-market,

Hatayli Oteli, LL-LLL; *Osman Gazi Caddesi 2; tel.* 880 18751.

Semi-luxury, with excellent rooftop terrace restaurant.

ULUÇINAR (ARSUZ)

The resort south of Iskenderun. South again from here there are several remote beaches worth exploring.

There are some over-priced hotels here, as well as a few rather modest *pansiyons*. In my view, the best is:

Arsuz Turistik Oteli, LL; *Uluçinar; tel.* 881 21782.

Old-style holiday hotel right by the beach. Most mod cons in working order.

• *Vilankale, Crusader castle east of Adana.*

with fountains and cool terraces. Arabic is spoken by many of the inhabitants, and quite a few still understand French from the 'old days,' which only came to an end just over 50 years ago. Also, there is a sizeable community of Syrian Orthodox Christians, following an independent faith which still clings jealously to its own version of the Arian heresy.

The north of this district is occupied by the **bazaar quarter**. At the edge of this, on the corner of Kemal Paşa Caddesi and Kurtuluş Caddesi is the **Habib Neccar Camii,** a mosque whose varied history reflects that of the city. It was originally the site of a Roman temple. The Byzantines recycled some its materials to build a Christian church, which was in turn partly rebuilt by the Crusaders in the Frankish style. Part of this, and the Byzantine church, have been incorporated into the present mosque, whose purpose-built minaret curiously resembles a Christian church tower (but only by accident).

If you're interested in looking further afield there's also a **Roman aqueduct** (1stC AD) to the south, and above the city to the east there's the **cave** once inhabited by the Islamic hermit-prophet Habib Neccar, after whom the ecumenical mosque is named.

But none of these is as rewarding as the city's two main sights: **Sen Piyer Kilisesi** (St Peter's Church) and the **Archaeological Museum.**

St Peter's Church was originally an early Christian cave church, though you wouldn't think so from its slightly ornate exterior, which was built by the Crusaders in the 11thC. Once inside, it is cool and dripping. But this is a historic spot. It's almost certain that St Peter himself preached here during the years when he lived in Antioch, on and off between 47 and 54 AD. Originally the Christians worshipped here in secret, fearing for their lives, while the other god-fearing members of the community honoured more acceptable deities such as the Emperor Nero or Caligula. Behind the altar there was a tunnel through which the worshippers could escape during a police raid.

The Archaeological Museum in Antioch has the finest collection of Roman mosaics you'll see anywhere in the world. They have an oriental delicacy seldom achieved anywhere else in the Roman Empire. The contents of this museum are too fine and varied to be merely listed. Go and see for yourself: you won't be disappointed. For those who wish to pick the cherries, my particular favourites are the mosaics of *Drunken Dionysus* and *Orpheus Charming the Wild Animals,* both in **Room 4**, and the pre-Roman coins in **Room 6**.

If you find Antioch too hot, try staying 7 km up in the mountains at the cool resort of **Harbiye** – see page 268.)

• *Opposite: Roman mosaics in the Archaeological Museum.*

DÖRTYOL

This town's name means simply 'cross-roads', which makes it sound as interesting as it is. However, history occasionally chooses such ordinary places for its most decisive moments.

Around 10 km north of here took place one of the most significant battles in world history. Alexander the Great defeated the Persian King Darius at the Battle of Issos. Alexander and his Greek army consisted of just 30,000 men, and were outnumbered three to one by the massive Persian army. The battle, which took place after a night of ominous thunderstorms and lightning bolts, soon developed into something of a confused slaughter on both sides, and it looked as if the Greeks were bound to lose – if only by the law of diminishing returns. Then Alexander himself led a cavalry charge right into the heart of the Persian forces, where Darius was attempting to direct his side of the battle. As Alexander fought towards him, Darius suddenly took fright and fled – abandoning his army as well as his wife and children. In his ensuing flight he even abandoned his armour, his sword and finally his chariot, with Alexander still in pursuit. Darius eventually escaped on horseback into the mountains under cover of darkness.

Meanwhile the Persian army had been inspired by its commander's example to similar feats of escapology. The referee and judges awarded a unanimous points victory to Alexander – who was now free to advance across Asia towards India for the world title.

According to contemporary records, the battle was fought beside a river. But the river in this plain has changed its course several times through the centuries, making the precise location of the battlefield difficult to identify. Fortunately, the plain of Issos is now more usefully employed growing citrus fruit. It is claimed by some historians that prior to this battle Alexander's only aim was to conquer the world as he knew it – i.e. the Hellenic world. Afterwards he decided to conquer the Persian Empire as well, and any other part of the world he happened to stumble across. This battle thus enters the Guinness Book of Records on several counts – including psychology. It so exacerbated Alexander's mental illness that it caused the world's worst case of megalomania until the arrival of Genghis Khan some 1,500 years later.

HARBIYE 🏖

Harbiye has been used as a holiday resort by the citizens of Antakya since before the Roman era, when it was known as Daphne. You approach through green hills with cyprus trees, climbing into the mountains. The setting is a wooded valley with pools and tumbling streams, and the climate is much pleasanter than the hot city.

This atmospheric spot has been identified as the location of a surprising number of mythological and quasi-historical events. Here the god Apollo, enamoured of the nymph Daphne, pursued her along the river bank – but when he caught her she turned into a laurel tree. From then on the disconsolate Apollo, the god of music, took to decorating his lyre with laurel leaves. (Daphne is the Greek name for laurel.) This is the origin of the laurel crown, which was first awarded at ancient Greek music contests.

The Romans erected a temple to Apollo here. In 40 BC Mark Antony and Cleopatra are said to have been married at Harbiye; and this spot was also the venue for the Antioch Games, which in the Roman era rivalled the Olympic Games in Greece.

ISKENDERUN 🏖 ✕

Iskender is the Turkish for Alexander – and this was the ancient port of Alexandretta, founded in 333 BC by Alexander the Great to celebrate his great victory over King Darius at the Battle of Issos. (See Dörtyol, page 266.) In all, Alexander named 16 cities after himself throughout his great empire – the best known of these being Alexandria, where he was eventually buried.

Iskender has had a varied but on the whole rather boring history – usually being overshadowed by neighbouring Antakya. In the 19thC it gained a measure of importance as the port for Aleppo (now Halab) in Syria. Until recently this was the end of the pipeline from the Iraqi oilfields. The Gulf of Iskenderun would be filled with lines of tankers from all over the world waiting to pick up oil (and meanwhile discharging pollutants, making this stretch of water one of the foulest in the world). This all came to an end in August 1990 with the Iraqi invasion of Kuwait, after which Turkey turned off the pipeline.

The city has a pleasant waterfront with cafés and restaurants where you are likely to encounter Arabs from all over the Middle East and North Africa. The Hatay is a much more cosmopolitan spot than other parts of eastern Turkey.

Iskenderun has a fine harbour, but there are no safe beaches for swimming nearby owing to the continuing pollution. If you're looking for some seaside activity you should head 30 km south to the village of Uluçinar, also known locally as Arsuz. This was formerly the site of the ancient Greek colony of Rhosopolis, which was founded in 300 BC and is mentioned by the historian Strabo. In later centuries it became a far-flung bishopric of the Byzantine Empire. It has a fine beach, also restaurants and hotels of all grades from tatty luxury to monastic dwellings for dwarfs. It used to be a favourite with the Middle Eastern smart set, but now attracts mainly holidaymakers from across the border in Syria.

SAMANDAĞI
Unfortunately the town centre is a mile or so from the beach. To compensate for this, there's a pleasant 5-km walk along the beach to the village of Çevlik, where you can see the ruins of Seleuceia Pieria, which was once the port of Antioch (Antakya).

Çevlik has an interesting underground channel more than 1,500 m long which dates from the Vespasian era. This was one of the great engineering feats of its time, and was used to prevent the nearby river from flooding the port.

ULUÇINAR (ARSUZ) 🛏
See Iskenderun, page 268 and Recommended Hotels, page 265.

YAKACIK
There has been a port here for more than 2,000 years. Two items of interest stand out. Above the harbour stands a **Crusader castle**, fortified by the Genoese and heavily rebuilt by Suleiman the Magnificent. The castle is surprisingly well preserved, and has a suitably gruesome deep dungeon whose short-term occupants were tossed in through a hole at the top and then left to contemplate its brilliant architectural features in ascetic solitude.

Nearby is an ancient *kervansaray,* a traditional inn for the camel caravans which put in here from the Middle East with goods to be shipped on across the Mediterranean.

Some 9 km S of here at Saraseki is a **Roman tower** known as Baba Yunus (Father Jonah). According to legend, Jonah was disgorged from the belly of the whale on to the shore here. Sadly, such is the pollution along this stretch of coast that nowadays any passing whale would probably vomit up a good deal more than the odd stowaway prophet.

RECOMMENDED RESTAURANTS

ANTAKYA
The best place for restaurants is along Hüriyet Caddesi, which runs east from the central bridge into the old town. Otherwise the best restaurants are in the hotels. Try the one at:

Atahan Oteli, LL; *Hürriyet Caddesi 28; tel. 891 11036.*
Serves some particularly original local dishes. In Antakya the *cuisine* takes on a distinctly Middle Eastern flavour, many dishes being served with mint and peppers.

ISKENDERUN
The best eating places in town tend to be the hotels, especially the restaurant in the **Hatayli Oteli, LL-LLL,** see Recommended Hotels, page 265. Hotels on the waterfront tend to be the most agreeable. One which combines both advantages is:

Kiyi Oteli, LL; *Atatürk Bulvari; tel. 880 13680.*
Serves a range of Turkish favourites, also some interesting regional dishes with a distinctly Arabic character.

INDEX